Reading Children

READING CHILDREN

Literacy, Property, and the Dilemmas
of Childhood in Nineteenth-Century America

Patricia Crain

PENN

University of Pennsylvania Press

Philadelphia

Published by
University of Pennsylvania Press
Philadelphia, Pennsylvania 19104-4112
www.upenn.edu/pennpress

Printed in the United States of America on acid-free paper
10 9 8 7 6 5 4 3 2 1

Library of Congress Cataloging-in-Publication Data
Names: Crain, Patricia, author.
Title: Reading children : literacy, property, and the dilemmas of childhood in nineteenth-century America / Patricia Crain.
Other titles: Material texts.
Description: Philadelphia : University of Pennsylvania Press, [2016] | "2016 | Series: Material texts | Includes bibliographical references and index.
Identifiers: LCCN 2015038843 | ISBN 978-0-8122-4796-1 (alk. paper)
Subjects: LCSH: Children—United States—Social conditions—19th century. | Literacy—United States—History—19th century. | Children—Books and reading—United States—History—19th century. | Socialization—United States—History—19th century. | Children's literature—History—19th century. | Social values in literature.
Classification: LCC HQ792.U6 C73 2016 | DDC 305.23097309/034—dc23
LC record available at http://lccn.loc.gov/2015038843

For Jack and Kate

Contents

Introduction

Children and Books

THIS IS a book about children and books, about children's reading practices and the discourses and narratives surrounding them, and about the way in which the so-called invention of childhood was also an invention of a new relation to books and reading. It has emerged from a long engagement with and skeptical interest in how children's reading and children's relationship to textuality has historically been represented. I've especially been struck by the ways in which, when new media or genres of textuality emerge and reading practices naturally transform with them, an alarm goes up about the menace to children or to the very concept of modern childhood that such shifts seem to threaten. Our contemporary concerns over screen reading might remind us of reactions against novels in the eighteenth and nineteenth centuries, against comic books and television in the twentieth, and worried debates over all sorts of genres of digital media today.[1] And yet, notwithstanding the cultural gravity of childhood reading, histories and theories of reading as well as histories and theories of childhood have tended to gloss children's relationship to books as a history of schoolroom practices alone.[2] The immersive reading practice that has long been the desideratum for middle-class reading in the United States emerged in an icon of a reading child at the end of the nineteenth century. But the literacy campaigns and the literature directed toward children in the eighteenth and nineteenth centuries first promoted quite different relationships between children and books. In the following chapters I explore this long and complex modern history through a series of texts and images, sites and pathways where we can observe aspects of these relationships unfold. Later in this Introduction, I will describe these diverse portals for thinking about children and books, children and reading. For starters, though, I'll begin with an image. For not only does everyone agree, it seems, that children should learn to read, but, for the past two hundred years, a scopophilic cultural imperative dictates that they should be *seen* reading.[3]

An Icon: Child-in-Window-Seat-with-Books

The image of a child absorbed in a book, a genre of picture belonging to the turn of the twentieth century, brings a new creature into the world (see Plate 1). "Head in a book," "lost in a book"—these are the epithets for a child face to face with the open pages of a codex. Books had long been occasional props in portraits and other visual representations of children, from sacred paintings of St. Ann and the Virgin, to images signaling the virtue or the class prestige of literacy to illustrations in children's primers.[4] The tradition of representing adult readers, men and women, saints and scholars, loungers, dozers, dreamers, has been beautifully explored by Garrett Stewart in *The Look of Reading*.[5] The earlier visual tropes of children reading and images of adult readers early and late are both evoked and transformed as the reading child gradually becomes a dominant figure for "childhood" during the nineteenth century. Coming at the end of the period I explore in this book, this 1905 image by Jessie Willcox Smith, created for Robert Louis Stevenson's *A Child's Garden of Verses*, which I return to in the Coda, offers a heuristic for thinking about the suturing of a new mode of literacy with a new style of childhood, a mode and style that still resonate today. Smith captures a small child, with a book propped against bent knees. The light comes from the window behind, but the child's forehead glows from that light reflected by the illuminated pages. All that is visible of the pages are bright blank triangles, whiter than almost everything else: whiter than the girl's smock and stockings, than the window seat and sill and the white background of the flowered upholstery; only the snow seen through the window-panes matches the bright whiteness of the pages. The child attends to the book in the midst of a material abundance that both supports reading and supplies distractions from it, including three other books, to which the child might turn fleeting attention. The image underscores a promised comfortable sameness of reading, its capacity for replication: the child was immersed in *that* book some other time, now *this* one, later that *other* one. The image evokes the perpetuation of face-to-page, page-to-face absorption in the codex, with its suggestion of an intense, private engagement with people and things present nowhere in the world but in those window-like pages, their words and images invisible beyond the charmed cone of a child's attention.

The opening scene of *Jane Eyre* is the locus classicus for scenes of absorbed, withdrawn, window-seat reading in literature, and though Smith's child is younger than Jane (who is ten as the novel begins), Jane's image might stand behind this one; one of this child's books is about birds, like Jane's copy of Bewick's *Birds*. The elision of the textual with the sheerly visual underscores the development of a kind of hypnotic optic absorption as a desired product of reading.

This image circulated well into the twentieth century in reprints of Stevenson's *A Child's Garden of Verses* and more recently as a birthday card and note card.[6] In its greeting card incarnation the image is lifted out of the book, where it illustrated the poem "Picture-books in Winter," and newly captioned "A girl reading." (In 1905 the child's gender would have been less certain.) The new title tilts away from the original's focus on the books being looked at to the act and fact of a child's reading. In its current form, the image's commercial value relies upon a nostalgic fantasy of interiority, as if to say, when one looks inside, one will see this benignant, safe, protected reading child: a primal and endlessly retrievable reading self. But of course the image has a cultural history and prehistory.

Reading in a window seat, for adults and children, is a nineteenth-century commonplace (and an interior design fantasy then and now).[7] For Victorians it even identified a leisure print genre—"parlor-window-seat books."[8] In or on a window seat, one might linger comfortably at a threshold, here and there, or perhaps, dreamily, neither here nor there; and yet a window seat isn't a doorway: you may look out, without the pressure or pleasure of venturing out. As it spans an elsewhere and a here, nookishly private and inward leaning, and yet referencing an external climate or landscape, it's a visual trope of reading.[9] As a window seat conceals, frames, and contains, it rhymes with the book that houses it. An illustration in a book, of a book and reader, intensifies the nook-like properties of the book one reads as well as the mirroring qualities of the child's posture, whether its reader is curled up also, like a "W," in a window seat, with the book in hand, or only longing to be—or longing to have been.

Among the scene's promises: an aspirational consumer economics of reading, in that costly-to-keep-clean whiteness, those fat downy cushions, that bespoke cabbage rose upholstery.[10] A parlor-window-seat book is décor, and a child perusing a child's parlor-window-seat book is the constitutive décor of domestic life. As an icon or hieroglyph it conveys a layered cultural fantasy: reading is easy, dreamy, natural, cozy, sleepy, safe, comfortable, comforting, desirable—and so are children. To put the myth the image refers to succinctly: a certain kind of child naturally reads.[11] Such a seemingly immersive, dreamy, self-forgetting, soft, childlike reading relies on deep pockets of cultural and social capital, and plain cash. For this is emphatically not the schoolhouse literacy that anyone can get in a public classroom. Instead it lifts the docile body out of the schoolroom and establishes an autonomous and yet protected and domestic child-with-books as an object of nostalgic reverie.

One of the things that make this image vibrate with iconicity is the child's absorption, so absorbing to observe.[12] An absorption seemingly without duration, it can change its object freely and easily.[13] The image indexes absorption as a quality of attention and suggests that it's an absorption that precedes or exceeds any particular object. This is a kind of absorption that nineteenth-century discourse attaches to two sites: children, as agents and objects of attention; and reading (or books), as absorbing activity or medium. This image captures the suturing of a model of romantic reading—absorptive, immersive, self-forgetting—with a romantic figure of childhood—absorbed and absorbing, immersed, self-forgetting.[14] The Smith image captures one of the emblematic combinations of posture, place, and person that reads as a certain kind of reading and importantly invokes a certain kind of childhood. Barnes and Noble's Nook (see Plate 2) shrewdly mimes this icon, invoking an architectural space for reading, implying that reading creates the space that used to be expressed by the codex form's container-like qualities.[15]

And yet, it was not always thus. This image offers a figuration of both childhood and reading circa 1900, whose characteristics were the result of the approximately century-long development that is the subject of this book.[16] These characteristics include a nostalgic regard for reveries of children and reveries about them, as I discuss in Chapters 2 and 6 and the Coda; a canon of literature for children and a boundless commercial stream of books (Chapters 1, 2, 4, and 5); an association of reading with dreaming and fantasy, on the one hand (Chapters 2, 6, and the Coda), and on the other, with self-ownership, property (Chapters 1, 3, and 4), and an array of signs and forms of material wealth, such as comfort, safety, and the leisure to dream. The historicity of this or any reading child is hidden in a haze of nostalgia, an emotion that belongs to reading practices promoted in the nineteenth century. If pictures like the one by Smith are now icons of pleasurable longing for imagined or real losses (of that kind of childhood and that kind of reading), the stories that I will tell in what follows will draw us away from this mesmeric image, to its prehistory in the eighteenth and nineteenth centuries.

In bringing together the Philadelphian artist Jessie Willcox Smith with the well-traveled Scotsman Robert Louis Stevenson, the image of the child reader captures too the ways in which so much of what we think about American childhood rests on translations, so to speak, from British originals, or, as in this case, transatlantic collaborations across time and space. And yet I write as an Americanist by training, and hope to elaborate a culturally American story. The artifacts, texts, images, and so on in the following pages embody and enact racial, class, and property relations that often mean quite otherwise in their U.S. context than within their culture of origin.

The Alphabetization of the Social Contract

As it has developed in the West modern childhood offers up the image of a child who is literate, dependent, and protected. As many scholars have understood, this concept emerged along with and, to a great extent, due to the invention and the subsequent democratization of print. This long and complicated conversation began with Philippe Ariès's *Centuries of Childhood* (1965), while Neil Postman's *Disappearance of Childhood* (1982) offers the most dramatic version of an argument for the constitution of "childhood" within print culture, written as a jeremiad about its vanishing under new media regimes.[17] What does modernity's child's posture in relation to reading, writing, and print—we might use the shorthand "books" here—have to do with the other qualities attributed to childhood? If it implies dependency, childhood in modernity implies at the same time the kind of self-possession that Locke described as the ground of autonomy in his famous assertion, "Every Man has a *Property* in his own *Person.*"[18] The influence of Locke's theories of sovereignty and social contract on early American political ideology have long been acknowledged. Since Jay Fliegelman's *Prodigals and Pilgrims* (1982) literary scholars have recognized the influence of Lockean psychology and pedagogy on the intimacies of family life. While Fliegelman described the new affective model of the family that was so important to what he called the "revolution against patriarchal authority," Gillian Brown more directly took up the materials of children's reading, finding in eighteenth-century children's books Lockean manuals for "promoting consensual individuals," the new subjects of the social contract.[19] In both of these accounts, from the revolutionary generation on, children were seen to be raised in an environment alive with the Lockean idea that their own persons and, hence, the argument goes, freedom and the capacity for consent were theirs by right. As Brown puts it: "Locke's political theory and psychology crucially revised the idea of children's subordinate position by envisioning that position as consensual. . . . Far from signifying a natural order of subjection, the dependent condition of a person's minority manifests the child's 'express or tacit Consent' to necessary parental governance."[20] In a powerfully illuminating reading of Locke, Courtney Weikle-Mills pursues the problem of children's consent and disentangles the paradox in Locke's *Two Treatises*, in which children are represented as free and yet at the same time under the subjection of their parents. She resolves this paradox by seeing that while the adult "citizen *consents* to [an] uneven trade"—that is, giving up liberty in return for protection of property—in the case of children "Locke's pedagogical texts further clarify that he relies on an irrational, hidden, and private force to carry out his model of citizenship: specifically the transfer of children's affectionate feelings, through education, from their parents to the law."[21] Weikle-Mills argues compellingly that for Locke it is parental affection that, transmitted in person and importantly circulated through children's books, seals the social compact, allowing the reading child of the early republic to become a model of what she calls "affectionate citizenship."

Not recognized in these rich analyses of Locke's powerful influence is that, from at least the mid-eighteenth century, what would later be styled the "acquisition of literacy" became the royal road to Lockean self-possession for children across ranks and classes. This was so not only because reading was associated with affection ("My Book and Heart / Shall never part," as the *New England Primer* verse has it), but, equally important, because it was associated with property. As I explore in Chapter 1, reading was promoted beginning in the eighteenth century as a symbolic property, a form of what, since Pierre Bourdieu, we have called "cultural capital,"[22] with the more or less fantastic capacity to migrate into real property (for example, the coach-and-six, the Cadillac Escalade of the eighteenth century, promised in early primers). Motile yet inalienable, this internalized property would provide a ballast against the vagaries of new economic relations that tended to dispossess children of traditional modes of inheritance and livelihood. Under an emergent concept of "childhood," children during this period were increasingly regarded as self-possessing humans, by virtue of an engagement with the materials and practices of literacy.

By 1800, especially in the United States, the child's position had begun to shift from the long-standing one of, in effect, father's chattel, with a self-evident value within the family or community, to what Peter Stearns calls the "modern model" of childhood, in which children are valued in abstract and affective rather than material and economic terms.[23] The traditional labors of children had been determined by the child's economic and social status; the work of schooling, of reading and writing, was increasingly (if unevenly) seen as the labor newly appropriated to and appropriate for children in the nineteenth century. If social contract theory underwrote and articulated the revolutionary transformation of social and economic relations from status to contract and, as Amy Dru Stanley has put it, from "bondage to contract"[24] over the course of the eighteenth and nineteenth centuries, children were both the vanguard and the forlorn hope of these transformations.

While social contract theory is, as Carol Pateman writes, a "conjectural history,"[25] it's an origin myth whose explanatory power has real-world consequences. For Pateman, the "sexual contract" had been the unacknowledged verso of the social contract's recto, binding "a very special kind of property, the property that individuals held in their own persons";[26] in her view, liberal reliance on contract as the basis of civil freedom is ultimately delegitimized by the dark tale of the dispossession of women she reads at its heart. In the case of children, I argue, literacy practices in the early national and antebellum periods function as both constituting and signifying ownership of the self, a supposed precondition of voluntary consent. The child's accession to the protocols of reading and writing establishes, I suggest in Chapter 4, a "literacy contract," whose restrictions, obligations, and assurances unfold not in codicils and constitutions but in the multiple codices and print and manuscript ephemera that are the materials of children's reading.[27] The nursery and schoolroom version of the social contract underwrites the child's entry not only into reading and writing but also into a world of commodity and property relations that a child engages by, for example, marking a flyleaf and linking her signature with "her book,"[28] as I show in Chapter 5. Literacy sets and dispenses the terms for self-ownership while at the same time threateningly revealing the potential for the alienation and commodification of this emergent self.

By the beginning of the nineteenth century in America, skill in literacy had become one of the key distinctions between enslaved and free and, in turn, was promoted as a sign of the "civilizing" of native populations, as if in extension of the old "benefit of clergy," which allowed felons a one-time escape from punishment if they could read.[29] As Cheryl I. Harris notes, "Although systems of oppression of blacks and Native Americans differed in form—the former involving seizure and appropriation of labor, the latter entailing the seizure and appropriation of land—undergirding both was a racialized conception of property implemented by force and ratified by law."[30] This property distinction underwrote access to literacy, which was encouraged for Native Americans, partly for the sake of acculturating them to white property customs, but was forbidden to slaves. Bans on slave literacy have often been regarded as being instrumental, designed to prevent incendiary reading or the writing of travel passes. But the prohibition also spoke to the promise and presumption of self-ownership signified by literacy practices, which are, theoretically at least, incompatible with the condition of slavery and whose presence might call servitude into question.

In the first half of the nineteenth century, the reading child, in his self-possession and tacit binding to the literacy contract, was presumed to be safe from serfdom, pauperism, and slavery. In the postbellum and, importantly, postemancipation decades, the ambitions and anxieties surrounding literacy and children changed. If self-possession was a central aim of antebellum literacy for white children, a privileged kind of self-loss or self-forgetting or a self-*dis*possession became the new readerly ideal postbellum. The children who

inhabited what by the end of the century was increasingly marked as a racialized, white "childhood" were supposedly being educated to become autonomous agents in the world, and yet at the same time were encouraged to be
escape artists who could imaginatively flee it. A chiastic relationship between
children and books emerged. That is, across the nineteenth century, reading and
writing became foundational to characteristics we now identify with childhood,
while, by the end of the century, the new discourse of childhood imbued reading
practices with the promise of an eternal return to the lost space and time of
childhood inhabited by seemingly salvific children. One of these redemptive
children, as the new science of psychoanalysis was discovering, would be the
most phantasmagoric and most desired child of all: oneself, in the past. As the
child's economic value as a producer declined, her value as an object of professional expertise, including the expertise of authors, rose.[31]

Chapters: Views of the Child Reader

In visual images as in cultural discourse, the reading child has a galvanic place
in nineteenth-century through early twentieth-first-century American culture,
bearing anxious fantasies about both children and books. The figure emerges
from and is writ large, I argue, through the language and crisscrossing genealogies of two key cultural concepts that help structure how we think of modernity
and even how we come to think ourselves modern: "literacy" and "childhood."[32] In these pages I consider the historical child as at once the site and the
material prompt for the abstractions of "literacy," and I consider the practices
and materials of reading and (to some extent) writing as essential to the formation of the abstraction "childhood," with consequences in the lives of children.
Moving between the child (and childhood) and literacy (and reading and writing practices), I pursue the linked genealogies of these two concepts, pointing
to the cultural and literary effects of their deep, if generally unremarked,
mutuality.

Reading Children explores the ways in which children's reading practices
were described and had values ascribed to them, in a range of images and texts,
before those practices coalesced toward the end of the nineteenth century as
"literacy."[33] Indeed, this book has grown in part out of my wish to understand
the surplus meanings of that long-lived bureaucratic catchphrase, "acquisition
of literacy." Benefiting from exhilarating recent work in children's literature
and childhood studies, the book is motivated by a desire to pursue the ways in
which the histories and discourses of childhood and of literacy, which have
been largely separated by disciplinary boundaries, share a cultural evolution

beginning in the eighteenth century. It considers some of the lasting effects of nineteenth century constructions of "literacy" and "childhood," through a focus on the media through which childhood is structured and the ways in which childhood itself becomes by the end of the century not only a medium and a signifier for adult memory but also a form of what we now call "media." By this I mean that the figure of the child often functions as a residual and conserving and at the same time emergent and creative means of accessing the "interiorised self" (in Carolyn Steedman's term)[34] of modernity. This child, then, to put it in medial terms, both stores and transmits the modern self.

The book follows a loose chronology from the middle of the eighteenth century (with a short detour to the seventeenth century) to the end of the nineteenth. Each chapter offers a distinct portal for investigating the discursive, rhetorical, and material relationships between children, books, and the practices that put them in the same imaginative or real spaces. The objects of study, then, vary, among texts and images, with their historical and sometimes biographical embeddedness and genealogies; pedagogical theory and practice; and the material object of the book. The first two chapters treat two key texts of the early children's literature canon that became bywords for their genres—the ballad of the "Babes in the Wood" and the novel *The History of Little Goody Two-Shoes*—exploring the genealogy of children's literature per se and the ideologies of literacy and of childhood that accompanied its formation. The third chapter, on Joseph Lancaster's monitorial system of education, shifts from literary canons to pedagogical practices and colonial notions of knowledge distribution, and from technologies of print media, which we have naturalized when thinking about children, to a previous vision of children that depended on other media technologies. Chapter 4 explores the contractualism that emerges from the 1830s to the Civil War, which narrativizes Lancaster's instrumental literacy in tales of middle-class and subaltern children's implicit consent to a "literacy contract," and the various consequences of evading or acceding to it. In Chapter 5, the material artifact of the book comes to the fore, in a reading of the inscriptions, ownership verses, marginalia, remembrances, and other eloquent marks and found objects in children's books. As one of the first commodities addressed to children, the codex emerges as one of the first dedicated childhood spaces; in laying claim to their books as personal property, child scribes (and sometimes adult inscribers) creatively engage and profoundly transform the expressive form of the book. The final chapter turns to Henry James, as a kind of expert witness and, to switch professional metaphors, a participant observer of the transformations of childhood and the shifting media of literacy practices in the second half of the century. His fictions of childhood bring into being what I call a "medial child," a figure whose anguished coming to knowledge allows the James narrator a channel through which the mediated complexities of scenes of composition are recast as scenes of instruction.[35] Claiming children and childhood as literary property intensifies and elaborates James's narrative explorations of interiority and of the threats posed by both the porosity and the inaccessibility of the self to others and of others to the self.

The first two chapters read an early children's literature canon that promotes children's literacy as a newly valuable form of cultural capital and establishes childhood as a newly precious form of literary property. Two famous if now rarely read steady sellers, so embedded in cultural memory that their titles have become catchphrases, uncover the ways in which their various redactions circulated evolving concepts of childhood and of the place and purpose of children's literacy over time. Chapter 1 describes the structuring of literacy as a form of property at the end of the eighteenth century. Chapter 2 reaches back to the Renaissance to trace the genealogy of a ballad that transforms into a staple of the children's literature canon throughout the nineteenth century. By identifying children with a putative lost orality, this ballad was reconfigured in line with changing concepts of childhood as well as the changing cultural and legal status of children.

The opening chapter focuses on *The History of Little Goody Two-Shoes*, published in 1765 by John Newbery and circulating in many American editions beginning in 1775. One of the first novels for children, *Goody* spread widely in England and America through the nineteenth century and beyond, narrating the fairy-godmother-less tale of a girl rising from orphaned poverty to riches and respect strictly by means of her mastery of the alphabet. Through *Goody*, this chapter articulates the ways in which property and literacy are theorized in the Anglo-American eighteenth century. Many scholars have recounted the transition from traditional modes of landed property to newer forms of property in an increasingly market-driven culture in both England and America at the end of the eighteenth century, noting the consequences of these transformations for both subject formation and public virtue. What's been lacking is the crucial function of literacy acquisition, a phenomenon that during the nineteenth century resulted in the supplanting of property by literacy as a foundation not only of political and private "virtue" but of subjectivity itself.

The History of Little Goody Two-Shoes beautifully elaborates, while it helps to invent and distribute, the literacy-property nexus as it emerges in the eighteenth century. Episodic, full of unlikely coincidences, immensely interested in the components of social class and success, *Goody* mirrors eighteenth-century novels and opens, as they tend to, with an economic crisis. The consolidation and commodification of farmland, elaborately polemicized in the novel's introduction, leaves the heroine, Margery Meanwell, orphaned and cast into pauperism. Her famous transformation into Goody Two-Shoes, the "trotting tutoress" who becomes "the mistress of ABC College," hinges on acquiring, first, proper footgear and then the alphabet. One of the story's ostensible lessons is how to navigate in a new economy, but the novel represents the economic catastrophe as a fortunate fall: Goody's acquisition of literacy emerges directly from the failure of her family to maintain its property; it's through her literacy that she restores and exceeds her family's original status. The collapse of traditional property relations motivates the creation of a new social network—a fantastic one, which embraces animals—founded on literacy, while the cultural capital of literacy translates, not by magic, but by the hidden hand of this new system, into real capital and land. *Goody* merrily promotes its own commodification, and it was widely read in its original and later elaborately illustrated versions throughout the nineteenth century.

Through the case of "Babes in the Wood" the second chapter explores the ways in which childhood becomes a valuable—indeed, an indispensable—literary property. Originating as a broadside ballad at the end of the sixteenth century, the artifact variously known as "The Norfolk Gentleman's Last Will and Testament," "The Children in the Wood," and "Babes in the Wood" (among others) had a long afterlife in the United States as a staple of the nineteenth-century juvenile market. The striking resilience of this unlikely candidate for children's literature canonization, in its evolution through many textual and pictorial manifestations, reveals a nostalgia for "traditional" orality in the formation of modern children's literature. Like *Goody*, the babes ballad owes its wide print circulation to the labors of Grub Street, but unlike *Goody* it doesn't thematize its relation to print literacy, at least not at first. Though this ballad may well have been written around the time of its first recorded printing in 1595, its genre inevitably evokes—through the practices both of ballad hawkers in the street and antiquarians in the study—a link to oral folk tradition. As originally printed, the babes ballad reads as a how-to manual in meter and rhyme for writers and executors of wills, its murdered children serving as ciphers for a tragedy of inheritance gone wrong, a lineage derailed, and poetic justice distributed. As the object of literary preservation in the eighteenth century, this ballad's legacy was imagined as testifying in and to a vox populi, a voice of "common people" in the past, increasingly associated with "little folk," as children were newly called. Taken up by antiquarians and romantic writers, the ballad became a touchstone for childhood memories and for a nostalgia associated with and indeed demanded by the concept of childhood.

By 1800 the ballad was almost always printed in editions for the new juvenile market. Redactions of the ballad—in prose and verse, variously illustrated, sentimentalized, politicized, moralized, infantilized—charted the transformations in the idea of childhood and in the function of children's reading. In one novelized version much reprinted in America in the early 1800s the children are rescued and enrolled in a "school of industry" to learn to "read, to write, and to work."[36] In the last decades of the nineteenth century the ballad's illustrations invoked a theatricalized, racially homogenous Anglo-Saxon past, as the inheritance of the child reader. Even when the language of the ballad was conveyed verbatim, the material conditions that sustained its existence—including its printed format, illustrations, price, and market—radically changed its meaning. In 1600 the broadside hawked in the street had represented a contemporary and monitory domestic tragedy. By1900, the ballad remediated in codex, marketed as a gift for children, now spoke of a phantasmagoric history, in antique language and through Pre-Raphaelite illustrations. If in the old broadside ballad the deaths of the babes thwarted a legacy, the late life of the ballad offered a fantastical heritage and genealogy; history had become a luxuriously melancholy space and time, lost in the past, and yet always uncannily present and accessible in the space-time of childhood. Here the two major themes of the present book emerge: the promotion of literacy as a necessity for children and the consolidation of romantic theories of language and memory around the figure of the child.[37]

Chapter 3, "Colonizing Childhood, Placing Cherokee Children," pursues the class and race politics in the representation and practice of reading and writing pedagogy in Joseph Lancaster's monitorial system, widely adopted across much of the British Empire, Western Europe, Russia, and Latin America between 1800 and 1850. Discredited as mechanistic by later theorists, and largely forgotten beyond specialized histories, the monitorial system was enormously successful for decades in the United States and had long-lasting effects on schooling. If *Goody Two-Shoes* and other early literature for children promised a notional personal property in and through literacy, by 1800 children themselves began for the first time to be regarded as something like what economists lately call "human capital." First imported to teach the urban poor in U.S. East Coast cities (Lancaster's London school claimed to manage five hundred students at a time), the monitorial system also found a home in American Indian mission schools on the frontier. Promoting a literacy not bound to books but modeled on new media technologies like the optical telegraph, Lancaster's system positioned children as living parts of a knowledge machine. Innovative technologies of literacy bound the alphabet to bodily disciplines through a classroom "telegraph," a system of coded signs that students responded to by performing such actions as removing their hats, sitting, standing, and so on. The classroom telegraph and other such props and gadgets transformed the schoolroom into a communications network and students into relay nodes.

In his urban schools, Lancaster identified students by number as well as by name; this bureaucratic cryptography, making the children legible as data, became sentimentalized in the Indian mission schools, where children were renamed after live benefactors and dead worthies. In their renaming, as in other classroom practices, such students were treated differently from the good Lockean subjects of middle-class white pedagogy, upon whom lessons were meant to be *impressed*. Rather, the Indian child, like the poor child, was figured as all exterior, less a surface to be written on than one upon which messages could be posted. Thus such children were always simultaneously both the objects of and the gazed-upon advertisements for the project of "civilizing." Especially for Cherokee children, an implied literacy contract, treaty-like, held out the promise of protection, as the letters mission students sent to President Andrew Jackson just pre-Removal poignantly demonstrate.

The status of children was transformed in the United States between about 1800 and 1830, under changing legal, social, and economic conditions. Once providing essential labor to the economic stability of their families, children now, due in part to increasing obligations for schooling, became a long-term financial burden. What did childhood mean in an increasingly market-driven culture? What were children for? Chapter 4, " 'Selling a Boy': Race, Class, and the Literacy Economy of Childhood," explores these questions through readings of two sets of narratives for children: the "lost child" fictions of the 1810s to 1830s, and Jacob Abbott's series books from the 1830s to the 1870s.

Though framed very differently, both *Goody Two-Shoes* and the "Babes in the Wood" ballad are tales of children abandoned through the force of economic pressure. But in *Goody* abandonment gives Margery Meanwell autonomy and a quasi-magical transformation into maturity and authority, bypassing the struggles of childish dependence, while in the traditional versions of the babes ballad, the children are barely out of infancy and toddlerdom, too young to survive without adult aid, feckless victims of adult avarice. These alternate visions of what happens to the child thrown from or torn from domestic life are joined in the early decades of the nineteenth century by monitory and sentimental narratives, both homegrown and London imports, that pose implicit questions for children about their status and role: What is your place? Who cares for you and on what terms? These are questions that childhood in transition from one form of value to another raises, especially in the social and economic context of the United States, where many poor and nonwhite children were routinely bought and sold, through slavery or pauperism, or had their homes destroyed, families killed, and property stolen, through Indian Removal.

With equal parts seductive charm and menace, paper-doll chapbooks pirated from London follow wayward children ("Little Fanny," "Little Eliza," et al.) stolen for their clothes as they bump down the urban ladder from their safe domestic perches to the beggar- and hawker-filled streets. Nathaniel Hawthorne exploits the plotline in "Little Annie's Ramble," turning it into a parable of adult usurpation—and authorial abduction—of childhood's properties. Jacob Abbott's version, "Selling a Boy," more boldly echoes slavery, as a poor father tries to sell his child but strikes an affectionate compact to keep him in the end. For Abbott, reading offers a deferred promise of self-ownership in line with the age of legal consent. Abbott directly engages race and contractualism in his later series books just before and just after the Civil War. These lively episodic narratives feature autonomous children navigating and mastering the mid-century economic landscape, arranging mortgages, hiring themselves out, negotiating for rights within their liminal status. Not only white children but immigrants and African American children as well are represented as similarly engaged in asserting self-possession. Abbott's narrative method, of accretion and accumulation, models a kind of economic realism, and in his last books Abbott channels this method through a young African American woman protagonist.

Like Lancaster before him, Abbott started out as an innovative educator and was, again like Lancaster, highly attuned to his medial environment. Thus his characters are identified with their skill at reading and writing but engage as well in the wide world of communications technology, learning, for example, how to send a telegram and how the telegraph works, learning how to read train timetables, riding the mail coach, and becoming a post rider. Series books rely for their success on an inviting and dependable everydayness, on the effect of depth, abundance, and reality that repetition of setting and character can provide, on the sense that the world is populated by and belongs to children. While these allurements incite consumer desire, Abbott's series books also circulate and instantiate both the new model of "childhood" and the new model of "literacy" across the mid-century.

Chapter 5, "Children in the Margins," considers the central medium of children's literacy in the nineteenth century—the printed codex—and reads the traces of children's marks of engagement with their books. These dedicated children's spaces register an array of children's experiences, and those of their friends and families, while, along the way, providing a space for reflection on the scholar's immersion in the archive of childhood. This chapter reads the

inscriptions, notes, blots, scribbles, spills, and other traces of children's engagement with the books that were avidly marketed to them in the nineteenth century. If scholars turn to children's literature to find out what the early culture
industry made of children, children answer back from the archive, making space
for themselves in the margins of their books. Reading the "social life" of books
uncovers their function as primers for property relations, as adjuncts to family
life, as surrogate selves, and as memorial artifacts. By the 1830s, some children's
books included a printed blank box on the frontispiece marked "property of,"
formalizing children's traditional ownership marks, by making them look like
grown-up contractual forms, requiring a signature. But children's appropriation
of their books exceeds the instrumental; their exuberance commands the space
of the book as a collaborative canvas, a treasure cache, and an external self. If
the book sometimes performs as what we might now call, following D. W.
Winnicott, a transitional object,[38] when children died such books were marked
"in memoriam" by parents or friends, adding to the haunted and haunting
quality such artifacts retain. Traces of child readers and their families and
friends on the commodity that is the outward form of the internalized property
of literacy provide a field for understanding the profound interdependence of
the shape of "childhood" and the construction of "literacy" in the nineteenth
century.

Chapter 6, "Raising 'Master James': The Medial Child and Phantasms of
Reading," turns to Henry James's fin-de-siècle literature of childhood, in which
the materials of literacy are eroticized and gothicized, and in which the self-
possession of children is rendered as possession by others—ghosts of the past,
projections of the present. The chapter treats Henry James as a highly attuned
reporter and his fictions of childhood, including "The Pupil" (1891), *What
Maisie Knew* (1897), and "The Turn of the Screw" (1898), along with his reflections on children's literature in his critical essays, as testimonies about the literary uses of new configurations of childhood and children's literacy by the end
of the century. James's biography (1843–1916) spans decades of transformation
in ideas of child raising, education, and childhood in England and America; by
the nineties, the child-study movement had made children objects of research
for the new academic disciplines of psychology and sociology, which engaged
James's brother, William. But children and childhood drew Henry James in the
nineties with more than scientific interest. Deaths among his family and friends,
along with the banal trappings of midlife anxiety—a crisis of vocation after
his failure in the theater, increasing physical ailments, money worries—turned
James's thoughts to his own childhood. These reminiscences, which would blos-
som in the two autobiographies he would write later in life, now turned up an
"untutored and unclaimed" child, which was how he described the hero of his

only novel focalized through a child, *What Maisie Knew*. James's attention to his friend Robert Louis Stevenson's novels and poems for children provided him with surprising models for the possibilities of his own narratives, along with an account of what adults stand to gain in belated encounters with the literature of childhood. His own fictive children—especially Morgan Moreen, Maisie Farange, and Miles—engage variously with the materials and practices of print literacy, but resonate as well with the rapidly changed medial environment of the late nineteenth century.

"The Turn of the Screw" followed *Maisie*, with orphaned and dispossessed siblings subject, like the original "babes in the wood," to a dodgy uncle, suspect hirelings, and fecklessly unprotecting adults. The major narratives of childhood by James coincided with a change in his working conditions; his injured writing hand led him to take up dictating to a typist, as he would do for the rest of his life. I argue that the medial shift in James's writing practice haunts the half-dictated *Maisie*, produces "The Turn of the Screw" 's ghosts, and helps create fictional children who enact the complex recuperative and mediating labors of late-century childhood. Since Shoshona Felman's analysis of the reading and writing effects in "The Turn of the Screw,"[39] scholars have recognized the tale's self-conscious investment in the materials of reading and writing. As I contend throughout this book, literacy is the technology of self-possession, the means through which modern subjects are assured that they belong to themselves. But while this self-possession had once seemed to underwrite freedom, the late nineteenth century's democratization of literacy and demotion of the scribal function to mechanical reproduction produced the modern intellectual worker, whose literacy skills could be alienated, rented out for a fee. The tale's narrative frame recapitulates James's scene of composition and, in its flurry of medial transitions, reads like a dark joke on the practice of dictation—the despairing reliance on interlocutors, the master-servant structure, and the layered sediment of composition.

The inside narrative maps this scene of composition onto a scene of instruction, temporally displaced into the 1850s, the period of James's own childhood. Here, abandoned children at a country house practice their reading and writing among the hired hands, ancestors of the knowledge workers who would fill stenographic agencies and telegraph offices in the nineties. James's reading children perform a literacy that materializes the dead, who, as his 1895 note from which the story emerged has it, "invite and solicit, from across dangerous places."[40] The governess suspects Miles and Flora of taking dictation from the ghosts of Miss Jessel and Quint, the mid-century equivalent of James's late-century amanuensis, who might be seen as artifacts of James's new conditions of composition. The "Christmastide toy," as James called his tale, is a game of chiastic substitutions: James is to his amanuensis as the ghosts are to the children, but at the same time the dictating ghosts represent the prehistory of the dictated-to amanuensis, and the children revive James's own childhood. (John La Farge's illustration for the *Collier's Weekly* serialization captures this chiasmus: both the governess and Miles look uncannily like La Farge's earlier drawings of the James children.) Carolyn Steedman has argued that by the end of the nineteenth century the "child-figure came to be used as an extension of the self, a resource for returning to one's own childhood."[41] James uses this prosthetic or medial child in "The Turn of the Screw" to depict and enact literacy practices, once a presumed ground of freedom, that have now become alienated and dispossessed.

In the Coda, "Bedtime Stories," I describe that new genre of children's literature and its companionate domestic reading practice, promoted first in the 1870s, just as "literacy" was becoming established as both a key cultural concept and a public good, through compulsory schooling. Advances in lighting technology, shifts in architectural styles, changing views of nighttime, a broadening of the middle-class—these and many other social and cultural changes transformed late-century late-night reading. But most important of all, the cultural discourse surrounding childhood reading now embraced what it had once feared—reading's association with sleeping, dreaming, fantasizing, and primal emotions—just as the child-study movement embraced play and the "primitive" in children themselves. A concluding return to Stevenson's *A Child's Garden of Verses*, a best seller in America from 1875 to 1895, finds a doubled child figure, bound in a book: a twinned effigy trying hard to contain at once the experience of its child reader and the longings of a ghostly adult.

This book engages with a well-developed "children's turn" in American studies, represented most notably by the work of Jay Fliegelman (*Prodigals and Pilgrims: The American Revolution Against Patriarchal Authority, 1750–1800*), Caroline Levander (*Cradle of Liberty: Race, the Child, and National Belonging from Thomas Jefferson to W. E. B. Du Bois*), Gillian Brown (*Consent of the Governed: The Lockean Legacy in Early American Culture*), and Karen Sánchez-Eppler (*Dependent States: The Child's Part in Nineteenth-Century American Culture*). They have been joined recently by Robin Bernstein (*Racial Innocence: Performing American Childhood from Slavery to Civil Rights*), Anna Mae Duane (*Suffering Childhood in Early America: Violence, Race, and the Making of the Child Victim*), and Courtney Weikle-Mills (*Imaginary Citizens: Child Readers and the Limits of Independence 1640–1868*), among others, as well as by a number of recent essay collections. This recent surge in Americanist scholarship parallels work in British literary studies (notably in romanticism) that have long seen the significance of children and childhood, especially by Alan Richardson (*Literature, Education, and Romanticism: Reading as Social Practice, 1780–1832*), Judith Plotz (*Romanticism and the Vocation of Childhood*), Ann Weirda Rowland (*Romanticism and Childhood: The Infantilization of British Literary Culture*), and Catherine Robson (*Men in Wonderland: The Lost Girlhood of the Victorian Gentleman* and *Heartbeats: Everyday Life and the Memorized Poem*). In her brilliant study of the figure of Mignon, *Strange Dislocations: Childhood and the Idea of Human Interiority, 1780–1930*, the British historian Carolyn Steedman offers an account of the ways in which the "child within was always both immanent . . . and at the same time always representative of a lost realm, lost in the individual past and in the past of the culture."[42] *Reading Children* shows the ways in which this interiorized self emerges and is sustained through literacy practices.

Reading Children counters the tendency of much scholarship to naturalize either, and sometimes both, childhood and literacy by arguing that these cultural concepts, and the practices surrounding them, are more fully understood when seen as mutually constitutive. While work in childhood studies, alive to the complexities of historical childhood, has so far failed to fully take account of the meanings of literacy, book history, for all its attention to the materiality of reading, has similarly failed to take account of discourses of childhood. With few exceptions (notably E. Jennifer Monaghan and Karen Sánchez-Eppler) scholarship in book history treats children almost exclusively as objects of pedagogy and childhood as a romantic or sentimental idea that helps to produce a market for books. By understanding the material artifact of the book as one of the first dedicated spaces of childhood, *Reading Children* brings book history into conversation with the history of childhood, uncovering the ways in which the allure of the codex is bound up with a cultural fantasy of childhood.

CHAPTER 1

Literacy, Commodities, and Cultural Capital

The Case of *Goody Two-Shoes*

> A shoemaker when he has finished one pair of shoes does not
> sit down and contemplate his work in idle satisfaction. . . . The
> shoemaker who so indulged himself would be without wages half
> his time. It is the same with a professional writer of books. . . . I
> had now quite accustomed myself to begin a second pair as soon
> as the first was out of my hands.
> —Anthony Trollope, *Autobiography* (1883)

ACCORDING TO its title page, *The History of Little Goody Two-Shoes*, published by John Newbery in London in 1765 and one of the earliest novels for children, recounts "the Means by which [Goody] acquired her Learning and Wisdom, and in consequence thereof her Estate."[1] To readers who know of the novel beyond its residue in the catchphrase,[2] *Goody* is largely remembered as a tale of educational and social advancement, a baby bildungsroman promoting Enlightenment virtues and values—rationality, self-sufficiency, literacy—which are rewarded in the end with the requisite "coach-and-six," a ubiquitous signifier of prosperity, here promised on the title page. Printed anonymously, like most early children's books, but variously attributed to Oliver Goldsmith or John Newbery among others, *Goody* became a staple of Anglo-American children's publishing for some one hundred and fifty years in its original and in later redactions, and it survives on the pantomime stage as well as in the schoolyard slur. Its long life in America began with Hugh Gaines's 1775 New York edition, Nathaniel Coverly's 1783 Boston edition, and Isaiah Thomas's 1787 Worcester edition, all more or less faithful to the London edition, followed by dozens of redacted, anthologized, sentimentalized, infantilized, remediated (toy books, poems, games, alphabets) and lushly illustrated versions throughout the nineteenth century. *Goody Two-Shoes* features centrally in every history of children's literature and children's publishing. The historian Isaac Kramnick sees *Goody* as an example of Anglo-American "radical bourgeois ideology," and literary scholars have offered nuanced readings in the context of eighteenth-century aesthetics, publishing history, legal history, and the history of childhood.[3] In this chapter, *Goody* offers an early example of the genre and format of a "children's book," whose novelistic plot and characters reveal some of the symbolic values and literary tropes associated with the practices of what will later fall under the key cultural concept "literacy."

We have come to think routinely of literacy as among the fundamental forms of cultural capital, and education has starkly been called "a process of human capital formation," a formula with ever-increasing pertinence to twenty-first-century policy makers.[4] Literacy is thus often to be found in the general neighborhood of capital, if never exactly nestled next to it in the vault. The literacy that comes to be represented to, through, in, and by children in the eighteenth century establishes a discursive relationship between, broadly speaking, literacy and property, when concepts of property were notably fluid, and long before the term "literacy" had come to represent, as it did only in the late nineteenth century, a fully consolidated object of "acquisition," as in the pat phrase "literacy acquisition." It is of course anachronistic to speak of "literacy" in the eighteenth century; in *Goody* what we might now call "literacy" is identified as sheer "learning" and manifests as the mechanics of alphabetization.[5] The literacy that *Goody* promotes and practices is largely reading and not writing. The eighteenth-century Anglo-American curriculum usually offered reading instruction before and in isolation from writing; few of *Goody*'s students would appear in the historian's archive of early modern literates, an archive dependent on signatures (on marriage registers, for example).[6]

The novel's plot takes up a rural orphan girl, who is motivated to learn her letters and to spread this knowledge through teaching; like many another heroine in a novel, near the end of her story the orphan marries well, and she lives to see those who reduced her to poverty reduced in their turn. *Goody* borrows the common property of the Cinderella/Dick Whittington formula and returns it with interest for circulation as a commodity in the eighteenth-century public sphere.[7] Like other children's books, *Goody* cannibalizes genres: satire, mock epic, ghost story, fairy tale, primer, courtesy or conduct book, picaresque, fable, adventure. *Goody* shares with other, "adult" eighteenth-century novels the trajectory of riches (or at least competency) to rags to riches, and an episodic, digressive narrative, and it even contains a mini-novel (a twelve-page *Vicar of Wakefield*-like tale), advertising the genre to the next generation of consumers.

Goody on the Commons, *Goody* in the Public Sphere

> The first idea which must be given him is therefore less that
> of liberty than that of property.
> —Jean-Jacques Rousseau, *Emile* (1762)

The half-title that appears over the first page of text reads: "The Renowned History of Little Goody Two-Shoes; Commonly called, Old Goody Two-Shoes," a naming that the novel's first words comically retract: "All the world must allow, that *Two Shoes* was not her real Name" (4). With this gesture, the narrative satirically both establishes and calls into question the identity of the heroine and begins with a genealogical, or an ontological, question mark. While the fairy tale's "once upon a time" opens onto the space-time of fantasy, an eternal elsewhere, "All the world must allow" marks the here and now of life lived out in public, and even in the print public sphere, with a nod toward a social contract; a knowing and worldly voice articulates and asserts the world's interest in the identity and the fate of a little girl.

Like so many novels, this one opens with a crisis of property, laid out in a self-consciously political "editor's introduction." The space of the novel is mapped as a farming village, tyrannized by the local lord and his lackey, who between them hold all the legal offices in the parish of Mouldwell: overseer, church warden, surveyor of highways, and justice of the peace. Farmer Meanwell has for a long time leased his land from Sir Timothy Gripe; Farmer Graspall gathers up the leases on all of Sir Timothy's farms; Meanwell gets embroiled in lawsuits to try to maintain his own lease and ends up in penury. "As soon as Mr. *Meanwell* had called together his Creditors, Sir *Timothy* seized for a Year's Rent, and turned the Farmer, his Wife, little *Margery*, and her Brother out of Doors, without any of the Necessaries of Life to support them" (9). Although this catastrophe is attributed in part to "the wicked Persecutions" of the two villains, it is also a result of "the Misfortunes which [Meanwell] met with in Business" (5), placing some of the responsibility on Farmer Meanwell himself and on a world in which business can have special, even fatal, dangers. As the legal historian Robert Gordon has put it, "To be in business at all [in the eighteenth century] . . . was to surrender a large discretionary authority over one's person and property."[8] The opening frame ends with a lament, or a jeremiad, about the consolidation of farmland: "These Reflections, Sir, have been rendered necessary, by the unaccountable and diabolical scheme which many Gentlemen now give into, of laying a number of farms into one, and very often a whole Parish into one Farm; which in the end must reduce the common People to a state of vassalage . . . and will in Time depopulate the Kingdom" (11–12). The introduction often has been read as evidence of authorship (echoes of "The Deserted Village" and *The Vicar of Wakefield* make Oliver Goldsmith a prime suspect) and as evidence of the mixed motives of and mixed audiences for early children's literature.[9] In later editions, it is often dropped, sometimes explicitly as being too radical, and its details get condensed to a sentence or two of text. Mary Jane Godwin (William's second wife), for example, adds an aspirational disclaimer: "Everybody knows, that, in this happy country, the poor are to the full as much protected by our excellent laws, as are the highest and the richest nobles in the land; and the humblest cottager enjoys an equal share of the blessings of English liberty with the sons of kings themselves" and Farmer Meanwell is "too noble-minded to retain a property which now could not justly be called his."[10] Some American editions of the 1790s add a patriotic motto: "Such is the state of things in Britain. AMERICANS, prize your Liberty, guard over your rights, and be happy."[11] But the local anxieties of the editor's polemic motivate the narrative's investment in elaborating an alternative to the shackles of land and leases and their inevitable losses on the shifting economic ground of the eighteenth century.

In the first chapter the parents die apace, leaving Margery and her sibling Tommy reduced to a Hogarthian—or Hobbesian—existence of begging in the street. Pushed to the spatial and social margins, Margery and Tommy must live on hedge berries and charity from the poor, who had once been the objects of their father's charity. If the center is inhabited by economic practices that the editor abhors, including, along with the land-grabbing, the ascension "by Marriage and by Death" (5) of Sir Timothy to his estate, Margery and Tommy's loss of family and exile to the margin promises a critique, perhaps a renovation, of the center. The orphaned child is perhaps the most vulnerable victim of the practices decried in the introduction.[12] Central among the deprivations of the orphan is the loss of private life, with its affection and protection, but also with its expectations, responsibilities, and duties; lacking these, Goody to some extent accesses the role and voice of the mythic orphan. Over the course of her narrative, Goody draws to herself the power of those whom she implicitly and explicitly supplants, or, of those whom she repossesses or forecloses on: the aristocrat, the witch, the spirit, the romance hero, Cinderella and her fairy godmother, the landlord, to name some of these. At the same time, as an entity by

Figure 1. "Pray look at him." Tommy in his new "Jacket and Trowsers." *Goody Two-Shoes: A Facsimile Reproduction of the Edition of 1766.* Intro. Charles Welsh. Detroit: Singing Tree Press, 1970.

definition inhabiting the commons—she belongs to no one and everyone—Goody emerges as a product of print and of the eighteenth-century public sphere.

Shoes

> I would also advise . . . to have his *Shooes* so thin, that they might leak and *let in Water.*
> —John Locke, *Some Thoughts Concerning Education* (1693)

How poor was Margery? She was so poor that she owned only one shoe. An unnamed gentleman brings the children to the attention of the clergyman Mr. Smith and offers to set Tommy up to make a living at sea, first by outfitting him in a new "Jacket and Trowsers"; the benefactor gives Mr. Smith money to buy Margery some clothes and orders for her "a new Pair of Shoes" (17). If the first function of Tommy's clothes is a published display ("Pray look at him," the narrator instructs, offering up an illustration [Figure 1]), the second is an intimate gesture: when Tommy and Margery part as he heads for London, he makes use of his new clothes by wiping her tears with "the End of his Jacket" (19). With Tommy gone, Margery was inconsolable: "She

cried out, *Two Shoes, Mame, see two Shoes.* And so she behaved to all the People she met, and by that Means obtained the Name of *Goody Two-Shoes,* though her Playmates called her *Old Goody Two-Shoes.*

Figure 2. "*Two Shoes, Mame, see two Shoes.*" *Goody Two-Shoes: A Facsimile Reproduction of the Edition of 1766.* Intro. Charles Welsh. Detroit: Singing Tree Press, 1970.

ran all round the Village, crying for her Brother" (20). Enter the shoemaker, bearing new shoes: "Nothing could have supported Little *Margery* under the Affliction she was in for the Loss of her Brother, but the Pleasure she took in her *two Shoes.* She ran out to Mrs. *Smith* as soon as they were put on, and stroking down her ragged Apron thus, cried out, *Two Shoes, Mame, see two Shoes*" (20–21) (Figure 2).[13] From this moment, she becomes "*Goody Two-Shoes.*"[14]

For Goody as for Tommy, the gift of clothing functions as an investiture. In their discussion of Renaissance clothing, Peter Stallybrass and Ann Jones note that "it was investiture, the putting on of clothes, that . . . constituted a person as a monarch or a freeman of a guild or a household servant. Investiture was . . . the means by which a person was given a form, a shape, a social function, a 'depth.'" Just as Tommy's proudly displayed new look dresses him for the sea of masculinity he is about to set sail on, Goody's shoes invest her with some to-be-specified new powers, along with her very name. Clothing, Stallybrass and Jones remind us, "reminds."[15] But if Tommy's new clothes make sense, what do Goody's shoes "remind" us of?

Powerful symbols, shoes, "totems of mobility and promise," as the theater critic John Lahr has called them.[16] Expensive necessities in the North, shoes define boundaries between genders and races and classes. Shoes, more vividly than any other garment, enact the melding of the sexual fetish with the commodity fetish. For us, if not quite yet for the eighteenth-century shopper, shoes practically signify "fetish." These erotics at the level of the state seem to have motivated Imelda Marcos, and before her Marie Antoinette, who is said to have owned five hundred pairs.[17] While their husbands provided boots for armies, these wives performed a glamorous, witchy burlesque of state power. Shoes, as these two shoppers must have known, are traditionally thought to bring good luck; hence their use in marriage rites and the phenomenon of "chimney shoes," embedded in houses presumably to ward off evil spirits.[18]

Magical shoes in fairy tales compress distances (seven-league boots) and enable revelation and elevation in the case of Cinderella. The Stith Thompson *Motif-Index of Folk Literature* notes 196 references to shoes;[19] one of these is a tale in which a task requires a hero to "come neither barefoot nor shod," a riddle that he solves by coming with one shoe on and one shoe off. The single shoe, then, might sometimes signal shrewdness. In her work on fairy tales, Marina Warner notes several fabulous (in every sense) shoes, including a cult of the Virgin's foot in Naples, where "Mary's own slipper" is rumored to reside.[20] Even the shoemaker has special status, not only for his role in fairy tales but also, as tradition has it, as one of the most literate of working people in the seventeenth and eighteenth centuries.[21]

Shoes resonate as both cultural icons and material artifacts, infused with powers to traverse real and symbolic distances, to attract, reveal, master, protect, and fascinate; a bare necessity, they are symbols as well of excess and accumulation. Goody Two-Shoes, then, is named for the shoes that have been given to her; more precisely, though, her name is echoed back to her from her oral repetition of delight in the shoes: "And so she behaved to all the People she met, and by that Means obtained the Name" (21). In the old-fashioned sense, she "published" her emotional investment in them, like a town crier. Biographically unhinged from genealogy, her name poetically or tropically shifts from the satiric allegory and metaphor of "Meanwell" to the synecdoche and metonymy of shoes. Her patronymic is overwritten by the metonym that her public gives her by acclamation. Goody as diva, perhaps. But also, in the repudiation of inheritance her rechristening represents, Goody stands as a new kind of child—the child as a kind of commons, not only resourceful in herself but a general resource as well. Goody's identity is established, or rather denominated, not by the Lockean fantasy of property in herself but rather by acceding to the common property in herself held by others.[22] And although the shoes set Goody on her peripatetic way, they also suggest a certain fixity and stability; the shoes render her the opposite of footloose or vagrant.

Goody's "*Two Shoes, Mame*" is the last passage in the text and the only really vivid one, in which, for the modern reader, Margery Meanwell resembles the kind of child we've grown used to encountering in literature. But the shoes, grounding and indispensable, function to transform that child, riven with emotion, into an adult-like agent. As "Two-Shoes" overwrites her surname, the generic "Goody" for "good wife" supplants her Christian name. This humble status marker, not normally given to children, makes her into a mini-woman overnight; indeed, her "Playmates called her *Old Goody Two-Shoes*" (21). Propelled from a world of virtues and vices (Meanwells and Graspalls) to a world of things, "Goody" bridges the two realms, embedding in the person of the child both goodness and goods. If metonymy is the trope of realism, as Roman Jakobson suggests, Goody's name also might shift her from one genre toward another, as the subsequent names in the novel are all nonallegorical.[23] Moreover, because shoes of course normally come in pairs, "Two-Shoes" names a tautology, which, by emphasizing Goody's new normative and wholesome status, calls attention to the disruption of poverty.

For her great losses (home, farm, parents, sibling) Goody's two shoes offer as a fully sufficient substitute an intimate commodity, which transforms her grief into an energizing delight associated with her new things. The sequence of actors in the biography of these shoes—her protectors, the Smiths; the mysterious philanthropist; the shoemaker—gives the impression that, made to measure and by hand, and purchased in benevolence, the shoes emerge from a preindustrial economy, imbued with practices of auratic artisanry and of a communal circle of gift, charity, deference, and obligation.[24] And yet they are commodities as well as gifts.[25]

Once the shoes are sutured to the child, they circulate her, not only through the episodes of her "history" but also across the pages of her book and onto the bookshelves of shops and into the hands of consumers— probably, rather frequently, as gifts.[26] Like the shoes, the book circulates and disseminates Goody. As two models of a commodity, shoe and book, each perhaps aspires to be like the other; the shoe might like the prestige and the distribution networks belonging to the book, while the book would like to be a necessity with built-in obsolescence, and a channel into the fashion system. Both commodities get their wish, over time. And the book is the model for the kind of commodity that shoes begin to turn into by the end of the eighteenth century: mass produced, branded, and distributed, rather than local and made to measure.[27]

Not long after getting back on her newly shod feet, Goody is made homeless once more. Graspall and Gripe reappear, threatening to ruin the kindly Smiths if they keep harboring Goody. The Smiths, becoming risk-averse at the thought that "the People who had ruined her Father could at any Time have ruined them" (23), throw Goody out. Immediately following this moment, the narrative recounts that "Little *Margery* saw how good, and how wise Mr. *Smith* was, and concluded, that this was owing to his great Learning" (24). Although Mr. Smith's goodness may seem a cloistered, even a merely "bookish," virtue, since he casts an orphan girl back onto the wide world, this observation motivates Goody to learn to read.

One might attribute this abrupt narrative illogic to the slapdash nature of hackwork. Whatever its source, the solecism lends an element of the dream or fantasy, which have this same paratactic quality: I was in my room, I was on the street. The narrative drops whatever anxiety it had about Goody's homelessness, as though the shoes now magically provide homelike protection; they don't ward off evil, but they do ward off the effects associated with it. It may not be paradoxical to say that the shoes provide an aura of hominess while at the same time they seem to rob Goody of affect; although she sobbed with grief when her brother went to sea and was delighted to the same degree by her shoes, she doesn't seem to register that she's cast out again. With this leap in narrative and emotional logic the homeless orphan girl propels herself into literacy, and in a way propels *Goody* into literary history.

The Alphabetic Fantastic

Goody's method for teaching herself aligns her with what will become a tradition of slave autodidacticism that Frederick Douglass records in his narrative eighty years later;[28] in Goody's version, "she used to meet the little Boys and Girls as they came from School, borrow their Books, and sit down and read till they returned" (25). Before long, she is teaching the alphabet to her playmates. Along with her shoes, then, Goody is associated with another interesting set of objects: the alphabet letters. Following Locke's prescription in *Some Thoughts Concerning Education* to make learning to read playful,[29] she calls her spelling lessons "the Game" (26) and carries around what the text calls her "rattletrap" letters,[30] which she has cut from wood: ten sets of lowercase and six sets of uppercase letters (25–26). Readers aren't likely to pause over this, but if they do, they will note that Goody is carrying around in her little basket some 420 pieces of wood.[31] Suddenly she's in the realm of the mythic, like the blues singer who says a matchbox holds his clothes. And though 420 pieces of wood are too many for a girl to carry, those sixteen sets of letters make for scarcity, once you begin to compose (as any printer would tell you). The narrative is silent on these contradictions, and, like the miracle of the loaves and fishes, the letters endlessly offer themselves, just as many as required, as the children make syllables with them (ba, be, bi, bo, bu [33]) and words (Bread, Apple-pye, Turnip [35]) and sentences (*"The Lord have Mercy upon me, and grant that I may honour my Father and Mother, and love my Brothers and Sifters, Relations and Friends, and all my Playmates, and every Body, and endeavour to make them happy"* [38]).

With Goody's materializing of the letters, bringing them into the world of bread and turnips and apple pies, the tale glides noiselessly across into the fantastic or the marvelous. The most interesting analyses of the novel have noted the force of the irrational in the text, finding that the narrative offers up to the reader the sensations associated with "raw-head and bloody-bones" while, following Locke, rationally debunking the content of the same superstitions. But the tendency is to assume that the alphabet is on the side of the rational, while the alphabet in fact, as the alphabet *will* do, initiates the fantastic in this novel.[32] Letters are, among other things, a spatializing technology; one of their stocks-in-trade is to be psychotropic, to distort, to bring far things close up, to make the absent present, to create tiny worlds that feel capacious, to bring the dead to life, and so on.

In a novel you can have as many things in a basket as you want to. And the printing of all the words and sentences that the letters in the basket are said to produce supports the fiction, or the lie, that Goody's letters are sufficient, a fiction further abetted by the often food-associated words that Goody has her charges spell: beef, turnip, plumb pudding. Indeed, in the illustrations of the original, she looks like Little Red Riding Hood, but rather than the dutiful, if dallying, daughter, carrying mother's food to grandmother, she's a little Cadmus, carrying letters instead, which can merely represent food (Figure 3). Yet this is seen not as their lack but as their bounty. Goody supplants and, in a way, repossesses the stock role of storyteller or old wife. But rather than producing ephemeral talk, she manufactures treen letters. In her role as type founder instructing the children in composing, she seems less like a dame-school teacher than like a stand-in for the printer and bookseller John Newbery.

I once went her Rounds with her, and was highly diverted, as you may be, if you please to look into the next Chapter.

C H A P. V.

How Little Two-Shoes *became a trot-ting* Tutoress, *and how she taught her young Pupils.*

IT was about seven o'Clock in the Morning when we set out on this important

important Business, and the first House we came to was Farmer *Wilson's.* See here it is.

Here *Margery* stopped, and ran up to the Door, *Tap, tap, tap.* Who's there? Only little goody *Two-Shoes,* answered *Margery,* come to teach *Billy.* Oh Little *Goody,* says Mrs. *Wilson,* with Pleasure in her Face, I am glad to see you, *Billy* wants you

Figure 3. The "trotting tutoress," with her magical basket. *Goody Two-Shoes: A Facsimile Reproduction of the Edition of 1766.* Intro. Charles Welsh. Detroit: Singing Tree Press, 1970.

Goody's Economic Bildung

> Send a treasure token token
> Write it on a pound note pound note
> —Adam Ant, "Goody Two-Shoes"

In his *Idler* essay number 19 (1758), Samuel Johnson satirized Newbery as "Jack Whirler"—"that great philosopher . . . whose business keeps him in perpetual motion, and whose motion always eludes his business; who is always to do what he never does, who cannot stand still because he is wanted in another place, and who is wanted in many places because he stays in none," and concludes that Jack Whirler "lives in perpetual fatigue . . . because he does not consider . . . that whoever is engaged in multiplicity of business must transact much by substitution, and leave something to hazard; and that he who attempts to do all will waste his life in doing little." Whirler's perpetual motion and breathless pursuit of commerce render him a phantom, "equally invisible to his friends and his customers," an emanation of a commercial economy devoted to the movement of commodities and of dematerialized property.[33]

Goody comes to embody the literacy that accompanies this new commercial figure, mirroring his ephemerality while supplying for him a kind of ballast. As she labors to materialize and distribute the letters, what she produces—the homemade letters, not intended for exchange, given freely— might be classed as what the anthropologist Annette Weiner has called "inalienable possessions," things that their creators "keep-while-giving." Like the cloth that circulates in Maori exchange, one of the subjects of classic anthropology that Weiner revises, the letters as conceived in *Goody* are the product of female labor. Such "inalienable possessions are the representation of how social identities are reconstituted through time. . . . These possessions then are the most potent force in the effort to subvert change, while at the same time they stand as the corpus of change."[34] As such, Goody's letters constitute a mainstay in the midst of dangerous speculative paper, a substitution for such previously inalienable possessions as land, for those who have lost, or could never have attained, an estate.

If, within the novel, Goody's letters are a hybrid kind of property, the novel *Goody* is merrily self-conscious about its own status as a print commodity and as an engine of commerce. The novel shares with other Newbery productions the aroma of the print shop and the apothecary (like many booksellers, Newbery also traded in patent medicines),[35] not only in the waggishness of the narrative voice but also in its marketing of the advantages of being "lettered" and of the sensual attractions of print. The illustrations engage the reader interactively, and the narrator demands a physical engagement with the text: "Pray look at him" (17); "as you see in the Print" (27); "See here it is" (29); and "Now, pray little Reader, take this Bodkin, and see if you can point out the Letters" (31), and so on. Such gestures insist on the fact that the story comes into being solely and unabashedly for the print marketplace; not just learning to read but an entire world of commerce becomes an interactive component in the book. In the most notorious example of this print-commodity effect,[36] after the editor's introduction, as chapter 1 opens, Goody's father was "seized with a violent fever in a Place where Dr. *James's* Powder was not to be had, and where he died miserably" (13). What is Dr. James's Powder? The back leaves of the Newbery editions advertise all manner of things found in Mr. Newbery's shop, including "Dr. James's Powders for Fevers, the Small-Pox, Measles, Colds, etc. 2

shillings 6."[37] Goody's father dies for lack of a commodity available at Newbery's shop; it's a condensed and displaced version of why he really does die: for lack of property. He dies, in fact, because he existed in a world in which subsistence and sustenance depended on real property, on expanses of land. Goody, it would seem, survives and thrives by establishing her identity in portable goods—shoes, for example—and, materialized as her quasi-magical "rattletrap alphabets," the inalienable property of literacy.

Thanks to her shoes and her rattletrap alphabets, her teaching becomes her livelihood, as she becomes a *"trotting Tutoress"* (28) "instructing those who were more ignorant than herself" (25). Goody soon becomes Mrs. Margery Two-Shoes, President of the A, B, C College (65–66). Much of the narrative is then given over to her pedagogy, which employs, among other things, a lamb, a lark, and a dog; a raven named Ralph, who can speak, read, and spell (70); and a pigeon named Tom, who can only spell and read. Except for two, who were, notably, gifts, the animals were all abused or menaced, and Goody purchases them from their abusers, removing them from what appears to be a dangerous commons, full of nasty little boys, and bringing them under the protective sign of the alphabet. The animals serve Goody and her students, in their turn, and are mentors in their own right: Tippy the Lark teaches early rising, Ralph the Raven supervises the capital letters (Figure 4), Tom the Pidgeon carries important messages and takes "Care of the small" letters (72), Will the Ba-lamb rewards good children by carrying their books (78), and Jumper the Dog is "the porter of the College" (77) and goes so far as to save the lives of Goody and all of her students when the schoolroom collapses (98).[38] The salvation of (and then by) the animals underscores the ethic that learning one's letters is meant to encourage (as in the somewhat shaky logic of Mr. Smith's goodness). Goody doesn't plead or beg for the animals or proceed legally to save them; she merely, without fanfare, lays out cash for them. It's one of few such transactions in the novel (the purchase of shoes and clothing, and the expenditures noted in Goody's will at the end are others), but it suggests a renovated purpose for money. Through this exchange, the animals are removed from circulation and brought into a space of safety identified with literacy, converting the old regime's landed estate into a virtual and portable protectorate, in which animals, like small children, will be safeguarded. (This even though for much of the narrative Goody's own material existence continues to be abject; like an impoverished aristocrat starving on his inalienable land, she continues to sleep in barns until at least chapter 5 [39]).[39]

Along with the safety of animals and children, the novel actively promotes the economic security of women. Toward the end of Goody's story, when Sir

Figure 4. Ralph the Raven, who looks after the large letters. *The History of Little Goody Two-Shoes.* Philadelphia: W. Young, 1793. Courtesy American Antiquarian Society.

Charles Jones proposed, "she would not consent to be made a Lady, till he had effectually provided for his Daughter" (130). Not only does the daughter receive a settlement, in a surprise move so does Goody: "Just as the Clergyman had opened his Book" at the wedding ceremony, "a Gentleman richly dressed ran into the Church, and cry'd, Stop! stop!" (132). The alarming stranger is "*Tom Two-Shoes,*" who insisted on seeing "that a proper Settlement was made on her" (133).[40] The careful details of property settled for the safety of women answers the economics of the opening, with its lesson of the recklessness of relying on the suspect promises of heritability. The novel's economic bildung goes one step further. Sir Charles dies (like Mr. Meanwell, of a "violent fever" [134], though no mention is made of Dr. James's Powder). "Lady Margery" purchased "the whole Manour of *Mouldwell*" and "threw it into different Farms"(136–37); in her will, she set aside a certain portion of land to be planted with potatoes for the use of the poor, "but if any took them to sell they were deprived of that Privilege ever after" (139). The poor are prohibited from com-modifying their potatoes;[41] if they break the taboo in order to rise up out of Mouldwell, they'd better keep walking. Cash is a worrisome matter in *Goody*. Though it purchased Goody's shoes, and Goody redeemed her animals with it, she has a King Midas nightmare after she acquires her wealth: after "seeing her Husband receive a very large Sum, her Heart went pit pat, pit pat, all the Evening, and she began to think that Guineas were pretty Things" (141–42). Associated with excitation and mobility, cash destabilizes, whereas Goody's transactions function as social balms and sedatives.

The final episode in the genealogy of Goody's marriage settlement, in a section of the "Appendix," recounts the adventures of Goody's long-lost brother,[42] who, as if acknowledging a new matriarchal regime, returns with Goody's surname. In this mini Robinsoniade, Tom Two-Shoes becomes a castaway "on that Part of the Coast of *Africa* inhabited by the *Hottentots*" (145). In the company of a lion, he explores "*Prester John's* Country," and in "*Utopia*" he comes upon a statue inscribed by an Arabian philosopher with a riddle ("*On May-Day . . . I shall have a Head of Gold*" [147]). Solving the puzzle, Tommy digs at the spot where the shadow of the statue's head falls on May 1, and uncovers a treasure chest, engraved "As thou hast got the GOLDEN HEAD, / Observe the *Golden Mean*, / Be *Good* and be happy" (150). It is this money that Tom settles on Goody. Her money, then, comes from the dead, like inherited wealth, but it's positioned in colonialist terms as emerging from a kind of commonwealth, a world-historical past, here figured as Africa and the "East," and as a boon marked as a legacy to the quick-witted, rather than to the high-born.

Spectral Literacy

> Can write my name in heaven in invisible ink.
> —Elvis Costello, "Little Goody Two-Shoes"

The sleight of hand that brings Goody her marriage portion underlies the economics of literacy throughout the text. Although the novel devotes many of its pages to the mechanics of alphabetic literacy, the representation of reading is not what we have since come to expect. Goody doesn't help tenants read their leases or their almanacs. It's not only that this is not the instrumental literacy that we might imagine for mercantilism; no one is reading the Bible, either. After the early scene of borrowing books, Goody is portrayed only once as reading anything herself. Her own literacy mainly serves to gain her employment to reproduce her own literacy. The economy of literacy Goody inhabits resembles nothing so much as a speculative bubble as her faith in literacy leads her to circulate her facility in literacy, which leads to more tutoring in literacy. The benefits that accrue to others are largely philanthropic and therapeutic, oblique consequences of the presence of the good and kind Goody. This enclosed system requires a faith in the association between literacy and respectability, virtue, wealth, safety. In other words, an association between literacy and the traditional attributes of inherited wealth in land.

The easy illogic of Goody's economy hints at magic, just as the episodes describing Goody's motives and Goody's basket opened fissures into the fantastic or the marvelous. But beginning in chapter 6 (about a third of the way into the novel), *Goody* the book situates Goody the girl more explicitly in relation to occult forces. The village attends the funeral of Lady Ducklington—"Who does not know Lady Ducklington," begins this chapter (45), echoing the opening's "All the world must allow"—about which the narrator (sounding very Newbery-like) moralizes that "the Money they squandered away, would have been better laid out in little Books for children, or in Meat, Drink, and Cloaths for the Poor" (46). After the funeral, "about Four o'Clock in the Morning, the Bells were heard to jingle in the Steeple, which frightened the People prodigiously, who all thought it was Lady *Ducklington*'s Ghost dancing among the Bell-ropes" (48). After much fearful hesitation the villagers unlock the church door, and "what Sort of a Ghost do ye think appeared? Why Little *Two-Shoes*, who . . . had fallen asleep in one of the Pews . . . and was shut in all Night" (49). Goody recounts being accosted by a mysterious presence which had "laid, as I thought, its Hands over my Shoulders" (52) and touched her neck with "something . . . as cold as Marble, ay, as cold as Ice" (52–53), a presence that is revealed to be Neighbour Saunderson's dog. Thus does the poor, diligent, homeless, ABC-toting little girl, envoy of a new form of property relations, disperse and displace the ghost of Lady Ducklington, emblem of the useless, spendthrift, aristocratic order.

If Goody here stands in the ghost position, assuming the prestige of both ghosts and ghostbusters, later in the narrative she supplants the hero of old romances. Goody invents something she calls a Considering Cap, a three-sided hat, each side of which bears a motto: "I MAY BE WRONG," "IT IS FIFTY TO ONE BUT YOU ARE," and "I'LL CONSIDER OF IT," while "the other parts on the out-side, were filled with odd Characters, as unintelligible as the Writings of the old *Egyptians*" (115). The cap functions as a "Charm for the Passions," a Dr. James's Powder for the temperament (115). But here, along with the rational messages, are illegible characters, supplementing the rational with the force of the ancient and the occult. The narrative notes that the Wishing Cap of the medieval romance of Fortunatus is "said to have conveyed People instantly from one Place to another" and lauds a Cap that instead transforms the "Temper and Disposition" (119). In the original romance of Fortunatus, the Wishing Cap and a bottomless purse, with which Goody's bountiful basket echoes, descended to the hero's sons, who lost the first and burned the second.[43] *Fortunatus* is, in effect, a monitory tale of inheritance. Goody's cap inverts the expected roles of inherited and acquired or created property. The hero's Wishing Cap induced mobility but led to exhaustion in the next generation; Goody's Considering Cap functions, by contrast, to stabilize and fix in place, to tranquilize, and to render productive. An invention of a self-made girl rather than a questionable legacy, Goody's Cap circumscribes the kind of mobility that her literacy promotes.

Among the novel's most appealing traits are Goody's animal familiars. In a famous episode, suspicious aspects of her husbandry and her role as a local weatherwoman, using a barometer to help the farmers figure out when to bring in the hay, lead to an accusation of witchcraft. The narrator characteristically moralizes, "It is impossible for a Woman to pass for a Witch, unless she is *very poor, very old,* and lives in the Neighbourhood where the People are *void of common Sense*" (127). Acquitted at the witch trial, Goody manages to charm Sir Charles Jones with her rationality, and she soon becomes his wife. For all the debunking of witchcraft, the original illustrator and all subsequent ones relish Goody's bewitching qualities, posing her with her creatures perched on her shoulders and arms (Figure 5; Plates 3–5).

When Goody died "a Monument, but without Inscription, was erected to her Memory in the Church-yard, over which the Poor as they pass weep continually, so that the Stone is ever bathed in Tears" (140). Despite Goody's good works, the poor are still poor. And though this passage echoes Thomas Gray's "Elegy" of 1751, even the "Elegy" permits the poor more than Goody is allotted: "frail memorial," for example, "uncouth rhymes," and "Their name, their years, spelt by th' unletter'd Muse." (Even a dormouse, earlier in Goody's narrative, receives an epitaph [114].) Why is Goody's monument uninscribed? Did the villagers in fact never learn how to read? Or did no local engraver learn how to write? Or is this the final melding of Goody the girl with Goody the commodity: she's an artifact like Jack Whirler, who exists only in circulation? I'll return to the question of Goody's lack of inscription.

In his essay on Gray's "Elegy" and Anna Letitia Barbauld's "Warrington Academy" (1773), John Guillory begins with the paradox that the vernacular canon "is at once conceived to be . . . 'common' property, while . . . literacy itself is by no means a universal possession." He notes the complex negotiation required to assign "the cultural value of a symbolic commodity such as vernacular literacy" and finds that "the distinction between classical and vernacular literacy corresponds roughly to the difference between two relations to property, to wit, entitlement and acquisition." In Anna Letitia Barbauld's poem about the Dissenting Academy at Warrington, an institution designed to educate a new class, the poet "insists upon the equation of knowledge with the form of property. Such property is acquired; it is not passed on like noble

Figure 5. An elegant Goody with her animal familiars. "The History of Little Goody-Two Shoes," in *A Treasury of Pleasure Books for Young Children: With More Than One Hundred Illustrations by John Absolon and Harrison Weir.* New York: D. Appleton, 1853. Courtesy American Antiquarian Society.

blood." Of the locodescriptive genre, the poem of place, to which the "Elegy" and "Warrington Academy" belong, Guillory writes that "it is uniquely situated between the [classical] commonplace book and the vernacular anthology" and provided "the new class of literate professionals" a site to "stand together in a common place, a place which was, at the same time, private property."[44]

More so than Gray and Barbauld, Goody, for all her country ways, inhabits and speaks from Grub Street, but the politics of literacy the novel promotes resonate with those that Guillory lays out. Directly addressing the new child of vernacular pedagogy and satirizing classical learning, Goody represents the alphabet as universally available, even to the most lowly; nature itself, in the person of Goody's mascots, seems to want to distribute the alphabet freely.[45] But, in its explicit framing of the narrative in terms of property, *Goody* at the same time expresses ambivalence over what kind of property literacy constitutes.

Property, as a concept, as a form of capital, and as a set of practices, is easily as layered and problematic in the eighteenth century as the practices associated with literacy. Many scholars have recounted the transition to new forms of property in an increasingly market-driven culture in both England and America across the eighteenth century. "In the late eighteenth century, property in contracts, property in hopes and expectations," writes Robert Gordon, noting a key aspect of this transformation, "was becoming the prevalent form of commercial property: paper money, shares of the public debt, certificates of stock in land or insurance companies, mortgages on land or inventory, bills of exchange, promissory notes, accounts receivable."[46] For the formation of both persons and publics, shifts in the meaning of property have profound consequences, since property in land grounds both the Lockean concept of identity and the republican formula for virtue. J. G. A. Pocock writes that "land and inheritance remained essential to virtue, and virtue to the ego's reality in its own sight," but "the ideal of personality-sustaining property was no sooner formulated than it was seen to be threatened"; and further that "the rise of forms of property seeming to rest on fantasy and false consciousness" made "the foundations of personality themselves appear imaginary."[47]

The mode of literacy that Goody, the girl and the novel, promotes and circulates is a kind of homeopathic remedy to the problems posed by property in the late eighteenth century. For the self haunted by forms of property passing away and frightened by the spectral nature of paper property and by the phantasmagoric nature of the commodity, Goody's therapy substitutes a literacy that incorporates and renovates these forms. Goody treats the dematerialization of property with the fantastic materiality of letters. In *Goody*, literacy is meant to be an inalienable property that can be absorbed into the person, supplementing the Lockean formulation that a person has "property in himself," and extending this entitlement to the smallest orphan girl. Unlike an estate or an heirloom, literacy lacks substance; it has nothing to offer but the paper it's written on, a promise of unspecified bounty. It's true no one can take it away from you, but chances are you can't trade it in for anything.[48] And what does it amount to once you have it? It's hard to say; certainly it's famously hard to quantify.[49]

If part of the work of *Goody* is to acclimate the reader to new forms of property, the problem it faces is to establish a site for alphabetization that will supply a mimetic form of property—internalized, spacious, timeless. Such mimetic property offers a purchase for subjectivity, especially for those for whom other forms of property, perhaps even especially property in the self, are problematic—the dispossessed, women, children, the poor, slaves. Goody's monument lacks inscription perhaps in order to return Goody to an undated and unnamed common property, to a world that maintains itself by talk and memory, and doesn't make the kind of distinctions implied by Gray's "Elegy" between simple and complicated, unlettered and lettered lives. Pierre Bourdieu writes of cultural capital, especially in its "embodied" state (that is, in the person, rather than in its "objectified" state in books and works of art), "It cannot be accumulated beyond the appropriating capacities of an individual agent; it declines and dies with its bearer. . . . It defies the old, deep-rooted distinction the Greek jurists made between inherited properties (*ta patroa*) and acquired properties (*epikteta*), i.e., those which an individual adds to his heritage. It thus manages to combine the prestige of innate property with the merits of acquisition."[50] In the case of Goody, the gift of the two shoes, which sets Goody's "history" properly in motion, might now be seen as an act of sympathetic magic by which the commodity confers on the recipient the accumulation of cultural capital. The literacy that is the legacy of this capital is constructed as a haunted piece of property, and Goody is the new old wife whose spells only seemed to have transformed entirely into spelling.

Afterlives of *Goody*

The original *Goody* renovated the traditional tale-taling old wife by making her an agent of literacy, while infusing the alphabetic letters (and, by extension, the act of reading) with some of her ancient allure. And yet, if *Goody* alphabetized the old wife, putting her out of a job, the old wife soon restaked her claim. The 1809 *Alphabet of Goody Two Shoes*, an elegantly engraved image-and-rhyme alphabet book, uses Goody's alphabetic brand prestige to promote its own circulation: "V was a Village, / Where liv'd near the brook, / The renown'd Goody Two-shoes, / Who sends you this book" (Figure 6).[51] This Goody bears no trace of the orphaned Margery Meanwell, or any echo of her story, melding her with Mother Goose, Old Mother Jumper, and other stock nursery figures. In the nineteenth century, even as the novel continued to circulate in redacted form for children, Goody was becoming a meme and a brand, evacuated of her political and narrative complexity and often, strikingly, of her girl and child power as well.[52] The narrative that promoted alphabetic literacy as a form of internalized property that could challenge and supersede aristocratic inheritance soon lost its urgency, becoming a souvenir of a fairy-tale past.[53] Thus, the original's opening salvo—"All the world must allow, that *Two Shoes* was not her real name"—

Figure 6. Within a few decades, "Goody Two-Shoes" had become linked in the cultural imagination to the traditional "old wife" figure, who now elided her orality with the alphabet letters and books. *Alphabet of Goody Two Shoes.* Philadelphia: Johnson and Warner, 1809. Courtesy American Antiquarian Society.

turns into this 1824 version: "Few histories, which have been written for the amusement and instruction of the little world, have been more read and esteemed than that of Goody Two-Shoes, and while shoes continue to be worn, this little book will never cease to be read."[54] "All the world" has collapsed into "the little world," and Goody has been reduced to someone who lives in a book.

Figure 7. This looming Goody offers her shoes with a suggestive lifting of her skirt. *Little Goody Two-Shoes* (Miss Merryheart's series). New York: McLoughlin Brothers [between 1859 and 1862?]. Courtesy American Antiquarian Society.

Goody's afterlife can be charted through the images that soon overtook her narrative. From its earliest editions *Goody* had warmly invited physical interplay by turning directly to the child reader in text and image: Tommy shows off his outfit; Goody travels as the "trotting tutoress"; Ralph the Raven and Tom the Pigeon sort their letters.[55] (See Figures 1–4.) But as image technology became more sophisticated and the market for children's books expanded in the nineteenth century, illustrations often offered a spectacle running parallel to the text. The fairy-tale motif of the miraculous recovery or mobility of an orphan girl who survives by her wits, teaching herself and then others to read, and finally coming into great wealth, might seem a resonant tale in the American setting. Certainly printers took advantage of its renown, but in *Goody*'s generic evolution, Goody herself lost her autodidact feistiness. In many editions she asks to be taught to read rather than scheming to learn on her own; Mr. Smith is often her teacher and takes on a new prominence in illustration and text.[56]

"I never supposed that any one here could be so weak as to believe that there was any such thing as a witch. But if I am a witch, here is my charm," she | the management of it, and educate his daughter also. She respectfully declined this handsome offer, for she thought it was her duty to continue teaching the chil-

Figure 8. The medievalism of some illustrations evokes the trial of Joan of Arc. *Story of Goody-Two Shoes*. New York: McLoughlin Brothers, 1869. Courtesy American Antiquarian Society.

Throughout the century, certain episodes were traditionally highlighted in images: the homemade alphabet letters, the trial, the relation to the animals, and, sometimes, an episode in which Goody foils thieves.[57] By the 1840s many editions of *Goody*, reluctant to imagine or encourage a poor, female autodidact in a contemporary American or English setting, gothicized the tale, situating it in a phantasmatic, theatrical Renaissance England, of "Good Queen Bess," wide white collars, and tricorne hats, a Disneyfication of childhood avant la lettre, leaping over even the original's contemporary eighteenth-century context.[58] Goody's witchery, in the original a playful Enlightenment riposte to persistent superstitions, which retained some of the enticements of magic, now became elaborately staged, à la Joan of Arc; what in the original was Goody's valorized wit and intelligence contrasted to rural ignorance now became a kind of frozen monumental saintliness (Plates 6–9 and Figures 7–8).

If twenty-first-century students find it hard to accept the original Goody as "childlike," the nineteenth-century redactions to a certain extent repudiated her. By the end of the century Goody was treated as a fairy tale, in lush picture books. Goody's attraction now relied at least as much on an absorption in these books' romantic and theatrical images, which read like history paintings, than in the spunky adventures of the orphaned girl. The nineteenth-century images, seductive and spectacular, ask little of the reader but awed admiration. They position Goody and her adventures as explicitly other and elsewhere, in the imaginative, hypnogogic zone that comes to be associated with childhood, as I will detail further in the next chapter.

CHAPTER 2

The Literary Property of Childhood

The Case of the "Babes in the Wood"

> "That means," said I, somewhat amused, "that we would have to eat of the tree of knowledge a second time to fall back into the state of innocence."
> —Heinrich Kleist, "On the Puppet Theater" (1810)

THE GENERIC evolution of *The History of Little Goody Two-Shoes* into a picture- and storybook staple in nineteenth-century America reflects a marketplace that had so thoroughly absorbed Goody's literacy lesson that it began to disavow its origins. In a sense, it's just the case that Goody's identification of literacy with the commodity form simply *took*. In her later incarnations, the political economy of Goody's adventures condensed down to an infantilized and domesticated "goodness," and Margery Meanwell's exuberant renaming, which acknowledged bonds to her community and a stage in her life's narrative, devolved into an epithet for a saccharine and cloistered virtue. This chapter reaches back to the Renaissance to trace the genealogy of a ballad that similarly became a staple of the children's literature canon throughout the nineteenth century. By contrast to Goody's promotion of children's literacy and identification of children with alphabetization, the history of the ballad "The Children in the Wood" charts an identification of childhood with a putative lost orality, which children and the literature for and about them are meant to preserve over time, whatever the cost to the children themselves.

In its image of small children, wandering helplessly, at the mercy of forces they don't understand and can't control, the expression "babes in the wood" uniquely conjures a familiar psychological state and social predicament. This evocative if now fossilized expression originates in one of the source texts (and tropes) of children's literature, which in turn emerged from an earlier literary tradition and developed into a topos for romanticism.[1] Across four centuries, on both sides of the Atlantic, "Babes in the Wood" has been a broadside ballad, a traditional folk song, a tale for children, a novel, a poem, a play, a musical, a holiday pantomime; it has provided the occasion for painting, sculpture, and book illustration; it's been an object of parody, a Disney cartoon, and a Cole Porter tune.[2] Though there's nothing unique in literary history about this extravagant medial and generic evolution and variety, "The Children in the Wood" (as it is also sometimes called) is at the high end of the spectrum along with *Hamlet*, for example, or Cinderella. Its afterlife as a catchphrase aligns it as well with *Goody Two-Shoes*. The mercurial and persistent relevance of "Babes in the Wood" bespeaks its unusual cultural suppleness, an uncanny ability to seem emergent even while becoming at the same time residual.[3] This chapter explores a few of the many phases of this artifact's long biography, especially its life as a printed text and its migration from the ballad canon to the children's literature canon, as a study of the ways in which such genre and format transformations converse and coordinate with shifting views and valuations of children's lives and deaths. Before about 1750 there were few items printed expressly for children other than the explicitly pedagogical—hornbook sheets, school primers, and grammars; children had, however, always been spectators, listeners, and eavesdroppers for ballad hawkers and singers, as well as erstwhile readers of their broadsides and other popular print offerings. If *children* formed only a marginal or minority market through the Renaissance, by the eighteenth century *childhood* had become a significant literary property, an object of philosophical consideration and an engine of narrative innovation, in the works of John Locke, Jean-Jacques Rousseau, and the authors of the new novel genre, the bildungsroman, among others. The ballad of the lost babes provides a rich site for observing the emerging cultural concept of childhood and of the print artifacts that form a crucial location in which it takes shape.

"Babes in the Wood" first appears in the print archive as a broadside ballad, registered in 1595 with the London Stationers' Company (Figure 9).[4] Through its many print versions, its baroque little plot remains fairly stable. Some of the early broadsides were illustrated with woodcut tableaux in which these episodes are enacted.[5] A dying gentleman and his wife write a will leaving their toddler daughter and son in the care of the father's brother; the ballad then telegraphs its central plot device: if "the children chanced to die / Ere they to age should come, / Their uncle should possess their wealth; / For so the will did run."[6] Not surprisingly, within "a twelvemonth and a day" and just one quatrain of ballad time after the parents die, the uncle hires "ruffians" to kill the babes. Charmed by the children's "prattle," the ruffians "relent";[7] the more mercenary one then

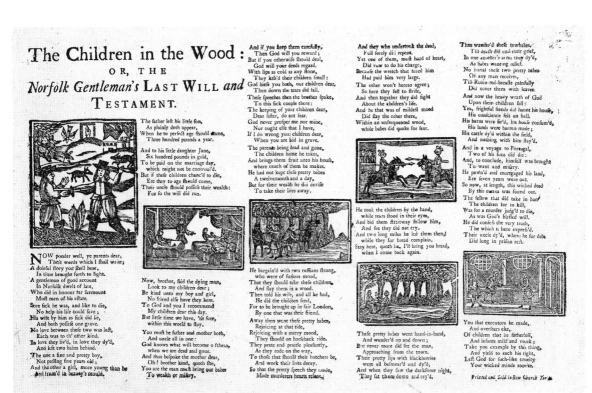

Figure 9. "The Children in the Wood: or, the Norfolk Gentleman's Last Will and / Testament." London: Printed and Sold in Bow Church Yard, [1770?]. The Bodleian Library, University of Oxford. Harding B 4 (30).

un-relents, which provokes the more repentant one to kill him (103). This good ruffian leads the children two more miles into the "unfrequented wood," and leaves them. The babes wander—"Their pretty lips with blackberries / Were all besmear'd and dyed" (117–18); they die, and "robin redbreast piously / Did cover them with leaves" (127–28).[8] The ruffian is hanged. "Fearful fiends did haunt [the uncle's] house"; his lands wither, his sons die, and, in prison for debt, the uncle dies.

    In its first print incarnations the ballad of the children in the wood addressed an adult audience, although, like other forms of popular art of the period, it would be heard and read by people of all ages; this is true as well of the two early theatrical versions—a tragedy from 1601 and a 1793 musical comedy that played into the 1850s.[9] But from the mid-eighteenth century the printed ballad "Babes in the Wood" began to be produced for the single audience to whom it would then belong: children. A version of the ballad is now firmly embedded in the historical children's literature canon, via the massive *Norton Anthology of Children's Literature*.[10] The plot of "The Children in the Wood" puts it on the far side of a gulf that separates twenty-first-century notions of childhood and children's literature from those of a premodern sensibility. Its story line shares with much early children's literature a scopophilic interest in dying, dead, abandoned, orphaned, kidnapped, neglected, or otherwise abject children. But it's not the violence, which doesn't rise to PG by twenty-first-century lights, that marks it as irretrievably previous. Rather, it's that almost every other aspect of this artifact—its diction, its ballad meter, its unusual address (to parents rather than to children), the fecklessness of the children themselves—is doing work that literature for children no longer quite does.

In this chapter, as I chart the social life of this artifact,[11] I'll suggest that one of the things "The Children in the Wood" *used* to do is bridge a gulf between historical eras and generations, between literary genres, and between traditions of, broadly speaking, "orality" and "literacy" or "print." Using "The Children in the Wood" as a lens, one might see some of the ways in which the modern idea of childhood, which we have inherited, takes shape, and the enormous work—indeed, the impossible work—that this concept, its literature, and its child subjects have historically been asked to do.

A Tragedy of Succession

The broadside ballad was known as the "Norfolk Gentleman's tragedy," and its twisted little plot is laconically described in the title that was registered with the Stationers' Company in 1595: "The Norfolk Gentleman, his Will and Testament, and howe he commytted the keeping of his children to his own brother whoe delte most wickedly with them, and how God plagued him for it."[12] Top billing goes to the gentleman, closely followed by the gentleman's will, as if to say that circa 1595, the death of children was suffered by and redounded to the patriarchal line.

In keeping with the focus of the title, the ballad opens with an address to parents:

Now ponder well, you parents dear,
These words which I shall write;
A doleful story you shall hear,
In time brought forth to light.

This opening thematizes what Paula McDowell has described as the hybrid oral/print nature of the ballad genre:[13] "these words which I shall *write*" and that "you shall *hear*." In the reminder that it has been *written*, the ballad speaks up for its self-interested transmission: the ballad hawker's task, after all, is to sell song as print, not as performance. More than this, writing is important because the first sixteen of the ballad's forty quatrains narrate the contents of the father's written will and his oral instructions to his executor, the uncle, making the ballad a kind of how-to manual. (Or, as it turns out, a how-not-to.)

The ballad then goes on to dispense with parents, babes, thugs, robins, uncle's fields, his cattle, his two sons (they drown on the way to Portugal), and uncle himself. After thirty-eight verses, it closes its frame, returning to the protocols of estate planning (39/40):

> You that executors be made,
> And overseërs eke,   (eke = also)
> Of children that be fatherless,
> And infants mild and meek,
>
> Take you example by this thing,
> And yield to each his right,
> Lest God for suchlike misery[14]
> Your wicked minds requite.[15]

This old broadside ballad, circulating circa 1600 and after, sung and hawked by peddlers for a halfpenny,[16] might remind us that in Tudor and Stuart England, though much ink was spilled over the guardianship of children, abandoned children were rather commonplace; as one history of childhood has it, "Parish records contain numerous entries concerning the desertion of unwanted children who were found dead on the roads from exposure and starvation."[17] The ballad babes, though, aren't "unwanted" but wanted all too much. And though these babes aren't royal, their story is a familiar literary property; it's the territory of Shakespeare's *Richard III* (c. 1592), of *King John* (c. 1595), even of *Hamlet* (c. 1603): the scheming uncle, the inheritance waylaid, the murders, the failure of succession. The future that the will is supposed to assure through the transfer of an estate to the next generation evaporates, *Hamlet*-like, in the deaths of virtually everyone the ballad brings on stage.[18] In its first print incarnations, the ballad presented itself as a tragedy of succession for a newly entitled, newly literate, will-writing, and broadside-reading class.

Always Already Old: Babes and Balladry

The ballad circulated in England and America through the seventeenth and eighteenth centuries, in broadside and, increasingly, in chapbook format.[19] The ballad of the babes seemed to be heading for the same fate as the hundreds of other ballads that we know of only because they were preserved by anthologists, collectors, and antiquarians, or have been passed down as song here and there, but virtually vanished from common knowledge by some point in the nineteenth century. But two related developments performed a kind of cultural rescue of the wandering babes ballad. The first development is that during the mid- to late eighteenth century, printers like Mary Cooper, John Newbery, and the Dicey firm began a lively trade in books for children.[20] The second and related development is that the genre of the popular or folk ballad became a locus of nostalgic fascination for literary intellectuals and for the collecting classes.

The eighteenth-century ballad revival, as it's been called, is marked by literary and antiquarian interest in popular print and folk genres, and in what Walter Scott would later call "a chapter in the history of the childhood of society."[21] Among the some three thousand separate ballads thought to be circulating in print and performance by 1600 (and that means at least a few *million* copies),[22] "The Children in the Wood" was frequently invoked in the seventeenth century into the nineteenth century as a synecdoche for the entire genre of the ballad. In the three examples that follow, spanning a century, the babes ballad became associated with contemporary discourses of a vanishing and valorized orality and an emerging discourse of childhood.

First, in a famous number of the *Spectator* in 1711, Joseph Addison finds a copy of the "Children in the Wood" broadside pasted to the wall of a public house; he's a great collector, he says, of scraps of print everywhere, and in this ballad he sees "one of the darling Songs of the common People, [that] has been the Delight of most Englishmen in some Part of their Age."[23] In capturing "The Two Children in the Wood" (as he calls it), Addison hints at collecting two other items: a darling something of the common people and a delightful something of one's own past—that is, something, we would say, of childhood.[24] Still, in 1711, for Addison the ballad *belonged* to "the common people"; not, that is, to children.[25] But he equates the common people with the past personal history, the childhood, of persons of his own class.[26]

William Wordsworth mentions this ballad in the Preface to *Lyrical Ballads* in 1800, using it as a counterweight to what he calls "the gaudiness" of modern writers.[27] He cites as "one of the most justly admired stanzas of the '*Babes* in the Wood'" this one:

These pretty Babes with hand in hand
Went wandering up and down;
But never more they saw the Man
Approaching from the town.[28]

In the ballad, this is the moment when the surviving "ruffian" who had seemed to be saving them in fact leaves the babes, and it is this final adult abandonment that seals their doom. It's not ostensibly the plot that attracts Wordsworth but the ballad's language, which, he says, "in no respect differ[s] from the most unimpassioned conversation."[29] In the poems of *Lyrical Ballads*,[30] as in the later "Immortality Ode" and "The Prelude," Wordsworth articulates what becomes the romantic vision of childhood, which converts a newly privileged (and newly imagined) children's innocence into an envied source of power and knowledge. In the 1800 Preface, though, Wordsworth only obliquely calls up childhood. He doesn't explicate what's so fetching about the passage or why it's admired or by whom; rather he invokes this devotion as the same kind of common property as the ballad itself. For Wordsworth, the ballad's bequest is a particular kind of language: words about children that have circulated orally for a long, long time, among plain-spoken people. And yet, the cited passage, it's worth emphasizing, is a lightly veiled scene of child murder.

Wordsworth's contemporary, Charles Lamb, made part of his living in the new children's print marketplace, most especially with the success of his and Mary Lamb's *Tales from Shakespeare* (1807 in London, and in 1813 by Mathew Carey in the United States).[31] In a little magazine essay in 1822 called "Dream Children: A Reverie,"[32] Lamb imagines his "little ones" gathering around to hear stories of their great-grandmother, caretaker of a Norfolk mansion claimed to be the very house of the tragic Norfolk gentleman. "The whole story of the children and their cruel uncle," Lamb writes, "was to be seen fairly carved out in wood upon the chimney-piece of the great hall . . . the whole story down to the Robin Redbreasts, till a foolish rich Person pulled it down to set up a marble one of modern invention in its stead, with no story upon it."[33]

More so than the broadsides pasted on country inn walls that cried out to Addison, here the ballad fully animates the old hearth (before the lamentable renovations). But as the reverie continues its speaker pulls the curtain back to reveal a literary stunt: he's not a paterfamilias after all but a bachelor, whose children are only dreams. These dream children nonetheless speak: "We are only what might have been," they say, "and must wait upon the tedious shores of Lethe millions of ages before we have existence, and a name."[34]

In this final example, the ballad of infanticide prompts a fantasy of generation, reproduction, and paternal intimacy. Lamb conjures spectral children who belong to a past of lost potential and to a distant future marked by forgetting. It's in the present that the children weirdly have no existence. For Lamb, the ballad of the babes is a vehicle for a fantasy of remembering childhood on behalf of imagined children who, he *imagines*, long to hear of the past.[35]

While the ballad form is often invoked as a stand-in for popular oral tradition, the fact is that when the babes ballad comes up it's just as often a stand-in for print. This is print with a particular affective and temporal resonance and a strangely animated quality: print that *speaks*—from a past that belongs to a putative "folk," which is increasingly aligned with those who begin to be called "little folk."[36] For Addison, it's a souvenir of bygone print and of past youthful delight, which he preserves in the amber of the *Spectator*. Wordsworth marshals a scene of forlorn children, about to die, captured in print, to represent everyday speech and a lyric ideal. Lamb does something that relies entirely on print for its effect: he dissolves the ballad into a hallucinogenic reading experience, cued by the genre designation "reverie." More so than Addison or Wordsworth, Lamb fully registers the movement of this ballad from a folk and antiquarian canon to the new canon of children's literature. Through the medium of the babes ballad, Lamb offers a tortured definition of childhood in modernity: as a fantasy that imagines it has to do with the desires of living children but in the end, perfectly brazenly, has nothing to do with children or their desires at all but everything to do with an adult's conflicted, aestheticized longing for the past. If the eighteenth century galvanized and circulated the modern "invention" of childhood, it did so by at the same time relishing a literary contemplation of the deaths of children.

Balladizing Childhood, Novelizing Ballads

These episodes from the ballad's reception and circulation in the literary field reveal its function as a synecdoche for a lost or threatened cultural form, whether printed or oral, and as a prompt for intricate, nostalgic reflections on childhood.[37] Once the ballad was marketed explicitly for children it sometimes shuffled off its ballad form and turned into a little novel, as, for example, *The Children in the Wood: An Instructive Tale* by a probably pseudonymous figure called Clara English.[38] First published in London in 1801 by Darton and Harvey, this version went into thirty-some editions in America from 1803 to 1842.[39] This little novel addresses children (rather than executors of wills) and opens with the two children reading stories to each other while their parents lie dying. As in the old ballad, when the parents die, the children are left to the uncle; avuncular though he appears in the illustrations that typically accompany these editions, his brand of wickedness is captured in the name of his estate, Bashaw Castle, suggesting "oriental" luxury and imperial spoils. The narrative dilates extravagantly on the uncle's character: he was idle, profligate, "seldom read his Bible," didn't go "any place for divine worship" (34), and engaged in cock fighting, drinking, and playing cards. Even so, on the way to his castle, the uncle stops off with the children to visit the "Vale of Content," a utopian woolen manufactory town,[40] where they see orphans "reading little story books, which had been given them as a reward for their diligence" (29). Still, the uncle goes on to plot the babes' kidnapping and murder in the usual thuggish way.

In the crucial plot revision of the Clara English versions, the abandoned children do not die. Rather, a poor spinster (literally—she spins) found them and "got admittance for them into the School of Industry" (45), where "Jane learned to read, to write, to work, to knit, and to spin; and Edgar was taught to read, to write, and to work in a garden" (46–47). The uncle meanwhile made off with their inheritance, but his "guilty conscience always tormented him" (47–48), and he and the surviving ruffian suffered the poetic justice of the original ballad. The babes were "put into possession of *Bashaw Park*, which soon changed its name for that of *Happy Dell*" (53).

The Clara English editions tend to print the traditional ballad at the end, editing out the children's death and, in a gesture that seems to insulate the old ballad from the new novel, often adding a few verses before the old ballad: "Our grandsires each have wept ere now, / Our grandsires and our grandams too / And shall to ages yet unborn / Who read the tale of these forlorn, / Still cause the tender tear to flow" (27).[41] These verses describe the weeping ballad audience as ancestors (grandsires, grandams) and descendants ("ages yet unborn"). Who are really forlorn here, it seems to me, are the current progeny, the contemporary child readers, positioned sheerly instrumentally or medially as something like executors of the ballad; that is, they are meant to guard it and transmit it, without exactly experiencing it.[42] Here, the old ballad becomes vestigial, and yet operates as a necessary signature or testimony for the new version.[43]

The traditional "old wife"—the storyteller, the nurse, the singer at the hearth—emblematizes a fertile reproduction of culture through artifacts like ballads and tales;[44] here, that reproduction is the job of the book, and the old wife becomes the solitary spinster who saves the children's lives—and ensures their literacy. And yet the cost of preserving the children is to make them blameworthy: in fact, in their survival, these texts say, they risk turning into the uncle who would murder them. After describing the profligate uncle, the narrator drives home an arresting moral: "And here my young friends, I have . . . placed before you the character of a very wicked man, and shown you what conduct it was that led him to the horrid crime of *intended murder*. You will, I am sure, turn from the picture with aversion; yet, I wish you to dwell upon it sufficiently, to avoid similar faults yourselves."[45] The admonition of the old ballad was, in essence, to guard children's lives and preserve legacies, which is nothing less than to make the future possible. The warning turns now toward the children readers: guard yourselves, it says, in effect: you're on your own and you're one unread Bible away from becoming a babes-murdering uncle.[46]

In the introduction to an 1832 Clara English edition, the publisher Mahlon Day sees his own livelihood dependent on children's potential for evil:

> The Story of the Babes in the Wood, has been handed down to us from generation to generation. The book was first printed in England, we believe, and again and again reprinted, in that and this country; so that we doubt if there is one man or woman in New-York, where this book is printed, but who has either read or heard of this affecting and entertaining story. It seems as if this book will sell as long as there are children to read, or a sixpence to spare to buy one: so as we want sixpences to pay our honest debts, we have concluded to add this also to our long list of Children's Books, with the hope that every child who reads of the dreadful deeds of the Uncle of those poor orphans, will take warning and watch closely their own tempers, and never do any bad act, however small, for fear they may go on, step by step, as did the Uncle, to commit the dreadful sin of hiring bad men to murder innocent babes. I say, dear children, while you read such a history of a wicked man, be watchful that you do not let in any bad thought into your minds; for from thoughts proceed actions, and wicked deeds will surely be punished in this life or that which is to come.[47]

Like the text of the novelized ballad, this publisher's puff highlights the transitory temporality and moral fragility of childhood. But the proximity of the slippery-slope warning to the marketing pitch links children's moral susceptibility to commerce. Here the reading child risks her innocence by engaging in the reading that instructs her in the protocols of innocence.

In one verse edition of the Babes in the Wood story,[48] Mahlon Day pictures himself with two little children, a common enough image in children's books, of the avuncular printer with his flock. But Day has used the image of the wicked uncle with the children, as if in acknowledgment of his own paradoxical role (Plate 10, Figures 10 and 11).

Like *Goody Two-Shoes,* which precedes them, these new versions underscore a futurity that relies not on inherited family property but on the internal property of literacy, as, for example, when the babes mirror their readers by being shown reading. While the uncle hopes to cash the children in for the monetary value of their legacy, the novelized ballad converts the children themselves into a new kind of self-generating cultural capital, as the reading and writing and usefully working inhabitants of Happy Dell. If children's innocence is always risked in the fall into language and literacy, the entry of the child into what the

Figure 10. On their way to Bashaw Castle, the uncle takes the children to see "the Vale of Content," before revealing his villainy. Clara English, *The Children in the Wood: An Instructive Tale.* Philadelphia: J. Johnson, 1807. Illustration "hand-colored, probably by a reader," according to the American Antiquarian Society catalog. AAS call number CL-Pam E58 C536 1807. Courtesy American Antiquarian Society.

era calls the "reading world," which is by definition commodified, increases the vulnerability of the children not to adult transgressions *against* them but to adult transgressiveness *by* them.

In effect, the text of the novelized version of "The Children in the Wood" preserves the children only in order to register the inevitable death of childhood itself.[49] Scholars have long noted the new consciousness circa 1800 of childhood as a privileged time and space inhabited by living children, if they have quibbled about the exact dates of this transition. But what makes children's literature possible is adult consciousness of childhood as a privileged time and space that's been lost, that's died, and that yet remains infinitely accessible to adult memory and imagination, through the medium of literature and the practices of literacy.

Gothicizing Childhood

While the ballad became rationalized and narrativized in some of its first incarnations as "children's literature," by the 1820s it became, like *Goody Two-Shoes*

THE
BABES IN THE WOOD,
IN VERSE.
AN AFFECTING TALE.

A NEW EDITION.

CORRECTED AND ENLARGED

BY A FRIEND TO YOUTH.

If you have a penny or two now to spend,
Look in at Day's Book-store, my kind little friend .

NEW-YORK:

PRINTED AND SOLD BY MAHLON DAY,
AT THE NEW JUVENILE BOOK-STORE,
NO. 374, PEARL-STREET.
. . . .
1833.

Figure 11. The avuncular printer echoes the dastardly uncle. *The Babes in the Wood, in Verse.*
New York: Mahlon Day, 1833. Courtesy American Antiquarian Society.

and other books for the children's market, an ever more intensely visual artifact, and a wide range of variations of the tale circulated, in verse and prose, in many formats. These early nineteenth-century illustrated versions of the ballad situated the action in contemporary settings, engaging the fates of contemporary children (Plates 11–13).

Such illustrations, current into the mid-century, convey, among other things, the plausibility of the plot's contemporaneity. "The Children in the Wood" speaks not just to but *of* its early nineteenth-century readers, these images seem to say, even when the tale is rendered in what was by then a somewhat archaic ballad form. That children could be vulnerable to sinister manipulation, that parents might die and guardians betray, that childish charm might only defer and not avert tragedy, that children might be regarded not as humans possessed of inalienable rights but as something like property themselves—these were more than plot devices to readers of the early national period.[50]

But beginning in the 1830s, most editions of the ballad took a turn away from contemporary representations, and, like those of *Goody Two-Shoes*, their illustrations became increasingly gothicized, theatricalized, "Shakespearized," and medievalized (Plates 14–16; Figure 12). In the mid- to late nineteenth century, as Lawrence Levine has shown, Shakespeare was the most popular playwright for the American stage, which was widespread entertainment in cities and towns and on the frontier. Popular children's publishers like Edward Dunigan and Turner and Fisher also traded in Shakespeare's plays, and Shakespeare was part of the grammar school curriculum. By the end of the century, Levine tells us, Shakespeare had largely migrated from popular to elite culture, becoming a marker of literary taste and a signifier of cultural capital, a process these images register. Relatively inexpensive books were soon joined by costlier and more elaborate ones, attuned to and marketed to an increasingly child-centered middle class.

The heavy shade of *Richard III*, the most popular Shakespeare play in America in the nineteenth century, hovers over many of the illustrations.[51] With the highbrowing of Shakespeare came a cultural fantasy of a pastoral Elizabethan past, in which children were staged as both tragic and historic: the domestic tragedy of the two little babes thus maps onto the national disgrace of the princes in the tower. While *Richard III*'s popularity could be a problem for contemporary intellectuals (James Russell Lowell attributed it to a taste for melodrama), everyone agreed that it was a play about overreaching ambition.[52] The ballad's domestic tragedy echoes the play's national tragedy. The ballad uncle's hiring of the ruffians, which occupies one quatrain, becomes a site of illustration, underscoring the parallel scene of Richard hiring Tyrrell to kill the

The Children in the Wood.

Their little hearts with terror sank,

With hunger too they cried;

At length upon a flowery bank

They laid them down and died.

The Children's Death.

The redbreasts in their clustering bowers

Sung mournful on each spray;

And there with leaves and fragrant flowers

O'erspread them as they lay.

Figure 12. Hand-colored wood engravings of the babes in an Elizabethan imaginary. *The Affecting History of the Children in the Wood.* Binghamton, N.Y.: J. and C. Orton, 1840. Courtesy American Antiquarian Society.

princes in the Tower (4.2) (Figure 13). The uncle's haunted conscience ("Fearful fiends did haunt his house, / His conscience felt an hell") is literalized in illustrations, bringing the children's ghosts as it were onstage (Figures 14–15; Plate 17). If the play is a parable of overweening ambition, which is how nineteenth-century commentators framed it, it is just as emphatically a drama of succession, a warning about the unreliability of primogeniture, about the failure of the law to protect children, and about the state's vulnerability to rupture—and to civil war.

But it's not only the Shakespeare of *Richard III* that these mid- to late-century editions of the ballad evoke. As the children are increasingly represented as verging toward adolescence, looking like so many little Hamlets and Ophelias

THE CHILDREN IN THE WOOD.

Now ponder well, you parents dear,
    These words which I shall write;
A doleful story you shall hear,
    In time brought forth to light.
A gentleman of good account
    In Norfolk dwelt of late,
Whose wealth and riches did surmount
    Most men of his estate.

Sore sick he was, and like to die,
    No help his life could save;
His wife by him as sick did lie,
    And both possess'd one grave.
No love between these two was lost,
    Each was to other kind,
In love they lived, in love they died,
    And left two babes behind:

Figure 13. The uncle as Richard III. *Little Lizzie and the Fairies; and Sunny Hair's Dream.* Boston: Crosby, Nichols [between 1852 and 1856?]. This miscellany includes a ballad version of "The Children in the Wood," illustrated with an engraving of a Richard III–like uncle paying for the murder of the children. Courtesy American Antiquarian Society.

Figure 14. Clara English, *The Children in the Wood: An Instructive Tale*. Philadelphia: J. Johnson, 1807. The mutual haunting of the babes ballad and *Richard III* was recognized early, as in this 1807 prose version, mirroring the play's dream sequence. Courtesy American Antiquarian Society.

and Romeos and Juliets, the scopophilic interest in them takes on a more distinctly erotic quality (Plates 18–20). The antiqued or "distressed"[53] style of such images isn't, of course, unique to this text but is common to mid-century and especially postbellum children's literature generally. These books are influenced not only by the popular Shakespearean theater but also by architectural, decorative arts, and painting traditions of gothicism from the 1830s on, and by the postbellum revivals of medieval and Renaissance scholarship.[54] There's more than an aesthetic fashion at stake in this retreat from one historical moment to another more-than-half-imaginary one; or rather, the aesthetic fashion has deep roots. The evocation of the past as a historically fluid Old English theme park links these representations not only to Shakespeare but also to mid- to late nineteenth-century racial Anglo-Saxonism.[55] The marble-white babes of Thomas Crawford's popular 1851 sculpture (Figure 16) might remind us that, as Caroline Levander has argued in *Cradle of Liberty*, the figure of the child in the nineteenth century "increasingly represents whiteness . . . as an unequivocally preeminent cornerstone of the nation's political identity to ensure that race will continue to organize national identity after slavery is abolished."[56]

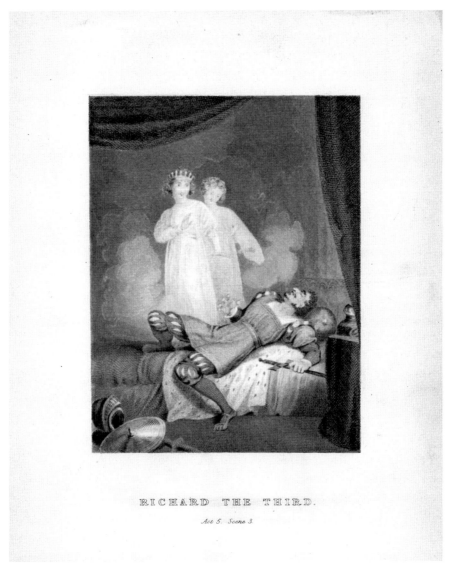

Figure 15. Print of Richard III haunted by the murder of the princes in the tower.
Shakespeare Fantasy Prints, Houghton Library, Harvard University.

Steve Newman has shown how the ballad genre became a fixture of the second-
ary school curriculum postbellum, at least in part to transmit racial Anglo-
Saxonism: "As with the philological scholarship in which it was rooted, the texts
that brought legends to American youth during this era often had a nativist and
racialist bent."[57]

Figure 16. Thomas Crawford, *The Babes in the Wood*. Carved 1851, marble. The Metropolitan Museum of Art. Bequest of Hamilton Fish, 1894. www.metmuseum.org.

Ante- and postbellum images of dead, white children, tricked out in Ye Olde English outfits, might seal the ballad off from associations with the children most at risk in this period: the urban poor and slave children and Indian children in the South and on the frontier. Such medievalized, gothicized, or otherwise historically displaced images accompanied a reanimation of the last will and testament that continued to frame the ballad. If wills are instruments of futurity,[58] voices from the past regulating the present (what legal commentators call the "dead hand"), the ballad assimilates this role, bequeathing a spectacularized "Anglo-Saxon" white past. Like the books that transmit this imaginary realm, late nineteenth-century childhood was becoming consolidated and commodified. That is to say, like these books, childhood was becoming a kind of heritable property, a something that only some people would get to *have*.

In becoming "children's literature" the ballad enacts a literary phenomenon that Jacqueline Rose has described like this: "There is a continuity in children's fiction . . . in which the child is constantly set up as the site of a lost truth and/ or moment in history, which it can therefore be used to retrieve."[59] A paradoxical chiastic relationship is conjured between the traditional "orality" of the old wife at the hearth and the literacy that is the signal marker of childhood as modernity has constructed it: the reading child is figured as the legatee and the archive and the medium all at once of a phantasmatic ballad orality now specifically styled Anglo-Saxon.[60] The child represented in these images models childhood itself as temporally isolated from the present moment: as "always already old," always already previous, always medieval.[61] This sequestered "childhood" is, as it were, protectively quarantined to the past and a cultural fantasy of racial homogeneity. In the temporal logic of these images, the child is both ancestor and inheritor at once.[62]

Dickinson's Robins and the Death of Childhood

In the winter of 1850, Emily Dickinson had just turned twenty—that birthday that definitively marks the end of childhood—when she wrote to Abiah Root, one of her best friends, at the end of the year. A friend and teacher had recently died, but she was also mourning the inevitable fading of childhood intimacies, especially with their mutual friend Abby Wood: "I am feeling lonely; some of my friends are gone and some of my friends are sleeping—sleeping the church-yard sleep. . . ." In a postscript to this melancholy letter she imagines this scene: "Oh you are both asleep, and your hand is fast in Abby's. I stand by the fond young bedside, and think of 'Babes in the Wood'—large babes—the ones we hear of were *small* ones—I seem to myself a robin covering you with leaves—the Babies we *were are* buried, and their shadows are plodding on."[63] Readers of her robin-filled poetry will be struck by Dickinson's identification with the ballad's robin, and struck as well, perhaps, by the aggression she betrays in tenderly abandoning, killing off, and burying her old friends.[64] Like Charles Lamb in his "Dream Children," Dickinson associates the ballad with a reverie of childhood. She manages the dizzying temporal and spatial layers the ballad imposes: we are large babes, we were small babes, those small babes are "buried," but "their shadows are plodding on." For Dickinson the ballad articulates the problematic of what I've been calling the death of childhood. If the babes can never really be quite tragic, they are always nonetheless a kind of elegiac property. This is the burden of the Children in the Wood tale in the nineteenth century: by assimilating the old ballad into the new children's literature it identifies childhood with a quaint antiquity that the literate child is asked to both mourn and preserve.

CHAPTER 3

Colonizing Childhood, Placing Cherokee Children

> Everywhere I turned I found a "squared world," a society so compartmentalized that life, including my own, had no room to move around. . . . I unwittingly internalized it—tore my life-web and stuffed the broken strands into the "boxes."
> —Marilou Awiakta, Cherokee (1997)

> We have got to become men and women and we have got to take our place in line in life. . . . You have got to march through this world; the world expects you to do something, not simply to play and not simply to have pleasure.
> —Richard Ballinger, secretary of the interior, addressing Indian students (1909)

IN LITTLE Goody's transformation from shoe-deprived orphan to the well-heeled "trotting tutoress" who spreads alphabetic learning, as in the Clara English reenvisioning of the "Babes in the Wood" ballad, pedagogies and institutions of reading (ABC College and the School of Industry) are represented as secularly salvific. The literacy events at the heart of these narratives save the children's lives and, exceeding the promises of learning's symbolic capital, position the children as a new-style landed gentry, whose property in land is fantastically conjured by the practices of literacy. From canonicity and the cultural capital of literacy, and from fictive representations of schooling, this chapter turns to schooling in theory and fact, and to children seemingly at the margins of emergent constructions of childhood, whose literacy engages them in deeply personal as well as critically political struggles. While theorists of the early republic hoped for a "more general diffusion of knowledge," schooling followed a localized and uneven development and continued to be ad hoc for many children well into the nineteenth century. But schooled or unschooled, white children along with some Native American and free black children were increasingly obliged to master reading and writing skills. This chapter examines a site for considering the form an emergent and tacit literacy contract could take and the consequences for children of entering into, negotiating, or escaping its demands.

Monitorial Media

Carrying the banal but wholly apposite motto "a place for every thing and every thing in its place," Joseph Lancaster's monitorial system penetrated hundreds of schoolrooms in the United States and across the British Empire, Western Europe, Russia, and Latin America between 1800 and 1850. Though his slogan has the texture of proverb, Lancaster coined the phrase, cannily translating Enlightenment rhetoric into the language of the schoolhouse.[1] In its echo of the "places"—*loci* or *topoi*—of rhetorical invention, the expression conveys a technique for organizing and transmitting knowledge. But far from the rhetorical training available to elites in Latin schools, academies, and colleges, Lancaster's system is stridently alphabetical, not only in its innovative methods of teaching elementary literacy but also in its anatomized and atomized classroom topography. At the same time, the motto begins to map the place of Lancaster's pedagogy among the media technologies of the early nineteenth century, including not only genres and formats of print but also an early form of telegraphy, in the optical telegraphs built, planned, or imagined by his contemporaries. In its tautology, Lancaster's motto captures the self-sufficiency of his system and its effacement of the power dynamic that motivates the placing (and displacing) of people and things. In this sense the phrase expresses the consonance between Lancaster's pedagogy and the discourse of colonialism.[2]

Originally fashioned to teach the London poor, Lancaster's monitorial system was widely adopted for missionary projects, particularly those of the American Board of Commissioners for Foreign Missions.[3] And in 1821 the Bureau of Indian Affairs, then a branch of the War Department, promoted it specifically for teaching American Indians.[4] That a pedagogy designed for the urban poor became a boon to missionaries on the southern frontier reveals the striking similarities between the child produced by Lancaster's system and the American Indian imagined by U.S. colonial discourse. It is not simply that the Indian was the "child of the forest," or that poor children and Indians both required the supplement of "civilization." In *Suffering Childhood in Early America: Violence,*

Race, and the Making of the Child Victim, Anna Mae Duane has demonstrated the discursive grounds of this conventional linking, as the production of childhood in the early national period aligns with the ways both Native Americans and African Americans were positioned, vacillating between dependency and victimhood on the one hand and the potential for autonomy and independence on the other. For children as for Indians, the representational techniques and technologies in Lancaster's manuals and classrooms, which "place" students and which create a template for their uncanny replication, translate well, if with delicate calibrations, to the mission project.

Joseph Lancaster was motivated by a missionary impulse from the start. Born in the artisan class in London in 1778, he read an abolitionist essay by Thomas Clarkson that determined him at the age of fourteen to go to Jamaica to teach African slaves.[5] The story goes that he put out to sea with a Bible and *Pilgrim's Progress* in his kit but was returned to his family after three weeks. In 1798, young and poor himself, Lancaster set up a school for the poor, supported by Quakers, his adopted sect. In part a figure of the late Enlightenment, in its missionary and Benthamite molds,[6] Lancaster is in part a figure of romanticism, a blowzy Byronic character. Profligate, spendthrift, overweight, paranoid, probably a sadist, possibly a pedophile, half altruist, half self-promoting snake-oil salesman, Lancaster was a ready-made American. When he was hounded out of England, he was embraced by the United States. By the time Lancaster arrived in 1818, an estimated one hundred and fifty schools followed his plan, from New York and Philadelphia, to Tennessee and North Carolina, to Cincinnati and Detroit.[7]

In the early national United States, as in England, pedagogical theory was haunted by the French Revolution, the monitory example of the revenge of the unalphabetized. The English solution to threat of unrest from below, as Carl Kaestle has noted, was to educate the poor only within strict limits, meant to impress upon them their place. In the early American republic, the poor, like the native population, were deemed capable of "civilization," and white middle-class culture was seen to benefit from their perceived rise.[8] While the United States didn't have a so-called peasant class, it did have, along with its growing slave, free black, and indigenous populations, a burgeoning white population whose class affiliations were worryingly indeterminate. As the promoters of a Philadelphia monitorial school put the case for education in 1810, "The idle habits and neglected education of a numerous class of poor children within the City of Philadelphia and its vicinity, suffered as they have been to range at will the streets and wharves, exciting one another to almost every species of vice and immorality, have long been a cause of painful regret to the well-disposed and benevolent mind."[9] Although the United States warmly promoted its "rising generation," it was a tide that rolled in a little too fast for comfort: the 1790 census found that 49 percent of the white population was under sixteen, which was also the median age of Americans from the 1790s to 1830.[10] How to cope with such an immigration from within? How to incorporate and acculturate all of these "little strangers"?

Lancaster's system promised wholesale acculturation and social control at discount prices.[11] As Carl Kaestle notes, however, it was not only the outcome that appealed to reformers but the very idea of method applied to the training of youth, an ambition of theorists of the republic from Thomas Jefferson to Noah Webster to Benjamin Rush, among many others.[12] Lancaster offered a "fundamentally new idea in education, informed by the image of the factory, the reality of technological advance, the incipient growth of bureaucracy in response to demographic growth, and, especially, a desire for order in response to the increasingly obvious threat of chaos in the lives of the working classes. The answer was a system that was the essence of technology: it was not simply efficient, as a single machine is, but, like the machine, it was infinitely replicable."[13] As Kaestle suggests, much of the promise of the system was embedded in the very terms of its promotion, communicating the soothing notion that rational principles of mechanization and manufacturing could apply to the thorny problem of education, for which organic metaphors of cultivation had long been the mainstay. The new terminology was taken to like a tonic, and its result seemed miraculous. Lancaster could cheaply instruct hundreds of children at a time; the school he established in London could tutor five hundred students, from the ABCs on up, in one great room.

Like a good manufactory, the Lancaster school could turn out product.[14] And as if to assure his clientele of his expertise at replication, Lancaster promoted his system through the repetition of images supplementing his texts. Lancaster's illustrated manuals are blueprints for pedagogues and school committees. The illustrations, along with specs for materials, buildings, furnishings, and apparatus, give his manuals a can-do aura: they are, in the new technological sense, "plans," as for architecture or manufacturing. What they designate and chart is the placement of children. The Lancasterian manual represents children arrayed in classrooms—standing in groups, performing tasks, circulating through space. In these images, there are almost always two notable truants. First, the absent teacher (Figure 17). Lancaster's revolutionary management trick is, after all, simply to delegate; the innovation that he shared with his British rival, Andrew Bell, is the "mutual" or "monitorial" (Lancaster's term) positioning of more experienced students as instructors, boys teaching other boys, in small groups organized by level of accomplishment.

The second truant in Lancasterian representation is the book. By printing large posters and occasional outsized volumes, visible by many at once,

Plate 2.

Plate of School when in Draughts.

Figure 17. Students in "draughts" at "reading stations." The sense of mise-en-abîme conveys the infinite replication of the system and the exchangeability of the students. *Manual of the Lancasterian System, of Teaching Reading, Writing, Arithmetic, and Needle-work: As Practised in the Schools of the Free-School Society, of New-York.* New York: Samuel Wood and Sons, 1820. Courtesy American Antiquarian Society.

Lancaster saved on book buying.[15] While Lancaster's system might be said to distill Western literacy practices into their most strenuous forms, emphasizing standardization, physical embodiments, repetition, routinization, and arbitrary but highly disciplined order, in this scheme these practices are not associated with the codex. In the long run, this lack may have contributed, if in unarticulated ways, to the monitorial system's falling out of fashion by mid-century, when explicitly affective pedagogy, centered around the sentimentalized artifact of the book, would hold sway. And it signals the fact that Lancaster's system intervenes in educational history at a moment when the status of the book form as the central vehicle and icon of literacy, particularly for a mass readership, is by no means assured.

If for Lancaster literacy is transmitted without the body of the book, so too general instruction is transmitted without the body of the teacher. But the absence of the master's person signals the ubiquity of his effect. Like a colonial administrator, this master is not subject to representation. Rather, all the powers of overview belong to him: to represent, to look, to inspect, to monitor: "The master should be a silent by-stander and inspector. What a master says

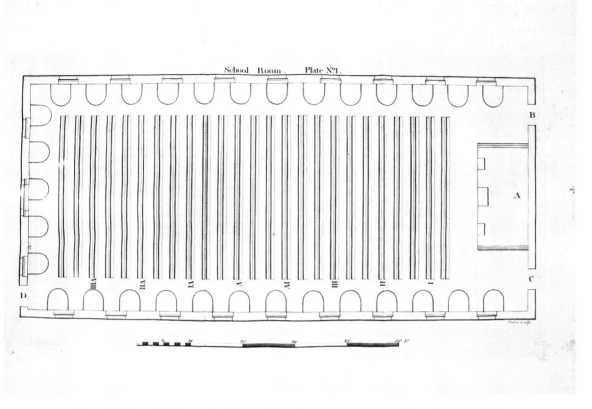

Figure 18. Floor plan. From the alpha position, the master can oversee the entire space. "The entrance door, should be on the side of the platform, at the master's end of the school, in order that the visitors on entering, may have a commanding view of all the children at once." From *Manual of the Lancasterian System, of Teaching Reading, Writing, Arithmetic, and Needle-work: As Practised in the Schools of the Free-School Society, of New-York.* New York: Samuel Wood and Sons, 1820, 6. Courtesy American Antiquarian Society.

should be done; but if he teaches on this system he will find the authority is not personal, that when the pupils, as well as the schoolmaster, understand how to act and learn on this system, *the system*, not the master's vague, discretionary, uncertain judgment, will be in practice."[16] Such a system demands an architecture in which all the children are visible at once (Figure 18). The floor slants, higher at the back, lower at the front, so that the master's elevated position offers a clear line of sight to the back of the room. The children are placed in order to be observed, first for purposes of discipline: "The consciousness of being under the master's eye," writes Lancaster, "has a tendency to prevent half the usual school offences."[17] Like nineteenth-century prisons, which were real tourist attractions,[18] Lancaster's schools were, to a lesser degree, also sights:

"This arrangement of the school has another advantage: visitors, on entering the school-room have a full view of the whole school at once: a sight to the benevolent heart, most interesting, and to the eye, one of the most pleasing which can be witnessed."[19]

Along with this panoptical visibility[20]—warming the heart as it disciplines someone else's body—Lancaster's system produces as well a certain legibility. In a classroom cryptography, students are identified not only by name but also by an arbitrarily assigned "mustering number," posted around the wall of the room; the students line up in the morning under their number, and in this way, the monitors can quickly note the truants.[21] In the Lancasterian system, the visibility of the child does not demand the transparency promoted by evangelicism, in which the child's comportment reveals the state of its soul.[22] Rather, these students are figured as all exterior, all surface. The time-honored pedagogical trope of the written-upon child is expressed most famously in Locke's "tabula rasa"; "impress" and "imprint" are keywords of eighteenth- and much nineteenth-century pedagogy. The Lancasterian student is emphatically not the impressible Lockean subject, which, as developed further by Rousseau and Pestalozzi, gradually became the standard for middle-class white schooling into the nineteenth century. Locke's is a trope that printing makes possible, while Lancaster incorporates a psychology aligned to a different communications technology. The Lancasterian student is not so much a surface to be written on as he is a surface upon which messages can be posted.

Among Lancaster's innovations are a number of media-technology gadgets, notably something he calls the "telegraph" (Figure 19). These are signs with a series of codes on them, giving commands; in Figure 19, "F" means to *face front* and "SS" to *show slates*. Leaving nothing to chance, Lancaster illustrates the actions that are meant to be motivated by these commands (Figure 20). Lancaster models his telegraph system not on the electromagnetic telegraph, which, though theorized in the eighteenth century, didn't come into use until Samuel Morse's practical innovations in the 1830s. Lancaster would be thinking instead of the system of optical or semaphore telegraphs that spread across Europe and parts of the United States in the 1790s and early 1800s (Figure 21). At first a military technology, invented in France by Claude Chappe, the optical telegraph encoded the alphabet in arrangements of articulated arms or shutters that could be witnessed by a telescope operator at the next station, some six miles (10 kilometers) away. Military and shipping news that would conventionally take days could be conveyed within hours, and by 1805 the French had lines from Paris to Brest, Boulogne, Lille, Brussels, Metz, Strasbourg, and Lyon. Between 1801 and 1807, a line was built from Martha's Vineyard to Boston, and others were proposed but never built between Maine and New Orleans.[23] In an era

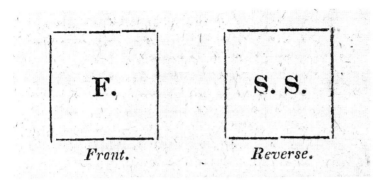

Figure 19. Telegraph. "The telegraph placed at the head of the school consists of six squares, each square about four inches by three. These squares play on pivots, in the sides of a wooden frame. On each side is a letter F. as *front*, on seeing which, the whole school face the master: or, S.S. as show slates, on which the whole school show slates. The attention of the school is called to this by means of a very small bell *affixed*, which does not require loud ringing, but has a sharp clear sound." *The Lancasterian System of Education, with Improvements.* Baltimore, 1821, 10. Courtesy American Antiquarian Society.

when technologies of communication and transportation were closely allied and tied to the same networks, those who were interested in the circulation of information—what the era called "the diffusion of knowledge" and what we would call information or data networks or media—were interested in both. The American Christopher Colles, who proposed an extensive system of optical telegraphs for the United States, was an important geographer and published the first book of U.S. roadmaps. Then as now, the desire for information went hand in hand with the categorizing and regulating impulse. Indeed, the optical telegraph and the analogous naval semaphore became famous for transmitting two imperial dicta: "Paris est tranquille et les bons citoyens sont contents" (Napoleon, from Paris to the Provinces, in 1799; "Paris is quiet and the good citizens are happy"); and Lord Nelson in 1805, to the fleet: "England expects every man will do his duty."[24] Both might be said to be translations into capital letters of Lancaster's classroom slogan; to put it another way, Lancaster's gift is to condense complex social regulation into statements whose proverbial ring makes them legible to the nursery crowd.

Having instituted the classroom telegraph, Lancaster found himself with an invention that exceeded his original motives; his telegraph was apparently being appropriated by his instructors for their own purposes: "With some teachers the rage is a telegraph for everything, and if a telegraph could have brains or communicate intellect, too much could not be said of its importance."[25] With

Figure 20. Postures. Here boys display the correct postures in response to the telegraph "S.S." (show slates). Notice the hats on their backs, attached by string, which they toss over their shoulders when commanded to "sling hats." *The Lancasterian System of Education, with Improvements.* Baltimore, 1821, 27. Courtesy American Antiquarian Society.

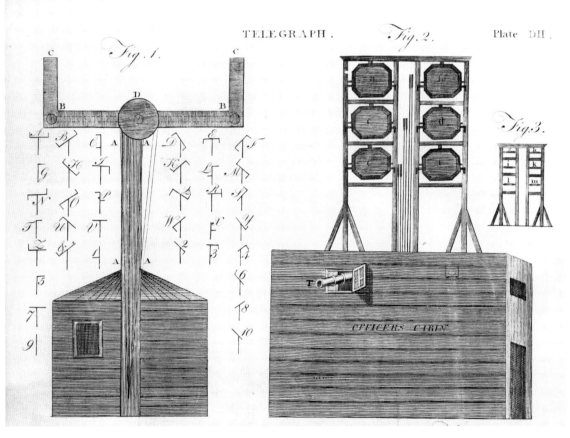

Figure 21. The optical telegraph. From *Encyclopaedia Britannica*, 3rd Edition. Philadelphia: Thomas Dobson, 1798. Rare Book and Manuscript Library, Columbia University.

the anxious if sardonic hint toward artificial intelligence, Lancaster expresses the paranoia that accompanies the valorization of media technology—a fear of the technology's seemingly self-authorized power. Lancaster lamented that his followers took to the term "telegraph" faddishly and was exasperated by those who would insist on using the word "telegraph" to refer to other classroom technologies that, by his lights, were certainly not telegraphs: "*Examination sticks*—These answer the purpose simply of shewing when an examination has been made; some ignorant persons call them telegraphs" (Figure 22).[26] The difference is, in fact, a crucial one, between the telegraph and the "examination stick" (which, in the example here, indicates simply that an exam is going on in class group number 8). The exam stick merely conveys data, while the telegraph literally incorporates the student into a network; only when the student performs the cued action can the network proceed. The Lancasterian child is thus

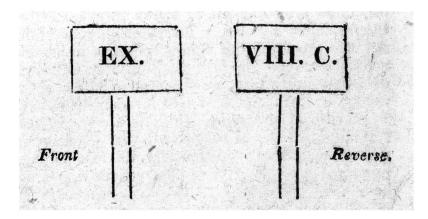

Figure 22. Examination sticks. (Not to be confused with telegraphs.) *The Lancasterian System of Education, with Improvements.* Baltimore, 1821, 3. Courtesy American Antiquarian Society.

positioned not only inside a kind of knowledge machine but also as a moving part within it.

Mainly used to communicate to a student the knowledge of his body's own movements and placement, the telegraph is part of Lancaster's general mania for spatial distortion as a means of regulation. The architectural historian Dell Upton has described the Lancasterian system as one which conceived "of human knowledge, orderly instruction, individual accomplishment, and spatial order as interlocking realms in which the material world could act as a tool for shaping the moral and intellectual faculties decisively and efficiently."[27] Lancaster manipulates these "interlocking realms" by shifting scale; he loves to expand, to contract, and in effect to create parodic, even gothicized, versions of ordinary human scale in a pedagogical *Castle of Otranto*. In his classroom, not fifteen or fifty but five hundred students in one room. Not just illustrations in his books but elaborate foldouts. Not ordinary schoolbooks, in the hands of the children, but outsized versions to be viewed from afar. Not everyday speech but sequences of coded commands, requiring specialized knowledge. These proto-cinematic effects—of zoom, close-up, long shot, and tracking—displace identity, keeping the child off-balance, so that he can only find his place within the system itself. I use the analogy to cinema advisedly, for Lancaster is attuned to the medial shifts of his own epoch, as expressed by his passion for the telegraph and disdain for books (other than his own). Shifts in scale like the ones he institutes regularly occur with shifts in media technology: the distant is brought close; the small is made large; the prolix is condensed.

What in the realm of literature for children, beginning in the eighteenth century, had been the miniature, became, in Lancaster's universe, the abbreviated, the literally telegraphed. While both modes signal a consensus that material for children ought to be scaled down and condensed, their differences mark the boundaries of an emerging normative view of childhood, which excludes the poor and children of color. As we saw in the last chapter, an imagined child, akin but not identical to the middle-class child, who was the object of the boom in children's publishing that produced the *Goody*s and the "Babes," was becoming a vehicle for adult memories and desires; as such he was (if often ambivalently) encouraged in a certain kind of sensuous, internalized reading experience. One 1827 children's book describes this mode of reading:

> Your attention was roused [by hearing others read], it was fixed before you were aware of it: . . . your heart bled for distant woes, or those which never had an existence.
>
> With what eagerness have you seized the book to read it yourself; and when you had once begun, you found you could not leave off, till you had read the whole. Not satisfied with this, you have read it over again and again; and have ruminated on the airy dream with pleasure when the book which contained it was worn out or lost.[28]

This advice for young Bible readers figures even sacred reading as compulsive, immersive, hallucinogenic, empathic. At the same time, vehicles of children's reading, the child's-palm-sized, decorative, little books and chapbooks, like many of the editions of *Goody Two-Shoes* and of *The Children in the Wood*, offered an additional sensual and tactile attraction. The story of Tom Thumb, toy books, tiny Bibles no larger than postage stamps—when adults market such objects to children they tap a realm that James Clifford has described as enacting a "bourgeois longing for inner experience."[29] The miniature, Susan Stewart writes, inspires an "infinite time of reverie" and creates an "'other' time, a type of transcendent time which negates change and the flux of lived reality."[30]

By contrast, the abbreviation is profoundly sublunary; far from slowing time down, the abbreviation willfully accelerates it. If the miniature allows for a kind of narcissistic flood, the abbreviation is grounded in the social. It even creates its own class around the literacy event that it inspires: you're "in the know" if you find the abbreviation legible. Indeed, Lancaster's system relied on insider knowledge: "A command will be obeyed by any boy, *because it is a command*, and the whole school will obey on the common, *known* commands of the school from being merely *known* as such, let who will give them."[31] The abbreviated command is one of the ways in which Lancaster's methods register and process the velocity of change in the early national period. That is, it displaces the anxiety inspired by modernity's plunge into futurity onto the very act of reading, transforming incompetency and inexperience into a sense of mastery, of knowingness, and of belonging. However condensed and restricting the data may be—*face front, show slates*—the bodily dance of decoding might have its consolations.

But at the same time that the telegraph and its methods constitute an accommodation to modernity—this is, after all, part of what made Lancaster's system popular—they also create a temporal and spatial density, quite different from readerly absorption, from which it is hard to remove oneself: no time for thought or privacy or interiority. These are for others. David Wallace Adams describes the boarding school experience of an Indian student, at a much later date, which neatly captures the Lancasterian ethic: "Every aspect of his day-to-day existence . . . would be rigidly scheduled, the hours of the day intermittently punctuated by a seemingly endless number of bugles and bells demanding this or that response."[32] Lancaster, too, like so many of his pedagogical heirs, was devoted to bells, which punctuated the day, and signaled when a "telegraph" was arriving.

Telegraph: literally, writing at a distance, from afar. But why do you need a telegraph when you are in the same room? When is proximity figured as distance? One answer is that protocols of communication tend to safeguard class, age, gender, or racial distinctions; but in this case, something more is at work. During the formation of the republic, education was conceived of as a component of the "diffusion of knowledge," essential to the transformation of "subjects" into "citizens."[33] Such "diffusion" implies an existing cache of "knowledge" requiring radiation from a center along metropolis-to-provinces routes.[34] Aligned with this mapping, the Lancasterian structure positions "monitors"[35] as relays between master and pupils; in the classroom telegraph, this relationship is distilled and refined into ever more narrow channels. The paradigm for education, formerly the guild and scholastic model of master and apprentice, of vertical ascent in a "tower of learning" or through degrees of mastery, is here represented as a horizontal network, where face-to-face interaction is increasingly reduced, authority is increasingly abstracted—and facelessly enforced—in a model suggested by the new media technology of the telegraph, supplanting both the rhetorical and the print-based models.

The abridgement of face-to-face communication in the monitorial system transforms punishment as well; while pedagogical norms of the time still supported corporal punishment, Lancaster's discipline was, by contrast, discursive and narrative. Lancaster describes his notions of disorder and the punishments designed to prevent it in biblical terms: "The attempt to promote learning without the principle of order, would be like the efforts of the eastern nations, when Nimrod, in the despotism and pride with which he built the *Tower of Babel*, only succeeded in producing confusion, and thereby founded the first *empire of ignorance*."[36] Here authority, linked with the telegraph as one of the means by which authority remains consistent and anonymous, is constituted through opposition to a disordered, Eastern "empire of ignorance."[37]

Lancaster's orientalism extends to his classroom literacy practices. Alphabetic technology in Lancaster's classroom reproduces an imagined history of alphabetic writing: the youngest children, the "alphabet boys," work at the "sand-table," a black sand-covered surface in which students would write with their fingers. Sand writing was an innovation of Andrew Bell, who reputedly learned it in India, by observing how the native children learned to write. Lancaster positioned the sand tables within the factory of the schoolroom, as the first step in a process. Once the letters were thus incorporated grittily into the body, the students were ready to engage with more advanced classroom technologies, including the telegraph and an "alphabet wheel," echoing Colles's telegraph (Figures 23 and 24).

The punishments that Lancaster substitutes for corporal discipline similarly rely on orientalist theatrics along with shaming written labels and are brought into play when an accompanying system of rewards and merits fails. While Lancaster fosters competition, mirroring the economy, with students continually changing places, his disciplines more rigidly place students. "Birds in a cage" are placed in baskets suspended from the rafters.[38] Often the placing is figurative and explicitly theatrical: "Instead of recurring to the rod, make him *a bashaw of three tails*. The use of the famous coat, called the fool's coat, is well known in schools; let such a coat be suspended in public schools, the name of the offender printed in large letters, that the whole school may read, and fasten on it the words 'Bashaw of three tails,' also on the back of the coat, and three birchen rods suspended from the tail of the coat, at due and regular distances. This punishment is excellent for the senior boys, and will not need many repetitions."[39] A mainstay of orientalist fiction and theater of the eighteenth and nineteenth centuries, the bashaw is a role with antic possibilities (if often sinister overtones, as in the wicked uncle's Bashaw Castle, in some versions of "Babes in the Wood"). But for the offending boy, the performance is framed by text, fixing it within the realm of regulation rather than misrule.[40]

Lancaster further deploys an urban marketplace effigy to penalize through ridicule: "When a boy gets into a singing tone in reading . . . decorate the offender with matches, ballads, &c. and, in this garb, send him round the school, with some boys before him, crying 'matches,' &c. exactly imitating

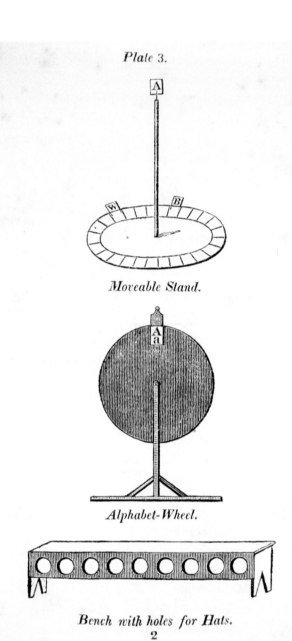

Figure 23. The alphabet wheel. Like the telegraph, this anticipates later inscription technologies such as the typewriter. *Manual of the Lancasterian System, of Teaching Reading, Writing, Arithmetic, and Needle-work: As Practised in the Schools of the Free-school Society, of New-York.* New York, 1820. Courtesy American Antiquarian Society.

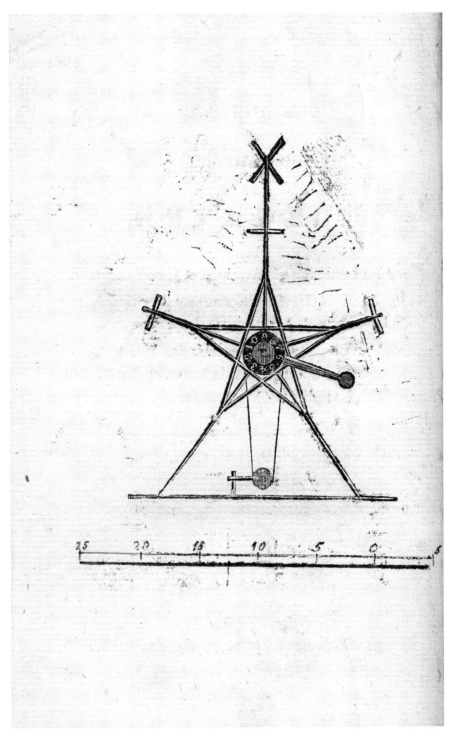

Figure 24. Christopher Colles's improvement on the optical telegraph, like Lancaster's alphabet wheel, relies on "a revolving index" on a circular board. This image forms the frontispiece for Colles's *Description of the Numerical Telegraph for Communicating Unexpected Intelligence by Figures, Letters, Words, and Sentences, with Directions for Writing the Correspondence Either Public or Private, and Shewing the Manner of Working the Machine with Perfect Accuracy and Despatch*. Brooklyn: Alden Spooner, 1813. Rare Book and Manuscript Library, Columbia University.

the dismal tones with which such things are hawked about the streets in London."[41] Sean Shesgreen points out that the crier of matches is "the poorest and most numerous of street sellers."[42] Both the Nimrod-like Bashaw and the abject hawker are figures of marketplace carnival; what the two have in common to the pedagogue's mind is their festive and oppositional relation to emergent norms of literacy and to the technologies that transmit it. And both suggest that the student metamorphoses into a racial and class "other" when he falls out of the network's order.

The monitorial classroom is, perhaps above all, a zone of mimicry;[43] indeed, "emulation" ("to copy or imitate with the object of equalling or excelling," according to the OED) is an important keyword of the system, as of much eighteenth- and nineteenth-century pedagogy. These disciplinary effigies are a variation on the theme of emulation. Given their widely discriminatory nature, one wonders how Lancaster's system could be translated to the project of educating children of color. And yet, the system was virtually designed to teach the sons of London's street hawkers, and to wean them from the streets. While the punishments are included in Lancaster's first U.S. manual (1812), and were therefore part of the training of missionaries who were sent into the field in the 1810s, they were dropped from the 1821 pamphlet (likely to have been circulated to mission schools).[44] In what follows, I turn to the case of the Brainerd School in the 1810s and 1820s, to consider some of the ways in which Lancasterian pedagogy, particularly its replicating and representational techniques, was adapted to suit the mission project.[45]

Cherokee Students in Their Places

A missionary and colonialist streak ran through Lancaster's life and work, from his first ambition to run away to Jamaica (Figure 25). Lancaster joined the Quakers not only because they could supply him with financial support but also because of their abolitionist and missionary work. When he got to the United States, he promoted his system explicitly to teach American Indians, and proposed to President Monroe that monitorial methods would "enlighten the mind's eye before it can be darkened by the gloom of the forest, and before the affections of the heart can be absorbed, by the furious feelings attendant to the love of the chase. Thus you will grasp a new power, which may operate on the minds of this interesting people, and render the yet unvitiated and undirected energies of their youth, subservient to the promotion of the general welfare."[46] For the purposes of schooling, missionaries and pedagogues, like later ethnographers, conflated Indians, Africans, and the

Figure 25. This broadside image from 1813 captures the imperialism of the mission project. Here King George hands the Bible to a generic dark-haired peasant/indigenous child. Transmitting the Lancasterian doctrine in a characteristically high-voltage rhetoric, the broadside declares that the "paternal wish of our King" to teach the Bible to the poor has replaced apathy with "energy, while operating with the speed of an electric stroke . . . has permanently conveyed light and knowledge at once into the cottages of poverty and industry." "Royal British System of Education." Courtesy American Antiquarian Society.

poor into an undifferentiated population, requiring the supplement of "civilization" (an eighteenth-century neologism) to render them fully human.[47] While each case—of the black, the poor white, the Indian—had its urgent claim to benevolence, the rhetoric surrounding the Indian juxtaposed, or opposed, to "civilization" the stringent "extermination" and "extinction" and "extinguish." While the spatial euphemism "removal" would come into play as a way to defer both "civilization" and "extermination," there was, strikingly, no other middle term. This situation created a particular emergency for the mission project.[48]

Confronted with the enormity of the problem of education, theorists tended to shiver under the weight of a kind of mathematical sublime. Sending missionaries off to teach American Indians in 1815 (in the Lancasterian system), the Rev. Elijah Parish worried that "there may be three million savages on this continent, perishing for the bread of life. Here then we have in our own country, as it were in our own neighborhood, in our own family, six million souls, sinking into ruin, crying to us for help, to pluck them as brands from the burning. Is not here a field of spiritual misery and death, far surpassing all our resources, far surpassing the labors of all our missionaries? Six million souls need six thousand missionaries. But where can half, where can one tenth part of this number be found?"[49] The occasion for this sermon was the ordination of Cyrus Kingsbury, who was being sent to the Cherokees by the American Board of Commissioners for Foreign Missions, the Massachusetts Congregationalist organization responsible, from its founding in 1810, for the largest number of missions to American Indians. By the time the mission school at Chickamauga, Tennessee, was opened in 1817, the Cherokees were in extremis, riven by internal pressures for and against assimilation and by external pressures exerted by the whites surrounding them.[50] As Margaret Szasz has pointed out, the "success" of mission projects depended largely on "the extent of disruption experienced by [the] native culture."[51] By this measure, Kingsbury's school would be destined for great things.

On a mission tour in 1818, the American Board's treasurer, Jeremiah Evarts, wrote from Kingsbury's newly christened Brainerd station that the Lancaster plan is "not only excellent in itself, but particularly suited to the attention of Indian children."[52] This assertion goes unelaborated, but in a later account of Brainerd, written for children, the narrator relates the visit of a Cherokee chief to the classroom: "The king [chief] addressed the scholars in Cherokee. . . . It was ascertained from the bi-lingual children that the king's sentiments corresponded exactly with his gestures, so that the missionaries understood what he uttered, by his gesticulations, almost as well as if he had made an address in correct English."[53] This widespread nineteenth-century notion of the gestural language of Indians, the idea that Indians can thus be fully and accurately read from the outside, without the wearisome bother of translation, is part of what made the Lancasterian system seem plausible to missionaries and policy makers.

At the same time that Indians were regularly drawn into English literacy as a constituent of the civilizing process, Anglo-Americans and Europeans consistently noted what they perceived as a special native gift for oratory. This characteristic veneration for Indian oratory has an elegiac cast. David Murray argues that here, as in much American discourse about Indians, the notion of Indian "nobility" aligns the Indian with the moribund aristocracies of Europe.[54]

Further, Murray points out, Indian speech, when not perceived as prelinguistic altogether, was essentialized as authentic nature; he cites an 1836 article entitled "Indian Eloquence" that remarks that the "'genius of eloquence bursts the swathing bands of custom, and the Indian stands forth accessible, natural, and legible.'"[55] It is by means of such putative "legibility" that this imagined Indian might be easily positioned within Lancaster's network. As in the case of the Lancasterian child noted above, the Indian is represented as lacking a unique interiority, a self or subjectivity, and therefore might be easily provided with a surrogate self—or, more precisely, a *representation* of a self—in its stead.

The Brainerd school at Chickamauga used the Lancasterian devices of monitors and merits, including gifts and money. Monitors functioned to relieve the small missionary staff, who were also responsible for every aspect of life for their families and the Indian students who boarded with them. Lancaster had a set of medals that he gave out to students, which attracted the waggery of his critics; in America these rewards, which began as leather or metal badges and medals, were supplemented and replaced by script, tickets, and tokens exchangeable for "such articles as the holders need[ed]," which "answer[ed] the purpose of a circulating medium among the boys."[56] These tokens drew upon and helped to firmly establish the genre of the "reward of merit," classroom premiums that became widespread in the nineteenth century. Combining rewards with codes echoing the telegraph system, Cyrus Kingsbury distributed "little cards bearing the initial letters of the words 'Punctual attendance,' 'Behavior,' and 'Diligence.'" These coded cards could then be redeemed for cash: one-half cent, one cent, and three and a half cents, respectively. The cash could be exchanged for books, knives, or toys.[57] Cherokees had long been incorporated into the white economy, but this system associates literacy and the high-rent "diligence" (a virtue much urged upon Indians who were thought to be "idle" and "indolent") with the consumption of goods.

It was not only in such commodity practices that Indians were brought into the white economy. Through the naming of both mission schools and mission students, Indians were incorporated into white culture through a kind of sentimental cryptography, in a code legible only to the whites. Brainerd, Dwight, Eliot—these American Board mission schools, to the Cherokees, Choctaws, and Creeks, were named to commemorate and perpetuate the work of the previous generations of missionaries and teachers: John Eliot (1604–1690) to the Massachusett Indians; David Brainerd (1718–1747) to the Seneca and Delaware Indians; and the educator and clergyman Timothy Dwight (1752–1817). Much is made in the nineteenth century of Indian place names. "How can the red man be forgotten," writes the poet Lydia Huntley Sigourney, "while so many of our states and territories, bays, lakes and rivers, are indelibly stamped by names of their giving?"[58] The carrying of the New England names into the Southeast reverses this process, imprinting the landscape with these cenotaph inscriptions.

Such names are replicated as well when the schools rename their Cherokee students after dead missionaries and living benefactors, incorporating them into an institutional (and heavily Christian) rather than a familial kinship structure.[59] Thus "Brainerd" becomes not only the name of the mission school but also the name of one of the Cherokee students—"David Brainerd"—in the school. This renaming places students within a new constellation, legible only from the outside; like little Bellerophons, they are, at first anyway, carrying a language that they can't read into a culture that wishes them ill.[60]

The particular force of the Cherokee children's renaming relies in part upon the cultural significance of a name in the narrative of a life. Novels, for example, mobilize this power in fictional naming and renaming; in *Goody Two-Shoes*, Margery Meanwell adopts and declares her new status and independence with a name that sheds her kinship ties and opens up her new role as someone whose shoes allow her to circulate in the community as the "trotting tutoress." Baptism, marriage (for women), adoption, religious ordination—these and many other life passages call for new names. These examples, though, posit agency or at least a community of shared interest. The renaming of the Cherokee children by white missionaries, then, also relies on what Eric Cheyfitz describes as "the translation of the Indians into proper English," which may serve as a kind of shorthand for Cheyfitz's longer argument in *The Poetics of Imperialism* about the colonial violence of translation, in all of its forms.[61] "Proper English" resonates with "property." For, as Cheyfitz further notes, the "European process of translation I am describing displaced or attempted to displace (for there was and still is enduring resistance) Native Americans into the realm of the proper, into that place where the relation between *property* and *identity* is inviolable," in the interests of dispossessing them of property in land.[62] The renaming intentionally asserted a claim on the children's identities, which were now aligned with Christian ideology, institutions, and charitable donors. Especially when children were named after their benefactors, children's new identities function as a kind of currency. The unselfconscious ease with which whites redenominated Indian children suggests as well that a model for what scholars have seen as the "hollow category" of childhood[63] was identified with the alterity of Indians and blacks. Indeed, as Anna Mae Duane has argued, the discursive production of white childhood in the eighteenth and nineteenth centuries occurred in conversation and coordination with the fluctuating and interlinked status of racial others. The renaming amounts to a reappropriation and a commodification of the children, who are treated as being accessible to what modern advertising would resonantly call rebranding.

In keeping with Lancasterian accounting procedures, Brainerd teachers tracked each student in their record books, listing the child's name and age, when he or she came to the school, his or her Cherokee name and its English translation, and in the "Character" column such attributes as "Respectable," "Pious," "Industrious"; "Mediocrity" or "Saucy"; and, once, "a wild creature just from the woods."[64] With a double-entry attention to the result of their investments, some records concluded with "Runaway" or "Died." The list of names reads like entries in the *Dictionary of American Biography*, dizzyingly replicating the American Board's theological, political, and literary taste, as though the students were to form a living canon. From the *Brainerd Journal*'s tables:[65] Samuel Worcester (twice); John Knox Witherspoon ("Run away"); Thomas L. McKenney ("Not so attentive as he should be"); Lydia Huntley; Lyman Beecher; Timothy Dwight; Jedidiah Morse; Jeremiah Evarts; Elias Boudinot; even Boston Recorder, after a newspaper.[66] The names ring a change on Lancaster's classroom cryptography described above. The poor are identified by number, but in a sentimentalizing of Lancaster's militaristic and bureaucratic "mustering," the Indians are identified with names richly enmeshed in the web of United States culture: its literacy practices, its memorializing customs, its affective demands, its patrilineal kinship structure, its institutional filiopiety, its processes of commodification. Names were, in effect, purchased with charitable donations.[67]

The renaming served several practical purposes, as this entry from the *Brainerd Journal* shows: "In compliance with the request of a society of young gentlemen in Southampton, Mass. a boy has been selected to bear the name of Vinson Gould, to be educated by them & at the request of a society of young ladies in the same place a girl has been selected to bear the name of Mindwell Woodbridge Gould, to be educated by them. The children are called after their pastor & his wife. . . . [The little girl] being destitute of a name that we could conveniently pronounce . . . has been called baby till the present time."[68] Here the names make good on a debt, memorialize a "pastor & his wife," and resolve the continually vexing problem of many missionaries' monolingualism. (Presumably "Mindwell Woodbridge Gould" would rarely have to pronounce her own name.) To affix a name was to fix the Indian within a new social space. The names also functioned as apotropaic charms to prevent the Indians from engaging in the kind of movement represented by the names Cherokees themselves gave their children, which often have an active and somewhat narrative quality.[69]

What did the students make of their new names?[70] Ethnographers suggest that for Cherokees, a name was not a kinship marker but was meant to carry particular information about the individual; it had an active, not a memorializing or retrospective, relation to the person, and was capable of being changed as the events of life unfolded, demanding a new name.[71] For most native Americans, a "degree of sensitivity to the use of the name or names of dead persons was so common that its absence is noted only a few times in the ethnographic literature. . . . Respect and consideration for the bereaved and fear of the dead entered into . . . restrictions" on being named for the dead.[72] But with their new missionary names and necronyms, the mission students became living monuments.

As the children became fluent readers and writers in English, their literacy was put to work in the hopes of warding off further harm. Cherokees and those in sympathy with them hoped that removal from their established homes and ancestral lands to unknown western territories could be forestalled by accumulating sufficient evidence of Cherokee civilization. To this end, children at Brainerd in the 1820s wrote to their benefactors, and copies of many of these letters (all from girls at the school) have been preserved. These child writers and their letters to their benefactors were advertisements for Indian progress. Hilary Wyss describes a type of "Readerly Indian" that emerged in mission-published memoirs from Brainerd and elsewhere, "crafted by missionaries looking for appealing fund-raising subjects."[73] Many of the children's letters almost formulaically refer to what white consensus of the period regarded as particular markers of civilization: girls and women sewing; men farming; children reading and writing at school. In the same spirit, some of the letters mention the Cherokee printing press, established in 1828. Lucy Campbell, for one of many examples, writes: "I think you would be pleased to hear about the improvement of the Cherokees. Many of them have large plantations and greater part of them keep a number of Cattle and some have large buildings but some live miserably they dont send their children to school and dont care anything about the Sabbath. We out to be thankful to the missionaries for what they done for us."[74] This passage shares the characteristic mix seen in many of the letters: a description of Cherokee "improvement" mingled with the letter writer's observation of lapses from the new Christian protocols, along with assertions of gratitude. The project of civilizing had long been associated with Western notions of personal property and land use.[75] Like the renaming, the looms and plows, buildings and cattle, books and printing press were advertisements for the Cherokees' becoming incorporated into an economy of private ownership that went hand in hand with the missionary project "to train them up, in families and schools, for comfort and usefulness on earth, and everlasting happiness in heaven," as one account described it.[76]

The letters are a lively mix of contemporary epistolary conventions, local mission news of presumed interest to benefactors (curriculum of the school, spiritual condition of the letter writer and others, gifts gratefully received, children named for benefactors, and so on), and accounts of other notable events at the station (the accidental death of a child, the capture of a horse thief), channeled through the particular style and élan of each letter writer, ranging in age from about eight years old to about fifteen. When Nancy Reece was nine the missionaries noted in their book that she was an "active child, apt to learn and apt to work";[77] by fourteen and fifteen she had grown into a prolific and gifted letter writer. While hitting most of the dutiful generic marks, her letters also seem to express pleasure in her acute visual imagination and in the mastery Reece has developed since she began writing only a few years earlier.[78] In one letter, she invites her correspondent into an imaginative visit to the school, aware of the visual interest such travel would hold for the benevolent tourist. In this June 1828, letter, after a rather awkward opening to Louisa Sanborn ("I have just finished a letter to Mrs. Colman, a relative of Mrs. Dean and I cannot think of much to write"), she finds her topics. She describes the after-school assistance given by all the girls to the teachers "in sewing and other work" and her studies ("Reading, Spelling, Writing, Woodbridge's Geography, and reading History of the United States, in the afternoon spell the words with the definitions in the spelling book"). She writes of walks "with our Teacher. It is very pleasant in the woods at this time of the year, the trees are green, and we can find flowers in almost every place. It is very warm. I should like to see you here, and I think you would like to walk with us.—I am alone in the school room writing while my Teacher has gone to the wash house with some of her scholars to see about the washing."[79] The vivid invitation to come take a walk with the students and the long dash leading to the small portrait of the girl alone in the schoolroom breathe the air of the place into the letter. Against the backdrop of all the routine housework the girls do, Reece conveys her escape from those labors into another kind of work, the work of writing to a stranger ("Altho I am a stranger to you and know nothing about you, yet I will write a few lines to you, because you are a relative of Mrs. Elsworth"). Engaging with the network of benefactors allows Reece to circulate beyond her place at the mission school and within her Cherokee family, while at the same time her correspondence is in the service of preserving the school and her Cherokee community. In another letter, she writes to one of her teacher's friends: "She has been telling me about your family and the place where you live. She says your door yard and garden are filled with rose bushes and flowers and that your house is kept neat just as she wishes us to keep our part of the house. We have a rose bush at our door but it is a wild one such as grows in the woods. It seems to me that I can see such things when Miss Ames is telling me about them."[80] Reece has traveled in her mind's eye to Miss Ames's New England town and engages her correspondent with the powers of her own visual imagination. To another "Respected Madam," she writes: "We have an interesting school. I think you would now be glad to step in at our door, and see us rise before you and see our dear teacher call up the first class and so on till the last, and then hear us recite our lessons in geography, Arithmetic, &c."[81] While all of the girls' letters movingly express their vibrant voices and presence, Reece situates herself directly in the present moment ("I am alone in the school room writing") and warmly engages the figure of enargia to bring her interlocutor into that present moment with her: "I think you would now be glad to step in at our door, and see us rise before you."

Many of these letters are, as it were, "cold calls" ("Altho I am a stranger to you . . . , yet I will write a few lines to you"), duty-bound outreach to benefactors, friends of the mission teachers, and others, which the children close with "your young friend," as Reece often does, with some version of "Your affectionate Cherokee friend"[82] or, if the child has been renamed, as Lucy Campbell closed a letter to Daniel Campbell, "from your adopted Cherokee daughter."[83] That the girls are writing to people they don't know and often know almost nothing about suggests that Reece's engagement comes less from her connection to her correspondents, or even her devotion to her teacher or to performing well as a student, than from a pleasure in her own capacities as a writer and as an observer. In a letter to her teacher's mother, Reece reveals something about her manner in person: "I can write more than I could say if you were here. I think more than I can talk. Sometimes Miss Ames laughs at me and tells me to let my thoughts come forth that people may know that I can talk."[84] In other letters, her imaginative engagement with the scenes at the mission and New England scenes she has only heard of are matched by a sympathetic engagement with others' grief and loss.[85]

These letters of Nancy Reece and her student colleagues are eloquent in themselves and are striking examples of the literature of childhood as well as of Cherokee literature. Even given the difficult circumstances of their composition, just pre-Removal during the Jacksonian transformation of Indian policy, these letters convey their writers' unique voices, as well as pointed expressions of political will, as do some letters in a batch of student writing sent to President Jackson. The central letter in that group decorously doesn't mention the crisis but instead offers gifts:

> Sir,
> We heard that the Cherokees were going to send you a mink skin and a
> pipe. We thought that it would make you laugh; and the Scholars asked

our teacher if they might make you a present and she told us that she did not know as there was anything suitable in the whole establishment. Then she looked among the articles of the girls society and told me that I might make you a pocket book. Will you please to accept it from a little Cherokee girl aged nine years.

Christiana McPherson[86]

Copies of the Brainerd letters were preserved in the interests of the mission project generally, but also to publicize the Cherokee crisis specifically and to offer a key marker of the "civilization" that would undergird and justify their legal rights and claims.

In an 1830 Massachusetts Sabbath Society children's book *Letters and Conversations on the Cherokee Mission*, for example, Sarah Tuttle imagines a family dialogue about the Cherokees and the missions, interspersed with letters from missionaries, including two from Brainerd students Nancy Reece and Christiana McPherson. Tuttle's choice of letters is telling. The letter from Nancy Reece recounts her effort to organize a charitable society among the Brainerd girls, "in the hours that were given us to play, on Saturdays," and modeled on the ones in the North that benefit them. The Cherokee students' society would be supported by selling some of their sewing and handicraft labor to Cherokee women, "such as making and fixing their bonnets, and such things."[87] The second letter, by the nine-year-old Christiana McPherson (who wrote to Andrew Jackson, quoted above) to Jeremiah Evarts, a founder and secretary of the American Board of Commisisoners for Foreign Missions, speaks of the recent accidental death of a young cousin, reflects on death in Christian terms, and then turns to school discipline: "I think you would like to hear if we are good children. We are not allowed to do bad things. When we get angry, we have to stand in the middle of the floor, before all the scholars, and say the twenty-ninth verse of the fourteenth chapter of Proverbs."[88] McPherson goes on to list several other child infractions and their punishments (lies: Proverbs 12:22 and Revelation 21:8; taking food "without leave": the eighth commandment and Corinthians 6:10; breaking the Sabbath: the fourth commandment). If in so many ways the Brainerd students' letters greatly exceed their prompts and seem far removed from Lancaster's original system and motives, Tuttle's choice of letters demonstrating the children's model capitalism and capitalist charity and assuring stand-and-recite discipline show how the children's literacy could be put to use.

Whatever else the letters may do, in Tuttle's narrative they position the students as vehicles of white pedagogy and as publicity agents for the missionary project of which they themselves are the object. Here the order of "civilization" is instituted by an inversion of the Lancasterian disciplinary effigies noted above; these Indian children are written into a masquerade in which they function as monuments and celebrations, as models and lessons, as replicas and repetitions. It is in this representational work that their letters display their consonance with the monitorial project, in which the child is produced as, in effect, a medium of communication. As Anna Mae Duane has argued, "childhood," as a condition not only of dependence but also of suffering and vulnerability in the early national period, relies on paradoxical associations with Indians and African Americans. But such overwriting of personhood by the social, however aggressive, is never the whole story.[89] Nancy Reece and Christiana McPherson and the other letter writers at Brainerd claim distinctions for themselves and express the fullness and presence of their own personalities.

Still, mission pedagogies like that at Brainerd highlight the easy enlistment of children as monuments to and memorials and living enactments of adult hopes and desires. The colonizing project posits a child that is capable of being transformed into a messenger circulating in the present and making claims on the future, which is the cultural logic of the construction of childhood more generally. Wyss's theory of the "Readerly Indian," produced by missionary propaganda, chimes with the child reader beginning to be produced in a different register—not to further the mission project but rather to distinguish the reading child from children at risk, like Nancy Reece and her student friends.

CHAPTER 4

"Selling a Boy"

Race, Class, and the Literacy Economy of Childhood

> We behold a child eight or ten months old. . . . Who is it? Whose
> is it? what is it? where is it? . . . Can you love it? . . . Where does
> it belong?
> —Sylvester Judd, *Margaret* (1845)

SCHOOLING OFFERED the uncertain benefits of reading and writing to free African American children and poor urban children as well as to Indian children
on the frontier, even at the risk of making them strangers to themselves, while
gathering them into both the moral strictures of nineteenth-century domesticity
and the economic structures of the marketplace. If most children were still likely
to contribute to the household economy, as they always had, working in and
around the home or farm, or in paid jobs beyond the home, more and more
children were also going to school, for at least part of the year. The transformation that Viviana Zelizer describes both as "the 'sacralization' of children's lives"
and, more provocatively, as "the construction of the economically worthless
child" was, she writes, "in large part accomplished among the American urban
middle class" by the mid-nineteenth century.[1] In imported, adopted, and
adapted children's literature, from Margery Meanwell and her shoes to Rosamond and her purple jar—heroes well known to American children—the mores
of consumption had begun to fuel narratives alongside the long-standing ethic
of work.[2] The autonomous orphans of *Goody Two-Shoes* were shown to thrive,
not only through learning, but also through careful husbanding and foreign
adventure; even the child tragedians of the traditional "Babes in the Wood"
were sometimes restored to life, liberty, and property via schooling in a popular
redaction of the old story.

While such tales engage the pervasive cultural fantasy of a symbolic value for literacy that translates to real capital, books for and about these schooled children in the early republic register anxiety about the class status of those newly identified by the endearment "little strangers," capturing some of the paradoxes surrounding childhood in the nineteenth century.[3] On the one hand, the authority of paternity and the assurances of heritability had decreased: "The ability of a father to transmit his 'status position' to his children declined. By the early nineteenth century, families were finding it increasingly difficult to pass on their status by bequeathing land or a family craft to their offspring."[4] But if fathers couldn't mark their children like books, signifying ownership, children didn't exactly own themselves either: "Although only children held as slaves were ever actually designated by law as 'chattels personal' . . . the laws applying to children as a group had much in common with the laws of property."[5]

To whom children belonged and how that belonging might be defined and adjudicated became crucial questions in a range of social and political venues, as the Lockean social compact was put under pressure by the expansion of the suffrage, by economic upheavals, and by the ongoing disasters of slavery and genocide. This chapter explores these issues through readings of two sets of narratives for children: popular books and tales of the 1810s to 1830s circulating anxieties about lost or stolen children, and Jacob Abbott's far-reaching and steady-selling series books from the 1830s to the 1870s that register and grapple with paradoxes of children's autonomy and dependency in a social, legal, and economic landscape shaped by both racial and age hierarchies.

Little Strangers

While the United States in the nineteenth century was the shattered home to many "stolen children"[6]—enslaved African Americans, Indians, and poor children—the lost or stolen children of popular narratives tend to be more or less prosperous and white. Monitory diversions, these child abductions are figured as "adventures," "histories," and "rambles." The "lost child" tales, cheerfully menacing children with kidnapping and death, ask their child readers: To whom do you belong and where do you belong? Texts like the "The Children in the Wood" (toddlers murdered by their uncle), "The History of Little Fanny" series (1812–1830s) (children stolen for their clothes), Jacob Abbott's "Selling a Boy" (1835) (a father offering his son for sale to neighbors), and Nathaniel Hawthorne's "Little Annie's Ramble" (1835) (a little girl abducted by an adult male stranger) position children in middling white families as always at risk of vagabondage, pauperism, or chattel slavery, conditions represented as lying just beyond the threshold of the middle-class home.[7] Children's traditional position as virtual property was inflected by an expanding commercial sector in the nineteenth century, and many children were still sold, not only as slaves, but also as apprentices (throughout the century) and in pauper auctions (until into the mid-century).[8] This chapter reads in such texts anxiety over the class, race, and property status of children in a period on the margin between one "style" of childhood and another, in which the legal condition of children is in transition, in which whiteness becomes consolidated as property, and in which reading and writing practices are advertised as protection against the threats these texts circulate.

Amounting to a small subgenre, linked both to fairy tales and bildungsromane, tales for children about lost children had a special resonance for Americans.[9] The chapbook trilogy *The History of Little Fanny, The History of Little Henry,* and *The History and Adventures of Little Eliza* was copied from the London S. and J. Fuller 1810 editions and reprinted from the 1810s to at least 1832.[10] Structured as conversion accounts, these are secular allegories of obedience and monitory tales of dependence, situating children in early consumer and commodity culture. *The History of Little Fanny* (Philadelphia, 1812) is one of the earliest paper doll books, a small blue pamphlet of seventeen pages, with hand-colored illustrations and a verse narrative.[11] Fanny echoes Maria Edgeworth's nearly contemporaneous Rosamond, a little girl who wants what she wants, and whose domestic adventures elicit maternal training in the regulation of desire. In her *History,* Fanny longs to wear her new clothes out to the park. When mother points out that it's too hot for a *"great coat, muff, and bonnet"* (5), Fanny pouts, and then goes out overdressed anyway with a careless maid. A beggar steals her for her expensive clothes,[12] and Fanny becomes a beggar herself, all "Tatter'd and torn" (9), until "a generous dame" helps her move up the ladder of child labor, from fishmonger to dairymaid. While Fanny "oft thinks of home, and of her mother dear" (13), it turns out that her mother has her in her sights all along: her eye

> Follow'd her close, and was for ever nigh,
> Longing once more her daughter to embrace,
> Hang on her neck, and kiss her smiling face,
> Whilst prudence still withheld maternal love,
> Till longer trial Fanny's virtue prove. (13–14)

At last Fanny is sent to deliver butter to her mother's house, and they are reunited. Fanny's history showcases the Rousseauvian mother, who produces a

theater from the materials of society in which to educate the child; the disciplining of the mother, in whom prudence must regulate love, goes without saying.
Among the paradoxical appeals of *Fanny* are the child's childlike vanity and
rebelliousness and the fact that her descent provides opportunities for new
paper doll outfits—beggar, dairymaid—parading a middle-class pastoral. The
final image shows a demure Fanny, "restored to her former station, modestly
dressed in a coloured frock, with a book in her hand" (17). (See Plates 21 and
22.) Her adventure has reconfigured her consumer desires, now channeled to
modest frocks and the possession that transcends consumerism: the book.
"Return'd to what she ought to be," Fanny is

> no longer idle, proud, or vain,
> Eager her own opinion to maintain;
> But pious, modest, diligent, and mild,
> Belov'd by all, a good and happy child. (17)

Fanny's punishment for her vain acquisitiveness is to become a working girl,
earning her keep, her bread, her clothes (both the cause of her downfall and the
attraction of the images). Her misstep precipitates a fall out of the class in which
childhood newly functions as a protected and dedicated temporal-spatial zone.
The class status of Fanny's parents seems secure, represented by an unchanging
address in an apparently prosperous neighborhood, but once she's beyond the
threshold Fanny's status is fluid, reflecting a kind of stadial theory of labor
history for the nursery set. The child, in these narratives, might be defined as
the entity whose class status you do not know. Or, to put it another way, it is
through the figure of the child that the nonessential nature of class is uncovered.

In the history of little Fanny, the book marks the child's redemption as well
as her return to the class with the leisure time to read. The book is a permissible
commodity, reading an activity that promotes a desirable stasis, in which real-
life adventure, with its connotations of chance, hazard, and the unadvisable, is
brought safely under the sign of "adventure," as a literary genre. *The History
and Adventures of Little Eliza* opens with Eliza reading, for "At school she learn'd
to spell and read with ease" (n.p.) (Plate 23). Her mother takes her to a fair and
buys her a doll (depicted as looking just like Eliza), and Eliza is wooed away to
the realms of pleasure, where she is stolen by Gypsies. Eliza's descent is like
Fanny's, with the difference that the prodigal's return depends not on maternal
surveillance but on a novelistic chance encounter. Eliza, herself a paper doll, is
devoted to a little doll, which seems to be a stand-in for her self: it's a version
of self-ownership that has more in common with amour propre, for Rousseau
the problematic self-regard which relies on the esteem of others, than with

Lockean self-ownership. In *The History and Adventures of Little Henry, a Companion to Little Fanny*, Henry, left alone by a negligent maid, is, like Fanny, stolen for his clothes by Gypsies, who put him to begging and then sell him to a chimney sweep. Henry runs away from the sweep, finally going to sea and returning home to be reunited with his parents as a hero (in the Tommy Two-Shoes line).

The children in these texts seem to attempt to be self-owning Lockean heroes, establishing themselves as autonomous agents; but their independence is figured as mere poverty, their labors as servitude and vagabondage. (In these examples, Henry, as the sole male child, grows up to embody the competent, consenting individual.) The children fulfill fantasies of self-ownership, represented by their dollness, while the dolls at the same time seem to function to objectify the children, and to "trouble the boundary between person and thing," as Robin Bernstein has put it, which denotes "the terror at the ontological core of slavery."[13] If books instruct the child in the mores of children in books, they also hauntingly present children as slavishly bound within and by books.[14]

Lost (in a Book)

Echoing Little Fanny and company, Nathaniel Hawthorne's 1835 "Little Annie's Ramble" engaged the lost-child genre for the children's gift-book market.[15] Like Fanny et al., Annie ventures into public, seemingly allured by the "Ding-dong! Ding-dong! Ding-dong" of the town crier's bell, in the tale's first words. Like them, she crosses the threshold between the safety and privacy of the domestic on the one hand and the charms and dangers (the "adventure") of the thoroughfare on the other, as she "stands on her father's door-steps" (228). Her original venue in *Youth's Keepsake: A Christmas and New Year's Gift for Young People* circulated her story along with others explicitly designed for the gift market; "keepsake" is a print genre entirely at ease with—indeed, banking upon—its status as a commodity. While most books are commodities, of course, the form of the gift book suggests that part of the festivity is in the purchase, for it often creates blank spaces for filling in the names of donor and recipient.[16]

Hawthorne's Little Annie transforms the lost child's "history" into a "ramble." As the genre changes from mock biography to mock picaresque the tone and address change too. Fanny and friends are playful and didactic à la Edgeworth, offering toy books and doll toys as décor and sweetener for admonitions. One of Hawthorne's addressees is also a child, but the lesson, such as it is, aims over her head: if Fanny is shadowed by her mother, Annie's reader is shadowed by an adult double. The crier's bell, alerting the town to the arrival of a circus or carnival, also alerts the narrator to the presence of the little girl, who he surmises is "weary of this wide and pleasant street" and "feels the impulse to go strolling away—that longing after the mystery of the great world"; he need only "hold out [his] hand" and she "comes bounding on tiptoe across the street" (228). Passing through "the busy town," they window-shop "silks of sunny hue," "burnished silver, and the chased gold, the rings of the wedlock . . . glistening at the window of the jeweller," and pies, cakes, and sugar plums (229). They pause at the bookseller, but "truth to tell, she is apt to turn away from the printed page, and keep gazing at the pretty pictures, such as the gay-colored ones which make this shop window the continual loitering place of children" (230). On their "ramble," the couple pass street hawkers ("Did Annie ever read the cries of London city?"), kin to the roles played out by Fanny's circle; a chimney sweep (one of little Henry's roles) emerges "from smoke and soot . . . into the upper air" (233). The tale closes as it began, with the crier's voice now calling on behalf of an "afflicted mother": "Strayed from her home, a LITTLE GIRL, of five years old." The child "after wandering a little way into the world . . . return[s] at the first summons, with an untainted and unwearied heart," to "be a happy child again." The narrator, however, has "gone too far astray" to be called back. Children's "influence on us is at least reciprocal with ours on them" (234), the narrator concludes. "After drinking from those fountains of still fresh existence, we shall return into the crowd . . . with a kinder and purer heart, and a spirit more lightly wise" (235). What Hawthorne represents as Annie's flânerie has come to an end, as it must, since flânerie itself is by definition an adult mode; the child flâneur is simply a stolen or strayed child.[17]

Though written for children, "Little Annie's Ramble" is monitory only to the degree to which all of Hawthorne's tales threaten—or promise—alienation. Karen Sánchez-Eppler reads the tale as, in part, an account of Hawthorne's conflicted self-consciousness as a writer for children; he feels, in a sense, to double duty bound, as both the children's "monitor and [their] playfellow."[18] If the narrator confesses doubleness, not to say duplicity, Annie emblematizes a temporal-spatial doubleness: the here-and-yet-elsewhere nature of books and reading. As Annie and the narrator linger at the bookstore window, he muses: "What would Annie think, if, in the book which I mean to send her, on New Year's day, she should find her sweet little self, bound up in silk or morocco with gilt edges, there to remain till she become a woman grown, with children of her own to read about their mother's childhood!" (230). Pressed into a book, like the keepsake of the gift book's title or like a paper doll, Annie is asked to think of her "sweet little self" as a paper-doll-like entity that can be split off

from Annie and retained for future delectation—not hers but that of her putative future children.

"Little Annie's Ramble" is a not-quite-lost-child tale, an abduction story
with a (perhaps) benignant, Wordsworthian vampire for a narrator, who only
wishes to "drink from those fountains of still fresh existence" (235). Twenty-
first-century readers tend to be appalled at the topos, with contemporary sex
panics in mind.[19] In the nineteenth century the tale circulated rather widely for
adults (at least twice, in Hawthorne's *Twice-told Tales* in 1837 and 1851), as well
as for children, in Whittier's *Child Life in Prose* (1873), in a Riverside edition of
Hawthorne tales in 1887, *Little Daffydowndilly: And Other Stories and Biographical Stories*, and in *McGuffey's Fifth Reader* (1901).[20] Variously situated, "Little
Annie's Ramble" addressed not only the child reader and the adult reader but
also the reader that such texts (like those of Charles Lamb's "Dream Children")
bring into existence: the child folded into the text, the "sweet little self" bound
within the book and within its adult reader, who must, however, go to the book
to recover it.

"Selling a Boy": The Literacy Contract

So far, I have described texts that imagine what happens when a child follows
an irresistible impulse to step beyond the domestic threshold. In each instance,
this starting point produces (and is produced by) fantasies of child theft and
abduction, leading, in the earlier texts, to class and status declension. In each
case the child is subjected to the acquisitive motives of an adult who's outside
of the parent-child compact. The vulnerable child of the earlier texts is represented as asserting a kind of self-ownership, as an independent laborer. Annie,
by contrast, is both more protected and more bound; hers is an erotic and
affective capital, upon which others may draw, but which she never quite pos-
sesses herself. And while the earlier children are, literally, alienated in the marketplace, Annie is existentially alienated, divided from herself by being bound
in a book.

By the 1830s, custody cases had begun to register shifts in the legal structure
of "childhood," as "the declining appeal of apprenticeship and other traditional
methods of placing out children and the rising concern for child welfare encouraged custody-law innovation."[21] Cindy Weinstein's study of the literature of
nineteenth-century family life traces the development of adoption law in the
first decades of the nineteenth century, in which as early as 1810, something
like "the best interests of the child," not codified until the 1830s, began to
take primacy.[22] By the 1830s, "courts began to conceive of children less as the

'inalienable' property of their parents and more as the inalienable property of themselves," and the antebellum family began to replace the "paternalism of consanguinity" with "a family that is based on affection and organized according to a paradigm of contract."[23]

In his best-selling series books, Jacob Abbott, arguably the most prolific and popular American children's writers of the nineteenth century, increasingly promoted contractualism for children, attuned to their shifting legal and cultural status, and to the problematic of self-ownership for white and African American children. Abbott devised an accretive narrative method ideally and perhaps uniquely suited to his themes. Born more or less with the century, in 1803 in Hallowell, Maine, he lived and worked into the 1870s. He went as a child of thirteen or fourteen to Bowdoin College, trained as a minister at Andover Seminary, but early on pursued teaching, a vocation in which he was gifted and innovative. He made a name for himself as a kind of liberal moralist with the best seller *The Young Christian* for the American Tract Society in 1832. But the turning point in his career from pedagogue to author occurred in 1834 when the Boston publisher T. H. Carter presented Abbott with a set of engravings and asked if he couldn't concoct a little book for children out of them.[24]

Abbott used each image as a prompt for a little episode. Hence, the picture of the little girl feeding chickens appears under the title "Feeding the Chickens." A picture of a shepherd prompts a plotless narrative entitled "The Shepherd." When Abbott got to a picture of another shepherd, he decided it was perfectly adequate to present "Another Shepherd." The picture of an explosion prompted a warning about bad boys and gunpowder. Originally published as *The Little Scholar Learning to Talk: a Picture Book for Rollo by His Father,* this became the first in the Rollo series, which grew to twenty-six volumes.

Abbott's episodic narrative method, most apparent in his books for small children, imitates Edgeworth's and Anna Letitia Barbauld's collections for children, popular until the Civil War, with bite-sized chapters. Abbott's dozens of novels for older children and adolescents pivot around episodes as well, stringing them together into narratives that lack the kind of arc one associates with the genre of the novel as it had developed in the nineteenth century. For Abbott the episode functions as a narrative engine that captures his brand of proto-realism, a diurnal or quotidian quality, in which incidentals rise to the level of incident, and the larger social and historical panorama is overwritten by the local and the timely. The episodic functions in Abbott's child-centered workaday world as a principle of accumulation, accretion, and repetition. Lyman Abbott described his father's method of composition like this: "He did not form a plot beforehand. Each incident led on to the next incident; it might also be said that each paragraph led on to the next paragraph; and when the allotted number of pages was finished, the story came to its end, much as the story-telling would come to an end when the clock struck nine and it was time for the children to go to bed."[25] Lyman Abbott positions this method as an echo of oral tale transmission, aligned with the practices of bedtime storytelling.[26] But it should also be seen as a typical method of printed narrative accumulation and accretion—pulling things off the shelf and tossing them into the basket of the text—and an imitation of the composite anthologies (including schoolbooks), gift books, and magazines that circulated for children (and, of course, for adults as well).[27]

Rollo Learning to Read, first published in 1835, the same year as "Little Annie's Ramble," is the second in Jacob Abbott's most famous series of books, about little Rollo Holiday and his family.[28] Republished in at least twenty-six editions into the 1890s, it contributed to the creation of Rollo as a fixture of and even a byword for nineteenth-century American childhood and children's reading.[29] In common with most of Abbott's books, *Rollo Learning to Read* is intended for home, not school, reading; it addresses and assumes an engaged middle-class parent. Marked though it is by Abbott's idiosyncratic style, *Rollo Learning to Read* is a thoroughgoing primer of contemporary attitudes toward children and childhood. Even in this early episodic collection of vignettes, directed at small children, Abbott highlights children's labor, children's social roles within and outside the family, and children's property. Moreover, he expresses here beliefs about the function of childhood reading and hence about the kind of narratives that suit children. If all reading lessons acculturate and initiate, Abbott's offer a practicum in navigating a world shaped by the liberal marketplace of the mid-century, as well as by the slave economy, and inflected by the shifting terms in which children and childhood were regarded.

Like many other children's books from the 1830s, *Rollo Learning to Read* directs its preface to the parental consumer: "In those intervals of rest which the serious cares and labors of life imperiously demand, a man may find the best amusement for himself in efforts for the amusement of children. This little work . . . [has] been written to this principle" (v).[30] Notionally at least, one of the new jobs of middle-class nineteenth-century children was to be amused and to amuse;[31] Rollo's last name, "Holiday," captures the new space-time of "childhood," with connotations of the festive, the restful, a time and place apart from the workaday world, with a lingering sense of the hallowed. The new discourse of childhood presumed that the amusement of children would bring benefits to the adults around them at least as much as to the adults they would become; as Hawthorne noted in "Little Annie's Ramble," children's "influence on us is at least reciprocal with ours on them" (234). Yet we also know that this model of childhood was emergent and aspirational, as most children still had *un*amusing work to do.[32]

Some of the twenty-six vignette-like chapters (the number may intentionally echo the ABCs) of *Rollo Learning to Read* do indeed describe a method for learning to read, emphatically presented by the genial narrator as a species of domestic labor for Rollo and his older sister, Mary. "It is very hard work to learn to read," reports the narrator of the first chapter, "How Rollo Learned to Read" (9); Rollo's father reiterates that "learning to read is hard work" (10), that it is "'harder work and will take longer time than you think'" (11), that it is "'a hard task for both'" Rollo and Mary (14). In keeping with the businesslike nature of the task, Mary "was to keep an account of every day . . . putting down, each day, the letters he learned that day" and report all to father. The book that Rollo learns from has columns of words, and "some very easy reading in large print, but no pictures" (12), that is, a typical speller of the day. The prohibition on pictures, which are here associated with play, underscores once again that "learning to read was hard work, and that [Rollo] must attend to it *as a duty*" (16, italics in original). Mr. Holiday produces alphabet picture cards only after Rollo is well under way with learning the alphabet. All in all, according to the opening chapter, Rollo's apprenticeship in reading lasts a full year.

Other chapters school Rollo variously in time management, pet keeping, letter writing, and the care of books, among other lessons in self-regulation. These chapters give a sense of Abbott's imaginarium, a combination of conventional antebellum views of children and childhood, with Abbott's particular brand of pragmatism, drawn on his work as a teacher in a variety of settings, as well as on his own childhood relationship to his father, and his own experience as a father of small boys. In the chapter nervously entitled "Tick,—Tick,—Tick," the narrator, who must get up early to meet the stagecoach schedule, wakes up in the night at three, at four, at five, and finally at six he puts on his spectacles to check the time on the ticking clock. "A Little Letter" does double duty: a letter to a boy from his uncle offers an example of the genre, while transmitting a new humane attitude toward animals by lamenting the killing of a robin: "'Poor robin; poor robin. . . . I am very sorry that any boy should kill the poor robin and spoil its nest. This is from your affectionate, Uncle" (43). In "Rollo's Dream," Rollo transforms into a series of animals to escape the labors of being a boy but finds that their lives are even harder, and more dangerous: the dream's final episode wakes him, when, as a robin, he is shot by a hunter. "How to Treat a Kitten" contrasts kindly pet keeping with the overmastering kind; "How to Read Right" highlights the materiality of print, noticing distinctions in type size and font, and the meaning of punctuation and marks for notes. "Rollo's Breakfast" echoes the dinner party scene in *Emile*, a common trope in nineteenth-century children's literature, in which the origins of everyday things are described ("'Where do the plates come from?' . . . 'They come from England. The men find a bank of white clay . . . make it into the shapes of plates . . . and paint them blue . . . and bake them hard . . . they pack them up . . . bring them over the waves, and over the hills, away to the town we live in, so that little Rollo may have a plate when he eats his breakfast'" [90]).

The child-centered utopia of the Rollo books, in which all of the labor of others and the resources of the earth are deployed for the middle-class American child, is one of the legacies of alphabetization, which brings all the goods of the world into the nursery and parlor. But the theme park of childhood has an entry fee. Other chapters register more starkly the precarious situation of even such a one as Rollo. Among the stories that tutor self-regulation, "Waking Up" introduces the contractual nature of Rollo's position. Rollo's father quizzes him:

> "Where are you going to get your breakfast?"
> "Oh I am going to get it down stairs, in the parlor."
> "But whose breakfast is that down in the parlor? Is it yours? . . . Did you buy it with your money?" (105)

When Rollo concedes that the breakfast is not his and he did not buy it with his money, his father points out, "Then it is not your breakfast; it is all my breakfast; but as you have not got any breakfast of your own, I believe I will let you have some of my breakfast. But what are you going to do for a house to live in all day?" (105). The unrelenting Mr. Holiday goes on: "I shall let you wear those clothes of mine then. I am very glad I have got a house, and some breakfast, and some clothes for my little Rollo boy, since you have not got any of your own. But I think if I get a house for you to live in, and breakfast for you to eat, and clothes for you to wear, you ought to be a very careful, faithful, obedient little boy" (108–9). Mr. Holiday, in short, strikes a deal with Rollo, detailing the obligations of both sides of the compact.

In the contractual structuring of this relationship, Abbott reflects the legal consensus of the day. The Maryland legal professor David Hoffman's 1836 *Legal Outlines*, a series of lectures for American and British students, noted "the dual nature of paternal authority," constituted of " 'the injunction imposed on parents by nature, of rearing, and carefully watching over the moral, religious, and physical education of their progeny, and the impracticality of advantageously discharging that duty, unless children yield implicit obedience to the dictates of parental concern, seeing that they are not of sufficient age and discretion to limit the measure of their submission or obedience.' "[33] Michael Grossberg points out that the second part of paternity's "dual nature" was, as Hoffman put it, " 'the presumed consent of the offspring,' " in which, as Hoffman continues, " 'a tacit compact between them is thus formed.' "[34] For the child's part, it would seem that the behaviors under the umbrella designation of duty—obedience, gratitude, and submission—are meant to enact rather than to articulate consent.

Other chapters of *Rollo Learning to Read* hint at the world beyond the paternal doorstep, which marks the notional boundary marker of "childhood," with its demanding but protective compacts. Rollo and his father meet up with a homeless boy from a nameless city who tells them that his father is dead and that he "never had any" mother (39). Rollo's father takes him home. No indentures, no adoption, no further mention of the boy's past: "Jonas lived with Rollo a long time and became a very industrious, useful boy" (41). Indeed, following generic conventions of series and spin-offs (which Abbott is helping to invent), Jonas becomes a key figure in subsequent books, a prodigy of self-education and autonomy, serving as a mentor for younger children, in a combination role as a kind of Juliet's nurse and Jean-Jacques-like panoptical tutor, and sometimes as a reliable slave, servant, or factotum. Jonas is the first of the autonomous orphans, usually marked by race as well, whom Abbott conjures repeatedly in later books.

The volume closes with a chapter called "Selling a Boy." Here a poor man who "found it very hard to get money enough to buy bread for himself, and his wife, and his little boy" (174) offers his child for sale around the neighborhood ("'Shoemaker,—Mr. Shoemaker,—do you want to buy a little boy?'"). When the shoemaker offers a dollar, the tale proceeds ritualistically, echoing accumulative verses like "The House That Jack Built": "'A dollar,' said the man, thinking, 'shall I take a dollar for my little boy?'" (175), and so on, until the father turns down the miller's offer of $100. He is about to offer him to a "rich gentleman," presumably for even more money. But at that moment he "looked into his little boy's face, and he was so pleasant, and looked so gentle and kind, that the man could not bear to sell him" (180): "'No, no, no,' said he, 'I will not sell my little boy at all. I have kept him a good while, and taken care of him, and I love him very much. No, I will not sell him. I will carry him home, and work very hard to get bread for him to eat. And he will be kind, and dutiful, and obedient, and when I grow old perhaps he will take care of me. No, no, I would not sell him for a thousand dollars'" (180). If the tale induces anxiety, the narrator reiterates the poor man's vow to love and care for the child, assuring the reader that "This is a *fictitious* story. It is written to teach children that if they are good, and kind and obedient, their fathers will love them, and work hard, if necessary, to get them bread, and will not sell them, even if any body should offer them a thousand dollars" (180, my emphasis).

Positioned as the conclusion to *Rollo Learning to Read*, this tale suggests that a missing term from the list of things a boy has to do to remain unsold is this one: to read. The tale highlights the contractual nature of the child's status, while also implying that the child's unremarked and seemingly protective white-ness is a property of the child reader, and one that is, in part, produced through the act of reading. Some children are alienable, the tale says, but you, dear reader, probably aren't. Here both Jonas and the unnamed son of the poor man are subject to the harsh economy of the 1830s, only slightly muted by Abbott's genial narration; in that economy many children were sold, not only as slaves, but also as apprentices and in pauper auctions, where the poor boy and Jonas might have ended up if they hadn't become objects of paternal or paternalistic care.[35]

The Business of Childhood

Abbott returned with increasing explicitness to the question of the economic value of children and to children's practical engagement with money, labor, and financial documents. Abbott's early series books—mostly geared to the very young—tend to underscore antebellum children's rites of obligation, centering around what I'm calling the "literacy contract," a translation of the social con-tract for children, through which learning to read emblematizes and enacts self-ownership. If Abbott's earlier books, like the tales of lost children with which I began this chapter, imply such a contract, hinting at the dangerous world that lies just beyond the boundaries of the middling white household, Abbott's later ones literalize and thematize ideas of contract, wages, and self-ownership, put-ting mortgages, notes, and labor agreements at the center of their narratives. Abbott sends his literary children to work precisely to save them from the abjec-tion of pauperism or slavery on the one hand or of privileged and useless idle-ness on the other.[36] Unlike much literature for and about children in the middle decades of the century, Abbott's narratives tend to promote children's social, legal, and economic agency. Abbott made a living from his prolific Harper's "story-books" for and about children, and to that extent inevitably positioned children instrumentally. As his narratives became economic engines and identi-fied children as inhabiting capitalism and inheriting its structures, at the same time they also strikingly resisted making children objects of adult longings and lacks, memories and memorializing. Abbott's fictional children were, instead, oriented toward a near future of their own making and an ethic of enterprise, as Abbott naturalized and narrated the practices and performance of market capitalism.[37]

Not quite bildungsromane, Abbott's novels nonetheless emplot experiences of education and development. And unlike virtually all other white writers for children in the period, Abbott included African Americans as key characters, protagonists or nearly so, in these works. As Mary Quinlivan has pointed out, Abbott was a lifelong abolitionist and as early as 1835 wrote against slavery in *New England and Its Institutions*, cowritten with his two brothers.[38] I have not detected the word "slave" in his children's fiction, but he takes up the menace of slave labor and of racial prejudice in his books of the 1850s, through African American characters, whom he depicts with varying degrees and kinds of racist condescension while also portraying them as acting with an expansive range of autonomy.[39]

Abbott's narratives provide a can-do tone and a how-to method. Their very lack of modulation creates a reality—or perhaps hyperreality—effect, lending an intensity to everyday practices that we associate with local color and realism, narrative modes to which the unsung Abbott importantly contributes. In an Abbott narrative, one learns, for example, how to sharpen a knife and how to send a telegram;[40] how to make a scrapbook and a panorama and a table out of paper for a doll;[41] how to run an auction, how to splice a clothesline, how to repair a book left out in the rain;[42] how a paper mill works, and a printing press and a type-foundry;[43] what a "jumping-bridge" is;[44] how to build a work-bench;[45] what a warrant is, and bail;[46] what "fishing for a compliment" means and why it's "a mean sort of artifice";[47] and why on New York City streets, when an omnibus is coming, you should allow enough time to "fall down twice" and get up again before you get to the other side.[48]

These novels imagine a manifestly knowable, secular world, whose materials and practices a child can learn to master, and whose regulations and mores he—and quite often she—can comprehend and navigate. Among the many detailed descriptions of technologies and manufacturing, agriculture and husbandry, and of a variety of social codes and institutional modes, Abbott often foregrounds questions of property and ownership; as value in itself, and as the foundation of all other value, property plays a crucial role in most of these novels, both as markers of character and as engines of (such as they are) plots.

Abbott's 1855 novel *Timboo and Joliba; or, The Art of Being Useful* introduces the boy Timboo, one of many homeless, itinerant, often immigrant and ethnically or racially distinguished orphans, like Jonas in *Rollo Learning to Read*. Timboo shows up one day at a middle-class house, befriends the children there, and, as the title promises, makes himself so useful that their father hires him to do small jobs. In return Timboo asks if he can have an old barrel abandoned in the yard. Timboo fixes it up as a little apartment for himself, in a secluded corner. One of the children objects to him that "my father gave you the hogshead, but he did not give you any leave to make a house of it on his land." Timboo replies, "He told me that I might keep it on his land as long as I pleased.

. . . And that I might keep any thing in it that belonged to me. I am going to keep myself in it. I am sure I myself belong to me."[49] Thus the dark-skinned boy from the South Sea Islands asserts a right of self-ownership.

It is often through the voice of such "other" children that Abbott lays a claim for the autonomy and agency of children. And it is such worldly subaltern children who have the job of mediating the law to the younger, domesticated ones, as if only children on the margin of the social narrative can dictate its protocols. These subaltern mentors are kin to the contemporaneous figure of the urban newsboy, the working child whom Karen Sánchez-Eppler has described as "seen to embody play, and who hence teaches the middle class about fun," one of the affects that an increasingly leisured ideal of childhood begins to privilege in this period. Sánchez-Eppler compellingly describes the ways in which "it is through depictions of working-class children that these middle-class ideals are first and most forcefully articulated."[50] Abbott's subaltern orphans, however, combine the picaro characteristics of working children like the newsboys with a mentor persona. Taken in by family patriarchs, they stand in and stand guard for them, as the fathers go out to business every day. They straddle the class boundary, protecting the middle-class children from the very experiences of worldliness from which they themselves seem to have learned their independence and manifold skills, parceling their wisdom in small manageable lessons. And yet, their own skill and intelligence can't lift them out of their own class position. So, for example, when Timboo appears again, a year or so later, in *The Alcove*, he has become a servant to the family that he originally befriended, formalizing and instantiating his role.[51]

But while race or national origin might limit a young person's access to childhood, whiteness and native birth are not always, in themselves, protective. When a white child's family's class status descends, he might have to give up his status as a child too. Abbott's *Willie and the Mortgage: Showing How Much May Be Accomplished by a Boy* (1855), his only full-on temperance novel, reads rather like an up-to-the-minute twenty-first-century young-adult novel.[52] Willie's father, lured into drinking by the new tavern owner in town, falls behind on the mortgage, held by the same man, who is about to foreclose. When Willie learns this, he literally puts away his toys: "'From this time, my father's and mother's work is to be my play, until we get out of this trouble'" (82). Willie sobers up, as it were, out of his childhood idyll (not that, in Abbott's universe, this wasn't full of useful work already), having to become alert to economic time, time measured out in payments.

Abbott excoriates the tavern owner's usury and exploitation of the vulnerable, as distortions of what's at heart a sound financial system, offering a primer on mortgaging, "one of the most convenient and useful customs of society":

"By means of it, a man who has a house and land can almost always obtain any sum of money which he may require for a temporary purpose, to the amount of at least half the value of his estate, without selling it. And there are innumerable cases where this is of very great advantage to the mortgager" (95). The system relies on the surety represented by collateral, and Abbott proposes that women "debar themselves" from the convenience of mortgages by making a fuss if they're foreclosed on (96). Hence, he continues, "I give all the readers of this book, therefore, whether boys or girls, this advice. When you grow up to be men and women, if you borrow money on a mortgage of your property which you may, in many cases, very wisely and properly do and then are unable to pay the money when the time for payment comes, give up the property that you had pledged in the most ready and good-natured manner" (96). In the end, due to Willie's labor, the redemption of the mortgage by a benevolent rich man (one Mr. Banks) and a series of unfortunate events for the tavern keeper save Willie's family from having to cheerfully leave their house behind.

At the end of the prewar decade, between 1859 and 1861, Abbott produced a series of five books for Harper and Brothers under the rubric "Stories of Rainbow and Lucky," featuring an African American protagonist (Rainbow, who tellingly shares billing with his horse, Lucky). The setting, as in most of Abbott's U.S. novels, is in unnamed New England towns and villages. In the opening book of the series, the narrative at first belongs to a white boy named Handie Level. A poor boy barely able to read the alphabet as the novel opens, Handie soon becomes known in his village for his good sense and handiness. He helps his ineffectual father and earns money for himself. But in a legalistic qualification, which recurs in Abbott's novels, "all the money which Handie earned, over and above what was required for his own clothing and other personal expenses, he paid regularly to his father, as he was in duty bound to do" (25).[53] When Handie discovers that his father has defaulted on the mortgage and will lose the house that Handie's labor has made homelike, the narrator characteristically explains at length and in detail what a mortgage is: "a formal writing, in which he solemnly promises that, if he does not repay the money at the time when he agrees, then he will give up the house, in order that it may be sold to raise money to pay the debt" (41). Handie "had some general ideas . . . floating in his mind in respect to the nature of a mortgage, and to the duties and obligations arising from such a contract," but is shocked to learn that his father is soon to be foreclosed upon (42).

By now in the narrative, the creditworthy Handie finds himself barred nonetheless, at just nineteen, from entering into a mortgage contract himself until he's twenty-one. The lawyer who's handling this business devises a friendly plan: "'I have thought of a piece of property which your father has, and which I think he might sell, and so raise money enough to pay off his mortgage'" (132). This invisible and unsuspected property turns out to be: "'Your *time*' said Mr. James." For, he continued, "'Your time for two years is quite a valuable piece of property'" (133). In a financial arrangement nearly as complex as any in twenty-first-century headlines, Handie then borrows money, "for three years on interest," arranging to purchase his own time from his father (134–35);[54] with the money from the so to speak mortgaged Handie, Mr. Level will pay off the actual mortgage on the house.

Abbott's striking description of these financial exchanges provides a thumbnail history of forms and sites of property, channeled through Abbott's liberal perspective. Property's first location, in real estate, a "home," proves not as "safe as houses" after all, since someone holds and calls in the mortgage. Property then seems to be located in the labor and creditworthiness of the reliable Handie, but he still, in essence, belongs to his father. Finally, property is located in Handie's "time"—the two years in which his labor is still the property of his father, a promise and potential he's able to use as collateral. The trajectory of this concept of property is from the traditional and material (house and land); to the "human capital" that Handie represents, a constellation of attributes, including Handie's able body and his reputation; to the abstract and future-oriented "time" of Handie's potential labor, which is the property of his father. In a virtual historical timeline of changing conceptions and locations of property, Abbott pursues modes of alienating and transferring real and human property. His narratives suggest questions that his plots then seem to implicitly settle or dispense with: What does it mean to own a thing? What does it mean to have property in oneself? To whom do children belong? What is their value?

By the end of this first novel in the series, Handie hires the fourteen-year-old Rainbow to help him work on a farm that he's inherited from his father's brother. In the subsequent four volumes, Rainbow takes center stage, eventually becoming a post rider for the U.S. mail. In the juxtaposing of the young white man buying himself (his labor and "time") from his master (his father) with the episodes in which Rainbow shows himself to be a paragon of middle-class virtues, Abbott addresses slavery in an oblique way by insisting on the contractual nature of labor, in all of its complexity, and on the contractualism embedded in family relations, as a model for human relations generally.[55] In *Rollo Learning to Read*, he suggested that his child readers engaged in an implicit contract that would protect them from pauperism, vagabondage, and slavery. Abbott promoted the self-ownership of children and a consequent freedom, shaped by the centrality of contract—as Amy Dru Stanley calls it, the "pith of social existence" in the antebellum United States and at the heart of debates about the nature and meaning of free labor during and after the Civil War: "For most abolitionists, the autonomy expressed in wage labor was . . . an offshoot of the underlying right of property in the self that constituted the taproot of contract freedom."[56] The only scene in the Rainbow and Lucky series in which a contract is explicitly drawn up and signed features Rainbow himself, signing on to deliver the mail, in a chapter called "The Contract," with an illustration captioned "Making the Contract," in the wryly titled last book in the series, *Up the River*, published just as the war began (see Plate 24).

Jeannine deLombard identifies "the trope of the self-purchase fraud" in slave narratives, whereby a slave discovers, after spending years accumulating the money to buy himself from his master, that he's legally unable to enter into a contract to perform the purchase: he isn't recognized as a legal subject. DeLombard concludes that "rather than demonstrations of the slave's competence to enter into contractual relations, these subsidiary agreements turn out to be status relations in disguise."[57] It's always the case that relations with children are status relations in disguise, all the more so when the child is African American. And yet, Abbott imagines a role for Rainbow that he couldn't in reality fulfill, as blacks were barred from riding for the post.[58]

In "Selling a Boy," Abbott was responding to anxieties about the status of children, within and beyond the white family, in the 1830s. In the late 1850s, he schooled his free black and white child characters in contract law, providing lessons in the central distinction between free and slave labor. Though Abbott represents Rainbow as a thoughtful, intelligent, highly skilled, and enterprising protagonist, placing him at or near the center of four action-filled novels, he fails to grant him the kind of full personhood that he assumes for the white Handie. Abbott identifies Rainbow with natural phenomena, denies him a surname, links him closely with his horse, and supposes certain limits in mental skills and life ambitions.[59] Rainbow is, however, represented as entirely self-possessed, unlike Abbott's first major black character, from the mid-fifties, the hired youth Congo, in the eponymous novel; its subtitle, *or, Jasper's Experience of Command*, gives the flavor of the narrative, in which the twelve-year-old Jasper, being trained up by his grandfather in white masculinity, learns how to manage his young black employee.[60]

Abbott's only other major African American character appears after the war, in a four-book series published in 1870 featuring Juno, a servant in a middle-class New England household. As in the Rainbow and Lucky series, Juno's race and status are highlighted in her name and in episodes that position her among white people: she enters the house of a benefactor through the kitchen; she is presumed by a haughty white woman on a crowded train to be ready to give up her seat; she starts a Sunday school, which she herself assumes only "colored" children will want to attend, though white children come as well. While her age isn't specified, she falls under the broad category of "girl" (for example, as "a nice and tidy-looking coloured girl" and "quite a pretty girl, and not very dark")[61] and seems to be in her late teens or early twenties, working as a nurse-maid and governess to a young boy. In this role, Juno functions like the subaltern mentors of Abbott's earlier books; "sensible" is one of her epithets, and as her young charge, Georgie, reports, "'Juno knows almost everything,'" testimony to an intelligence and competency that she proves again and again.[62]

Just as the subaltern mentors of the earlier books provided voices of both alterity and worldly experience, while modeling ethical behavior and yet remaining outside the social order of the family, Juno too inhabits a social and narrative margin, even as she is cast as protagonist. Abbott evades the period's most egregious stereotypes while still restricting Juno's autonomy and mobility to the range of her guardianship position. Juno teaches her young students in the traditional curriculum of reading, writing, and reckoning but is also counted upon to instruct them in ethical behavior; Georgie's parents serve mainly to bolster and legitimate Juno's authority.[63]

Indeed, Juno's authority expands into a kind of authorship, as she becomes a channel for an explication of Abbott's narrative method. Juno feels she can't tell stories well but knows how useful they are in engaging and educating children. In *Juno and Georgie* her white benefactor, Mary Osborne, counsels Juno not to overworry her plots: "People think there must be a connection and a sense in what is told to children, in order to interest them; and they think so, because they do not understand the *nature* of the interest which they feel. It is in the *images themselves* and not in the manner in which they are connected, that the charm lies."[64] In a "story-telling" lesson, Mary Osborne advises Juno to "relate something that is so far connected as to form a continuous narrative . . . but which shall have no *point* whatever,—no plot, no remarkable occurrence, no beginning or ending, but designed only to bring a series of *agreeable images before their minds*."[65] For older children, "a thread of connection,—a beginning, middle, and end,—or a *unity* as it is called in the books on rhetoric that I studied in school, is all very well."[66] For them, Mary Osborne suggests having a minimal plot or plan (she gives the example of a field mouse stowing away in a boy's pocket), but she advises that "all that you have to do in telling it is simply introduce abundance of details."[67] With her mentor's theory in hand, Juno puts the method into practice successfully, becoming something of a proxy narrator, finding that she is able to conjure copious incidents and details when she tries the experiment with Georgie. Mary Osborne assures her that "it is of no consequence" when or even whether she ever gets to the incident that motivated the story: "Authors, sometimes, in writing a book, find that what they intended as only the introduction, expands as they write it and becomes the whole book, so that the plot they originally formed for it is not brought in at all."[68] The novel itself ends on the next page, in just the way that Mary Osborne might advise, for Juno "soon acquired great skill in making up narratives that pleased the children who heard them very much indeed."[69] Through her marginal social status as guardian of and mentor to white youth, Juno is thus authorized and credentialed as a narrator and author: she creates her narratives in "chapters" and makes lists of incidents that she might make use of for future stories. If Abbott restricts her to a trusted and highly respected and respectable position as a teacher, he also situates her narratively as among the "agreeable images" of everyday life that he promotes as values.

Postbellum, Abbott resolves the problem of contract by dismissing it; the circumstances that had so demanded that children be schooled in their contractual rights and obligations had changed. Instead, he makes a claim for the value of the sheer everyday observations of his proxy narrator Juno, which she transmits to her charges. Abbott's a moralist but no sentimentalist; though sharing most of the racial and gender biases of white Protestant New England, Abbott lacks many of their more florid distortions. For all of her intellectual and ethical gifts, Juno is ordinary; she channels no special wisdom, her speech is not depicted as dialect, and she enacts no redemptive sacrifice.[70] The experiences she recounts are distinctly and intentionally minor, offering a moment of the literary intersection of race and childhood in which dailiness leaves little room for melodrama or mythologizing.[71] As Juno embodies Abbott's method toward the end of his career, she embodies the paradoxes—both the reach and the limits—of his progressivism.

After the war, the little strangers of the early national period had been overtaken by European and Asian immigrants and freed African Americans as objects of class and status anxiety. With emancipation, the question of whom children belonged to had lost its currency, and the spread of compulsory schooling had changed the terms in which literacy was being thought. Juno's—and Abbott's—narrative method of the accretion of incident was being incorporated into an expanded periodical market for serialization and into late-century realism. Abbott situated children in an imagined and idealized workaday capitalist world, in which, so his narratives insist, their own agency and autonomy would have consequences, and in which, if they were still too young to be recognized as legal persons, they could nonetheless claim and act upon the authority of their labor and expertise.

CHAPTER 5

Children in the Margins

ACROSS THE early decades of the nineteenth century, new genres of children's literature emerged from multiple origins at once: they mirrored primers' and gift books' composite, anthology form, the bildungsroman's narratives of progress, and traditional ballads' access to memorializing. Romanticism's legacy produced reveries of childhood that seemed only to serve adult memory, and to deny children their rights to a generative present reality, while at the same time, the demands of capitalism and threats of a slave economy insisted on the kind of new economic bildung for children exemplified in the books produced by Jacob Abbott. But how did children engage with their books? What did books mean not only to "childhood" but to individual children, and what, in turn, did children mean to books? This chapter explores the cultural forms that emerged from the encounter between child and book, writ large and small, and the ways in which that encounter shaped both the relation between them and the individual status of both child and book in the aggregate. In the variety of marks left in children's books, children in the past come alive as historical actors, inhabiting and transforming long-lived forms of children's culture. Their own writing and other indications of their own and others' engagement with their books bring to the surface the ways in which the new properties of childhood in the nineteenth century had begun to emphasize with increasing intensity two aspects of children's increasingly literate lives: the ways in which their literacy enacted and enabled practices of ownership, and, once claimed as their own, the ways in which their books became repositories, registers, and mediums for social and emotional attachments. If these categories, broadly economic and affective, seem somewhat at odds, it might be helpful to think of them in terms of what the sociologist Eva Illouz calls "emotional capitalism," when, she writes, "affect is made an essential aspect of economic behavior and in which emotional life—especially that of the middle classes—follows the logic of economic relations and exchange."[1] At the same time, Seth Lerer has drawn attention to "an as-yet-unexplored relationship between the biblio-graphical challenges and the scholarly exhilaration behind marginal discov-ery."[2] Thus, for the scholar and the reader, the incitements and excitements of the affective aura that children's artifacts retain offer invitations while posing challenges to interpretation.

Marks in books, which in this chapter include inscriptions, annotations, graffiti, ink blots, pen testing, shreds of leaves and flowers, crumbs of food, mash notes, and unidentifiable stains, among other things, often remain ineluc-tably mysterious.[3] A scene of inscription in a mid-nineteenth-century American novel offers a heuristic for thinking about these traces.[4] Early in Susan Warner's 1850 best seller, *The Wide, Wide World*, little Ellen Montgomery's dying mother inscribes her daughter's new Bible. Mrs. Montgomery "wrote Ellen's name, and the date of the gift. The pen played a moment in her fingers, and then she wrote below the date: 'I love them that love me; and they that seek me early shall find me.'"[5] She wrote another verse and then "as if bowed by an unseen force Mrs. Montgomery's head sank upon the open page" and she prayed: "'Let these words be my memorial, that I have trusted in thee.'"[6] Ellen has little idea of what her mother is investing in her inscription; even Mrs. Montgomery won-ders why she's written some of it: "The next words were not for [Ellen]; what made her write them? . . . They were written almost unconsciously."[7] The novel has prepared the scene with a vivid account of the financial and spiritual eco-nomics of the Bible's purchase—an heirloom's sale funds it, and Ellen suffers the frenzy of consumer choice amid many alluring Bibles. Mrs. Montgomery's presentation inscription decommodifies the book, transferring it from the mar-ketplace to a gift economy, with its chain of obligations and ceremonies. Along with the marks that other guardians make in Ellen's books, her mother's inscription guides the child's spiritual journey as she replicates and transmits the mother's lessons, first embodied in the miniaturized maternal and homelike book.

If Ellen Montgomery's Bible had found its way into an archive, we would have Ellen's first and possibly last name, the date, with or without the year, and the Bible verses, from which we might suppose something about the evangelism of the inscriber; but we might not know Ellen's age or where she lived, might know nothing of the mother, and less than nothing about the exact meaning that the book had for mother or daughter. We might reasonably think the writ-ing was Ellen's. But never mind, because the marks made by Ellen's mother would likely be illegible, bathed as they are in tears. Or they would have been foxed with damp and mildew or obscured by a bookplate or the marks of a dealer or librarian. Case in point: in a first edition of *The Wide, Wide World* held by the American Antiquarian Society pencil marks on the last front flyleaf of the first volume have been erased. When looking at and for marginalia, one often finds oneself contemplating the erasure.

Yet even such an erasure is a reminder of ways in which a book is a registry of human encounters.[8] While bibliographers and book historians have long understood this about book artifacts and have explored the material, social, legal, and economic conditions of their composition, production, and circulation and categorized their size, look, provenance, and condition, recently scholars have turned their attention to marginalia. In his work on Renaissance reader's marks, William Sherman reminds us that "readers' marks provide some of the most interesting links between books as texts and books as artifacts of material culture: they provide evidence of a wide variety of reading and writing practices as well as pointing to the disparate ways in which books could be used."[9] Still, the affective expressiveness of these artifacts has been largely sidelined as somewhat infra dig for literary or historical scholarship, belonging rather to the book-fetish shelf in the belles lettres case—the memoirs and essays of collectors, the love letters of bibliophiles.[10] And books marked by, to, and on behalf of long-dead children may strike one as especially charged objects. Old books and dead children make a perfect storm for an access of emotion. Such sentiment (and its access) is rooted in the nineteenth century's intersecting cults of reading and of childhood. One is aware too of the full stop that's been put to their lives, both of the children (some of whom died in childhood) and of the artifacts; as putting the brakes on hurls everyone clumsily forward, shards of the former liveliness break through. As for the books, their writing days are over, and their reading days are curtailed (children of course are banned from reading so-called children's books in rare book collections, and adult readers are constrained). Modern conservators usually respect the often wracked condition of these artifacts, hoping to keep them from further harm and decay rather than to restore them.[11] The marks in them are hence in a permanently suspended state, transformed from event to artifact, from acts of self-fashioning, sociability, or testament to misdirected or entirely inscrutable traces, inviting readerly projection. While such projection is perhaps inescapable, and writes its own important chapter in the afterlife of these books, children's encounters with their books often leave legible traces of an affective history that invites exploration.

Some things we can say with confidence about these marks.[12] First, we are not their intended addressee; our presence in the chain of readership depends on their having entered, sometimes by accident, a stage of life that brings us into the same room. The books in which these marks appear, which we encounter in libraries, in second-hand bookstores, and on our own shelves, had and still have a life, which can be read and written in terms of what the anthropologists Arjun

Appadurai and Igor Kopytoff have called "the social life" and "the cultural biography" of things: Kopytoff describes the commoditization of things (more or less following Marx) as well as their "singularization"—the way in which they can be removed from the commodity sphere, as in the fictional case of Ellen Montgomery's Bible. Indeed, he writes, "When the commodity is effectively out of the commodity sphere, its status is inevitably ambiguous and open to the push and pull of events and desires, as it is shuffled about in the flux of social life." He continues: "For Marx, the worth of commodities is determined by the social relations of their production; but the existence of the exchange system makes the production process remote and misperceived, and it 'masks' the commodity's true worth. . . . This allows the commodity to be socially endowed with a fetishlike 'power' that is unrelated to its true worth. Our analysis suggests, however, that some of that power is attributed to commodities after they are produced, and this by way of an autonomous cognitive and cultural process of singularization."[13] A book is an always already animated thing, a notorious fetish object, easily masking its nature as commodity, while begging to be decommodified; it was one of the first industrial consumer objects to be produced and marketed explicitly as a gift, such that its "singularization" became a further incentive to commodification.[14] To see the thingness of books helps as well in trying to see more clearly the ways in which children are brought into a relationship with these things, a relationship that has been powerfully naturalized and displaced, not to say fetishized, as an aspect of temperament, personality, or character, rather than as a historical event.

Recent accounts of things *in* books—by Elaine Freedgood and Bill Brown, among others—attend to the material lives and cultural and historical genealogy of the things encountered in texts, proposing "new thoughts about how inanimate objects constitute human subjects, how they move them, how they threaten them, how they facilitate or threaten their relation to other subjects."[15] These things have more substance, they argue compellingly, than what Roland Barthes called the "reality effect," in which objects punctuate narrative with a richly itemized illusion of material presence. Rather, things in books, these critics suggest, are more like punctures in the narrative, flowing out into the world and allowing the world in turn to seep into the narrative. Marks in books are "things" in book-things, with a difference; they prompt a procedure for interpretation that similarly reads them as belonging to and emerging in the midst of the material and artifactual world.

Children's marks in their books and adults' marks in children's books, unlike other writing for, by, and about children, are a site of children's own engagement with, encounter with, the "thing" and the "other" that constitute the book. H. J. Jackson, whose two books about marginalia in the romantic period have attended to such geniuses of the marginal riposte as Coleridge and Blake, as well as to the anonymous or obscure "ordinary" reader, notes in passing the importance of children's marginalia: "A case can be made for their revealing fundamental readers' attitudes in a particularly raw state."[16] All reading enacts prosopopoeia, the figure that describes the imagined presence of absent others; but, paradoxically, reading also has the effect of dematerializing the book that one becomes lost in. To read the margins is to shift attention away from the text toward the material presence of the artifact, or to oscillate between printed text and the variety of marginal paratexts. There, other presences make themselves known, other authors emerge, chronicling other events and experiences. The result is a palimpsest of prosopopoeia, the other upon other that constitutes the life of a book. In our encounter with the traces of this encounter we can't pretend to be reading over a shoulder; the effect is something closer to a mutual haunting.[17] If the book has often been understood as a metaphor for a life and a symbol (a mirror, a vessel) of interiority, I want to literalize these aspects of the book: rather than resembling a life mimetically, the book lives a life; rather than symbolizing interiority, the book opens and closes upon surrogate selves, embodied (as this chapter will show) in things like paper dolls and locks of hair. In what follows, then, I describe what amounts to a life cycle of the child's book, from cradle to grave, and beyond, to the afterlife of the archive.[18]

Property of . . .

Many inscriptions on the inside cover and flyleaves of children's books take the form that Abiah Chapin used to mark her copy of an 1809 Windsor, Vermont, prose chapbook version of the old ballad, *The Affecting History of the Children in the Wood:* "The / Property / of Abiah / Chapin" (Figure 26).[19] Discussions of marginalia often assume that the inscriber wishes first to declare ownership: "All marginalia are extensions of the ownership inscription, which itself expresses the primary impulse of claiming the book as one's own."[20] The child writer does often leave a trace of a property claim in her book (or, as in cases like Ellen Montgomery's, has it asserted by proxy). But rather than assuming that all child writers share a "primary impulse" or proprietary instinct, it's helpful to think instead of the ownership mark as registering the cultural and social situation in which the child and the book meet. A frequent variation of this mark takes this form: "Alice Comfort, Jr., her book / 5th May 1826" and "Joseph Bowers his Book." Here is English trying hard to make a genitive case, and such attempts often elide into the simple possessive: "Maria W. Bullard's

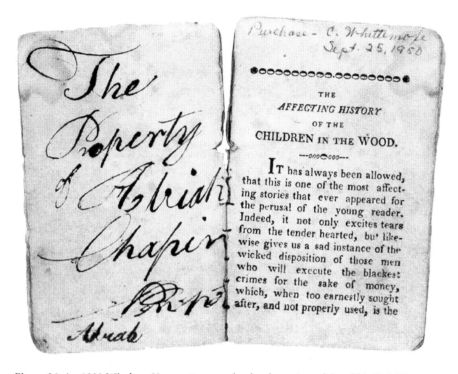

Figure 26. An 1809 Windsor, Vermont, prose chapbook version of the old ballad *The Affecting History of the Children in the Wood:* "The / Property / of Abiah / Chapin." AAS call number CL-Pam C5365 A257 1809. Courtesy American Antiquarian Society.

Book." Occasionally, an inscriber drops the possessive altogether, perhaps uncertain about how it works, asserting a property claim by metonymically sidling up to the substantive. Grammatically, "Decimus White Book" defies parsing, but the sense is clear, as if Decimus White is rubbing shoulders with the book syntactically, as he's scratching its cover with his pen physically (Plate 25).[21]

"Her book" and "property of" have a formal, quasi-contractual and performative quality to them, embodying and enacting the literacy contract discussed in the previous chapter. For a child, as for many adults, the idiom declares ownership not only in the book at hand but in the constellation of experiences, and of rights and privileges, that the book represents, and that are represented by the fact of writing. Until the nineteenth century—and, in some places, well into the century—learning to read was a skill that preceded and was quite separate from learning to write.[22] As E. Jennifer Monaghan has pointed out, in colonial and early national America one learned to read at home or in a dame school, often while still a toddler. Writing belonged to a later stage of schooling, and until 1750, belonged almost exclusively to boys. For boys writing was a signifier of maturity, like wearing long pants, and denoted future property rights; while the reality of such future rights for girls and women was more restricted, training in penmanship often made no gender distinction.[23] During the period of most of these inscriptions—circa 1800 to 1860—schooling continued to be sporadic and class-based, though literacy rates steadily rose.[24] The ownership inscription asserts that the inscriber reads, writes, and owns, with an associated logic. The claim over and in the book transforms the notional cultural capital of literacy into a grounding of ownership more generally; it is a claim to a principle of ownership, to, that is, the very capacity to own something.[25]

The book is one of the first consumer objects addressed specifically to children, marketed and advertised especially to them, specially designed, and purchased from a store or a peddler. Some inscribers note that the book was "bought," sometimes with the price. The tautology of such declarations suggests the novelty and importance of the event that warranted marking it. Along the way, the signature transfers the book from its commodity form in the shop into something individuated and associated with the person.[26] The book also represents one of the child's first encounters with private property, as such—as a vocabulary word, as a thing, as a concept, as a practice. A solely instrumental claim of ownership would be served by signing the book, and many books are, simply, signed, inscribed with a name. The child who performs even this starkest of scribal gestures participates in the knowledge system that requires the repetition of that authorizing signature. The contours of this naturalized regime are made visible in accounts of those outside it; one thinks, for example, of the opening of Frederick Douglass's 1845 *Narrative*, in which many of the facts of names and dates are unavailable to the enslaved child. Then as now, children like adults, would have increasingly had occasion to put their signature to other papers, domestic and public, with varying degrees of separation from the subjective engagement that the ownership signature suggests. When children signed their books, they often did so repeatedly, on assorted flyleaves, in seemingly arbitrary margins and gutters, as though practicing the iterability that, as Jacques Derrida describes it, is one of the signature's characteristics.[27] One might say that the modern child is positively identified as one who owns—or, more strictly, as one who performs the rites of ownership. For there's some question whether these books could be said to belong, legally, to these children, whose own ambiguous status is the subtext of many fifth commandment exhortations in the books made for them, and, as we saw in the previous chapter, who don't have full possession of their own labor. The performance of the property rite asserts a right to property, and implicitly makes a claim for one's status as not owned oneself.[28]

Anathema: The Rites of Property

In the early nineteenth century, children often posted at the boundaries of their books, especially schoolbooks (often uniformly bound in leather or primer-blue paper boards), the formulaic poems that bibliographers and cataloguers call "ownership verses" or, in some cases, anathemas.[29] Mary Lucretia Shelton of Bridgeport, Connecticut, for example, extensively marked up her 1816 New York edition of Lindley Murray's *Introduction to the English Reader*, in 1821. Like other volumes of Murray's vastly popular anthologies, staples in the marketplace into the 1830s, this one gathers short excerpts in prose and poetry from a Scottish Enlightenment and British sentimental and romantic canon for reading aloud, memorizing, and performing, and for learning prosody.[30] Shelton writes on the first flyleaf (Figure 27):

> Steal not this Book my honest
> friend for fear the gallows will
> be your end For god will say in
> the judgement day where
> is that Book you stole away

The rhyme heavily burdens the potential thief; the addressee is reminded of his honesty, of the obligations of friendship, of the extremes of punishment, of God's fastidious accounting at the end of days. Shelton repeats her conventional anathema on a back flyleaf, where it's upside down for good measure and good luck.

The gallows rhyme urges, in the tradition of slippery-slope didacticism, that the consequences for stealing a book will be death. Conventional though it may be, the trope bears a chilling element of truth: in England and in America children could still be executed for theft into the nineteenth century.[31] The schoolbook anathema, then, like all curses, has a prayerful subtext: "Let me stay in (or join) the propertied classes," it would seem to say, "and save me from the fate of unprotected children." Still, many versions in the same period, in the spirit of romantic pedagogy, rely on shame instead of the threat of capital punishment: "Steal not this book / Book [sic] for fear of / Shame for in it / you see the / owners name."[32]

In *An Abridgment of L. Murray's English Grammar* "Nahum Newton, jun," of Shrewsbury, Massachusetts, inscribed a version of the verse on January 18, 1817 (see Plate 26):

> Steel [sic] not this book my
> good old friend for fear
> the gallows will be your
> end

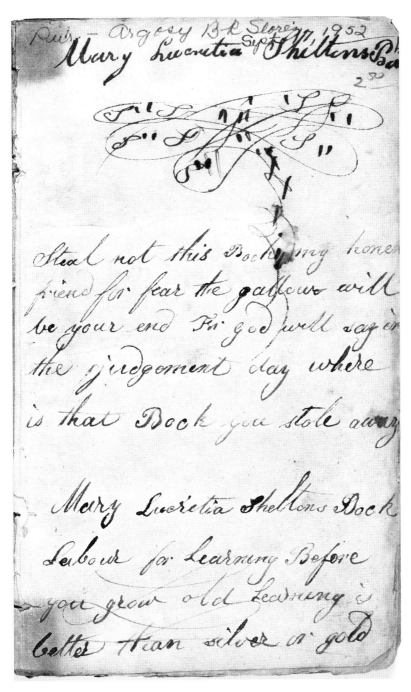

Figure 27. *Introduction to the English Reader: Or, A Selection of Pieces, in Prose and Poetry.*
New York: Collins, 1816. Inscribed by Mary Lucretia Shelton. AAS call number Dated Books.
Courtesy American Antiquarian Society.

The appealing modernist poetics in the visual fall of the last line probably results from Nahum Newton's inscribing to the edge of the page in the previous lines; the final line is filled out with penmanship flourishes, deemphasizing the falling "end." Despite a section on prosody in Murray's grammar, these verses are, in general, attuned to the material demands of the page rather than to the conventions of the poetic line. The seemingly random line breaks also signal that these verses are in transition between the rhythmic, lineless orality of children's schoolyard verses and the printed realm to which these little poems are the gatekeepers.

The "honest friend" of these warnings is only one of their addressees. The first reader is of course the inscriber; every time she opens her book, she has the pleasure of seeing her handiwork, which, among other things, has safeguarded the book for another day. But these verses address as well the reader invoked by every act of writing: the unknown ghostly reader, the one both feared (the thief) and desired (the sympathetic, penitent reader), the one whose presence would be proved only by the absence of the book inscribed to him (Figure 28).

<blockquote>

/ find

If any one this Book should
I write to you unknown
Consider Hourly in your
            / mind
Each one Should have his
            / Own[33]

</blockquote>

This inscriber intimately beseeches the "unknown" reader to do the right thing. If the first addressee is always oneself, here the inscriber makes herself strange. This very estrangement, however, has the effect of including far-flung addressees. I know, for example, that I am not Mary Shelton's sociably addressed "honest friend," but this inscriber's more abstract "you unknown" describes me well enough. In shearing off the contemporary sociality of these artifacts, the archive allows them to speak in surprising ways.

While it warns, this writing's display of conventional wit places it within the ancient traditions and genres of schoolchild culture. As such it associates the writer with a group, a culture, and a history, establishing her as cued to and clued into the inside lingo, jokes, curses, and taboos. These rhymes ward off not just theft but all sorts of evil, keeping the child within the charmed cultural circle that the book represents. Some verses sidestep convention—or take it all too literally. In his 1819 copy of Noah Webster's *The American Spelling Book*,

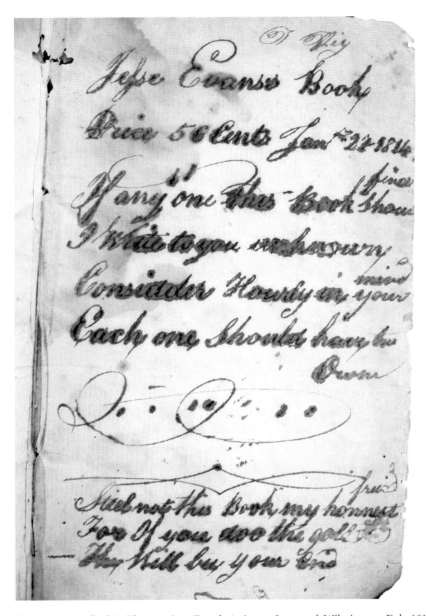

Figure 28. Inscribed in *The American Tutor's Assistant, Improved.* Wilmington, Del., 1811. AAS call number Dated Books. The inscription continues, after a space, with a version of a more conventional rhyme, in a ritual doubling that is frequent in these books: "Steal not this Book my honnest / friend / For if you do the gallows / They will be your end." Courtesy American Antiquarian Society.

David H. Hooper, of Bridgewater, Massachusetts, writes: "Don't steal this / Book if you do I will / Beat your Brains / out" (Figure 29).[34] Hooper's edgy, vigilante spin on the forensic or theocratic "the gallows will be your end" underscores the conventional, generic, and hence social nature of the standard version.

These rhymes help to constitute the book as valuable, both in memory of its life as a commodity and as a token of membership in the club. The warning against theft raises the object's value, making it a more desirable article to own and a tempting one to covet. One book owner ingenuously appeals, "Please don't steal, it is a valuable book."[35] The most seemingly abject little items are posted with no-trespassing signs. The owner of an 1810 twenty-five-page ready reckoner writes simply, "Steal not this."[36] Though pocket-sized to begin with (just over three inches square), this pamphlet was further condensed, folded into quarters, postage-stamp size, giving the impression of having been regularly tucked into some small watch- or vest-pocket. Utterly utilitarian, physically intimate, close to the body, and even, who can say, a loved object.

By at least the 1830s publishers for children began to give some inches of real estate to the property question.[37] In an 1832 prose version of "The Children in the Wood" ballad, the prominent New York children's book publisher Mahlon Day provides a frontispiece with a rectangular border composed of printer's ornaments, imprinted with "THE PROPERTY OF" over a space for signing, which, in this case, Harvey Copeland has taken advantage of (Figure 30).[38] The incorporation of the job-printing blank form, the economic staple of print shops, associates the children's book with legal and mercantile printed ephemera.[39] Publishers were shrewd to link these genres, for the explicit identification of the book, no matter how small or meek, *as* property, served the interests of the institutions associated with it: printers, publishers, authors, and schools. The child who inscribes himself under the sign "THE PROPERTY OF" in his book practices the kind of consent associated with the contractual obligations and ideology of ownership discussed in the previous chapter. And it hints at what's sometimes stated explicitly about the relationship between literacy—what the era usually called, simply, "learning"—and real estate or other forms of capital accumulation. "Labor for learning Before / you grow old, Learning is / better than silver or gold," Mary Lucretia Shelton writes, circa 1821, in her Murray's *Introduction to the English Reader*, a value-added inscription to the two owner's verses with which she protected her book (see Figure 27). Echoing this sentiment, an eight-year-old girl writes in her 1811 copy of Murray's *The English Reader: Or, Pieces in Prose and Poetry, Selected from the Best Writers*: "Grace Comforts Book wherein / she ought to look not / only look but understand / that learning is before / house and land when / land is gone, and money spent / good learning is most exlent."[40] As in the proverb current in the eighteenth

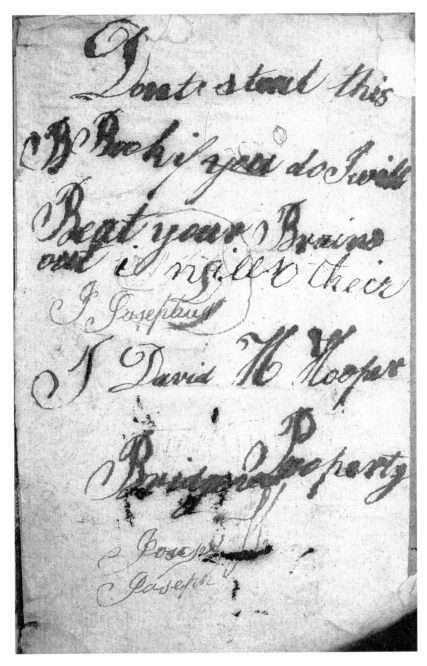

Figure 29. Noah Webster, *The American Spelling Book: Containing the Rudiments of the English Language, for the use of Schools in the United States.* Brattleborough, Vt.: John Holbrook, 1819. AAS call number Dated Books, copy 1. Courtesy American Antiquarian Society.

Figure 30. *The Children in the Wood, To Which Is Added, My Mother's Grave, a Pathetic Story.* New York: Mahlon Day, at the New Juvenile Book-store, no. 376 Pearl-Street, 1832. AAS call number CL-Pam C5365 C536 1832. Courtesy American Antiquarian Society.

century, "learning better than house and land," literacy is here imagined as a more stable currency than the traditional forms of real estate that until the mid-eighteenth century had been widely regarded as inalienable.[41]

The Space of Childhood

Like other books, a schoolbook circa 1810 or 1820, such as Lindley Murray's *English Reader,* typically has a few blank pages of front and back matter, filling out the printer's signature. Children claim this space for all sorts of uses. In accord with what the psychoanalyst Adam Phillips has called the child's "ecstasy of opportunity,"[42] many child book taggers go in for excess and superfluity, as they exploit and appropriate the physical form of the book—that it opens onto blank pages and white spaces, and that it closes up again, concealing whatever is inside it. These books are marked by sequential owners, handed down to cousins and siblings, or shared by them, as a common, if occasionally privatized, social space (as a family today might share some "devices," sometimes, but not others). Many books are shared along a chain of siblings, cousins, and sometimes parent-child axes, so that the signature represents a node in a social network that connects horizontally among age peers and vertically through time.[43] If books, as the material sign and external measure of learning or literacy, are "better than house or land," they tend to function like the traditional versions of both, as a space that one enters and inhabits as well as a site for cultivation, for labor, and for passing along a legacy.

A typically sturdy leather-bound 1819 copy of Murray's *English Reader* was written in by Elizabeth, Benjamin, Mary, Sara, Samuel, David, and William Miller, and one Joseph with no last name mentioned, and was dated by them variously in 1829, in 1837, and 1838.[44] Together, over at least a decade and possibly two, the Miller children commandeered, edge to edge, every millimeter of space of the inside front and back covers, and all available flyleaves (see Plate 27, Figure 31).[45] Some children—especially those collaborating with others over time—rise to the level of graffiti artists or taggers, creating dense expressionist palimpsests, ancestors of Jackson Pollocks or Cy Twomblys, that invite one into all of their interesting corners. They make a fitting frame for the genre they're inscribing: Lindley Murray's anthology brings together dozens of authors, in short pieces; it's a book of fragments the student takes in bit by assigned bit, reading aloud here, memorizing there, skipping this passage, zeroing in on that one. (I have yet to find this kind of rock 'n' roll inscription in any other kind of book.)[46] These inscriptions seem to address multiple potential readers, mostly within a school and family network. But they include, in one uncanny instance,

Figure 31. Miller graffiti in Lindley Murray's *The English Reader: Or, Pieces in Prose and Poetry, Selected from the Best Writers.* Fredericktown, Md.: George Kolb, 1819. Inscribed by Benjamin Miller et al. AAS call number Dated Books. Courtesy American Antiquarian Society.

a proto-Whitmanian "you," which seems to hail the twenty-first-century reader from the stained but otherwise strikingly blank page (Figure 32).

Among the internal graffiti in this book, Benjamin Miller positions his name and the year 1829 beneath William Cowper's much-recited poem about Alexander Selkirk, the castaway who was the model for Robinson Crusoe.[47] The poem opens famously with "I am the monarch of all I survey," but it quickly despairs at Selkirk's lonely fate: "Better dwell in the midst of alarms, / Than reign in this horrible place." Miller's dated signature might be read as a castaway within the space of schoolbook or schoolroom hailing his literary other, and yet the child does reign on the page, and asserts his mastery.

The Lamborn family similarly collaborated, into at least the 1830s, on an 1802 edition of Murray's *Grammar,* another stock schoolbook, marked by Carson, Sarah Ann, Mary H., Edith B., and Jacob Lamborn, as well as by James and Samuel Mendenhall and C. Pyle, all related to the Lamborns, and by Thomas

Figure 32. Hailed by a nineteenth-century young person, from the Millers' copy of Murray's *English Reader*. Courtesy American Antiquarian Society.

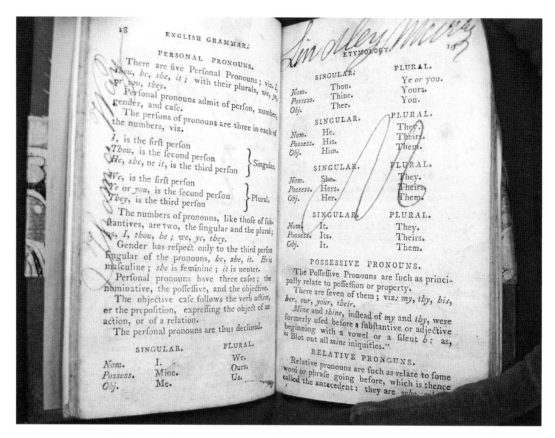

Figure 33. The Lamborns comment on Lindley Murray's *An Abridgment of Murray's English Grammar*. Philadelphia: Benjamin Johnson and Jacob Johnson, 1802. AAS call number Dated Books. Courtesy American Antiquarian Society.

Way, James Miller, William Steel, Ellis W. and John S.[48] The Lamborns remind us that there's nothing magically "authentic" about inscriptions—or about children, for that matter—for amid the dozens of student tags is the "signature" of Lindley Murray himself (Figure 33). Some of the Lamborn marks exaggerate the reorientation of space that all inscriptions perform. An inscribed ABCs, a partial alphabet stretched out, one large letter per page, creates a kind of scrim over the text, and make of it a backdrop—a chorus or a chorus line—to the inscriber's own grammatology. But here the inscriber and the original author are talking about the same thing: the inscriber writes the ABCs across a dozen pages of printed text devoted to the alphabet— orthography, pronunciation, grammar. A good-boy-and-girl piece of graffiti, it draws attention to itself by rescaling the space and shifting perspective, without actually changing the topic.

Like the Lamborns, many children mark not only on inside covers and fly-leaves but in more remote places, internally, within the book. In such cases the printed text, which is the occasion for the signature or other mark, its condition of possibility, becomes momentarily marginalized, as the space it has created gets appropriated for other writing. Marginalia within books, rather than on inside covers and blank flyleaves, ambush the reader and create the special effect of reorienting the page. The printed text recedes, becoming only a part of the book, rather than the entire event. To read gutter signatures, and many other inscriptions, we have to turn the book upside down or sideways. If learning to read and write demands of the child a strenuous array of physical disciplines—sitting still, standing to recite, elaborate rituals and paraphernalia and postures of penmanship—here's a kind of payback: the child stage-manages his latter-day readers, asking, through this distant collaboration, that they too now play with the book.

While many inscriptions establish the writer's place geographically, they also command the space of the book and turn it into one of the first dedicated childhood spaces, following the nursery and the schoolroom, and before the advent of the playground movement at the end of the nineteenth century. Books like Murray's *Grammar* and *Reader* tell the child what he's supposed to do with his mind, his memory, and, especially, his mouth and vocal organs, as they are devoted to the performance of the English language. With his writing, the child brackets the taming space of the book, letting in something wild. And yet, not all that wild. The wild child of the nineteenth century is represented as "truant," the one who throws his books away altogether, not the Lamborns and the Millers, who appear to have identified with their books, played in them, and treated them both as extensions of the self and as tokens and adjuncts of sociality.

Marginal Events: "I Should Chouse Dissipation"

Children often date not only their ownership inscriptions but annotations within their books as well, apropos of nothing apparent in the text, marking the time of year: in the Lamborns' copy of Murray "the end of March" is written along one page; in another book "October" appears in a margin.[49] While there's no telling exactly what motivates such notes, they are reminders that a child read and wrote in a particular time and place, and they evoke the here-and-now quality of the child's attention to seasons and the passing of time. Such time stamps constitute datelines, and if they seem to fall short of journalistic precision—the exact time and geographic place of a reported event—they in fact register that the book itself is the place in which the events of reading, writing, dating, and signing occurred.

In her 1816 copy of Murray's *Introduction to the English Reader*, Mary Lucretia Shelton signs several times, with place and date, "Bridgport November 26th 1821." Her marginal remarks replicate dialogue, and sometimes include a penciled response from another young writer, to whom a lightly penciled signature may also belong.[50] Like much schoolbook marginalia, her remarks are pertinent and responsive, engaging the text, disputing with it, idly commenting upon it, exercising her wit and intelligence upon it.[51] She is often diligent and comments, "I love to repeat poetry / don't you" at the beginning of the poetry section (115). In response to the Isaac Watts chestnut "The Sluggard," rather than sharing the speaker's horror at the sluggard's desperate fate, Shelton finds "I am a sluggard for I love / to lie abed very much in / the morning."[52] Another hand has written in pencil, "So do I like to liy in / bed in the / morn- / ing" (137) (Figure 34). In this and similar instances, one can't know whether this is, for example, a schoolmate, side by side with Shelton, sharing notes, or a later owner, joining in the conversation; we can know only that the comment, like the printed text, had a responsive reader. Elsewhere, Shelton seems to solicit a response, but none emerges in writing: "This is interesting to [*sic*] but I have / not time to read it now but / I am sorry have you time?" (38).

Shelton sympathizes with an enslaved European ("don't you feal for them" [74]); but above a poem about an African slave suicide, following the printed word "slave," she adds "of fashion" (164). She conveys a conventional sense of duty and writes "I am charitable" over a piece on charity (63) but is not always up to what it demands of her: next to a piece called "Gratitude," she writes: "I learnt Gratitude all by heart / but I don't know as it will do / me any good" (64). (Indeed, the piece on gratitude is a bloodless couple of paragraphs from Robert Doddsley's *Economy of Human Life*.) In a similar vein, Shelton reads an essay by Anna Laetitia Aiken Barbauld, the eighteenth-century poet and essayist, who is well represented in Murray's *Readers*. In Barbauld's "Female Choice" a girl dreams that two women approach her. A glamorous creature holds out a fancy dress and a ticket to a ball; her name is "Dissipation." The other, dressed in brown, carrying a distaff and a workbasket, is "Housewifery." The dreaming girl watches as Dissipation's mask falls away and she turns "wan and ghastly with sickness, and soured by fretfulness." Hence the girl "gave her hand unreluctantly" to "her sober and sincere companion" (43). Mary Shelton writes above this essay: "I should chouse Dissipation." Shelton takes up the disingenuous democratic pretense of the title, "Female Choice," and submits her vote. Scary though she makes the figure of dissipation, Barbauld seems unable to

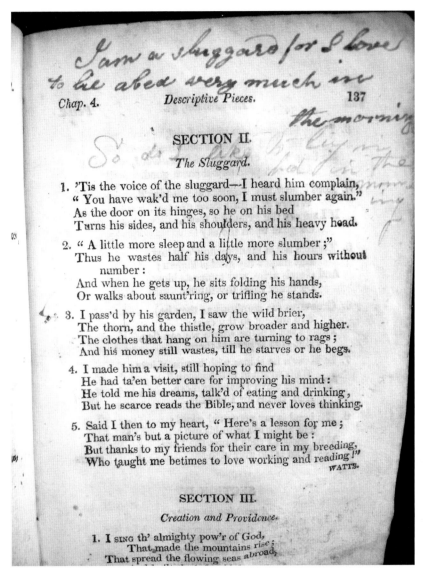

Figure 34. Mary Lucretia Shelton in penciled dialogue within her Murray's. Courtesy American Antiquarian Society.

produce a housewife that one can follow with anything more than "unreluctance," and Shelton, perhaps, sees through this (Figure 35).

If Mary Shelton displays schoolgirl savvy, one typically finds schoolboy wit too, with its long Latin school provenance.[53] In the Lamborns' grammar book, a wag has annotated a lesson in verb moods and tenses—"Let me be . . . Let him be," "We may . . . Ye or you may . . . I might . . . They might, could would,

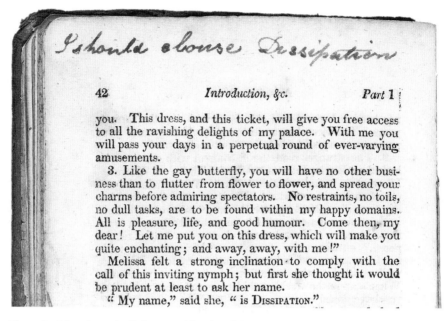

Figure 35. Mary Lucretia Shelton would rather "chouse Dissipation." Courtesy American Antiquarian Society.

or should be"—by completing the sentence fragments with "in haste to / the tavern."[54] The social and cultural capital associated with the book is not only, or even perhaps primarily, "knowledge" but rather a kind of knowingness, a canniness, that beyond its content also says: I know my way around a book so well that I can treat it wryly.

Sometimes one finds a more raucous encounter with the text. In a much traveled, multiply-owned and marked-up 1802 edition of *Fables of Aesop*, one inscriber seems fascinated by the fable "The Ape and the Fox."[55] The ape lobbies to acquire some of the fox's tail to cover his "poor naked backside," and the fox declines to give "the least Bit to cover the Ape's nasty stinking Posteriors."[56] The inscriber has scrawled "Ape-Stink posteriors" in large letters in the lower margin. As such practice and play with words might illustrate, the book offers a socially sanctioned private space in which to read and write with some freedom from surveillance, a capacity of the book that allows for all kinds of intimate uses.

The New Work of Childhood

Three tiny chapbooks were given to Lucy Watson Draper of Spencer, Massachusetts, beginning in September 1817, when Lucy was not quite four years old.

Figure 36. One of three small (3.5 x 2 inches) chapbooks inscribed to Lucy Draper by Eunice Underwood. *Childhood*. New York: Samuel Wood, 1815. AAS call number CL-Pam C536 N532 1815.

The first, *Childhood*, was inscribed, with ceremony, "Lucy Draper's / Property / Presented by / Miss Eunice / Underwood" (Figure 36).[57] Eunice Underwood, twenty-five at the time, may have been a relative, a family friend, or a teacher (in any case, she married in 1819 and moved to Maine). This bite-sized book has been carefully covered in wallpaper, by Eunice Underwood, perhaps, as part of the gift, or later by Lucy or her older sisters. Published by the notable Quaker printer in New York, Samuel Wood, an early and vigorous marketer to children, *Childhood* provides a commentary on the duties and privileges of this form of life circa 1814. A standard chapbook engraving on the title page shows a boy posed at mother's knee with a book; in the pages that follow, childhood is defined as the period of schooling that comes after "the days and dangers of infancy," during which the child learns reading, writing, and "cyphering," plays healthful games, and decides on a livelihood (preferably farming, in this account). Underwood inscribes the book as the property of Lucy, as she does with two other little books in the same chapbook series, *Manhood* and *Spring*, that she gives to Lucy over the next two years. The elaborate care of these small books seems a trope for the care of Lucy, the youngest of four daughters and seemingly the object of doting paternal care, as evidenced by a poem James Draper wrote for her: "Lucy Draper's very good, / She picks up chips and brings in wood; / Washes dishes, makes a bed, / Sweeps the house and learns to read" (see Plate 29).[58] Lucy's father likely wrote this verse around the time of the gift of the little books.[59] Written legibly for a young reader of print, the verse figures reading as one of the newly assumed labors of middle-class childhood. It opens with Lucy's goodness, shown in her age-appropriate duties, and ends with the era's outward signifier of virtue: she's learning to read. Along with the performative inscriptions, denoting the books as Lucy's property, the labor of learning to read in them is what further constitutes these books, however wittily, as property. While it may have been Miss Underwood, or a slightly older Lucy, or one of her older sisters, who made the bright wrappers for these artifacts, the care of the book became, along with reading and writing, an aspect of the new work of childhood (Plate 28).

Britannia Anthony, wife of a prosperous Providence merchant, gave books to her two little girls, Kate and Sarah, aged five and six, on June 3, 1857. In *Little Kitty Clover and Her Friends* she wrote, "Kate J. Anthony / May this book be kept / very nice." Kate was the third of the Anthonys' eight children, one of the three who survived childhood. Aside from two torn pages and a soiled (possibly chewed upon?) corner of the front cover, the book has indeed been "kept very nice" by Kate, the Anthony heirs, and the library the book was given to a century later.[60] Like many books compiled for the bustling children's market of the mid-century, the text of this thirty-cent, eighty-five-page book was composed to make use of the variety of engravings that the printer must have had to hand ("Illustrated with nearly one hundred woodcuts"). Holding the image-prompted fragments together is "little Kitty Clover" herself, the outline of whose biography rhymes with Kate Anthony's (perhaps also, sometimes, "Kitty"?). "She lives in a pleasant home with kind parents, two brothers, and one sister, who all love her very much. Being the youngest, and a very pleasant, good little girl, she is consequently the pet of the whole house."[61] (Kate in 1857 had one older brother, one older sister, and a baby brother; a year-old sister had died in 1855.) Like Jacob Abbott's first book for young children and many other such books, this one's method of composition or compilation creates a narrative that follows the arbitrary persons and things dropped into it. Mirroring its own commodity status, it is heavily reliant on consumer objects, which naturally include books: "Charles brings his last new book, and wooden horse on wheels. Little Willie comes,

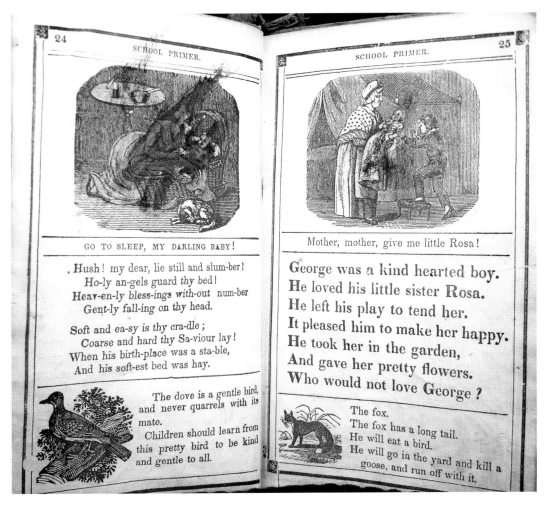

Figure 37. Possibly Edgar Anthony's response to siblings in general in his *Blue Pictorial Primer*. New York: Geo. F. Cooledge and Brother, 1839. AAAS call number Primers B658 P611 1840. Courtesy American Antiquarian Society.

bringing his pet cap, with the long tassel, and dissected map, that his mamma brought from Philadelphia."[62]

Possibly Kate's mother wasn't thinking so much of Kate when she wrote her inscription as of Kate's older brother Edgar, whose *Blue Pictorial Primer* has also survived—barely (Plate 30). The primer might have been purchased to be shared over time among siblings, but Edgar Anthony appears to have all but consumed it on his own; indeed, passages that encourage sibling harmony ("George was a kind hearted boy. He loved his little sister Rosa") have been evocatively blotted by this eldest child in a growing family (Figure 37).[63] That it was preserved and formed part of the legacy to a library testifies to the value placed on such artifacts in nineteenth-century families. Books were a crucial adjunct to family life for the Anthony children, who numbered them and kept them as a family library; sixteen books inscribed to and by the Anthony children are in the American Antiquarian Society collection, along with a few uninscribed children's books and schoolbooks and a few issues of a children's magazine. This collecting practice was common among middle-class children, influenced by marketers' promoting of such consumer goods as Ellen Montgomery's Library, Harper's Story Books, Mrs. Leslie's Juvenile Series, and Pleasure Books for Children (volumes from these series, by the popular writers Anna Bartlett Warner, the sister of the *Wide, Wide World* author, and Jacob Abbott, among others, are in the Anthonys' library). *The Blue Pictorial Primer* contains a page detailing the fate of "Idle Tom," aka "Tom Truant," the stock bad boy of tracts and primers; his downward slide begins the day he plays with ducks at the pond instead of going to school. In the spirit of "the gallows will be your end," the anecdote concludes, "Ignorance and vice always go hand in hand. If Tom does not die in a prison, or in the poor-house, it will be a wonder."[64] As anathemas protect the child-inscriber from the projected thief and his threat of poverty, so Tom Truant figures exclusion as transgression. Whether stealing books or repudiating them, the figure of the truant is really a specter of poverty, neglect, abandonment, and orphanhood transformed into an object of discipline.

Kate Anthony seems to have taken to heart her mother's message to keep her book "very nice." For her eighth birthday in 1854, she was given *Mamma's Gift Book*, which has been wrapped in a homemade brown packing paper cover, with the title inscribed on the cover and spine, in imitation of a binding.[65] Though clearly much read—it opens easily and is marked inside with small stains of use—it remains in "very nice" condition. The text of *Mamma's Gift Book* is, even by nineteenth-century standards, hair-raising. It opens benignly, the anonymous writer vowing "to write a story book for all good children. It will have some pictures in, and many stories about dogs, horses, birds, and little boys. It will be written so plainly, that all children may understand it; and I hope that after reading it, they will be both wiser and better."[66] Among these is the story of a Russian woman who flees wolves in her sled, placating them by throwing one after another of her children to them; when she is found by her husband and villagers, she herself is axed to death. In another tale a wicked cat's mischief is repaid by the community of cats who "tore him to pieces"; a fable tells of a hare who is too vain to believe that dogs can hurt him, but they break his back anyway with one bite: "Children sometimes act as foolishly as did this hare."[67] It's hard to say what's to love in this book, whose mean-spirited stories lack the fairy tale's fantastic space-time or psychological coherence. And yet, if loved it has been, it is due to its nature as a gift and as a surrogate, externalized self: cared for but wicked; punished but surviving; horrible but fascinating; full of death but infinitely accessible to revisiting. As an adjunct to the self, the book is eligible for the same kind of attention and care that the self is owed. Other, seemingly neutral and benignant objects receive similar treatment: Laura Newton has swathed her 1813 *Abridgment of Murray's Grammar* in brown paper and inscribed the cover with a heraldic flourish; Prudence Varnum has enveloped hers in a pretty span of flowered wallpaper (see Plates 31 and 32).[68]

Caskets and Cenotaphs: The Life and Afterlife of Children's Books

If in the social life of the book it transforms from a commodity, to a gift, to a teacher, to a transitional object, to something like a self, it sometimes demonstrates along the way one of the signal traits of a self: the capacity to keep a secret.[69] In her handsomely kept *Mamma's Gift Book* Kate Anthony has cached a set of paper doll clothes, cut from wallpaper (Kate's father was in the hardware business and perhaps brought home samples) (see Plate 33). Children routinely exploit the material qualities of the codex that printers had long captured in titles that identify books as "caskets," "cabinets," "treasuries," and the like: its portability, its intimately miniature size, its tidy boxlike structure.

In a heavily and dutifully marked-up 1806 copy of Murray's *Grammar*, which Nancy Smyth of Virginia inscribed in 1824, something is tucked into the leaves, where, reading the stain it's made on the pages, it had rested for some time.[70] It's a small slip of paper with a printed message: "If you approve of my love, in your bosom put this, / Thus assenting to love, you'll perfect my bliss." A shadow between two other pages shows that the slip had once rested there as well, where there are also fragments of a flower. That it has stained these pages dates it to long after Nancy Smyth's schooldays, at least to the 1840s, when wood-pulp paper was first produced.[71] The form of the book, its aptitude for both privacy and sociability, invites use as a postbox for a mash note, transforming the book from one kind of medium to another—from the fixity and long duration of print to the liveliness and temporal urgency of a post or telegraph office.[72]

Like erased inscriptions, some things in books leave only spectral traces. In her 1872 botany book, Hattie S. Putnam of Worcester, pressed flowers. They are long gone but have left their photograph-like shadows, formed of the same wood-pulp acid that spilled from the love note.[73] These remnants—perhaps specimens prompted by her textbook—like the Lamborns' ABC graffiti described above, seem to emanate from the book, adding fullness or presence to the abstraction of words. Sometimes the thing within the book remains intact, but one becomes conscious of all the possibilities for misreading it. An 1845 *New England Primer* was given to Helen Spalding when she was eight, and she used it to store "my young / est brother locks," as she wrote in ink within a curl of hair; in pencil (in another hand perhaps) are the words "Edward" and "hair."[74] Helen Spalding's younger brother Edward seems to have lived at least long enough to marry in 1871; but her youngest brother, George, died at four months, in 1841. Is this a memorial lock of the baby's hair, kept and then pasted into the primer four years later? Or is it, as the penciled note says, Edward's? Was he ill and near death? Was he going away and so locks were exchanged? Or did Helen Spalding simply want to store a token of her brother in her book? Does this lock memorialize a child who died in childhood, or is it instead a memorial of the *fact* of childhood, marking what Henry James would call "the death of . . . childhood"?[75]

If this last might describe what any children's book that has survived seems to convey, some books are specifically kept, cared for, willed, and donated to archives in memory of a child who did not survive. A tiny pamphlet, hand-covered in brilliant red paper, is inscribed: "Relief Crouch / her Book She / was Born—— / September the 12/1803// and died—— / September the 3/1805."[76] The little pamphlet's plot is telegraphed in its title: *The History of Miss Kitty Pride*. A proud spoiled little rich girl looks down on everyone, and when her father is eventually ruined, Kitty is reduced to seeking the charity of her former servant, who takes her in and teaches her to "read and work." In other words, it's not really a two-year-old's book in any sense except the one that has accounted for its preservation. As often in such inscriptions, the adult handwriting seems expressive; here the *t*'s of September are left uncrossed.

"Homer S. Wire / Aged three years, Seven Months, One day / *died 1851* / his Present to M. C. Wire." This appears on the front flyleaf of an 1843 book called *Coverings for the Head and Feet, in All Ages and All Countries*, another perhaps surprising choice of reading for a toddler (Figure 38).[77] The inscription suggests that the child may have asked on his deathbed that the book be given away. Stains on the inside cover facing the inscription reveal that the inscriber closed the book before the ink could dry.

On the cover of *Rollo's Philosophy: Air*, a volume in Jacob Abbott's "Rollo" series, are barely visible embossed figures: a boy with a book and two other children, one a girl with a hoop and a bonnet, the other a littler girl or boy in a dress.[78] The inscription reads: "Presented to / Howard Littlefield / from his deceased / cousin Leroy by / his parents in token / of their affection for / each

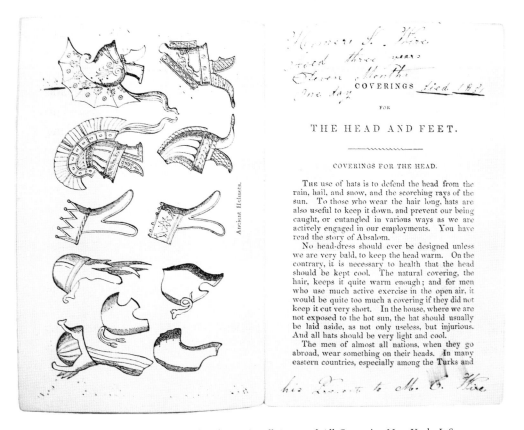

Figure 38. *Coverings for the Head and Feet, in All Ages and All Countries.* New York: J. S. Redfield [between 1843 and 1851?]. Inscribed to M. C. Wire. AAS call number CL-Pam C873 F692 1843. Courtesy American Antiquarian Society.

other when alive" (Figure 39). The agonized syntax struggles to chart the gift's genealogy and rationale. Dashes of ink on the facing cover suggest that it was closed before the inscription had had a chance to dry.

The Pearl Story Book, an 1850 collection, fetchingly turned out in its red cover, in keeping with its gift-book genre, mixes such grim fare as Hans Christian Andersen's gory "The Red Shoes" with more festive stories and poems. Inscribed in light pencil on the first flyleaf is: "A little book that / I used to read from / to Carrie my little / girl 2 years old when she / died." Who wrote this? What happened to Carrie? We only know that Carrie seemed to have liked a certain poem, marked in pencil "Her favorite piece." The plot of this poem, "Naughty Marian," is a familiar one in such anthologies: adults jokingly pretend that sulky Marian is not really Marian at all. Spread over two pages, the poem ends: "When my own little girl comes back, / Just send her in to me!"

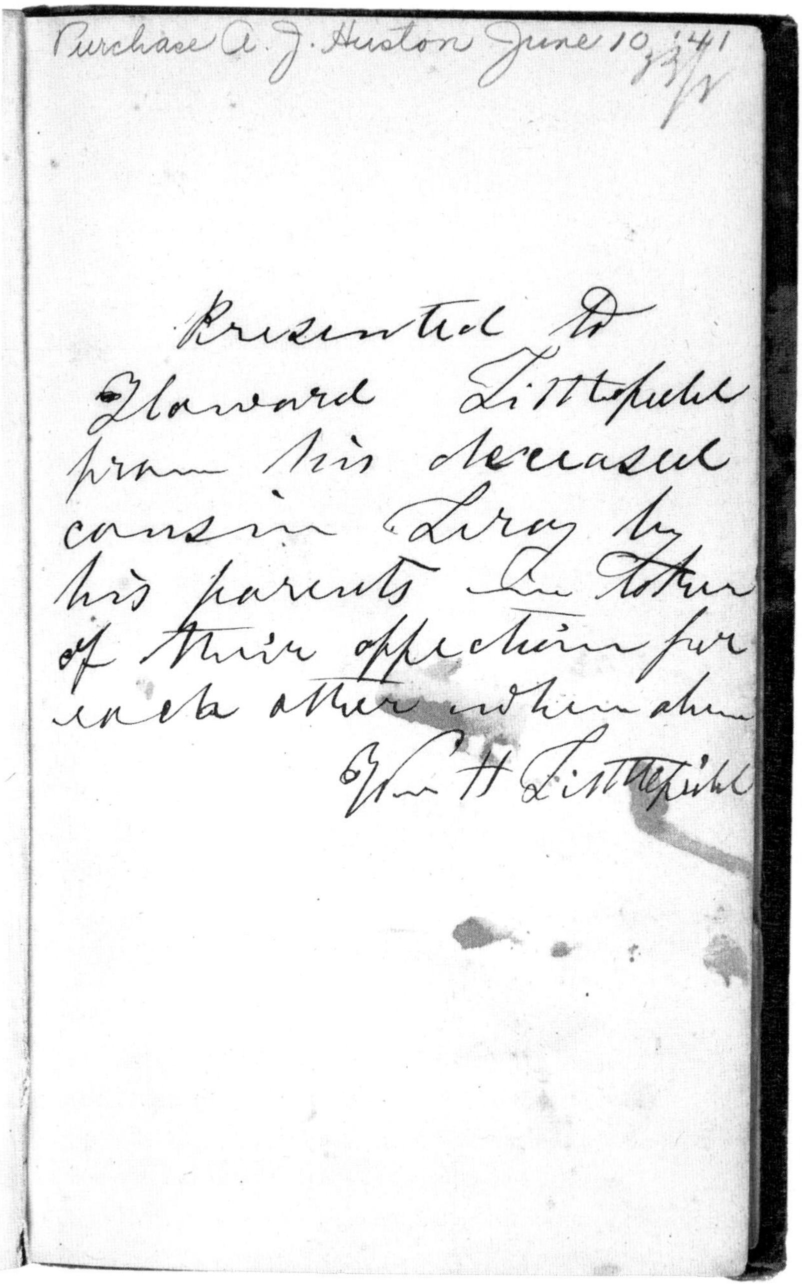
Purchase A. J. Huston June 10, '41
Presented to
Howard Littlefield
from his deceased
cousin Leroy by
his parents in token
of their affection for
each other when alive
Wm H Littlefield

Figure 39. Jacob Abbott, *Rollo's Philosophy: Air.* Philadelphia: B. F. Jackson, 1853. Inscribed to Howard Littlefield. AAS call number CL A132 R757 1853. Courtesy American Antiquarian Society.

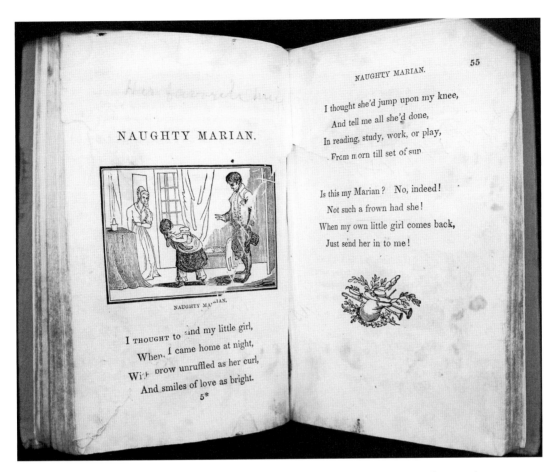

Figure 40. "Naughty Marian," in Mrs. Colman, *The Pearl Story Book*. New York: Samuel Raynor, 1850. Inscribed in memory of Carrie. AAS call number CL P359 S884 1850. Courtesy American Antiquarian Society.

(Figure 40). Originally playful (if disciplinary), the poem is transformed—by the inscription, and by the news it conveys—into a stark cry of loss. Such sketches of grief are striking for the degree to which they differ from the elegiac tradition, at least in its nineteenth-century sentimental mode, in not taking any special pains to be moving. The intimacy of their gestures and the sheer materiality of the book itself—and the way, in whatever fashion, it had mingled its DNA with that of a child—seem to be regarded as eloquence enough.

A copy of *Little Annie's ABC*, published in New York in 1851, was annotated by Harriet Rose Chandler of Worcester, Massachusetts, who was born on June 6, 1847, and died on July 1, 1857 (Figure 41).[79] This prettily produced but spare ABC book lacks even the predictable alphabet images, relying only on printed

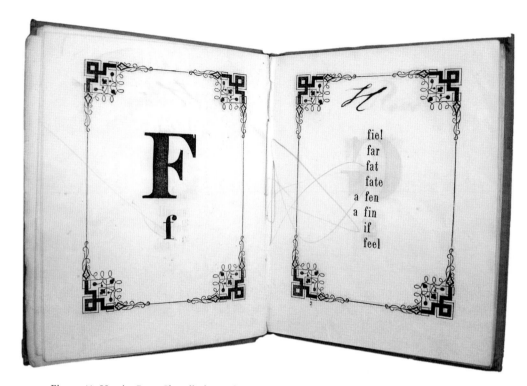

Figure 41. Harriet Rose Chandler's marks in her copy of *Little Annie's ABC*. Philadelphia: Appleton, 1851. AAS call number CL L7781 A6131 1851. Courtesy American Antiquarian Society.

letters and associated words for interest. Similarly, the child's marks in it have the least possible semantic content—"H," for example. But this attunes them to the printed pre-text and context of the alphabet book. And their very sparseness gives them a lyric and proleptic quality: tucked within the border of the page, Harriet Rose asserts her own initial against the *F* for "fie!" and "fate." Unlike Carrie's life (or that of the other children mentioned in this chapter), Harriet Rose Chandler's life has been well documented by her prominent Worcester family. On the flyleaf of *Little Annie's ABC*, her sister Fanny Chandler Lincoln has written in pencil: "Belonged to/ Harriet Rose Chandler./ My sister—F. C. Lincoln/ She was said to be, by / Dr. Joseph Sargent of Worcester,/ the most beautiful child/ he ever saw—" Indeed, a heavily annotated and extra-illustrated family genealogy includes a tiny fetching cameo-like photograph of the girl as a toddler (Figure 42), along with a paper cutout of her infant footprint. The genealogy quotes her father's account of Harriet Rose in life and death: "She was large of her age, had dark hair, dark hazel eyes, and very red

Figure 42. Photograph of Harriet Rose Chandler, from George Chandler, *The Chandler Family: The Descendants of William and Annis Chandler, Who Settled in Roxbury, Mass., 1637.* Boston: D. Clapp and Son, 1872. Courtesy American Antiquarian Society.

cheeks. She was quiet, amiable, confiding, sensitive, and honored her parents. She excelled with her needle, and made great progress in school; was diffident, and had extreme delicacy of feeling, yet was ambitious." In June 1857,

during the closing exercises of the dancing school quarter . . . she was pushed across a settee by her mates but continued to dance afterward. On coming home she complained of feeling ill and went to bed. Inflammation of the bowels came on, and she sank on the morning of July 1st. The last hours of her life were singularly calm and serene. She tried to comfort those weeping around her, and when told she could not live long, she replied, "Do you think so, father? Oh! then I shall see Jesus." She then gave her two sisters each "half of all she had," naming the articles for each. She bade "all come to heaven," and said, "Tell grandmother to come." While sick, her schoolmates serenaded her under her window, and at her funeral they sang a hymn at the house and a dirge at the grave, besides strewing her coffin with flowers.[80]

The account of this child's shocking illness and death, written for a family history, is consonant with scenes from one of Harriet Rose Chandler's own books, a bound set of tracts called *The Newfoundland Fishermen*, inscribed "Miss Harriet-Rose Chandler, with best love from cousin May."[81] Following the immensely popular evangelical genre established by James Janeway's *Token for Children* (1700), tales of the pious deaths of young children make up about half the volume. "'I love them that love me, and those who seek me early shall find me,'" the verse that Mrs. Montgomery inscribes in Ellen's Bible, is predictably quoted in more than one tale. In "The Withered Flower," when the fourteen-year-old Martha was told she was dying, "she . . . desired her sisters to be called, and addressed them earnestly and affectionately." In the "Memoir of Mary Jane," as this eight-year-old was dying, "she requested her mother . . . to distribute her books among various members of the family, specifying the particular book or books which she wished each to have. She was at a loss to fix on a suitable book for her sister Ellen, who was only two months old, and of whom she had seen but little. On her mamma saying, 'Ellen will never remember you my dear,' she replied, 'No, mamma, but I wish to remember her.'"[82] These accounts—of the unremembered but lovingly remembering child—and the account of Harriet Rose Chandler's death echo one another so thoroughly partly because the genre so powerfully shapes the printed record, which would have one believe that thousands of children died *exactly* like this. And yet some of them surely did, perhaps Harriet Rose Chandler, having learned all about death from cousin May's gift of *The Newfoundland Fishermen*. If nineteenth-century children are increasingly told by their books how to live—how, that is, to perform the work of this new creature in the world, a child, or, strictly speaking, a child-in-a-book—they are told as well how to die.

Little Annie's ABC, like many of the books discussed in this chapter, was preserved as a kind of miniature cenotaph of Harriet Rose Chandler, in a literalizing of prosopopoeia. In this unusual case, the child's biography can be linked to that of the artifact. In this and in all of the cases of memorial inscriptions, the death of the child marks a new stage in the life of the artifact. I close this chapter with these books because in a way they offer a fulfillment of what all of the other marked children's books leave fragmented and unresolved. For one thing, here the scholar or reader's melancholic or nostalgic projection can take a holiday, for here grief is the text, not a troubled or illusory subtext; one is obliged with these artifacts to acknowledge or even to invite rather than disavow or suppress sensations of "presence" or the auratic. But more important, these artifacts express in an emphatic form the extent to which children in the nine-teenth century became identified with books. Through children's marks we can chart the transformation of these commodities into primers for modern prop-erty relations, into spaces children appropriate for an array of reasons and uses, into objects of nostalgic and sentimental fascination, and finally, whether explic-itly or implicitly, into souvenirs—whether of dead children or of that peculiarly modern affliction, the death of childhood itself.

CHAPTER 6

Raising "Master James"

The Medial Child and Phantasms of Reading

"He was serious with children," observed G. K. Chesterton. "I saw a little boy gravely present him with a crushed and dirty dandelion. He bowed; but did not smile."
—Simon Nowell-Smith, *The Legend of the Master* (1947)

To look back at all is to meet the apparitional and to find in its ghostly face the silent stare of an appeal. When I fix it, the hovering shade, whether of person or place, it fixes me back and seems the less lost—not to my consciousness, for that is nothing, but to its own—by my stopping however idly for it.
—Henry James, *A Small Boy and Others* (1913)

The child's own importance, spreading and contagiously acting, has determined the *total* value otherwise.
—Henry James, Preface to *What Maisie Knew* (1908)

I have been a child.
—Henry James, "The Art of Fiction" (1884)

THE ASSOCIATION of children with books and reading found expression in the schoolroom and parlor, in visual motifs, in genres and formats of children's literature and belles lettres, and, as the previous chapter explored, in the ways that the material artifact of the book became a registry of the child-book matrix, not only for the child herself but for her guardians, friends, and family, and, across time, for their extended progeny (of descendants, but also of librarians, collectors, and scholars, for example). By the last decades of the century, it could go without saying that the middle-class white child, real, ideal, or aspirational, was a book reader. For that figure, books and reading constituted a reflective and projective spaciousness; to lose oneself in a book was the means to finding and asserting subjectivity and interiority. It may seem a strange self-possession that thrives on self-loss, but this was part of childhood's new work: to model and preserve a reading practice that resembled reverie. For everyone else, there was "literacy," a neologism of the 1880s, a term that referred to putatively quantifiable instrumental practices of reading and writing suitable, in the bureaucratic imagination, for a post-Reconstruction America with a growing immigrant population.[1] At the same time that children's immersive reading was valorized, the book as an artifact of typographic media was beginning to face competition from other forms of communication, from telegraphy and the telephone to the photography and chromolithography that filled magazines and children's books, to the emergent cinema.

This chapter turns from works produced, intended, or adopted for or by children, to narratives that claim children as literary property. In this final chapter, I've been drawn to explore Henry James's child-centered texts of the 1890s not so much as culmination but as critique and complication. James's imagination of childhood and his child-centered theories of reading form a record by this highly attuned nineteenth-century cultural witness of an accumulated wealth of observation about children and childhood, providing a kind of expert testimony about—in broad strokes—what children might mean for reading and what reading might mean for children. Contemporaneous with Freud's studies in the formation of children's consciousness, the use of childhood memory, and individual children's own desires and the desires of those around them, James's child-centered narratives rival Freud's, while working in a strictly literary register, in the domain of books and reading. This chapter is equally interested in the ways in which the childhood that emerged in the nineteenth century presented James with a new ground for narrative exploration. The admixture of James's two nationalities—his ineluctable Americanness, his adopted mantle of Britishness—resonates with the fluid transatlanticism of so many texts discussed in these pages. In this chapter, in fact, childhood is suspended between national literatures. In his multiple allegiances, to his own New York childhood, to his eccentric, experimental, European education and upbringing, and to his adopted English home, James echoes, without resolving, the transatlantic hybridity of nineteenth-century childhood—its ideology, its representation, and its literature. By writing against the grain of conventional childhood and in a distinctly antinostalgic mode, James explores and exposes the impossible symbolic labors burdening children and childhood by century's end.

In the works I take up in this chapter—"The Pupil" (1891), *What Maisie Knew* (1897), and "The Turn of the Screw" (1898), along with some of his critical essays—James found potent literary value in representing his precocious young protagonists; found, that is, a portal or channel for an expansive and recuperative narrative energy in a difficult decade. For James, the nineties were years of loss and depression, of vocational questioning and self-refashioning, of removal from London to Rye in Sussex, and of increasing dependence on a mediating typist in his writing room. In what remains the only study dedicated to the topic, in *The Fictional Children of Henry James* (1969) Muriel Shine observes acutely that in the decade of the 1890s James "undertook a penetrating study of the young sensibility; and his gift to his persecuted young people was to be the gift of awareness."[2] In the end, Shine concludes that while James treats his "too watchful and precious" child-heroes "symbolically" and his children are "tactically engaged in giving formal expression to their creator's philosophy of childhood," he is also presciently attuned to child psychology avant la lettre.[3]

Tales of teaching all, "The Pupil," *What Maisie Knew*, and "The Turn of the Screw" engage the tropes of nineteenth-century childhood in relation to books and reading that I have been exploring in previous chapters. Especially concerning modes and effects of literacy, genres of literature, and technologies of communication, I will argue that James's young heroes do the work of a figure that might be described as a "medial child." In this rubric, I am drawing on Dorothea von Mücke's description of the "medial woman," which she sees operating in romantic tales like Poe's "Ligeia." For von Mücke, the medial woman, a mysterious, seductive character in eighteenth- and nineteenth-century tales, offers access for the male authorial protagonist to a realm of bliss, as a "conduit to an artificial paradise, a site of sensuous enjoyment without a body."[4] James's medial child, seductive, vulnerable, and fragile or ill, as the medial woman often is, similarly poses at the cusp between living and dying in a literal but also in a figurative sense, as she inhabits with temporal fluidity the transitions between life stages. Like von Mücke's medial woman, the medial child provides a channel to a sought-after realm; though these phantasmatic destinations offer different attractions, they each hold a promise of narrative fecundity. By "medial," in this formulation, I mean to specifically evoke the transactions and practices of what we now call "communications media" or simply "media." That is, in the medial child one would find, in varying degrees of explicitness, capacities of receptivity and containment, storage and transmission, of relaying and circulation, of connecting and mediating across space and time. In the late-century media landscape, in which telegraphy, phonography, film, and typewriting interrupt the exclusivity of print, the book-bound symbolic territory of childhood expanded. For Henry James—and his narrators—the medial child promised access to a reparative narrative mode, which, with the writing of *What Maisie Knew* (1897), his only major novel since *The Tragic Muse* in 1890, opened up to him what we now call his late style.[5] In what follows, then, I turn first to James's illuminating critical statements about the children's literature of Robert Louis Stevenson and then offer readings of "The Pupil," *What Maisie Knew*, and "The Turn of the Screw" as exercises in a kind of authorial rearing of children as literary property, with attention to what their child characters allow these narratives to explore and imagine.

"The Pupil," the "Boy's Book," and the Spectral Boy Reader

James's interest in children and childhood is usually located in his fictional narratives and their protagonists and in his evocations of his own childhood in the late memoirs. And yet in what is among his most valued and cited critical statements, "The Art of Fiction" (1884), James invoked his friend Robert Louis Stevenson's *Treasure Island* as an exemplary novel that "succeeded wonderfully in what it attempts." He contrasted it to Edmond de Goncourt's *Chérie*, which he regarded as an unsuccessful attempt to depict "the moral consciousness of a child," a subject, he goes on to say, that is nonetheless "as much a part of life [and hence of fiction writing] as the islands of the Spanish Main."[6] A surprising touchstone for James and a heuristic for his thinking about the genre of the novel, *Treasure Island* recurs in a striking theory of reading in an 1888 essay on Stevenson. Here that novel is figured as "a 'boy's book' in the sense that it embodies a boy's vision of the extraordinary, but it is unique in this, and calculated to fascinate the weary mind of experience, that what we see in it is not only the ideal fable but, as part and parcel of that, as it were, the young reader himself and his state of mind: we seem to read it over his shoulder, with an arm around his neck."[7] Adopting something of Stevenson's "imagination for physical states" that he admires in the same essay,[8] James vividly conjures a boy reader that Stevenson's uniquely more-than-a-boy's-book itself conjures, a boy with whom to intimately ("with an arm around his neck") share the reading experience. Perhaps moved by Stevenson's own interest in doubles, in this arresting theory of reading James lifts a boy out of the text to accompany his reading, as if folded into the "boy's book" is the book-owning boy ("Boy, his book"), a virtual companion and a channel into that "young reader himself and his state of mind." More than a mere genre marker, then, "boy's book" now offered up to the adult reader a prepossessing boy, who would "fascinate the weary mind of experience," just as Little Annie (and numberless other Victorian child characters) could. It may be surprising to find James engaged in any way whatever with a reading effect that might equally be applied to or encouraged by, say, *Little Lord Fauntleroy* (1886), whose protagonist notoriously revivifies the stony heart of his grandfather. But James is describing an effect on the reader more complex and mysterious than that of a fictional boy in a book, moving or engaging though he be (as James clearly found Jim Hawkins, if not Cedric). A certain kind of narrative, according to this theory of reading, produces an interposition between the skillful writer and the susceptible reader of a spectral third party over whose shoulder one could affectionately read, in an enriching triangulation of desire. This longed-for reading companion was not quite oneself in the past but someone better, a medium through whom to safely explore the joys and terrors of boyhood adventures. With "boy's book," James invokes the term of art for children's literature and its subgenres: a children's, boy's, girl's *book*. Though a conventional genre marker, the scare-quoted "boy's book" hints that it's the book *form*, the codex container, from which, under the right conditions, the specter arises.

The Houghton Library holds the copy of *Treasure Island* that James held (that held him) and that gave rise to the mediating boy reader.[9] This copy *looks* well read, with a swollen spine and pages thickened and stained here and there with use.[10] As *X*'s mark spots on the frontispiece map of the island, James marked " + " next to one passage, and commented on another page's "truthful detail" in a note written in the margin of the publisher's advertisement on the back page.[11] He signed the book, in his usual fashion, in ink on the half-title page, in the formal hand with which he typically marked his ownership of his books. But very unusually, possibly uniquely, he also signed on the title page, boyishly, in pencil, a mode of double signing that, as we saw in the previous chapter, children, but not adults, routinely practice. It's as if for a moment the "young reader" possessed the adult, guided his hand, and asserted his rights across time and space.

James's critical appreciation of *Treasure Island* and his account of his hypnogogic experience of reading that novel serve not only to expand what has been a too narrow understanding of James's engagement with the literature of childhood, they also undergird his narrative approach to children and childhood in the nineties. In 1892, a few years after James published this essay on Stevenson, he was invited to share his thoughts on children in an unlikely venue. The Board of Lady Managers for the World's Columbia Exposition asked dozens of literary and political figures to contribute "sentiments dedicated to little children by famous men and women," which were to be published in "fac-simile," to raise money for a children's building (Figure 43).[12] Amid such characteristic Victorian sentiments as "fill their little hearts with sunshine" (from President

Figure 43. By "children," this title-page image suggests, the editors mean "children with books." *Fame's Tribute to Children*. Chicago: A. C. McClurg, 1892.

Benjamin Harrison) was James's handwritten offering: "When he tried to figure to himself the morning twilight of childhood, so as to deal with it safely, he perceived that it was never fixed, never arrested, that ignorance, at the instant one touched it, was already flushing faintly into knowledge, that there was nothing that at a given moment you could say a clever child didn't know."[13] If James's *Treasure Island*–inspired reverie produced a theory of "boy's book" reading, this passage offered a method of reading the very child himself (a boy as it happens), in the long "morning twilight of childhood." James had recently published his tale of the abandonment and death of a child, "The Pupil," from which this striking passage comes, in *Longman's Magazine* in March and April 1891 (the only piece other than "The Art of Fiction" that he published there), and then in the collection *Lessons of the Master* in 1892. It's a tribute perhaps to the ecumenism of the editors of *Fame's Tribute to Children*, along with their need for well-known names, that many other contributions were just as unsentimentally particular, countering the general sunny mood; indeed, as a whole, the volume provides a rich and varied record of contemporary attitudes toward children and the idea of childhood.[14] The Lady Managers' editorial decision to publish in facsimile rather than typesetting the handwritten notes, sketches, and, in one case, musical notation, suggests a desire to identify the seeming freshness, authenticity, and authority of the authorial hand with similar qualities of Victorian childhood. Such autograph "tributes" transfer some of the aura of celebrity from the "laurel-crowned" to the children.[15]

That James responded to the request with a passage from "The Pupil" offers a window onto his particular relation to conventional terms of nineteenth-century childhood. James's pupil might find echoes in the young Henry James himself, but he is unlike any of the real or imagined students of previous chapters—whether projected objects of pedagogy or the imagined beneficiaries of Abbott's economic bildung or even the marginal scribes of Murray's school-books, though *their* wit approaches that of the tale's hero. James's pupil, by contrast, like most of James's very young protagonists, is marked not only by charm and intelligence but also by solitude and peerlessness, by his status as an only child even amid a family, and by his affiliation to a fascinated teacher. "The Pupil" narrates the affectionate relationship between a young Oxford-educated American tutor, Pemberton, and his precocious and frail student, Morgan Moreen, the youngest of a feckless impecunious clan of Bohemian Americans living in hotels up and down Europe; when the Moreens' inevitable financial crisis arrives and they try to abandon Morgan entirely to Pemberton, Morgan's fragile heart apparently gives out, and he dies.

While James evidently thought the passage and its view of children's mental life as capacious and motile suitable for the Lady Managers, the tale's first reader balked at the whole thing. James had offered it to the new editor at the *Atlantic Monthly*, Horace Scudder, who, though eagerly soliciting work from James, turned it down, in the magazine's first ever rejection of James over nearly three decades. The tale was, Scudder wrote to James, too long, "lacking in interest, in precision and in effectiveness," weak in structure; it concerned a "situation . . . too delicate to permit quick handling," for "with such a family to exploit I should suppose a volume would be necessary."[16] Leon Edel thought that "the prosaic Scudder" may have worried that *Atlantic* readers would "resent a story about an American family" like the Moreens or that Scudder may have reacted to "the possible hint of unconscious homosexuality" between Pemberton and Morgan.[17] But it's likely too that Scudder was reacting more specifically to James's pointed representation of children and childhood in the tale. Before taking over at the *Atlantic*, Scudder had long been a successful writer of children's books, had edited the *Riverside Magazine for Young People,* and while at the *Atlantic* would publish *Childhood in Literature and Art* (1894), his historical analysis and meditation. Scudder's own series of books about the cheerful and wholesome New England Bodley family—some of which take them to Europe, like (yet so unlike) the Moreens and the James family—contain examples of just the "obvious little Anglo-Saxons who had misrepresented childhood to Pemberton," to which "The Pupil" offers a counterexample.[18]

When, in the *Fame's Tribute* passage from "The Pupil," James cites "ignorance . . . flushing faintly into knowledge," he implicitly repudiates "innocence" as a term of art in the representation of childhood. But if he refuses to complacently identify childhood with "innocence," that "morning twilight of childhood" hints at a temporal and atmospheric enchantment that the figure of the child performs.[19] The very name of the child in question in the tale, Morgan (German *Morgen,* morning), suggests his potential as the subject—or even the embodiment—of a kind of aubade, the poetic genre that figures lovers' poignant dawn leave-taking.[20] Precocious and enchanting, Morgan Moreen is oppressed by poor health and a dodgy if devoted family. His tutor, Pemberton, through whom the tale is focalized, has been on one hand "beguiled, bewildered, defrauded, unremunerated" by the Moreens "yet after all richly repaid" on the other in his "subjection" to his young charge.[21] The temporal vigilance that James assigns to Pemberton in the "morning twilight" passage echoes the chronological dislocation that James often registers about his fictional children (if not only about them). The "quaint" or "old-fashioned" child is a sentimental commonplace by the 1890s; children's temporal labors became more onerous by the end of the century as they became discursive vessels of cultural and personal memory. "The Pupil" ironizes these terms: Morgan *isn't* "'old-fashioned,' as the word is of children—quaint or wizened or offensive" (153).[22] Not old-fashioned, perhaps, and yet as the tale opens, Morgan, aged eleven, had "the air in his elderly shoulders of a boy who didn't play" (134), and his "small satiric face seemed to change its time of life," sometimes "infantine" but also "under the influence of curious intuitions and knowledges" (135). As in *What Maisie Knew* and even more so in "The Turn of the Screw," presumptions about chronological age map unevenly onto the "curious intuitions and knowledges," the internal, receptive, and perceptive experiences of particular fictional children, in whom James reposes so much narrative potential.

For his tutor, Morgan evokes books, periodicals, and scribal labors, along with temporal dislocations. First Morgan was "as puzzling as a page in an unknown language—altogether different from the obvious little Anglo-Saxons who had misrepresented childhood to Pemberton." Like Hawthorne's Little Annie (discussed in previous chapters), Morgan is represented as both legible (in someone's language anyway) and book-bound: "The whole mystic volume in which the boy had been bound demanded some practice in translation" (137).[23] Like the passage in "Little Annie's Ramble," this passage too, in an analeptic prolepsis, telegraphs ahead in order to flash back:[24] "Today, after a considerable interval, there is something phantasmagoric, like a prismatic reflection or a serial novel, in Pemberton's memory of the queerness of the Moreens" (137). For his tutor, the memory of his time with Morgan is dream-like and disjunct, like a memory of certain kinds of reading. But the description poses an odd conjunction; how is a prismatic reflection like a serial novel? Both, like the original magic lantern's phantasmagoria, represent a whole through its pieces—the optical fragments arrayed in space of the prismatic reflection, the episodes aligned in sequence over time of the serial. Flowing along different temporal axes, both are medial and mimetic, not quite the "real thing" but reproductions and representations. And while the "prismatic reflection" is by definition recursive and self-referential, so in this case is the serial: "The Pupil" appeared serially, in fact, in two issues of *Longman's*.

If in obvious ways "quite alien to the spirit of the magazine," which devoted a good half of its serial space to novels "of action and adventure" by Stevenson, H. Rider Haggard, and others,[25] in other ways the tale obliquely participates in that crucial subset of the genre represented for James by *Treasure Island*: the "boy's book." Once Pemberton has been lured back to Paris for the sake of Morgan's health by Mrs. Moreen (after the tutor's economizing flight to England to prep a dull "'opulent youth'" for Balliol [161]), Morgan "talked of their escape . . . as if they were making up a 'boy's book' together" (166). When in the final crisis "the thing was a good deal less like a boy's book," the scare quotes drop and the boy's book gets violently rewritten as a crude reality when "the 'escape' [now cordoned off in quotation marks] was left on their hands" (170). Self-consciously reflecting upon its own genre, "The Pupil" offers itself as a kind of meta-boy's-book: it talks about boy's books, imagines a boy's longing to flee into one, and asks what boys really like. (To leap ahead to "The Turn of the Screw," would Miles, one wonders, have given it to "those he liked"?) While the "reversed conventions of the Moreens . . . struck [Pemberton] as topsyturvy," the tale reverses the boy's book's generic conventions: it's the tutor

Plate 1. Jessie Willcox Smith, illustration for "Picture-books in Winter," in Robert Louis Stevenson, *A Child's Garden of Verses*. New York: Scribner's, 1905.

Plate 2. Barnes and Noble Nook advertisement. Reproduced in "Tales of Reading in Reintroducing a Color Device," *New York Times*, 25 April 2011, B7. Used with permission of barnesandnoble.com, LLC. Barnes and Noble and NOOK are trademarks owned by or licensed to barnesandnoble.com LLC or its affiliates. All rights reserved.

Now there was a Miser,
　So surly and rich,
Did accuse our poor Madge
　Of being a witch;
Before Squire Trueworth
　The action was tried,
And he found her so virtuous
　He made her his Bride.

In the mean time poor Thomas,
　By sad tempests tost,
Was wreck'd at a distance,
　On a Foreign Coast;
The Indians however,
　Prov'd kind to the Boy,
Who in hunting and fishing
　His time did employ.

Plate 3. Goody, with familiars, accused, on the left; Tommy, anomalously rescued by American Indians, updating and possibly for the first time combining Goody and Tommy's stories, while bringing them to America. *Goody Two Shoes*. Baltimore: Bayly and Burns, 1837. Courtesy American Antiquarian Society.

Plate 4. This frontispiece has Goody in seventeenth-century dress. Note Ralph carrying the letter *B*. *Goody Two-Shoes. Illuminated with Ten Pictures*. New York: H. W. Hewet, engraver and printer [between 1855 and 1856?]. Courtesy American Antiquarian Society.

Plate 5. The back cover of this late chromolithographed version depicts Goody, with familiars, accused by "Gaffer Goosecap." *Goody Two Shoes*. New York: McLoughlin Brothers 1898. Courtesy American Antiquarian Society.

Plate 6 and 7. The poet Lydia Very published a die-cut edition, whose illustrations suggest a monumental and saintly Goody. *Goody Two Shoes*. Boston: L. Prang [between 1863 and 1868?]. Courtesy American Antiquarian Society.

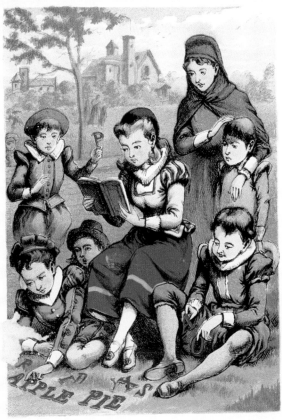

APPLE PIE
Margery Teaching.
order to comfort her, promised he would not fail to come back to see her, when he should return from foreign coun-

Plate 8. A young womanly Elizabethan Goody shows off her shoes, while children (notably all boys) spell out the traditional "Apple Pie," both a quotation from the original text and an invocation of the alphabet rhyme "*A Apple Pye*." *Goody Two Shoes*. New York: McLoughlin Brothers [between 1881 and 1882?]. Courtesy American Antiquarian Society.

APPLE PIE
The spelling Lesson.

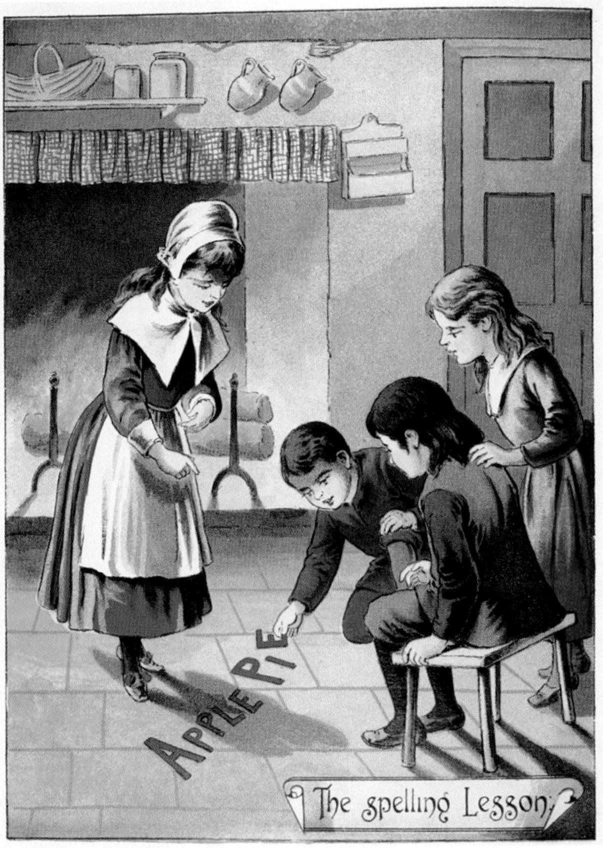

Plate 9. Puritan Goody and her "spelling lesson." In *Child's Delight: Cock Robin, Goody Two Shoes, Tom Thumb*. New York: McLoughlin Brothers, 1888. Courtesy American Antiquarian Society.

Plate 10. On their way to Bashaw Castle, the uncle takes the children to see "the Vale of Content," before revealing his villainy. Clara English, *The Children in the Wood: An Instructive Tale*. Philadelphia: J. Johnson, 1807. Illustration "hand-colored, probably by a reader," according to the American Antiquarian Society catalog. AAS call number CL-Pam E58 C536 1807. Courtesy American Antiquarian Society.

ed with elegant houses, and grounds beautifully laid out. On alighting from the carriage, they inquired the name of this delightful village. It was the Vale of Content. The beauty and good order of it were really remarkable; and, notwithstanding the number of poor cottages, there was not one beggar or idle person. Now, how do you think this happened?—-Because that the rich took care to assist the poor, and see that their children were well em-

B 2

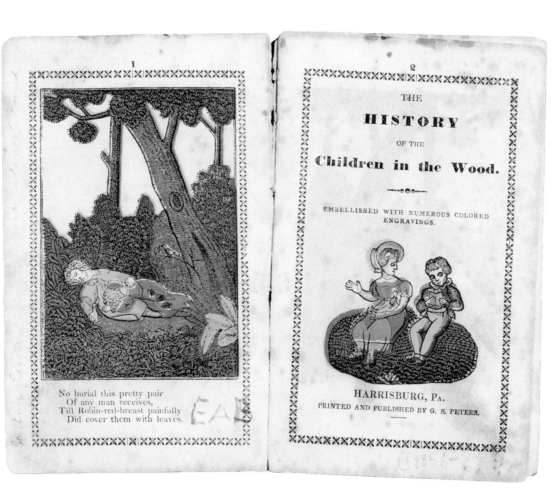

No burial this pretty pair
Of any man receives,
Till Robin-red-breast painfully
Did cover them with leaves.

THE

HISTORY

OF THE

Children in the Wood.

EMBELLISHED WITH NUMEROUS COLORED
ENGRAVINGS.

HARRISBURG, Pa.
PRINTED AND PUBLISHED BY G. S. PETERS.

Plate 11. The babes imagined as contemporary. *The History of the Children in the Wood*. Harrisburg, Pa.: G. S. Peters [not before 1834?]. Wood engravings printed in color, per catalog. Courtesy American Antiquarian Society.

Plate 12. Nineteenth-century babes, with dove-like robins. *The Tragical History of the Children in the Wood.* Philadelphia: Morgan and Sons [between 1828 and 1834]. Courtesy American Antiquarian Society.

The Ruffians quarrel'd on the Road,
One said the Babes he'd save
The other said that they should die
The reward resolved to have.

The Babes they both fied in the Wood,
To fight the Men began
One kill'd the other in A trice
And than away he Ran

Plate 13. Solomon King's engraved babes, imagined as contemporary.
History of the Babes in the Wood. New York: Solomon King [between 1822 and 1825]. Courtesy American Antiquarian Society.

Behind the rogues the babes were placed,
    And set out side by side,
Delighted as they went along,
    On horseback thus to ride.

Their pretty prattle, by the way,
    Made one of them relent;
That ere he undertook the deed,
    He sorely did repent.

The other being hard of heart,
    Was not at all aggrieved,
But vowed that he would do his part,
    For what he had received.

To save their lives, the milder rogue
    Did fight the other there,
And killed him before the babes
    Who quaking stood with fear.

He led the children by the hand,
    While tears stood in their eyes;
And, for the scheme which he had planned,
    He stifled all their cries.

For two long miles he did them lead;
    Of hunger they complain:
"Stay here," says he, "I'll go for bread,
    And soon return again."

Plate 14. By the 1830s, the babes retreated to an imagined historical ballad past. *Babes in the Wood: Embellished with Coloured Engravings.* Baltimore: J. S. Horton, 1836. Courtesy American Antiquarian Society.

TURNER & FISHER:–PUBLISHERS OF EVERY
VARIETY OF COLORED TOY BOOKS.

AFFECTING HISTORY

OF THE

CHILDREN

IN THE

WOODS

Deep seated in a flowery vale,
Beside a woody dell,
Stood Shrubland Hall, where says the tale
A worthy pair did dwel

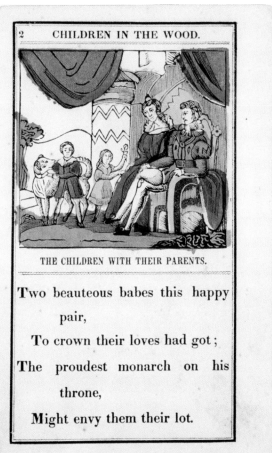

2   CHILDREN IN THE WOOD.

THE CHILDREN WITH THEIR PARENTS.

Two beauteous babes this happy
pair,
To crown their loves had got;
The proudest monarch on his
throne,
Might envy them their lot.

Plate 15. Staging the babes. *Affecting History of the Children in the Wood*.
New York: Turner and Fisher [between 1837 and 1841?]. A publisher
of "toy books," Turner and Fisher put the babes on stage, echoing
contemporary toy theaters, with the proscenium title page. Courtesy
American Antiquarian Society.

The parents anticipating sickness and death to overcome them, they summon their lawyer to draw up a will. The father having implicit confidence in the honesty of his brother, selected him as guardian for his little children. He amply provides for their future well-being: The boy £300 a year on arriving at maturity; and the girl £500 on her marriage-day.

Plate 16. The will signing represented in gothic revival style. *Children in the Wood* (Aunt Matilda's series). New York: McLoughlin Brothers [1875?]. The will signing becomes an object of illustration in some of the late-century editions, as in this lushly colored engraving. Courtesy American Antiquarian Society.

Plate 17. *Aunt Louisa's Oft Told Tales, Comprising Robinson Crusoe. Children in the Wood. Hare and Tortoise. World Wide Fables. With Twenty-four Pages of Illustrations. Printed in Colors.* New York: McLoughlin Brothers [1875?]. This lush chromolithograph illustration captures the Shakespearized and eroticized babes looking like Romeo and Juliet, hovering over, as though haunting, the Richard III–like uncle. Courtesy American Antiquarian Society.

THE CHILDREN DEAD.

Plate 18. Captioned starkly "The Children Dead," this image figures the babes in a romantic, erotic, theatrical Shakespearean fantasy. *The Babes in the Wood* (Little Folks series). New York: McLoughlin [between 1871 and 1874?]. Courtesy American Antiquarian Society.

Plate 19. Just post–Civil War, in a mash-up of Arthurian romance and Elizabethan fantasy, Richard Henry Stoddard reimagines the tale "Back in the days of good Queen Bess, / Old England's maiden Queen," and names his son "To bear his ancient name; / A young Sir Arthur, like himself." *The Children in the Wood, Told in Verse* by Richard Henry Stoddard, illustrated by H. L. Stephens. New York: Hurd and Houghton, 1866. Courtesy American Antiquarian Society.

Plate 20. Prolific illustrator Richard André imagines a gothic scene for the two babes dressed like the two princes in the Tower. *The Babes in the Wood, the Pictures by R. André*. New York: McLoughlin Brothers [1888?]. Courtesy American Antiquarian Society.

Plate 21. Fanny's redemption is signified by her book in hand. *The History of Little Fanny: Exemplified in a Series of Figures, Engraved on Copperplate*. Second edition. Philadelphia: Morgan and Yeager, 1825. "Metal-engraved illustrations are presumably by William Charles," according to the catalog record. Courtesy American Antiquarian Society.

Plate 22. The paper doll postures underscore the economics of Fanny's valorized bookishness: the book replaces the beggar's hat. *The History of Little Fanny: Exemplified in a Series of Figures, Engraved on Copperplate*. Second edition. Philadelphia: Morgan and Yeager, 1825. Courtesy American Antiquarian Society.

Plate 23. Little Eliza, like Fanny, shows her docility and claims her place in the home, by holding a book. *The History and Adventures of Little Eliza, a Companion to Little William; Illustrated with a Series of Elegant Figures.* Philadelphia: William Charles, 1811. Courtesy American Antiquarian Society.

Plate 24. Rainbow, an African American youth, signs a contract. The illustrations in this edition are all hand-colored, presumably by a child reader. Stories of Rainbow and Lucky, volume 5: *Up the River*, by Jacob Abbott (New York: Harper and Brothers, 1860). Courtesy Pat Pflieger, merrycoz.org.

The fireplace. Making the contract. Terms of the agreement.

was a small fire burning in an open iron stove, which had been built into the fireplace. The fireplace was surmounted with a broad oval funnel which turned at right angles, and entered the chimney just above the mantel-piece.

MAKING THE CONTRACT.

Rainbow took his seat by the fire, and then Trigget resumed.

"In the first place, it is understood that you are to carry the mail up the river as far as No. 5 twice a week—up Mondays and down Wednesdays; up Thursdays and down Saturdays, for eight dollars a week."

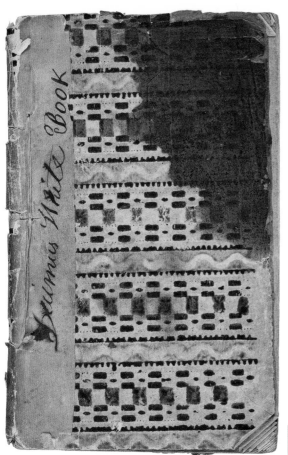

Plate 25. Decimus White inscribes his copy of Clara English, *The Children in the Wood: An Instructive Tale*. Baltimore: Warner and Hanna, 1806. AAS call number CL-Pam E58 C536 1806. Courtesy American Antiquarian Society.

Plate 26. *An Abridgment of L. Murray's English Grammar*. Boston: Manning and Loring, 1813. Laura Newton's copy, inscribed also by Nahum Newton jun. AAS call number Dated Books. Courtesy American Antiquarian Society.

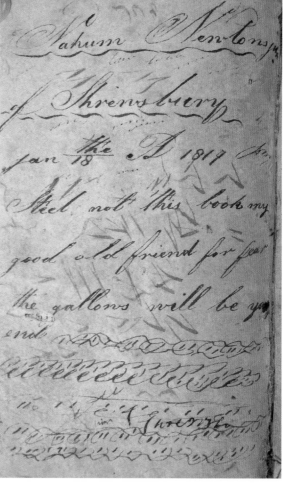

Plate 27. The Millers went to town on Lindley Murray's *The English Reader: Or, Pieces in Prose and Poetry, Selected from the Best Writers.* Fredericktown, Md.: George Kolb, 1819. Inscribed by Benjamin Miller et al. AAS call number Dated Books. Courtesy American Antiquarian Society.

Plate 28. Bright wallpaper cover preserving a tiny chapbook impressively entitled *Manhood*, and ceremoniously inscribed: "Lucy Drapers / property presented / to her by Miss / E Underwood," probably when Lucy (b. 1813) is about five years old. *Manhood*. New York: Samuel Wood, 1818. AAS call number CL-Pam M2685 N532 1818a. Courtesy American Antiquarian Society.

Lucy Draper's very good,

She picks up chips and brings in wood;

Washes dishes, makes a bed,

Sweeps the house and learns to read.

James Draper

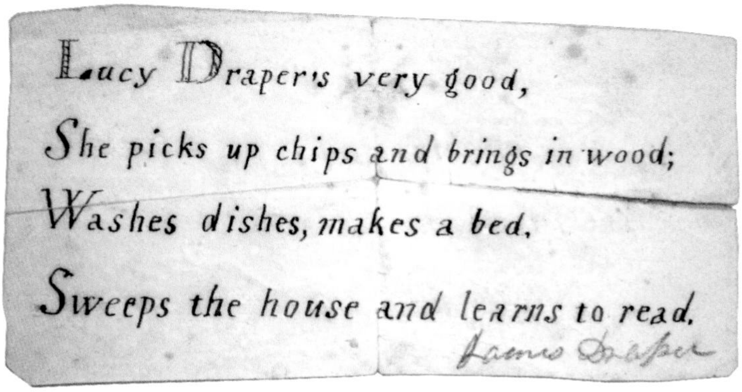

Plate 29. James Draper wrote this reading-ready poem for his little daughter. Courtesy American Antiquarian Society.

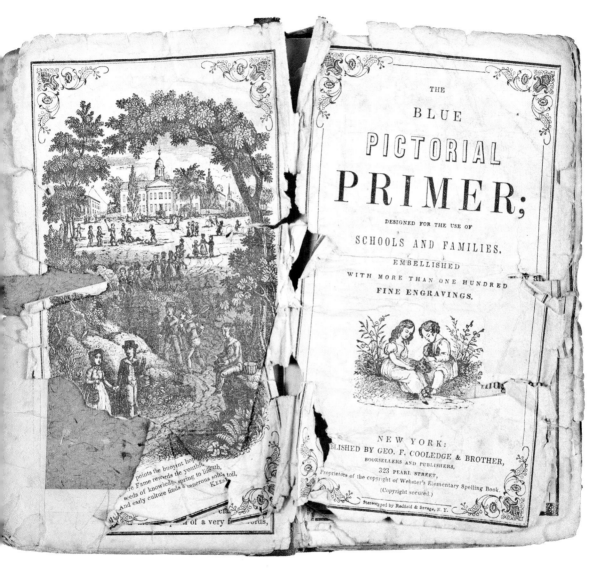

Plate 30. Edgar Anthony's tattered and torn *The Blue Pictorial Primer; Designed for the Use of Schools and Families*. New York: Geo. F. Cooledge and Brother, 1839. AAS call number Primers B658 P611 1840. Courtesy American Antiquarian Society.

Plates 31 and 32. Prudence Varnum's abridged *Grammar* protected and decorated in wallpaper. Prudence Varnum died at seventeen, on the same day (according to familysearch.org) as a younger sibling, which in part may account for the long life of her book. Lindley Murray, *An Abridgment of L. Murray's English Grammar*. Hallowell, Me.: E. Goodale, 1813. AAS call number Dated Books. Courtesy American Antiquarian Society.

Plate 33. Hidden inside Kate Anthony's brown-paper-wrapped copy of
Mamma's Gift Book, a set of homemade doll clothes. *Mamma's Gift Book.
The Little Gift Book. Winter Holidays. Christmas Stories*. New York: D.
Appleton, 1854. Inscribed to Kate Anthony. AAS call number CL M263
G456 1854. Courtesy American Antiquarian Society.

Plate 34. Seymour Joseph Guy (American, 1824–1910), *Story of Golden Locks* (c. 1870). Oil on canvas, 34 × 28 in. The Metropolitan Museum of Art. Gift of Daniel Wolf and Mathew Wolf, in memory of their sister, the Honorable Diane R. Wolf, 2013. www.metmuseum.org

Plate 35. Seymour Joseph Guy, *A Bedtime Story* (1878). Oil on canvas, 34 × 27½ in. Private collection.

who has run away with the "gipsies" (137); his employers are a "migratory
tribe" (140), a "band of adventurers" (146); they're like "strolling players"
(138). The tutor disreputably wanders the Parisian streets with his student, sup-
posing "they were looked at askance, as if it might be a suspected case of kidnapping" (144).[26] Stevenson's *Kidnapped* (1886), the notable "boy's book" hinted
at here, is the novel that James thought was his younger friend's best. The
fantasy that emerged for James in reading *Treasure Island* is echoed by the way
Pemberton remembers his time with Morgan—prismatically, phantasmagoric-
ally, intimately, and as a type of reading experience. Indeed, Morgan and Pemberton's mutual affection seems to me to have some of the flavor of James and
Stevenson's: the older man (James was forty-two when their friendship began
in 1885), authoritative yet admiring; the younger (Stevenson was thirty-four),
brilliant, enchanting, devoted, adventurous but ill, destined to die young.[27]

The genre of "The Pupil" tilts away from the boy's book at the close, as if a
sentimental plot, barely suppressed beneath the narrative, extrudes itself in the
end. As the denouement approaches, the "morning twilight" of Pemberton's
musing about Morgan's interiority becomes externalized in "the cold lemon-
coloured sunset" of the "splendid" Paris evening the two share before they
arrive back at the family's current hotel apartments to find that the Moreens
are being evicted (168–69). At the Moreens' "public exposure," Morgan "blushes
to the roots of his hair" and cries "tears of bitter shame" (169). The exposure
is at first financial and social, no small things to a young person; but when
Morgan's parents abandon him, "exposure" hints at its ancient infanticidal
meaning. To the revelation that his parents want to give him up to Pemberton,
Morgan first expresses "boyish joy," which James captures in boyish idiom with
a childlike, fairy-tale-like repetition: "'Do you mean that he may take me to
live with him—for ever and ever . . . Away, away, anywhere he likes?'" In the
flurry of responses to crisis in the final scene, Pemberton twice wonders
"whether he might successfully pretend not to understand," first for the boy's
sake (169). But the second time, when the Moreens abandon Morgan, Pemberton demurs in the face of the full force of Morgan's reality and the exposure of
the boy's humiliation, of his "gratitude and affection" (170), and of the boyish
joy that Pemberton can't in the moment bring himself to embrace.

In the startling pietà with which the tale ends, Mrs. Moreen "bound forward[,] . . . caught [Morgan] ardently in her arms," and then "still holding
him, sprang up." Pemberton "pulled him half out of his mother's hands" and
"while they held him together, they looked, in their dismay, into each other's
eyes" (170–71). If part of the shock for Morgan was that "the 'escape' was left
on their hands" (170), the shock for his survivors is that the boy's escape now
leaves them with Morgan stretched between them, his body literally on their

hands. Culminating thus with the mother's and tutor's hands on the boy, the tale has been interested throughout in things, including Morgan's body, that can be grasped and handled and touched.[28] In the final scene, Mrs. Moreen rubs her "plump white hands" together while trying to give her child away. Then, in his dying gesture, Morgan "raised his hand to his left side" (170). Earlier in the narrative, as Pemberton calls up his relationship with Morgan in his memory, it is only a lock of hair and letters—such "tangible tokens"—that keep the whole experience from seeming to have come from that phantasmagoric "dreamland" (137) mentioned above. In the "morning twilight" passage, Eric Savoy has noted the "spectral hand" that is implied there as well.[29]

As Michael Moon reads the closing scene, Morgan's body "occupies precisely the place of the dirty suede gloves" at the tale's opening that Mrs. Moreen draws "through a fat, jeweled hand."[30] Hearing in "suede" its English translation, "undressed kid," Moon reads Mrs. Moreen's gesture as expressive of an "erotic wish encrypted, mimed but unspoken, in the text of 'The Pupil.'" Moon urges readers to recognize "the access to 'perverse' energies that [James's] writing frequently affords us."[31] Gloves, with their suggestive skin-to-skin and penetrative intimacy, open the tale with an erotic charge, even without the unveiling of "suede."[32] As Mrs. Moreen draws her gloves "and, at once pressing and gliding, [she] repeated over and over everything but the thing [Pemberton] would have liked to hear. He would have liked to hear the figure of his salary" (133). The "pressing and gliding" describes the actions of her hands on the gloves but also forms a grammatical hinge to the question of money. "What Pemberton does not see at the beginning of the story," as Moon points out, "is that while his salary is not being discussed, his real compensation for his work—an invitation to desire Morgan—is being repeatedly issued in mime by Mrs. Moreen. His intense but unnamed relationship to her little son . . . will partake of the mixed character of her 'soiled' gloves."[33] Keeping Morgan with them had required first a nurse, then a tutor; the Moreens clear the ledgers by paying in kind, not in currency, for these employees' devotion. Previous chapters have found children willy-nilly engaged in economic transactions and their affects (victimized in the "Babes in the Wood" ballad, triumphing in *Goody Two-Shoes*, living and learning by them in Abbott's narratives, marking and valuing ownership in book inscriptions), sometimes with an implied or monitory erotics (little Fanny's *History*, "Little Annie's Ramble"). Here, in a kind of apotheosis, Morgan's attractiveness and lovability make him an intimate kind of economic medium: he pays for his own care with the caring of his caretakers.

In Robert Louis Stevenson's work James had experienced something enticing, a companionable and embraceable boy reader projected out of the book. This recuperative imagined child reader, emerging in the space between reader and text, would be a boy, one feels, who might have wrapped Morgan in his arms and leapt off into a boy's book with him. But as much as Pemberton hopes (in the "morning twilight" passage) to "safely deal" with him, Morgan Moreen is stuck in a James tale, a narrative realm from which boys do not escape with their lives. The temporal dislocations in "The Pupil," a signal marker of James's style as it develops in the nineties and beyond, speak to the impossibility of that boy-to-boy relation in the temporality to which it belongs. That is, it's belatedly fulfilling; yet in the moment, it was never quite possible.[34] For the reader of James's boy-killing tales ("The Turn of the Screw" is of course another one)[35] such a denouement feels like a punishing reversal of James's theory of boy-book reading, and in truth it is. There, the reading provides superabundant prosopopoeia—not just a boy *in* a book but an extra boy *with* a book, a medium through and with whom to enjoy the text. Here, in "The Pupil," the object of our affection by proxy is wrenchingly destroyed. What lesson to take from this strenuous tutorial? By contrast with what *Treasure Island* offered James, James's own narrative produces an unredeemable boy who has to remain within the text. "The Pupil," then, performs a gloss on James's observations about what happens when you read a "boy's book" by enacting what happens when you read a tale *about* "boy's books." For the adult reader of *Treasure Island* belatedness—reading at the wrong yet oh-so-right late time of life—produces a spectral, curatorial boy companion. But in "The Pupil," belatedness, figured in Pemberton's flashing forward to flash back as the narrative unfolds through his eyes and in his pained hesitation as Morgan dies, serves to entomb the boy in the text. For the adult reader of the adult tale, belatedness means it will always have been too late. No friendly ghost here. But along the way, James had begun the narrative and psychological explorations, through child characters and the evocation of genres of childhood reading, that he would turn to again, first in a novel entirely focalized through a child, and soon after in a tale focused once more on small pupils, presumed this time to be haunted by the ghosts the narrative raises for them.

Maisie, MacAlpine, and Master James

In the spectral boy that James had conjured over *Treasure Island* he had imagined a "young reader" offering an essential ("part and parcel") mediation between adult reader and boy's book. Here was a version of what I'm calling the "medial child," presented, in somewhat theorized form ("as it were"), as a reading experience, rather than as an element of a fictional narration. "The Pupil," I suggest, begins enacting this figure, as Morgan provides for Pemberton experiences that he analogizes to contemporary media: the serial novel, the magic lantern, the boy's book. But James withholds or perhaps disavows the promise that Morgan represents, making him into the tragic object of Pemberton's melancholic remembering. "Untutored and unclaimed" children, both boys and girls, continued to draw James as objects of inquiry, subjects for narrative experimentation, and laboratories for theories of reading throughout the 1890s.[36]

The depression following the losses he suffered in that decade—the deaths of his sister Alice (1892), of Constance Fenimore Woolson, and of Stevenson (both in 1894) and his discouragement with the theater (especially in 1895)— often turned his thoughts to his own childhood and to childhood generally.[37] After a hiatus of several years, which were busy with dramatic, critical, and shorter fictional works, James fully returned to novel writing with *What Maisie Knew*.[38] No boy's book here, in the story of a child of a bitter divorce; abandoned first by her egregious parents to her adulterous stepparents (her mother's dashing young husband and her father's wife, her own erstwhile young governess), Maisie at the end abandons them in turn, choosing to come under the protection of an elderly governess. And yet *Maisie* is, among other things, James's reply to *Treasure Island*. James had seen in Stevenson "an artist accomplished even to sophistication, whose constant theme is the unsophisticated."[39] Writing about Stevenson's *A Child's Garden of Verses,* James notes "the extraordinary vividness with which it reproduces early impressions; a child might have written it if a child could see childhood from the outside. . . . He speaks as a contemporary absorbed in his own game. That game is almost always a vision of dangers and triumphs." This could be a prospectus for *What Maisie Knew,* for what James wrote of Stevenson became true of his own procedure—that is, a "view of life from the level of the nursery-fender."[40]

In an affectionate reply in *Longman's* to James's remark in "The Art of Fiction," that he, James, had "been a child in fact, but I have been on a quest for buried treasure only in supposition,"[41] Stevenson had written, "Here is, indeed, a wilful paradox; for if he has never been on a quest for buried treasure it can be demonstrated that he has never been a child. There never was a child (unless Master James) but has hunted gold, and been a pirate, and a military commander, and a bandit of the mountains."[42] Written before James would have been routinely called "the Master," as he was by the mid-nineties, "Master" here tweakingly calls up James as a child.[43] If he hadn't been a boy as Stevenson defined a boy, he had nevertheless been a child, and never more so than in recollection, as when, for example, reading *Treasure Island*. In Maisie Farange, James created a hero whose experiences, all lacking in boyish adventure, allowed him to further explore the "geography" constituted by the "moral consciousness of a child" he wrote of in "The Art of Fiction."[44] In the New York Edition preface to *What Maisie Knew* (1908), James recognized "that my light vessel of consciousness . . . couldn't be with verisimilitude a rude little boy," since "little boys are never so 'present'" and "the sensibility of the female young is . . . the greater."[45] It's a poignant observation and would seem to cry out against the evidence, when one considers not only Morgan Moreen but James's own manifest sensibility and the degree to which he was to become the supremely "present" small boy in his later memoirs. But for James, the boy could only *become* "present" by being approached in the past, while little girls were temporally gifted, with the capacity to be present in real time.[46]

What Maisie Knew shares volume 11 of the New York Edition with "The Pupil" and "In the Cage" (1898) to make up "three Tales," combined, not strictly chronologically ("The Pupil" of 1891 is especially out of sequence), but thematically, in their interest in the vision and forms of knowledge of young and very young persons, and narratively, in their exploration of focalization.[47] They also might be said to share a response to forms of media and mediation. The character of Maisie offers to James the writer something like what that spectral boy offered to James the reader. As early as 1892 James began making notes for *Maisie,* envisioning the ways in which her stepparents would come into relation "through the child—over and on account of and by means of the child."[48] Nearly a year later, continuing to muse over this scenario, he noted that the "original parents . . . transmit the girl" to the stepparents, who "meet on the common ground" of the child.[49] James's preparatory schematics thus position the child as a "means," a "ground," a something that one can "transmit," as Maisie becomes the medium through whom the quartet of adults (quintet, really, counting the devoted old governess, Mrs. Wix) communicate and even intimately relate to one another. Her role in her author's life is analogous, as she offers access to a mode of narration that offers access to the consciousness of a child; and it turns out that such a mode becomes a model for accessing consciousness at all (Strether's, Maggie Verver's, and so on).[50]

After a preface detailing the legal outcome of the Faranges' divorce, *Maisie* opens with a glance back at "The Pupil":

> It was to be the fate of this patient little girl to see much more than she at first understood, but also even at first to understand much more than any little girl, however patient, had perhaps ever understood before. Only a drummer-boy in a ballad or a story could have been so in the thick of the fight. She was taken into the confidence of passions on which she fixed just the stare she might have had for images bounding across the wall in the slide of a magic-lantern. Her little world was

phantasmagoric—strange shadows dancing on a sheet. It was as if the
whole performance had been given for her—a mite of a half-scared
infant in a great dim theatre. (18)

Just as the "boy's book" emerges in "The Pupil" as an object of longing and a
space of escape, lending the aura of literary adventure to the scrappy existence
of tutor and boy, here Maisie's life experience is aligned with the popular print
genres a six-year-old (her age at the outset) might encounter. If not quite in a
"boy's book" she's boyishly still as much "in the thick of the fight" as a
"drummer-boy in a ballad or a story." Print genres might analogize Maisie's
predicament, but they can't adequately represent her visual perception, which
works like a magic lantern performance: she sees vividly and yet in a fragmented, prismatic way. The laying down of memories for Maisie echoes the
retrieval of memories for Pemberton. That favorite device—analeptic prolepsis—is rarely to be found in the novel. Maisie remembers things and sometimes
looks forward, but she never breaks the temporal frame of the narrative. We
never lose sight of Maisie, never see her leap into the future, from which she
looks back, nor ever become aware of her tale as a past from which she can
make observations that will inform some far-future reflection. The narrative
demands a temporality in line with the view from "the nursery-fender," as
James attends to the child's own "present" consciousness, the perceptions and
impressions that form it, rather than the traces that she leaves on other people's
memories or even on her own to be revisited at some future date.

James invokes nineteenth-century children's media—popular print, magic
lanterns—to capture the heightened, even martial, drama of Maisie's life. As
many scholars have noted, the enlarged medial landscape of the 1890s intimately affected James.[51] About halfway through composing *What Maisie Knew*,
beginning in February 1897, he hired the stenographer and typist William
MacAlpine to take dictation, which soon evolved into MacAlpine's taking
James's words down directly by typewriter.[52] James had made intermittent use
of stenographers previously, but this was now a permanent arrangement. If
thinking about and through the minds of children allowed him one portal for
narrative possibility, dictating aloud to a typist with whom he now shared the
writing room allowed him another, oddly congruent one.

The role of the typist-stenographer, though analogous to previous scribal
positions, carried distinct burdens. A typewriting manual of 1888 explicitly
reminded the novice, "The amanuensis must keep his ears open and his mouth
closed. He must remember that he is the hand and not the head, and that what
is entrusted to his brain is not his property."[53] The manual addresses the new

class of clerks and telegraphists, secretaries and stenographers and typists, literate knowledge workers, that had sprung up thanks to common schools in America and to the Education Act of 1870 in England. If literacy had once been a ground of self-possession, however, here the worker's mind, dispossessed, figures only as a safe-deposit box or a postbox—a space marked "to let"—instrumentalized for use by others. The admonition to become all ear and hand, stopping the mouth and keeping without owning the contents of his brain, extends the reach of the employer's property into the worker's mind, cordoning off a space there for use by the other.[54]

Critics and readers have occasionally suggested that the style of *Maisie* changes with dictation at about the halfway point; some pinpoint chapter 17, which coincides with the first of the few extant typescripts.[55] Others, attuned to the cultural significance of Maisie's stage of life, have pursued the particular narrative effects that James explores through Maisie and throughout *What Maisie Knew* that are possible because Maisie is a child. What I'm suggesting is that we think of Maisie as a child who shares with MacAlpine and the other new knowledge workers (a position that the title gives to Maisie too, after all) a self-consciousness about the ownership of the contents of one's mind. Without here undertaking a reading of the novel as a whole, I would like to note the ways in which James establishes for Maisie a "light vessel of consciousness," which his preface asserted as a crucial narrative value, along with her way of being "present," having "no end of sensibility" and a capacity to "see [him] through the whole course of [his] design."[56] The trope of the "vessel" identifies the child from the outset, when Maisie "was the little feathered shuttlecock" her parents "could fiercely keep flying between them. The evil they had the gift of thinking or pretending to think of each other they poured into her gravely-gazing soul as into a boundless receptacle" (22). Maisie's figuration as a container is each parent's "safeguard against the other." When one hurls an "objurgation" in response to a message Maisie delivered from the other, it "was a missive that dropped into her memory with the dry rattle of a letter falling into a pillar-box," and "as part of the contents of a well-stuffed post-bag" it was in turn "delivered in due course at the right address" (22). Thus it goes for Maisie "for a couple of years" (22), while the real letters Maisie gets from her mother, "wild" as they may have been, her father "chucked . . . across the room, bang into the fire" (18).

The narrative marks "a great date in her small still life," when Maisie understands "the strange office she had filled" (22). In the realization that she's being used as a relay between her vicious parents, she awakens to the appropriation of her voice—and her mind and memory—as instruments of abuse, and lays claim to the possession of her inner life:

> It was literally a moral revolution and accomplished in the depths of her
> nature. The stiff dolls on the dusky shelves began to move their arms
> and legs; old forms and phrases began to have a sense that frightened
> her. She had a new feeling, the feeling of danger; on which a new remedy
> rose to meet it, the idea of an inner self or, in other words, of conceal-
> ment. She puzzled out with imperfect signs, but with a prodigious spirit,
> that she had been a centre of hatred and a messenger of insult, and that
> everything was bad because she had been employed to make it so. Her
> parted lips locked themselves with the determination to be employed no
> longer. (22–23)

In one of the painfully few mentions of any childhood objects in Maisie's world,
the animation of cast-aside dolls captures a sensation of "danger." The dolls'
vivification arises not from Maisie's own play but from something uncannily
other; if dolls are a medium of a child's imagination (elsewhere Maisie plays
with her doll Lissette, miming her mother's waspish tone), Maisie senses the
menace in their coming alive out of sequence and out of place, separate from
her will. Like the dolls' frighteningly motivated gestures, Maisie's interiority has
been "employed" by others—put to use, like a stenographer's or a typist's or a
telegraphist's.

Maisie is always on the lookout for "the effects of so great a cause," as the
narrator puts it in the opening of the first chapter (18), and in this instance,
when she determines "that everything was bad because she had been employed
to make it so," she shuts down her little postal operation. In reclaiming an
interior space that had been appropriated by others, she is awakened to her
"inner self," which James identifies with "concealment." Maisie's gift of "presence" allows her first to refuse and conceal and then, throughout the novel, to
be conscious of being at the center of relations among adults, and to achieve
from that center a position and a point of view. "Presence," then, becomes
presence of mind, the self-possession that saves Maisie from the fate of James's
dispossessed boys, Morgan and Miles among them. When Maisie closes the
book on her parents she opens it for James; as this medial child redirects "her
little stream of life," it pours into the great stream of James's narration.

Reading, Writing, and Revenants

In the near rhyme of the title and the thematic rhyme of its off-kilter parable
of pedagogy, "The Turn of the Screw" continues James's pursuit of orphaned
or dispossessed children, and his rewriting of the genres that traditionally treat

of them—boy's books, ballads, fairy stories. (This tale's uncle and its abandoned, menaced orphans recalls "Babes in the Wood.") The opening of "The Turn of the Screw" plays upon a prevailing Victorian romance of childhood, in which the child acts upon the adults he encounters, by awakening them to their derailed or decayed emotions, a performance that James imagines only for the spectral boy reader conjured out of *Treasure Island*, who "fascinate[s] the weary mind of experience." But even of that boy it must be said that to "fascinate" the weary mind is not to refresh or redeem it, and the fictional children James positions in the place of the salvific child tend to fascinate according to the verb's oldest meanings: "To affect by witchcraft or magic; to bewitch, enchant, lay under a spell" (OED).

James offers up a style of adult-child dyad different from that of weary adult spiritually awakened by a child, in the first lines of "The Turn of the Screw":

> The story had held us, round the fire, sufficiently breathless, but except the obvious remark that it was gruesome, as on Christmas Eve in an old house a strange tale should essentially be, I remember no comment uttered till somebody happened to note it as the only case he had met in which such a visitation had fallen on a child. The case, I may mention, was that of an apparition in just such an old house as had gathered us for the occasion—an appearance, of a dreadful kind, to a little boy sleeping in the room with his mother and waking her up in the terror of it; waking her not to dissipate his dread and soothe him to sleep again, but to encounter also herself, before she had succeeded in doing so, the same sight that had shocked him.[57]

Here the child wakes the adult to show her something shocking and dreadful, from which there is no protection. If one strand of the romantic vision of childhood that developed during the nineteenth century posited a child that was a vessel of special knowledge that adults could access (partly by delimiting childhood as just such a zone of preservation), James's vision at the opening of the tale posits a child whose access to knowledge opens on to a scene of terror and dread that torques the figure of the soothing bedtime story into a night terror, reversing its direction from child to adult. Indeed, throughout "The Turn of the Screw" James cannily uses the Victorian fantasy of child as repository to expose its treachery—and not only for children. In response to the tale described in this opening, another guest, Douglas, ups the ante: "'If the child gives the effect another turn of the screw, what do you say to *two* children—?'" (1). This is met avidly, with "'Oh how delicious!'" (2). The opening frames a child's access to dreadfulness and terror as a narrative to thrill and titillate adults. Thus, the first tale that James composed entirely in dictation to his typist opens with an image of a "medial child," a figure that was emergent in "The Pupil" and developed further in *Maisie* comes more fully to life in "The Turn of the Screw."

The media environment from which the tale emerges surrounds the typewriter (invented in 1874 but not in wide use till the late 1880s)[58] with a distinct atmosphere in the 1880s and 1890s, expressed in the ephemera that immediately grew up around it.[59] Penny press fictions and sheet music from the period feature the typewriting woman as sexually available: "Kitty, the Typewriter Girl" (1894), for example, "plays click-er-ti click and click-er-ti click all day— / Before her machine like a sweet little queen, she passes the hours away, /—All the fellows they smile and call her the neat little pearl, / —She's ever so pret-ty, so gay and so wit-ty, is Kit-ty, the type-writer girl."[60] Kitty is the raucous and triumphant music-hall version of the sexually exploited typewriter girl who appears in romantic novels and tabloid fiction.[61] If these display the erotics of the machine age, along with the rapid gendering of typewriting decades before women actually outnumbered men in these jobs, another subgenre displays its enchantment. In occult fantasies, such as *The Enchanted Typewriter* (1899) and *Reciprocity, an Essay from the Spirit World* (1896), the typewriter itself becomes animate, generates automatic writing, and accesses another world, bypassing the operator, the typist, altogether.[62] In all of these texts, when the typist isn't figured either as all-too-irresistibly present, she is rushed off the stage disavowed, making room for the typewriter itself to directly record the thoughts of the dead, in modern "ghost complaints."[63] Labor—of both the typist and the writer—is effaced, or displaced, in these pop narratives of sex and death. In each instance the typewriting machine is represented as a kind of portal through which one can directly access an "other"—sexually, spiritually, or in some nec-romantic mélange of the two.[64]

In his own dictated correspondence during the first months of working with William MacAlpine as James completed *Maisie* and began "The Turn of the Screw," the typist appears as an emphatic and yet (like the telegraphist of "In the Cage" and the governess of "The Turn of the Screw") consistently unnamed presence. James feels obliged to comment on his letters' new medium as typescript rather than manuscript, and MacAlpine is sometimes acknowledged by the metonymic and servile, if entirely conventional, "amanuensis." Often he's conflated with the machine itself; "I dictate straight to Remington," James "writes" in a letter to his brother, echoing the conventional practice in which the operator and the machine were both called "typewriter," here substituting the brand name for the man's name.[65]

For James, during his transition from handwriting to dictation (he still handwrote some letters), the typed letter signifies a breach of etiquette in the cold withholding of the usually so-willing writer's hand. But the letters register as well, in their elaborations, the breach of the silent solitude of the workroom. Out of these violations of courtesy and of privacy, MacAlpine's presence generates narrative: James felt obliged to comment on the still exceptional medium of type, to infuse his letters with the clicks and ticks of the machine, and to remark by extension and metonymically on the presence of the typing "other." In the act of composition by dictation, James exposes his own intimate relations to MacAlpine; at the same time, he articulates his consciousness of the other inhabiting the room with him and struggles to efface him, creating an only half-suppressed ghostly presence in the letters.[66]

If the mini-narratives that frame many of James's letters from this period offer an *account* of mediation, they also should be read as an *artifact* of mediation by which the distant are brought near, or materialized, while the near are distanced or made invisible and dematerialized. One of the much remarked upon effects of medial shifts is the way in which new media imitate previous ones. A less often noted but pervasive effect is the "user's" (as we now say) nervous, self-conscious, and rueful abandonment of the previous mode. Thus James comments with elaborate, even enthusiastic, bewilderment on his *not-writing*.[67]

Before "The Turn of the Screw" arrives at the governess's tale of abandoned and haunted children for which it is conventionally remembered, its narrative frame recapitulates its scene of composition, reading like a dark joke on the practice of dictation. Folding in upon itself and upon the subsequent story, the frame brims with the self-consciousness of its own multiple media; in its elaboration of the media and materialities of its own composition and circulation, it compiles an encyclopedia of reading and writing technologies. Following the opening passage, Douglas says there's a *manuscript*, under lock and key, back in London. The story was *told* by the governess some forty years earlier; before her death, the governess sent Douglas the *handwritten* pages (2); Douglas took its *impression* "'here'—he tapped his heart" (2); Douglas sends a key to a locked drawer by *post* to his servant in London, who sends back the *manuscript*, which Douglas then *reads* to the party. His performance is not, then, a traditional festive storytelling, or a theatrical feat of memory or improvisation, but rather a kind of dictation, in the pedagogical sense of a *dictée*, from a set text.[68] Finally, before his own death, Douglas sends the manuscript to the narrator, who makes "an exact *transcript* of my own" (4). A dizzying series of deferrals and transfers[69] and a fanatical alertness to media—voice to script, to internalization, to a postal exchange of key for manuscript ("'I could write to my man'" [2]), to oral performance of the script, to the narrator's scrivenerish copy of the original manuscript.

Medially speaking, here are means and modes of inscription and transcription, copying and replication, circulation and transmission. In genre terms, James is tweaking the venerable frame tale, in which travelers gather to pass the time with storytelling, with an obsessive digressive attention to the tale's multiply mediated provenance. At the same time, he connects this traditional tale form to the mass-market genre he's actually producing for *Collier's Illustrated Weekly*. That story of "Griffin's ghost," with which the frame opens, is, the narrator says, "like the mere opening of a serial" (3), to which the governess's tale will presumably provide the later episodes. The frame narrative's tumble into the chain of mediations works spatially, as it traces the tale's itinerary, and temporally, as it transports us backward in time. The characteristic Jamesian deferral serves here to push the event of Douglas's reading into the future, but that reading, when it comes, sinks us into the past, to an earlier medial setting—characterized by writing by hand and mailing by post. We are in the prehistory of late nineteenth-century media revolutions, in the 1840s or 1850s, the Trollopian heyday of what Bernhard Siegert calls the "postal epoch," before the everydayness of the telegraph or—in this telling anyway—even of railways.[70] This is the temporal neighborhood of James's own childhood.[71]

In this mid-century, the provincial, cash-strapped parson's daughter, the unnamed "I" of the inside narrative, would have had virtually no other employment choices than to spend her young adulthood in the nursery and schoolroom. By the 1890s, she could become a telegraphist or a typewriter, leaving children behind with her own childhood and enabling new connections. The governess as well as her predecessor Miss Jessel and Jessel's consort Peter Quint might be read as MacAlpine's professional ancestors.[72] With the translation of the medial setting and its dramatis personae of the 1890s into the period of James's childhood, the riot of media in the frame identifies the materials and practices of composition with the materials and practices of instruction, as it maps the space of the writing room onto the space of the schoolroom and nursery.

When at last Douglas read, says the frame's narrator, he did so "with a fine clearness that was like a rendering to the ear of the beauty of his author's hand" (6). Douglas channels the "hand" of the governess through his voice. If the amanuensis is the human medium through which the voice passes into the hand that touches the typewriter keys, Douglas becomes the actor-like medium who revivifies script with his voice, suggesting here the spirit sense of "medium" as well. James invokes through this reversal his own procedure in the writing room; where the touch of the author's hand is lacking, James inserts the hand of the dead servant/governess. It's part of the joke that the writing hand was and is a signifier of authorship; as the "Master," James was often portrayed, long after his central mode of composition was dictating to typists, at a writing desk, pen in hand, in the ongoing cultural fantasy of the direct and silent solitary contact between hand and page. And yet as the narrator of the frame acts first as an auditor and then as a scrivener, James gives primacy to Douglas, presumably a Scot, like MacAlpine, to dictate the story, as though distributing its authorship among all of the transcribers. Douglas, like the governess, dies within the frame, leaving the story as a kind of legacy to the narrator, as the governess had left it to Douglas. While letters—alphabetical and epistolary—will take primacy in the governess's tale, suitable to its scene of instruction, the writing represented within the frame suggests wills, testaments, and legacies, in line with its allusive literariness. (For all the deaths noted in both the frame and the inside story, no one grieves or mourns—unless we readers do, with Miles on our hands at the end.)

Whatever else it may be, the inside narrative of "The Turn of the Screw" is a tale of teaching. Early in the narrative, before any spectral visitations, James shows the governess at her craft. The scene is set when, within days of arriving at Bly, she receives her employer's letter enclosing a sealed letter from a school headmaster, revealing that Miles has been expelled, echoing the enfolded media of the frame. Deciding to "open herself" (like a letter) to Mrs. Grose, the governess unfolds the letter to her, but when Mrs. Grose puts her hands behind her back, the governess, realizing that Mrs. Grose can't read, opens "the letter again to repeat it to her; then faltering in the act and folding it up once more" (10), she puts it away. This scene is brought to an end when "Flora, whom, ten minutes before, I had established in the schoolroom with a sheet of white paper, a pencil and a copy of nice 'round O's,' now presented herself to view at the open door. She expressed in her little way an extraordinary detachment from disagreeable duties" (11). In the tale's recurrent dual obsessions with the opaque materiality of letters and with the consequences of literacy, this scene of elaborate openings and closings, and of multiple dictations (in both senses of dictating), unfolds along a chain of command—the headmaster to the master (as the governess characterizes her employer) to the governess to Mrs. Grose. Flora meanwhile has refused to do her homework, as if to say (perhaps in attunement with Mrs. Grose), the letter stops here. Flora's appearance "at the open door" seems almost a conjuring act; she is drawn like an apparition to the letter the adults are discussing even though, Bartleby-like, she herself prefers not to copy her "O's," radically echoing Maisie's refusal of adult appropriation of a child's mind. The text makes up for Flora's lack: as though a repeated dictation, the vocalized exclamation "Oh!" appears, by my count, an extravagant sixty-eight times in the text.[73] In *not* writing her *O*'s, Flora is obeying the dictum of the entire inside narrative, which emerges from the injunction *not* to write: the Master's main stipulation to the governess is to "'never trouble him . . . neither appeal nor complain nor write'" (6).

With this perverse dictée, which recurs throughout the tale, James makes reference to and turns on its head the period's love of bureaucratic surveillance, of reports and papers and statistics, especially when it comes to children and education.[74] For the Master, these children, so richly and troublingly documented in the governess's narrative, are intended to go entirely undocumented. Miles and Flora, as Graham McMaster has pointed out, are orphans from India, a stock Victorian character, linked to the spoils of empire (which the Harley Street Master is said to have a supply of), to the exoticism of its races, and to the colonial enterprise. The desire of the Master back in Harley Street—to be left alone—begins to look like the opposite of colonial oversight: here the metropolis precisely does not want to know what horrors might be going on in the colonies. We might take this to apply as well to the colonizing of childhood itself, in which for all their surveillance, adults may not really want to know what children know, or to suffer the shocks of such knowledge.

Flora refuses to write, and Miles has been expelled from school, as if they're both becoming unalphabetized, opting out of the great spelling bee, refusing the discipline of the letters. Letters, of course, are inimical to children's utopia/dystopia (as J. M. Barrie also knew—Peter Pan can't read). If the tale seems to threaten to unwrite itself, still, as many others have seen, especially following Shoshana Felman's reading, letters drive the tale; but these are at-risk letters, letters left behind.[75] Among these are the letter from the Master, enclosing the headmaster's letter, which the governess then locks away in a drawer (as, in the frame narrative, her manuscript had been locked away); Flora and Miles write letters to their uncle, which are never sent; Miles steals the governess's letter to his uncle to find out what she says about him, which proves to be the same "nothing" as Flora's unwritten *O*'s. It's not that these letters are illegible; it's that they are unwritten or otherwise inaccessible, locked away or with hard-to-break seals.

While Flora's unwritten *O*'s translate into the cries of "Oh!" within the narrative, conversely many of the written but unsent letters in the tale emerge from varieties of oral dictation, in an echo of Douglas's reading out of the manuscript in the frame, which in turn echoes James's work with MacAlpine.[76] To send a letter herself, the governess discovers, the illiterate Mrs. Grose would have to *tell* the bailiff: and then "'*He* writes,'" Mrs. Grose says (59). Miles's sin at school was not that he took letters and other things, as the governess suspects, but rather that he "*said things*" (83, my italics) to those he liked, who in turn repeated them to those they liked. At play here is an affiliation of dictation with disreputable speech, like old wives' tales and, as the governess puts it, "the criminality of those caretakers of the young who minister to superstitions and fears" (45). While the tale evokes dictation throughout, strictly speaking only one person is said to actually "dictate" within the tale. Near its conclusion, when the governess and Mrs. Grose find little Flora mysteriously on the far side of the hard-to-traverse pond, the dead former governess, Miss Jessel, makes her final appearance. When Flora denies this vision, the governess responds: "'Of course I've lost you: I've interfered, and you've seen, under *her* dictation'—with which I faced, over the pool again, our infernal witness—'the easy and perfect way to meet it'" (70). The live governess accuses the dead one of putting words into Flora's mouth, just as this now dead governess's words are in Douglas's, and the governess's manuscript is in the narrator's hands (and *by* his hand, for he has transcribed the governess's tale), and James's words are in MacAlpine's hands. In reply to the governess's accusation, Flora echoes Morgan's plea to Pemberton ("Take me away, take me away" [70]), but hers is a wish to fly from, not with, her teacher. Later Flora continues to "say things" of a shocking nature, which becomes Mrs. Grose's version of spectral evidence (74). As someone immune to what Shoshana Felman calls reading and writing effects, the house-keeper is exempted from seeing the ghosts, but she can hear what they've dictated.[77]

In the inside narrative, then, writing is enabled by its prohibition and dictation risks being either shameful or scandalous, or both. "Shame," Eve Kosofsky Sedgwick writes in an essay about James's prefaces to the New York Edition, "mantles the threshold between absorption and theatricality"[78]—the movement, that is, from the inside self to its performance; or, in this context, from the private absorptions of reading and writing to the intersubjective display of dictation. At the same time, dictation opens the self to a potentially menacing eroticized transaction with another upon whom one is dependent.

In "The Turn of the Screw," the absorptions of reading are represented as being just as dangerously productive as dictation; indeed, reading projects the ghosts into the narrative. If the ghost of Miss Jessel is figured as having dictated to Flora in that final contest between the two governesses, Jessel herself may have originated as a specter conjured out of a book. In her influential reading of the tale, Shoshona Felman notices the ways in which "the ghosts are consistently associated in the governess's mind with the novels she has read," and they even "seem[] to spring out of the pages of the book" the governess reads.[79] Thus, the governess's reading of romances precedes the first vision of Quint; her reading of Fielding's *Amelia* precedes her third encounter with him. Felman positions these moments as ways in which "the ghost itself . . . constitutes a possible interpretation of the novel just read."[80] But if we read somewhat more literally, so to speak, more materially and artifactually, recalling James's experience with *Treasure Island*, we might see something else. Before her first encounter with Jessel, the governess leaves Miles "on the red cushion of a deep window-seat . . . to finish a book" (27). In miming the opening scene of *Jane Eyre*, the passage suggests as well what Miles is reading.[81] That 1847 novel had come to the governess's mind just after her first sighting of Quint, when she wonders if there was a "'secret' at Bly—a mystery of Udolpho or an insane, an unmentionable relative kept in unsuspected confinement" (17). Leaving Miles absorbed in his window-seat reading, the governess takes Flora to play at the pond, noting, "I walked in a world of their [the children's] invention" (28). While the governess's account of her other encounters suggests that reading raises specters for oneself, a *child's* reading might not only conjure but even broadcast them to others, a reading effect James had envisioned over *Treasure Island* here taken to uncannier lengths.[82] His encounter with what he regarded as the exemplary boy's book amplified the prosopopoeia that reading routinely engenders, and in doing so produced or restored a longed-for boy that belonged to another time. Alone with Flora, the governess soon "began to take in with certitude and yet without direct vision, the presence, a good way off, of a third person" (28); eventually, at the end of a long procrastinating paragraph, she "faced what I had to face" (29). As if a kind of residue of Miles's reading, the authorial governess's literary, historical, and emplotted predecessor rises up in the narrative.

When *Collier's Illustrated Weekly* contracted with James to write "something seasonable," a "Christmas-tide toy," as he describes the request in the preface to the New York Edition, they commissioned James's old friend and mentor John La Farge to provide the opening illustration (Figure 44).[83] The headpiece's double portrait of the governess and Miles in a clutch, mirroring each other, evokes James's theory of boy's-book reading. Here, the adult, reading not a boy's *book* but rather a boy directly, "with an arm around his neck," invokes not a companionable third party but rather a fatal ghostly presence (note the skeletal hand) that dooms the boy. That is, when the authorial governess encounters the small boy face to face, it's the small boy, with his knowledge and desires, who must be disavowed. Like Morgan, Miles, as an object of desire and as a desiring subject himself, can't outlive the telling of the tale, while Flora, like Maisie, exerts her self-possession to exit, and survive, the scene.

As the governess says of Miles and Flora, "'While they pretend to be lost in their fairy-tale they're steeped in their vision of the dead restored to them'" (46). James's narrative itself is steeped in the ways in which reading materializes

Figure 44. John La Farge, *The Child Magnetized by the Nurse*, for the *Collier's* serialization of "The Turn of the Screw," 1898. Watercolor, black ink, and white gouache on off-white card. Harvard Art Museums/Fogg Museum, Gift of Grenville L. Winthrop, Class of 1886, 1942.13. Photo: Imaging Department © President and Fellows of Harvard College.

the dead. These dead, however, as James writes in the note from which the story emerged, "invite and solicit, from across dangerous places."[84] Echoing Miles and Flora's reading, in his 1908 preface James called "The Turn of the Screw" itself a "fairy-tale" whose "charm . . . for the distracted modern mind is in the clear field of experience, as I call it, over which we are thus led to roam; an annexed but independent world in which nothing is right save as we rightly imagine it."[85] Occult fantasies of automatic typewriters dematerialize the typist but also imagine a source exterior to oneself for the production of text. With the interventions of new techniques and technicians of literacy, "others" are seemingly brought into existence, becoming a presence that the composing self might wish to efface. James's children, who, in their motile "morning twilight," share with MacAlpine a posture of mediation, register this awareness and provide narrative with means of exploring it.

The intrusion into the private, silent space of composition by another adult male required elaborate and yet narratively productive evasions. These evasions, as I suggested in reference to James's letter dictating, gave James the paradoxical freedom to not write: to tell rather than write, to divide the labor of the practice, outsourcing part of it to a kind of double. That the time travel of the frame lands us with the governess in the era of James's own childhood transmits the children as ghosts in the writing room in a chiastic exchange that might go like this: While MacAlpine, the intrusive yet inaccessible (because one doesn't want to access him) and yet crucial mediating presence in the writing room, transmogrifies into the workers in the tale—the governess and also the ghosts of Jessel and Quint—so the children in turn haunt the writing room, enacting what Eve Sedgwick describes in James's prefaces as "the writing subject's seductive bond with an unmerged but unrepudiated 'inner child.'"[86] Like Morgan, Miles succumbs to the narrative's consuming appropriation, by the governess or Quint or both. Like Maisie, Flora repudiates these dictations; if she has taken them in, she throws them out again, in the "horrors" that Mrs. Grose finally admits that Flora tells her (74).

The intersection of childhood with a newly mediated mode of composition allows us to see, through the filter of James's narrative experiments, the ways in which "the child" by the end of the century had become available for representing both the accessibility and the porosity, and, by contrast, the inaccessibility and opacity, of others. More than this, the particular fictive children I've discussed in this chapter ring some changes on the relation of children to reading and books I've been exploring. The theory of reading that James offers when he thinks about his own belated encounter with *Treasure Island* might serve as a model of one kind of adult engagement with the materials of childhood. This engagement has been described well by Carolyn Steedman in her work on the idea of childhood in the nineteenth century, which she traces through the figure of Goethe's Mignon: "In the literary representation of children this implicit understanding of human subjectivity [that is, *as* interiority] showed in the way the child-figure came to be used as an extension of the self, a resource for returning to one's own childhood, and as an image of one's extension in time."[87] In Steedman's account, "The child within was always both immanent, ready to be drawn on in various ways, and at the same time, always representative of a lost realm, lost in the individual past and in the past of the culture."[88] In claiming childhood as a literary property in alternating narratives of belatedness and presence James conjured medial children who provided models for the narrative exploration of consciousness—of the self and uncanny others—that at the same time testify to new forms of displacement and dispossession at the heart of late-century literacy practices.

Coda

Bedtime Stories

> I can see very distinctly the child that I was, and I know how the
> world looked to her, far off as she is now. She seems to me like my
> little sister, at play in a garden where I can at any time return and
> find her. I have enjoyed bringing her back, and letting her tell her
> story, almost as if she were somebody else. I like her better than I
> did when I was really a child, and I hope never to part company
> with her.
>
> —Lucy Larcom, *A New England Girlhood, Outlined*
>   *from Memory* (1889)

TOWARD THE end of the nineteenth century, a new custom of reading to children in bed was coming into fashion. The "bedtime story," the genre named for this practice, identifies reading with sleeping and dreaming, a nostalgic nursery fulfillment of the romantic ideal of reading as productive of both self-possessed interiority and self-loss. In his study of "the bibliographic subject" circa 1800, resonantly entitled *Dreaming in Books*, Andrew Piper describes that earlier process for the literary or scholarly adult reader: "To dream in books . . . was not only to dream *while* reading, to engage in a kind of hallucinatory reading experience in which the book itself was forgotten. To dream in books also meant to dream *in the shape of* the book as well."[1] As a neologism of the 1870s, "bedtime story" engaged romanticism's romance with books, which depended on the capacity of the material artifact of the book to allow for reading-as-dreaming's hypnogogic dissolution of the book. For "bedtime story" was first a print-genre term that emerged when Louisa Moulton began publishing stories under that title in the 1870s. The term took a while to catch on, and so did the practice. (The OED missed Moulton's books and gives a first citation of 1894.) Adults have been reading in bed—and occasionally going up in flames—for centuries.[2]

In the nineteenth century there's ample evidence for evening Bible reading and other kinds of evening social reading in the parlor, but scant reference to reading to a child in bed in any source, before the turn of the twentieth century.[3] A little earlier than Moulton, one "Aunt Fanny" used "Nightcaps" as the rubric for a series of books in the 1860s. That catchword didn't catch on the way "bedtime story" did, although, as historians recount, nineteenth-century children were often simply drugged to sleep with opium and morphine potions.[4]

What happened toward the end of the nineteenth century that brought books to children's bedsides? Two paintings from the 1870s by the British-born American genre painter Seymour Joseph Guy register the emergence of the new language and the new practice. In 1870 Guy painted *Story of Golden Locks* (see Plate 34). When he revised the composition, possibly for a private commission, in 1878, he scaled it upmarket, renaming it *A Bedtime Story* (see Plate 35).[5] Bedtime reading harks back to traditional storytelling practices, as Maria Tatar has recounted.[6] The bedroom setting of the earlier painting doesn't dispel traces of such age-old tale-telling around the hearth; the children's companion seems less a reader than an oracle for whom the book is a mere prop. In its reframing of a storytelling tradition, as well as in its Miles-and-Flora or Babes-in-the-Wood-like sibling pair, both paintings evoke and echo childhood literary traditions. But the later picture underscores the way in which it domesticates them, aligning the old wife's voice with a modern interiority, and reminding us that reading to a child in bed is one of the last locations of nineteenth-century social reading, with its affectionate bonds of what Richard Brodhead called "disciplinary intimacy."[7]

If, in its sibylline white-nightgowned reader and frightened children, the *Story of Golden Locks* invokes round-the-hearth fairy-and-ghost-tale performance, the book substitutes for that tradition's festive sociality.[8] Aglow at the center of the composition, the book seems a talisman, even an omphalos, as if uniquely producing the scene surrounding it. But of course the real magic of books by the nineteenth century lies in their ubiquity: the book reproduces the same scene of private communication in countless rooms, with countless children. The scene's under-the-eaves marginality and isolation, the asymmetry of the upright seated reader's and the prone vulnerable children's postures, with the oversized shadow the reader casts on the wall, highlight the erotic and violent instinctual realms associated with sleeping and dreaming.

As the scene moves from the world of garrets to one of well-appointed, carpeted private bedchambers, *A Bedtime Story* presages the cozy reader-readiness of the window seat in the Jessie Willcox Smith image, of some two and a half decades later, with which this book began. As the still wide-awake children have prospered materially, their affect seems to have shifted from the terror of the first painting to something more subdued and dazed, aligning a domestication or taming of emotions with the soft safety of their bedroom. As if defending against the more darkly charged nighttime realms, the revised reader of *A Bedtime Story* appears not so much well dressed as well encased head to toe in her clothing. She leans a little forward, angles her head and eyes a little downward, toward the children, and seems to lend more attention to the book than does her predecessor. Remove the storybook from that *Bedtime Story* reader, and the slight downward angle of her face and gaze might suggest not absorbed reading but rather the emotion of shame that shares with reading this posture, or "proto-form," as Eve Kosofsky Sedgwick calls it, of downcast eyes and bent head. Sedgwick has described shame as arising in "the moment when the circuit of mirroring expressions between the child's face and the caregiver's recognized face . . . is broken: the moment when the adult face fails or refuses to play its part in the continuation of mutual gaze; when, for any one of many reasons, it fails to be recognizable to, or recognizing of, the infant who has been, so to speak, 'giving face' based on a faith in the continuity of this circuit."[9] The bedtime ritual that brings the adult to the child's bedside functions to focus, contain, and channel the adult gaze toward the mirroring book, which mediates between adult and child, maintaining the circuit between them. In the bedroom performance of story reading, the older reader's eyes turn down toward the book, one that perhaps she read as a child, or one steeped in late-century nostalgic imaginings of childhood. As with other bedtime activities for adults and children in that era, the representational veil is drawn over these scenes, and with the exception of the Guy paintings, the scenes do not seem to have generated art or illustration.

If, in the uneven development that I've been pursuing in previous chapters, books and children became increasingly identified with one another, children's leisure time was becoming increasingly identified with books.[10] Now sleep too would become a space-time of the book. Certainly, sweeping technological and cultural forces were also in play: safer lighting in bedrooms; separate bedrooms for children; ever cheaper and ever more books; smaller families, with more leisure and more attention to particular children; regulated industrial clock time in home and school that increased a focus on sleeping habits.[11] Along the way, between the democratization of schooling and the spread of public libraries, store-bought books in the home increased their value as social capital.[12] So did middle-class children, safely tucked into bed, as distinct from working-class children who played in the streets into the night.[13]

But it was also that the space-time of childhood, newly sequestered, demarcated, and miniaturized—in such catchphrases as "The Children's Hour" and "The Golden Hour"—had a captive quality.[14] The bedtime story thus formalizes, through a literary genre, the extension of reading's reach into the night, and into dreams and the unconscious. As the child had become, by the end of the century, a figure for interiority, she had also become a privileged site of reading's reach circa 1900.

The Child in the Book

The book that Henry James praised as one "a child might have written . . . if a child could see childhood from the outside,"[15] Robert Louis Stevenson's *A Child's Garden of Verses* was one of the ten best-selling books for children or adults between 1875 and 1895 in America.[16] Stevenson's collection makes a lively case for itself as bedtime reading: seventeen of its sixty-five poems, some 25 percent of them, are about bedtime, sleeping, or being in bed ill. By tucking the child not into bed but into the book itself, the closing poem, with which I will close my own book, captures some of the troubling, and doubling, complexity of childhood reading in the period of its establishment as a cultural value (Figure 45).

To Any Reader

As from the house your mother sees
You playing round the garden trees,
So you may see, if you will look
Through the windows of this book,
Another child, far, far away,
And in another garden, play.
But do not think you can at all,
By knocking on the window, call
That child to hear you. He intent
Is all on his play-business bent.
He does not hear; he will not look,
Nor yet be lured out of this book.
For, long ago, the truth to say,
He has grown up and gone away,
And it is but a child of air
That lingers in the garden there.

Following the dedication poem to Stevenson's old nurse at the beginning of the volume, and five specifically dedicated envoys, this final poem capaciously addresses "Any Reader." And yet not entirely inclusively: this is a child reader,

VI

TO ANY READER

A S from the house your mother sees
      You playing round the garden trees,
      So you may see, if you will look
Through the windows of this book,
Another child, far, far away,
And in another garden, play.
But do not think you can at all,
By knocking on the window, call
That child to hear you. He intent
Is all on his play-business bent.

[124]

Figure 45. Illustration by Jessie Willcox Smith for "To Any Reader," in Robert Louis Stevenson, *A Child's Garden of Verses.* New York: Scribner's, 1905.

whom Stevenson compares to "your mother" looking out to see *you* "playing round the garden trees." Like her, "you may see, if you will look / Through the windows of this book, / Another child, far, far away / And in another garden, play." But, while the analogy suggests that "Any Reader" will have a maternal interest in that other child, unlike the mother, the reader can't get his attention "By knocking at the window": "He does not hear, he will not look, / Nor yet be lured out of this book." Because that child "has grown up and gone away, / And is but a child of air," he has become divided and inaccessible. Absorbed in his "play-business," the child within the book is both too busy with play to be "lured" and at the same time too spectral, a mere apparition of the child who has since transformed into an adult and "gone away."

Stevenson, in common with other writers for and about children by the late nineteenth century, articulates a disconcerting, displacing condition of book-ness, or in-bookness, of children. Here the child-in-the-book, which the child reader is asked to identify with—*there he is,* the poem says, *out in the garden, just like you*—is stuck inside the book, eternally absorbed in his play. *You,* the poem seems to say to the child reader, *are like the boy in the garden, absorbed in the play of this poem, but, in a moment's time, you will be irretrievable, even to yourself.*[17] Judith Plotz has identified in the work of British romantics, especially Wordsworth and Lamb, an idea of childhood as "sequestered" that "operates as both an adult imaginary kingdom and a research institute."[18] For such writers and their adult readers, the introjected child survives within the adult, "sequestered" and protected. What's new about the romance with books and reading by the end of the century is that the child reader is asked to perform this doubling on himself. "Read forever," as one e-reader's advertisement commands; apparently it's the only way to have or to *have had* a childhood.

Appendix

"The Children in the Wood"

From Sir Arthur Thomas Quiller-Couch, ed., *The Oxford Book of Ballads* (Oxford: Clarendon, 1910; Bartleby.com, 2001. www.bartleby.com/243/. August 4, 2009).

I

NOW ponder well, you parents dear,
  These words which I shall write;
A doleful story you shall hear,
  In time brought forth to light.
A gentleman of good account   5
  In Norfolk dwelt of late,
Who did in honour far surmount
  Most men of his estate.

II

Sore sick he was and like to die,
  No help his life could save;   10
His wife by him as sick did lie,
  And both possest one grave.
No love between these two was lost,
  Each was to other kind;
In love they lived, in love they died,   15
  And left two babes behind:

III

The one a fine and pretty boy

Not passing three years old,
The other a girl more young than he,
  And framed in beauty's mould.   20
The father left his little son,
  As plainly did appear,
When he to perfect age should come,
  Three hundred pounds a year;

IV

And to his little daughter Jane   25
  Five hundred pounds in gold,
To be paid down on marriage-day,
  Which might not be controll'd.
But if the children chanced to die
  Ere they to age should come,   30
Their uncle should possess their wealth;
  For so the will did run.

V

"Now, brother," said the dying man,
  "Look to my children dear;
Be good unto my boy and girl,   35
  No friends else have they here:

To God and you I recommend
  My children dear this day;
But little while be sure we have
  Within this world to stay.   40

VI

"You must be father and mother both,
  And uncle, all in one;
God knows what will become of them
  When I am dead and gone."
With that bespake their mother dear: 45
  "O brother kind," quoth she,
"You are the man must bring our babes
  To wealth or misery!

VII

"And if you keep them carefully,
  Then God will you reward;   50
But if you otherwise should deal,
  God will your deeds regard."
With lips as cold as any stone,
  They kiss'd their children small:
"God bless you both, my children dear!"   55
  With that the tears did fall.

VIII

These speeches then their brother spake
  To this sick couple there:
"The keeping of your little ones,
  Sweet sister, do not fear;   60
God never prosper me nor mine,
  Nor aught else that I have,
If I do wrong your children dear
  When you are laid in grave!"

IX

The parents being dead and gone,   65
  The children home he takes,
And brings them straight unto his house,
  Where much of them he makes.
He had not kept these pretty babes
  A twelvemonth and a day,   70
But, for their wealth, he did devise
  To make them both away.

X

He bargain'd with two ruffians strong,
  Which were of furious mood,
That they should take these children young, 75
  And slay them in a wood.
He told his wife an artful tale:
  He would the children send
To be brought up in London town
  With one that was his friend.   80

XI

Away then went those pretty babes,
  Rejoicing at that tide,
Rejoicing with a merry mind
  They should on cock-horse ride.
They prate and prattle pleasantly,   85
  As they ride on the way,
To those that should their butchers be
  And work their lives' decay:

XII

So that the pretty speech they had
  Made Murder's heart relent;   90
And they that undertook the deed
  Full sore did now repent.
Yet one of them, more hard of heart,

Did vow to do his charge,
Because the wretch that hirèd him   95
  Had paid him very large.

XIII

The other won't agree thereto,
  So here they fall to strife;
With one another they did fight
  About the children's life: 100
And he that was of mildest mood
  Did slay the other there,
Within an unfrequented wood.—
  The babes did quake for fear!

XIV

He took the children by the hand,   105
  Tears standing in their eye,
And bade them straightway follow him,
  And look they did not cry;
And two long miles he led them on,
  While they for food complain: 110
"Stay here," quoth he; "I'll bring you bread
  When I come back again."

XV

These pretty babes, with hand in hand,
  Went wandering up and down;
But never more could see the man   115
  Approaching from the town.
Their pretty lips with blackberries
  Were all besmear'd and dyed;
And when they saw the darksome night,
  They sat them down and cried.   120

XVI

Thus wander'd these poor innocents,
  Till death did end their grief;

In one another's arms they died,
  As wanting due relief:
No burial this pretty pair   125
  From any man receives,
Till Robin Redbreast piously
  Did cover them with leaves.

XVII

And now the heavy wrath of God
  Upon their uncle fell;   130
Yea, fearful fiends did haunt his house,
  His conscience felt an hell:
His barns were fired, his goods consumed,
  His lands were barren made,
His cattle died within the field,   135
  And nothing with him stay'd.

XVIII

And in a voyage to Portugal
  Two of his sons did die;
And, to conclude, himself was brought
  To want and misery: 140
He pawn'd and mortgaged all his land
  Ere seven years came about.
And now at last his wicked act
  Did by this means come out.

XIX

The fellow that did take in hand   145
  These children for to kill,
Was for a robbery judged to die,
  Such was God's blessed will:
Who did confess the very truth,
  As here hath been display'd: 150
The uncle having died in jail,
  Where he for debt was laid.

XX

You that executors be made,
  And overseërs eke,
Of children that be fatherless,   155
  And infants mild and meek,
Take you example by this thing,
  And yield to each his right,
Lest God with suchlike misery
  Your wicked minds requite.   160

Notes

Introduction

1. As Andrew Piper was the most recent to point out, "Everything that has been said about life in an online world has already been said about books"—and, one might add, about just about every other form of media. *Book There Was: Reading in Electronic Times* (Chicago: University of Chicago Press, 2012), xi.

2. Belletristic memoirs of course often invoke childhood reading. But major scholarship on the history of books and reading in the main overlooks childhood reading beyond occasional explicit considerations of schooling. See, for example, the five-volume *History of the Book in America* (Chapel Hill: University of North Carolina Press, 2010).

3. In the nineteenth century, the imperative that *all* children read is of course only a postemancipation one, and even then thwarted for many African Americans during Jim Crow.

4. See Sarah Dowhower's "Picturing the Word: A Literacy Odyssey in Paintings of Children, Youth, and Families" for a survey of some of these images (*American Reading Forum Online Yearbook, 22*. Retrieved May 13, 2009, http://americanreadingforum.org/Yearbooks/02_yearbook/html/06_Dowhower_final.htm).

5. Garrett Stewart, *The Look of Reading: Book, Painting, Text* (Chicago: University of Chicago Press, 2006). I am indebted to Stewart's wonderfully observed insights about and attention to postures, places, and spaces of adult reading represented in easel painting. See also Kate Flint, *The Woman Reader, 1837–1914* (New York: Oxford University Press, 1995).

6. Published as "A Girl Reading" in "The Classics Collection" of "The Museums & Galleries Collection," copyright Trustees of the National Library of Scotland.

7. For example, the Amherst College journal had a section called "The Window-Seat": "In my window-seat . . . you can chat with our friends in the room, . . . enjoy the hills and valleys and sunsets, . . . indulge in long *tête-à-têtes* with your favorite authors, you can dream your favorite dreams." *Amherst Sketches: Being Selections of Light Prose from the Amherst Literary Monthly*, ed. Leroy Phillips and Robert Stuart Smith (Amherst, 1892), 7.

8. In an apparently much-reprinted article, Leigh Hunt is referred to as a writer of "parlor-window-seat" books. *Chambers Edinburgh Journal*, August 7, 1847, vols. 7–8, 96.

9. Garrett Stewart notes that the "cross-barred window is a nearly inexhaustible trope in the scene of reading" and that "windows are simply the most pronounced of escape hatches from the intimate to the undelimited. . . . From inside a closed space, they delineate ocular access, . . . for vision and the mind's eye . . . They offer the continuous presence of reading's other scene." Stewart, *The Look of Reading*, 173, 166.

10. The image shares the "leisured stasis" that Garrett Stewart ascribes to Renoir images of reading. *The Look of Reading*, 198.

11. I borrow the notion of such a posture as a "hieroglyph" from Garrett Stewart in *The Look of Reading*. It may go without saying that the kind of myth I mean is the kind Roland Barthes outlined in *Mythologies* (trans. Annette Lavers [New York: Farrar, Straus and Giroux, 1972]).

12. Gillian Brown sees the absorbed child as a key figure for sentimentality: "From the nineteenth century American discourse about children and absorption to which sentimental fiction significantly contributed, children emerge as emblems of both penetrability and impenetrability, figures for the states that absorption entails." "Child's Play," *Differences: A Journal of Feminist Cultural Studies* 11.3 (1999–2000), 80.

13. Jonathan Crary notes, contra Walter Benjamin's notion of "reception in a state of distraction," that "modern distraction was *not* a disruption of stable or 'natural' kinds of sustained, value-laden perception that had existed for centuries but was an *effect*, and in many cases a constituent element, of the many attempts to produce attentiveness in human subjects." For Crary "attention and distraction cannot be thought outside of a continuum in which the two ceaselessly flow into one another, as part of a social field in which the same imperatives and forces incite one another." *Suspensions of Perception: Attention, Spectacle and Modern Culture* (Cambridge, Mass.: MIT Press, 2001), 49, 51.

14. Judith Plotz describes the figure of the child that male romantic writers made into a "vocation" or a "habitat" in *Romanticism and the Vocation of Childhood* (New York: Palgrave Macmillan, 2001). For a compelling account of the origins of romantic reading practices and "bibliographic subjectivity" see Andrew Piper, *Dreaming in Books: The Making of the Bibliographic Imagination in the Romantic Age* (Chicago: University of Chicago Press, 2009).

15. Nook advertisement, illustrating an article in the business section of the *New York Times* online, "Tales of Reading in Reintroducing a Color Device," April 25, 2011. (Because the verb "to read" marks its tense by changing its sound but not its spelling, the ad's "Read Forever" might be—even more ominously—in the past tense.) Amazon's Kindle similarly deploys a textual figure for childhood reading, in the "once upon a time" that appears on the zipper pull tabs in all of its packaging. Nicholson Baker described opening a new Kindle: "I'd entered some nesting Italo Calvino folktale world of packaging." "A New Page," *New Yorker*, August 3, 2009, 25.

16. See my "Postures and Places: The Child Reader in Nineteenth-Century U.S. Popular Print" (*ELH* 80:2 [Summer 201], 343–372) for a survey of visual imagery of child readers in the nineteenth century, and "Reading Childishly? A Codicology of the Modern Self," in *Comparative Textual Media: Transforming the Humanities in the Postprint Era,* ed. N. Katherine Hayles and Jessica Pressman (Minneapolis: University of Minnesota Press, 2013), 155–182, for an argument about the link between the codex form, child readers, and ideas of subjectivity.

17. Ann Wierda Rowland's *Romanticism and Childhood: The Infantilization of British Literary Culture* (Cambridge: Cambridge University Press, 2012) offers a very fine roundup of the scholarship on "the discovery of childhood" in its introduction (6–12). See also thorough introductions in Susan Honeyman, *Elusive Childhood: Impossible Representations in Modern Fiction* (Columbus: Ohio State University Press, 2005) and Ellen Pifer, *Demon or Doll: Images of the Child in Contemporary Writing and Culture* (Charlottesville: University of Virginia Press, 2000).

18. John Locke, *Second Treatise* in *Two Treatises of Government,* ed. Peter Laslett (Cambridge: Cambridge University Press, 1960), 287.

19. Gillian Brown, *Consent of the Governed: The Lockean Legacy in Early American Culture* (Cambridge, Mass.: Harvard University Press, 2001), 30.

20. Brown, *Consent of the Governed,* 19. Brown cites the Locke quotation, book IV, 74, 17; with chapter, section, lines, and pagination in Locke, *Second Treatise,* ed. Laslett, 335.

21. Courtney Weikle-Mills, "'Learn to Love Your Book': The Child Reader and Affectionate Citizenship," *Early American Literature* 43:1 (2008), 35–61, 43.

22. See, for example, Pierre Bourdieu, "Forms of Capital," in John Richardson, ed., *Handbook of Theory and Research for the Sociology of Education* (Westport, Conn.: Greenwood, 1986), 241–58. See also John Guillory on cultural capital in the literary field in *Cultural Capital: The Problem of Literary Canon Formation* (Chicago: University of Chicago Press, 1993).

23. I take this useful category from Peter Stearns's historical survey, *Childhood in World History* (New York: Routledge, 2006). As Stearns describes the evolution of the "modern model," the pivotal shift was "from work to schooling," which "meant, as many parents quickly realized, that children turned from being . . . economic assets, to becoming absolute economic liabilities" (55). For a later

period, the sociologist Viviana Zelizer has examined the shift in the child's economic status in the family, in effect from producer to consumer of resources (*Pricing the Priceless Child: The Changing Social Value of Children* [Princeton: Princeton University Press, 1994]).

24. Amy Dru Stanley, *From Bondage to Contract: Wage Labor, Marriage, and the Market in the Age of Slave Emancipation* (Chicago: University of Chicago Press, 1998).

25. Carole Pateman, *The Sexual Contract* (Cambridge: Polity Press, 1988), 1.

26. Pateman, *The Sexual Contract,* 5.

27. In the formulation "literacy contract," I am indebted to the work of Carole Pateman and of Charles Mills, whose "sexual contract" and "racial contract," respectively, have been outlined in their books of those titles (Pateman, *The Sexual Contract,* and Mills, *The Racial Contract* [Ithaca: Cornell University Press, 1999]), and also in their shared collection of essays, *Contract and Domination* (Cambridge: Polity, 2007). I am indebted further both to Courtney Weikle-Mills's brilliant elaborations of "affectionate citizenship" and "republican childhood" and to Gillian Brown's analysis of the emergence and significance of Lockean consent in the print artifacts of childhood. "Reading," Brown writes, "thus crucially helped generate American national identity by circulating and typifying the acts of understanding in which Locke had anchored consent, the political principle by which a people forms and authorizes its government." *Consent of the Governed,* 4.

28. As far as the actual contracts that children could legally engage in, according to Holly Brewer, in English law children's "ability to bind themselves by their own consent is clearest with respect to their ability to bind themselves, their own bodies, in labor contracts" (242); in common law, in the colonies and in the new nation, children's ability to enter into contracts was restricted by age, and the specifics varied widely by region, by rank, and by nature of the contract. Brewer, *By Birth or Consent: Children, Law, and the Anglo-American Revolution in Authority* (Chapel Hill: University of North Carolina Press, 2007), 238–46. In the eighteenth century jurors had to be older than fourteen (and also had to be property owners) in Virginia and Pennsylvania; only after the Revolution was twenty-one established as a minimum age for jurors (Brewer, 142–49), and as a standard of "maturity." See also Caroline Levander's review article, "Consenting Fictions, Fictions of Consent," *American Literary History* 16:2 (2004), 318–38, and related chapter in *Cradle of Liberty: Race, the Child, and National Belonging from Thomas Jefferson to W. E. B. Du Bois* (Durham: Duke University Press, 2006), 78–110.

29. See Brewer, *By Birth or Consent,* 184, for "benefit of clergy."

30. Cheryl I. Harris, "Whiteness as Property," *Harvard Law Review* 106 (June 1993), 1715.

31. Viviana Zelizer notes the postbellum shift to the widespread affectionately valued child. Indeed, after emancipation, it's as if self-possession as a value changed when there was nothing left to contrast it to.

32. For "literacy," see Raymond Williams, *Keywords: A Vocabulary of Culture and Society, s.v.* "literature." For "childhood," see Karen Sánchez-Eppler, "Childhood," in *Keywords for Children's Literature,* ed. Philip Nel and Lissa Paul (New York: New York University Press, 2011), 35–41.

33. The OED's first citation for "literacy" is from an 1883 item in the *New England Journal of Education* blaming a statistical decrease in literacy rates in Massachusetts on immigration. For a genealogy of the term, see my "New Histories of Literacy" in *A Companion to the History of the Book,* ed. Simon Eliot and Jonathan Rose (London: Blackwell, 2007), 467–79,

34. Carolyn Steedman, *Strange Dislocations: Childhood and the Idea of Human Interiority, 1780–1930* (Cambridge, Mass.: Harvard University Press, 1995), 5.

35. In the "medial child," I echo and gratefully acknowledge Dorothea von Mücke's formulation of the "medial woman" in romantic tales like Poe's "Ligeia," which I describe in more detail in Chapter 6. *The Seduction of the Occult and the Rise of the Fantastic Tale* (Stanford: Stanford University Press, 2003), 148.

36. Clara English, *The Children in the Wood* (Baltimore, 1806), 45, 46–47.

37. For brilliant elaborations of the romantic idea of childhood, see Plotz, *Romanticism and the Vocation of Childhood,* and Rowland, *Romanticism and Childhood.*

38. D. W. Winnicott, "Transitional Objects and Transitional Phenomena," in *Playing and Reality* (New York: Routledge, 1971), 1–34.

39. Shoshona Felman, "Turning the Screw of Interpretation," *Yale French Studies* 55–56 (1977), 94–207.

40. *The Notebooks of Henry James*, ed. F. O. Matthiessen and Kenneth B. Murdock (Chicago: University of Chicago Press, 1947, 1981), 178.

41. Carolyn Steedman, *Past Tenses: Essays on Writing, Autobiography and History* (London: Rivers Oram Press, 1992), 129.

42. Steedman, *Strange Dislocations*, 12.

Chapter 1. Literacy, Commodities, and Cultural Capital

Epigraph. Anthony Trollope, *An Autobiography* (1883; New York: Oxford University Press, 2008), 323.

1. Unless otherwise noted, I will be referring to *Goody Two-Shoes: A Facsimile Reproduction of the Edition of 1766.* Intro. Charles Welsh (Detroit: Singing Tree Press, 1970). This is the London Third Edition, published by John Newbery, which early American editions follow closely. Subsequent page references appear parenthetically in the text.

2. The history of the catchphrase has been difficult to trace. *Brewer's Dictionary* naturally attributes it to the novel, but it seems unlikely that the expression had currency before the mid- to late nineteenth century, and probably evolved from pantomimes and sentimental versions of the novel. Adam Ant and Elvis Costello have built lyrics around "Goody Two-Shoes," which remains a vital element of popular speech.

3. Isaac Kramnick, *Republicanism and Bourgeois Radicalism: Political Ideology in Late Eighteenth-Century England and America* (Ithaca: Cornell University Press, 1990). Ronald Paulson reads the novel in a chapter on children's literature in *The Beautiful, Novel, and Strange*, which sees the child as "an intriguing but strange . . . subject matter for writers . . . with the built-in poignance of victimization and the nostalgia for a freedom from 'custom, or borrowed opinions' of the Lockean child in pursuit of the word"; his reading is especially alert to the narrative effects of alphabetization. *The Beautiful, Novel, and Strange: Aesthetics and Heterodoxy* (Baltimore: Johns Hopkins University Press, 1966), 197. Jan Fergus's interest in Goody emerges from her analysis of "the bookselling records of the Clays of Daventry, Rugby, Lutterworth, and Warwick," in which she finds that *Goody* is a big seller to the boys at Rugby and speculates interestingly about the model of subjectivity the novel presents. Fergus, *Provincial Readers in Eighteenth-Century England* (New York: Oxford University Press, 2006), 139. Martin Kayman reads Goody as "an agent for Lockean culture" who reclaims imaginative and legal rights of possession; "Lawful Possession: Violence, The Polite Imagination and Goody Two-Shoes," in *Violência e possessão: Estudos ingleses contemporâneos*, ed. David Callahan et al. (Aveiro: Universidade de Aveiro, 1998), 21–28, 24. Seniel Lucien offers a sensitive and acute psychoanalytic reading; see "Little Goody Two-Shoes: An Early Model of Child Development," *International Journal of Women's Studies* 6:2 (March–April 1983), 148–61, and Lucien's three-part article "'Goody Two-Shoes' Variations on a Theme: From Cinderella Through Horatio Alger and Beyond," *Folklore* (Calcutta, India) 23:8 (August 1982), 163–74; 23:9 (September 1982), 194–98; 23:10 (October 1982), 235–20. Gillian Brown notes Goody as an example of "stories of children who made their lives into moral and economic success." *Consent of the Governed: The Lockean Legacy in Early American Culture* (Cambridge, Mass.: Harvard University Press, 2001), 36. Courtney Weikle-Mills reads Goody's alphabet letters as mediating between the personal and legal realms, with children transferring their affectionate attachment to the playful letters to law and nation. *Imaginary Citizens*, 76–77. Many other references to the novel seem to be to later redactions, as in Maria Tatar's mention of Goody among works that "presented idealized and sentimentalized versions of reality." Tatar, *Off with Their Heads! Fairytales and the Culture of Childhood* (Princeton: Princeton University Press, 1992), 72.

4. The quotation is from R. S. Schofield, "Dimensions of Literacy, 1750–1350," *Explorations in Economic History* 10:4 (1973), 437. Pierre Bourdieu describes the three "guises" in which "capital can present itself": "as *economic capital*, which is immediately and directly convertible into money and may be institutionalized in the form of property rights; as *cultural capital*, which is convertible, on certain conditions, into economic capital and may be institutionalized in the form of educational

qualifications; and as *social capital*, made up of social obligations ('connections'), which is convertible, in certain conditions, into economic capital and may be institutionalized in the form of a title of nobility." Bourdieu is writing partly in response to what he sees as the inadequacy of economists' quantifying of education in simplistically monetary terms. Bourdieu, "Forms of Capital," in John Richardson, ed., *Handbook of Theory and Research for the Sociology of Education* (Westport, Conn.: Greenwood Press, 1986), 241–58, 243–44. John Guillory theorizes cultural capital specifically for the literary field in *Cultural Capital: The Problem of Literary Canon Formation* (Chicago: University of Chicago Press, 1993).

5. This "literacy," according to the OED, is an American coinage of c. 1883 and a back-formation from "illiteracy" (s.v. "literacy"). Social energies seem to coalesce around the term in the late nineteenth century; as Jenny Cook-Gumperz describes the general trajectory of literacy, "it can be argued that the shift from the eighteenth century onwards has not been from total illiteracy to literacy, but from a hard-to-estimate multiplicity of literacies, a *pluralistic* idea about literacy as a composite of different skills related to reading and writing for many different purposes and sections of a society's population, to a twentieth-century notion of a single, standardized *schooled literacy*." *The Social Construction of Literacy* (Cambridge: Cambridge University Press, 1986), 22.

6. See, for one of many examples of the literacy-as-signing method and its discontents, Lawrence Stone's classic "Literacy and Education in England, 1640–1900": "Throughout this chapter, the word 'literacy' should be understood to mean the capacity to sign one's name, which for periods before the nineteenth century is nearly all we now know or indeed are ever likely to know in the future. We do not know now, and may never know, the precise relationship between the capacity to sign one's name—'alphabetism'—might be a better word for it—and true literacy, that is the ability to use the written word as a means of communication." *Past and Present* 42 (1969), 98. Margaret Ferguson, among others, critiques this approach to measuring historical literacy, as it relies on an almost exclusively male demographic. *Dido's Daughters: Literacy, Gender, and Empire in Early Modern England and France* (Chicago: University of Chicago Press, 2007), 74–80.

7. Dick Whittington comes into print as a ballad in 1605. James Raven, *Judging New Wealth: Popular Publishing and Responses to Commerce in England, 1750–1800* (Oxford: Clarendon Press, 1992), 8; Cinderella comes into English in the 1729 translation of Perrault's *Histories, or Tales of Past Times*. For a discussion of the meeting between the traditional fairy tale and the print marketplace, of the appropriation of fairy-tale motifs by "didactic" writers of the eighteenth century, and the romantic valorization and misreading of the fairy tale, see Alan Richardson, *Literature, Education, and Romanticism: Reading as Social Practice, 1780–1832* (Cambridge: Cambridge University Press, 1994), 122–27.

8. Robert Gordon, "Paradoxical Property," in John Brewer and Susan Staves, eds., *Early Modern Conceptions of Property* (New York: Routledge, 1996), 95–110, quote on 99.

9. In addition to Oliver Goldsmith, who was a member of the Newbery stable, the printer Newbery himself is a likely candidate, as is Giles Jones, another Newbery regular. See Sylvia Patterson Iskander, "*Goody Two-Shoes* and *The Vicar of Wakefield*," *Children's Literature Association Quarterly* 33:4 (Winter 1988), 165–68; S. Roscoe, *John Newbery and His Successors 1740–1814* (Wormley, Hertfordshire: Five Owls Press, 1973); John Rowe Townsend, ed., *John Newbery and His Books: Trade and Plumb-Cake for Ever, Huzza!* (Metuchen, N.J.: Scarecrow, 1994); Wilbur Macey Stone, "The History of Little Goody Two-Shoes," *Proceedings of the American Antiquarian Society* 49:2 (October 1939), 333–70, and Charles Welsh, Introduction to *Goody Two-Shoes: A Facsimile Reprint of the Edition of 1766* (Detroit: Singing Tree Press, 1970), iii–xxiv.

10. *The History of Goody Two-Shoes and The Adventures of Tommy Two-Shoes* (London: Tabart, 1804), 3, 4.

11. *The History of little Goody Two-Shoes* (Philadelphia: W. Young [1793]), 13. See also *The History of Little Goody Two-Shoes* (Wilmington, Del.: Peter Brynberg, 1796).

12. Eighteenth-century Poor Laws allowed parishes to apprentice out their wards, and preindustrial poor children were subject to the same kinds of miserable labor conditions as they were in later, more visible industrial scandals. See Ivy Pinchbeck and Margaret Hewitt, *Children in English Society, Vol. I: From Tudor Times to the Eighteenth Century* (London: Routledge, 1969), 308–12. Children on

their own were easily exploited; their own crimes could subject them to capital punishment from the age of seven, and crimes against children were not normally punished severely in a culture that routinely employed children as chimneysweeps and prostitutes. Pinchbeck and Hewitt, *Children in English Society, Volume II: From the Eighteenth Century to the Children Act of 1948* (London: Routledge, 1973), 251–52, 355–61.

13. Seniel Lucien reads this as the substitution for Goody's brother, as well as for her sexual lack in contrast to Tommy, who, the narrative points out, had two shoes all along. Lucien sees this as part of the maturation process represented by the text. "Little Goody Two-Shoes: An Early Model of Child Development" and "'Goody Two-Shoes' Variations on a Theme." The incest that hovers around Goody and Tommy in this reading is emphasized in Victorian sentimentalized versions of the text. (And Goody becomes progressively more deprived, ending up barefoot in some retellings.)

14. Although she here acquires the name that makes her name, Goody is called by many variations on her name; Jan Fergus has noted a total of seventeen names that she goes by. *Provincial Readers,* 114.

15. Peter Stallybrass and Ann Jones, *Renaissance Clothing and the Materials of Memory* (Cambridge: Cambridge University Press, 2000), 2, 3.

16. John Lahr, "*Ma Rainey's Black Bottom,*" *New Yorker*, February 17 and 24, 2003, 191. For a shrewd reading of shoes as "powerful symbols of mobility and icons of and for desire," see Paula Rabinowitz's *Black and White and Noir: America's Pop Modernism* (New York: Columbia University Press, 2002), 172, 171–192.

17. Shari Benstock and Suzanne Ferriss, eds., *Footnotes: On Shoes* (New Brunswick, N.J.: Rutgers University Press, 2001), 1.

18. Lucy Pratt and Linda Woolley, *Shoes* (London: V&A Publications, 1999), 25.

19. A few of the "Shoe" entries in the *Motif-Index of Folk Literature* are to horseshoes. Stith Thompson, *Motif-Index of Folk Literature: A Classification of Narrative Elements in Folk Tales, Ballads, Myths, Fables, Mediaeval Romances,* CD-ROM ed. (Bloomington: Indiana University Press, 1993). Film has inherited the focus on shoes as a marker, particularly for women. Rabinowitz, *Black and White and Noir,* identifies a closetful of examples in American noir films. In addition, in Agnès Varda's *Vagabond* (1986), the heroine's fatal downward skid seems inevitable once the zipper on her boot breaks; she's literally hobbled from there on, until her death. Maureen Turin notices the visual trope of women with one shoe on and one shoe off in Fellini's *Nights of Cabiria* (1957) and Visconti's *Ossessione* (1942). "High Angles on Shoes," in Benstock and Ferriss, *Footnotes,* 58–90, quote on 77.

20. Marina Warner, *From the Beast to the Blonde: On Fairy Tales and Their Tellers* (London: Chatto and Windus, 1994), 203.

21. John Campbell, "Occupation and Literacy in Bristol and Gloucestershire, 1755–1870," *Studies in the History of Literacy: England and North America,* ed. W. B. Stephens, Educational Administration and History Monographs, no. 13 (Leeds: Museum of the History of Education, University of Leeds, 1983), 20–36, quotes on 20, 27. Shoemakers, like the more radical weavers, as village or town folk rather than country folk, had more access to and uses for reading and writing than farmers and laborers. The shoemaker persistently figures in philosophy; in his introduction to Jacques Rancière's *The Philosopher and His Poor,* Andrew Parker notes the philosophical position of the shoemaker, both in his own right and as a ubiquitous exemplum. For Rancière, workers' archives revealed that "the most militant trades were those, like the shoemakers, . . . whose work allowed them to imagine doing something else than that to which they seemingly were fated, while for philosophers from Plato on, the shoemaker is a figure against whom philosophy constitutes itself." Andrew Parker, "Editor's Introduction: Mimesis and the Division of Labor," in Jacques Rancière, *The Philosopher and His Poor* (Durham, N.C.: Duke University Press, 2003), xi.

22. Although children were not technically property, the "right to" them belonged to the father and before 1814 "child stealing" was treated as a crime against property, and was usually punishable only if the perpetrator was stealing the child's clothes (Pinchbeck and Hewitt, *Children,* 2:360, 362). See also Mary Ann Mason, *From Father's Property to Children's Rights: A History of Child Custody in the United States* (New York: Columbia University Press, 1994), 6–10, for the comparable situation in the American colonies.

23. Roman Jakobson, "Two Aspects of Language and Two Types of Aphasic Disturbance," in Jakobson and Morris Halle, *Fundamentals of Language*, (The Hague: Mouton, 1956, 55–82), 76–82. The exception to the shift from the allegorical is Mr. Lovewell, the hero of the novel within the novel that Goody tells (82–94). Other Newbery books' heroic names are metonyms with metaphoric tendencies: Giles Gingerbread (who "lives on learning"), Tommy Telescope, Tommy Thumb.

24. Aside from the classic work of Marcel Mauss on the gift (*The Gift: The Form and Reason for Exchange in Archaic Societies*, tr. W. D. Halls [New York: Norton, 1990]), I am relying on the following for thinking about the economic, social, and affective lives of things: James Carrier, *Gifts and Commodities: Exchange and Western Capitalism Since 1700* (New York: Routledge, 1995); John Frow, "Gift and Commodity," in *Time and Commodity Culture: Essays in Cultural Theory and Postmodernity* (Oxford: Clarendon Press, 1997), 102–217; and Annette Weiner, *Inalienable Possessions: The Paradox of Keeping-While-Giving* (Berkeley: University of California Press, 1992).

25. Arjun Appadurai offers a biographical definition of the commodity: "The commodity situation in the social life of any 'thing' [is] defined as the situation in which its exchangeability (past, present, or future) for some other thing is its socially relevant feature." "Introduction: Commodities and the Politics of Value," in *The Social Life of Things: Commodities in Cultural Perspective*, ed. Arjun Appadurai (Cambridge: Cambridge University Press, 1986), 3–63, 17. See also Igor Kopytoff, "The Cultural Biography of Things: Commoditization as Process," in *The Social Life of Things*, ed. Appadurai, 64–94. It's also worth contrasting Goody's shoes with later literary children's shoes. The shoes in Edgeworth's much-reprinted "The Purple Jar," for example, which Rosamond rejects in favor of a perfect image of the enchanting commodity: a jar whose pretty color turns out to be only the water it contains (in *The Parent's Assistant* [Dublin: Chalmers, 1798]). And of course Dorothy's shoes, the spoils of her violent descent into Oz: currency silver in Baum's original, they become glittering Technicolor red for the film and are finally auctioned in 1970 for $15,000. Salman Rushdie, *The Wizard of Oz* (London: British Film Institute, 1992), 46; see also Turin, "High Angles on Shoes." In Rushdie's fantasy of the auction, "orphans arrive, hoping that the ruby slippers might transport them back through time as well as space, and reunite them with their deceased parents" (60).

26. See Stephen Nissenbaum on the tradition of giving books as presents (*The Battle for Christmas* [New York: Knopf, 1996], 140–50). My impression from looking at archives of children's books is that a high percentage of them are inscribed as gifts by relatives and teachers, the sentimental value added making them most likely to survive as bequests to libraries. In the advertisements at the back of *Goody* Newbery lists gift books specially titled for Christmas, New Year's, Easter, Whitsuntide, Twelfth-Day, Valentine's Day, and one all-purpose Fairing. Jan Fergus has discovered that Goody was a steady seller to the boys at Rugby, some of whose purchases may have been as gifts as well. *Provincial Readers*, 246.

27. See Carrier on "changing circulation relations" in the eighteenth century. *Gifts and Commodities*, 61–83.

28. "The plan which I adopted, and the one by which I was most successful, was that of making friends of all the little white boys whom I met in the street. As many of these as I could, I converted into teachers. With their kindly aid, obtained at different times and in different places, I finally succeeded in learning to read." Douglass similarly purloins his writing skills at the shipyard where he works by noting that timber is marked with letters signifying what part of the ship each is meant for and making lessons for himself by reading the lettered city around him. *Narrative of the Life of Frederick Douglass, an American Slave* (New York: Penguin, 1986), 82, 86–87.

29. John Locke, *Some Thoughts Concerning Education* (1693), ed. John W. and Jean S. Yolton. (Oxford: Clarendon Press, 1989), 210–11. Weikle-Mills points out that Rousseau also promoted this method, which he refers to in *Emile* as "bureaux" for the case containing the letters. *Imaginary Citizens*, 76. Gillian Brown importantly notes that Locke's "educational pleasure principle stresses the intimacy between mental operations and material objects," a pleasure and intimacy Newbery exploits. "The Metamorphic Book: Children's Print Culture in the Eighteenth Century," *Eighteenth-Century Studies* 39:3 (2006), 352.

30. The first citation in the OED is to *Goody,* and defines it as "nick-nacks, trifles, odds and ends, curiosities, small or worthless articles." In the nineteenth century the word becomes slang for "mouth" (OED, s.v. "rattletrap").

31. If we treat Goody's rattletrap letters quite literally, the arithmetic would yield 420 pieces because Goody's lowercase alphabet adds the long *s* to the twenty-six letters, while her uppercase alphabet uses *I* for both *i* and *j*, resulting in a twenty-five letter alphabet (26). But of course the text has no interest in this arithmetical logic.

32. In Ronald Paulson's reading, for example, "the order Two-Shoes gives to experience, alphabetizing it and using reading as a child's defense against hardship, is followed by . . . the supernatural explanation and the prudential one, invoking, respectively, witchcraft and wisdom . . . that ask for a sense of both/and instead of either/or, a kind of randomness that includes the irrational and is far outside the order of Two-Shoes's alphabet." *The Beautiful, Novel, and Strange*, 197.

33. Samuel Johnson, *The Idler and The Adventurer*, ed. W. J. Bate et al., *The Yale Edition of the Works of Samuel Johnson,* vol. 2 (New Haven: Yale University Press, 1963), 60, 62, 60. According to Johnson's editors (xv–xix), Newbery may have been the publisher of the *Universal Chronicle* that ran the *Idler* essays and may have even suggested the idea of the series to Johnson; Newbery published the first collected *Idler* in 1767.

34. Weiner, *Inalienable Possessions*, 44–65, 11.

35. "Booksellers had been associated with the sale of patent medicines since the mid-17th cent. [*sic*], as described in John Alden, 'Pills and Publishing: Some Notes on the English Book Trade, 1660–1715,' *Library*, 5th ser., 7/1 (Mar. 1952), 21–37." Raven, *Judging New Wealth*, 51n29.

36. Throughout, the narrative uses as a conceit this production transparency. For example, the final text before the advertisements at the back of the book, "A Letter from the Printer, which he desires may be inserted," adds a few anecdotes about the "sagacity" of dogs and begins: "Sir, I Have done with your Copy, if you please; and pray tell Mr. Angelo to brush up the cuts, that, in the next Edition, they may give us a good Impression" (155). The "Mr. Angelo" reference completes the joke on the title page, probably by the same compositor-wit: "See the original Manuscript in the Vatican at Rome, and the cuts by Michael Angelo."

37. A pricey formula, equivalent to today's prescription drugs (about £10), costing a couple of days' wages for a laborer, while the book itself is only sixpence. Even this, according to S. Roscoe, was "a fairly stiff price in an age when the wages of a skilled workman were seldom more than 7s 6d a week and often as low as 5s." *John Newbery and His Successors*, 13. According to James Raven, in "1760 two shillings could buy a stone of beef or a pair of shoes." *Judging New Wealth*, 57. Newbery was at least as famous for his patent medicines as for his books. According to Townsend, Dr. James's Powder was a widely used (by, among others, King George III) if toxic remedy, which is thought to have been responsible for the death of Goldsmith; it seems to have consisted of "phosphate of lime and oxide of antimony," and continued to be produced by Newbery heirs until 1941. *John Newbery and His Books*, 21, 22, 159. Eighteenth-century American printers tended not to bother inserting their own name for Newbery's—with the unsurprising exception of Isaiah Thomas.

38. This event echoes the story that appears in Cicero's *De oratore* of the poet Simonides, who was called away from a banquet hall just before its roof fell in; his ability to clearly remember where everyone was sitting and hence identify the dead is said to be the foundation of the rhetorical memory art. See Frances Yates, *The Art of Memory* (Chicago: University of Chicago Press, 1966), 1–2. Is Goody's version renewing the story for alphabetic and vernacular pedagogy?

39. Thomas Laqueur suggests that eighteenth-century charity school teachers received in the range of £6 to £10 a year, although Goody for much of the narrative is freelance and so even poorer. "In Bilton, New Ainstey, a parish with 123 families and no endowed or charity school, we learn of 'two poor, honest, sober and well-meaning persons who teach children to read, and instruct them in ye Church catechism'; in Bainton, Harthill, there was no school, but there were 'two poor women [who] teach a few children to read.'" "The Cultural Origins of Popular Literacy in England, 1500–1800," *Oxford Review of Education* 2:3 (1976), 257–58.

40. Teresa Michals notes of this scene that "property law plays a spectacular role at her wedding" and that "Margery's legal rights to property . . . establish for her a new kind of agency." *Books for Children, Books for Adults: Age and the Novel from Defoe to James* (Cambridge: Cambridge University Press, 2014), 87.

41. They are also prevented from becoming, themselves, intermediaries—pedlars, in effect—a suspicious class for a moral economist like Goody. See Carrier, *Gifts and Commodities*, 66ff., on the

regulation of market transactions to privilege the local, direct sale in the seventeenth and eighteenth centuries.

42. Tommy's adventures become a more visible feature of nineteenth-century redactions, whose illustrators especially take up the image of the Africans, as such images circulated as part of the colonial and racialized discourse of children's primers, geographies, and natural histories. Mary Belson Elliott published an entire book devoted to Tommy's adventures, sending Tommy to Jamaica instead of Africa and embroiling him in a slave uprising there; Tommy's skill, seemingly gender appropriate, is writing rather than reading, though he has the same affinity with animals as Goody (London: Tabart, 1809). An 1837 Baltimore verse edition (Bayly and Burns) illustrates Tommy with American Indians.

43. According to an English translation of *The History, of the Birth, Travels, Strange Adventures, and Death of Fortunatus* (London, 1682), although at least one children's redaction, in *The Child's New Play-Thing* (Boston, 1750), compresses the tale into one generation. David Blamires notes that Fortunatus appears in print in German in 1509 and remains a popular children's chapbook and tale into the nineteenth century. *Fortunatus in His Many English Guises* (Lewiston: Mellen Press, 1996), 1–9. Newbery, as usual, is both plugging and cannibalizing one of his own products, the *Pretty Book for Children* (1761), which contained a version of the story.

44. John Guillory, "Literary Capital, Gray's 'Elegy,' Anna Laetitia Barbauld, and the Vernacular Canon," in John Brewer and Susan Staves, eds., *Early Modern Conceptions of Property* (New York: Routledge, 1996, 389–410) 389, 402, 407.

45. An already alphabetized natural world is a familiar fantasy of theorists and pedagogues; see Crain, *The Story of A: The Alphabetization of America from* The New England Primer *to* the Scarlet Letter (Stanford: Stanford University Press, 2000), for some earlier versions in Comenius's *Orbis Pictus* and *The New England Primer*.

46. Gordon, "Paradoxical Property," 99. See also Gregory S. Alexander's analysis of early American property debates: "So transformed [that is, into commodities], property might become a solvent that dissolves the political bonds of the community." Alexander, *Commodity and Propriety: Competing Visions of Property in American Legal Thought 1776–1970* (Chicago: University of Chicago Press, 1997), 35. James Raven notes that during "the second half of the eighteenth century, new manufacturers guided industrial expansion, extending the depth and diversity of the domestic market. At the same time, short-term credit crises provoked urgent discussion both of the causes and results of economic instability and of the definition of legitimate risk-taking. . . . In another commercial sector, the fundamental question posed by writers of didactic, imaginative literature was whether value in society was to be measured by wealth, station, or behaviour. In reality, late eighteenth-century society was dominated by monetary considerations." *Judging New Wealth*, 252.

47. J. G. A. Pocock, *The Machiavellian Moment: Florentine Political Thought and the Atlantic Republican Tradition* (Princeton: Princeton University Press, 1975), 463–64.

48. Other forms of nonmaterial property in the eighteenth century with which this construction of literacy is affiliated are "skill" and "liberty." On the former, see John Rule, "The Property of Skill in the Period of Manufacture," in Patrick Joyce, ed. *The Historical Meanings of Work,* (Cambridge: Cambridge University Press, 1987); on the latter, see John Phillip Reid, *Constitutional History of the American Revolution: The Authority of Rights* (Madison: University of Wisconsin Press, 1986), 31–33. Both skill and liberty began to have some protection under law; literacy too, under the general rubric of "education," emerged in the early American republic as an equivalent of property, and a potential substitute for it. See especially Robert Coram, *Political Inquiries: To Which Is Added a Plan for the Establishment of Schools Throughout the United States* (Wilmington, Del., 1791).

49. Historians of literacy have attested to a disconnect between economic development and literacy acquisition in the seventeenth to nineteenth centuries. See, for example, Kenneth Lockridge, *Literacy in Colonial New England: An Enquiry into the Social Context of Literacy in the Early Modern West* (New York: Norton, 1974). "Literacy did not march forward with commercialization and social development," according to Harvey Graff, "Literacy and Social Development in North America: On Ideology and History," in Stephens, *Studies in the History of Literacy*, 82–97, quote on 88. Indeed some historians of literacy chart a descent in literacy rates that accompanies increased population density and industrialization.

50. Bourdieu, "Forms of Capital," 245.

51. In this example, Goody embodies the now literate "old wife," but it would seem that she sometimes travels simply as a traditional story-teller. Matthew ("Monk") Lewis records in his Jamaican journal the "Nancy" story of the local "Goody Two-Shoes" "called by the negroes, 'Goosee Shoo-shoo'": "A glass of rum, or a roll of *backy*, is sure to unpack Goosee Shoo-shoo's budget." *Journal of a West India Proprietor, 1815–1817,* ed. Mona Wilson (London: Routledge, 1929), 212. In this figure, Goody's alphabet basket loops back into an oral copia. See also Lawrence Needham's interesting account of the story Lewis takes from Goosee, which shares some of the central concerns of the original Goody (though Needham treats the novel as a generic "nursery tale"), including the substitution for a lack (in Goosee's story, the hero wonderfully is missing his head) and proper rules for marriage. Lawrence Needham, "'Goody Two-Shoes'/ 'Goosee Shoo-shoo': Translated Tales of Resistance in Matthew Lewis's *Journal of a West India Proprietor*," in *Between Languages and Cultures: Translation and Cross-Cultural Texts*, ed. Anuradha Dingwaney and Carol Maier (Pittsburgh: University of Pittsburgh Press, 1995), 103–18.

52. McLoughlin Bros., who published at least fourteen editions of *Goody*, inaugurated a "Goody Two Shoes" series in their 1867 catalog, according to the American Antiquarian Society catalog.

53. For Charles Lamb, in a notorious letter to Coleridge, *Goody* seems to have stood for his own childhood memories of reading. He laments that it is "almost out of print," pushed out he claims by books by Anna Letitia Barbauld and others who promote, he claims, "knowledge" over "wild tales" and "poetry" (quoted in Welsh, Introduction, *Goody Two-Shoes* [1766]), viii–x. Others have noted that this screed is unfair to Barbauld, Edgeworth, Fenn, Trimmer, and other women writers he seems to be attacking; see, for example, Norma Clarke, "Women Writers and Writing for Children in the Late Eighteenth Century," in *Opening the Nursery Door*, ed. Mary Hilton, Morag Styles, and Victor Watson (New York: Routledge, 1997), 91–92. But it underscores the degree to which *Goody* was *read* by its first readers in the fantastical terms I've described.

54. Philadelphia, Ash and Mason, 1824 edition, 3.

55. Gillian Brown notes Newberry's Lockean attunement in all of his productions to "the physicality of reading." "Metaphoric Book," 357.

56. The tradition of infantilizing Goody begins with the greatly condensed (to some twenty pages) London 1804 Tabart Popular Stories edition, which in other ways too defangs the radicalism of the original, and continues in many though not all editions in America through the century. For an essay about and access to images of the Tabart edition, see the Hockliffe Project http://www.sd-editions.com/hockliffeNew/items/0123.html.

57. In a somewhat contradictory concession to realism, Goody sometimes cuts the letters from cardboard.

58. An 1881 McLoughlin version opens like this: "In the reign of good Queen Bess, there was an honest, industrious countryman named Meanwell" (1).

Chapter 2. The Literary Property of Childhood

Epigraph. Heinrich von Kleist, "On the Puppet Theater" (1810), in *An Abyss Deep Enough: Letters of Heinrich von Kleist with a Selection of Essays and Anecdotes,* ed. and tr. Phillip B. Miller (New York: E. P. Dutton, 1982), 217.

1. Aside from the other ways in which the Babes ballad figures romanticism, Ann Weirda Rowland points out that the so-called Babes in the Wood topos describes the moment in Enlightenment philosophies of the origins of language arising from "two primitive beings . . . trying to communicate." It seems a striking rubric for that topos, since the virtually speechless babes of the ballad exist in an intensely civilized milieu, ringed around by the law, and far from navigating a "savage" state, they die in it. That said, the figure underscores the ballad's persistent association—and by extension, children's persistent association—with a putative orality, that has a capacity for being stored and even restored. Rowland, *Romanticism and Childhood: The Infantilization of British Literary Culture* (Cambridge: Cambridge University Press, 2012), 71.

2. For a genealogy and bibliography of this ballad, see Dianne Dugaw, "On the 'Darling Songs' of Poets, Scholars, and Singers: An Introduction," *The Eighteenth Century: Theory and Interpretation*

47:2–3, (2006), 97–113, and Maureen McLane, "Dating Orality, Thinking Balladry," in the same issue, 131–49. See also Susan L. Porter, " 'Children in the Wood': The Odyssey of an Anglo-American Ballad," in Porter and John Graziano, eds., *Vistas of American Music: Essays and Compositions in Honor of William K. Kearns* (Warren, Mich.: Harmonie Park Press, 1999), 77–95. For visual arts representations, see Barton Levi St. Armand, "Emily Dickinson's 'Babes in the Wood': A Ballad Reborn," *Journal of American Folklore* 90:358 (October–December 1977), 430–41. The Disney cartoon, in the Silly Symphony series from 1932, is a raucous and self-parodying hybrid of "Hansel and Gretel" and "Babes in the Wood." Thanks to an audience member at the American Antiquarian Society for bringing the Cole Porter tune to my attention, and to Mary Poovey for lyrics and Porter's own rendition ("Two Little Babes in the Wood," written for *Greenwich Village Follies*, 1924).

3. The terms are from Raymond Williams's description of the temporality of cultural forms in *Marxism and Literature* (New York: Oxford University Press, 1978), 121–25. For consideration of the residual (and the emergent and the dominant) particularly in relation to media and mediation, see the introduction to and the essays in *Residual Media*, ed. Charles R. Acland (Minneapolis: University of Minnesota Press, 2007).

4. The ballad was registered on October 15, 1595.

5. There are a few broadsides, with recordings of sung performances, at the University of California, Santa Barbara, English Broadside Ballad Archive site, http://ebba.english.ucsb.edu/.

6. References to the traditional ballad will be to Arthur Quiller-Couch, ed., *The Oxford Book of Ballads* (1910), available online at bartleby.com (see the section of my bibliography listing the editions cited in Chapter 2 and see Appendix, p. 177). While there are local variants, the plot, verse structure, and most details remain strikingly stable over more than three centuries of the ballad's publication.

7. This scene in particular resonates with Shakespeare's *King John*, 4.1.25–26, in which Hubert relents to the child Arthur: "If I talk to him with his innocent prate / He will awake my mercy, which lies dead." I say more about the ballad and Shakespeare later in this chapter.

8. Sometimes the robins cover the children "painfully"—but always very famously. This is the moment in the ballad that circulates the most widely and that intersects the most with folk and popular culture and with the folk song as it is still sung.

9. While it may seem self-evident that children were members of the early ballad audience, their presence is confirmed, according to Nicholas Orme, by the Protestant writers who worried about the influence of more raucous and romantic ballads on children. *Medieval Children* (New Haven: Yale University Press, 2003), 287–89. The 1601 play is *Two Lamentable Tragedies,* Robert Yarington (London); the musical is *The Children in the Wood: An Opera in Two Acts*, by Thomas Morton.

10. Subtitled *The Traditions in English*. Edited by Jack Zipes et al. (New York: Norton, 2005), 57–60. The editors chose a London chapbook version, circa 1800, with twenty-four stanzas, instead of the traditional ballad's forty (this chapbook leaves out both the uncle's and the ruffian's punishments as well as the closing frame addressed to executors).

11. See Arjun Appadurai and Igor Kopytoff, *The Social Life of Things: Commodities in Cultural Perspective* (Cambridge: Cambridge University Press, 1986).

12. Quoted in Porter, " 'Children in the Wood,' " 77.

13. Paula McDowell, " 'The Manufacture and Lingua-facture of Ballad-Making': Broadside Ballads in Long Eighteenth-Century Ballad Discourse," *The Eighteenth Century: Theory and Interpretation* 47:2–3 (2006), 151–78, 151.

14. Often "by suchlike cruelty."

15. Sometimes "deeds" rather than "minds."

16. For London ballad hawkers' practices and prices, see Sean Shesgreen, ed., *The Criers and Hawkers of London: Engravings and Drawings by Marcellus Laroon* (Aldershot, Hants.: Scolar Press, 1990), 100.

17. Ivy Pinchbeck and Margaret Hewitt, *Children in English Society, Vol. 1: From Tudor Times to the Eighteenth Century* (London: Routledge, 1969), 22. Pinchbeck and Hewitt note as well the traffic in royal wardships (that is, orphaned children under the protection of the Crown) through the Court of Wards, and, for orphans with less property, regional Courts of Orphans, in the Tudor and Stuart legal system (58–90). For the history of child exposure and abandonment, see John Boswell, *The*

Kindness of Strangers: The Abandonment of Children in Western Europe from Late Antiquity to the Renaissance (Chicago: University of Chicago Press, 1988).

18. The innocent wife of the uncle ("He told his wife an artful tale: / He would the children send / To be brought up in London town / With one that was his friend") is the only character whose fate is not mentioned. (The ballad is its own Horatio, willing itself to itself.)

19. The rhyme of "always already old" with media historian Lisa Gitelman's *Always Already New* is meant to underscore the sense of mediality always linked to discourses of modern childhood.

20. The best account of the rise of children's literature is still F. J. Harvey Darton, *Children's Books in England: Five Centuries of Social Life* (Cambridge: Cambridge University Press, 1932 [3rd edition, revised by Brian Alderson, 1982]).

21. Walter Scott in 1830, quoted in Dianne Dugaw, ed., *The Anglo-American Ballad* (New York, 1995), 33. For the ballad revival, see, for example, *The Eighteenth Century: Theory and Interpretation*, special issue on the ballad, 47:2–3 (2006). See also Steve Newman, *Ballad Collection, Lyric, and the Canon: The Call of the Popular from the Restoration to the New Criticism* (Philadelphia: University of Pennsylvania Press, 2007), and Adam Fox, *Oral and Literate Culture in England 1500–1700* (Oxford: Oxford University Press, 2000).

22. Tessa Watt, *Cheap Print and Popular Piety, 1540–1640* (Cambridge: Cambridge University Press, 1991), 25, 42.

23. *Spectator* 85, from *The Spectator Project: A Hypermedia Research Archive of Eighteenth-Century Periodicals*, www2.scc.rutgers.edu/spectator/text/june1711/no85.html (accessed January 7, 2016). Addison opens the essay by comparing himself to a "Mussulman" who treats all written papers as sacred in case they might contain a bit of the Koran.

24. While Addison doesn't memorialize his own childhood, John Aubrey, the early scholar of oral tradition, relates his own childhood memories of the 1630s and 1640s, noting, as later ballad collectors will repeatedly do, the importance of women's talk (Fox, *Oral and Literate Culture,* 179).

25. Within a decade or two of Addison's remarks, the London Dicey firm began to advertise ballads and chapbooks explicitly for children. Victor Neuberg, "The Diceys and the Chapbook Trade," Transactions of the Bibliographic Society, *The Library*, September 1969, 219–31.

26. In Steve Newman's reading of Addison's reading of "Children in the Wood" and the ballad "Chevy Chase" (the latter in *Spectator* 70 and 74), "Addison's view of the subject as individual and as type is linked to a narrative of personal and national development. For him, the ballad is part of a crucial pedagogical project: It initiates a process of aesthetic reflection that coordinates personal ontogeny with national phylogeny. . . . The ballad is the unreflective delight 'of the Common People and has been the Delight of most Englishmen in some Part of their Age' allowing more sophisticated readers to measure the progress of their own tastes and that of the nation in general." Newman, *Ballad Collection*, 42.

27. *The Prose Works of William Wordsworth*, ed. W. J. B. Owen and Jane Worthington Smyser (Oxford: Oxford University Press, 1974), 154.

28. James Beattie invokes the ballad (and highlights the same stanza) in his 1771 "Minstrel," as a formative song from a "beldam." No one, he writes, "hears their dying cry: / 'For from the town the man returns no more'" (quoted in McLane). Maureen McLane sees Beattie creating "the illusion of oral mimesis." "Dating Orality," 137.

29. Specifically, it's the "order of the words" that Wordsworth attends to; in this passage he is defending what he sees as a plain-spoken poetics against critics, using a parodically vacuous verse by Samuel Johnson for a foil. In "Lucy Gray," he echoes this stanza: "The storm came on before its time, / She wandered up and down, / And many a hill did Lucy climb / But never reached the Town," *Selected Poems*, ed. Stephen Gill (New York: Penguin, 2004), 74. James Averill notes this echo, attributing it to Wordsworth's interest in Thomas Percy's *Reliques of Ancient English Poetry: Wordsworth and the Poetry of Human Suffering* (Ithaca: Cornell University Press, 1980), 188. Duncan Wu attributes it to Vicesimus Knox's *Elegant Extracts: Wordsworth's Reading 1800–1815* (Cambridge: Cambridge University Press, 2007), 125.

30. In, for example, "The Pet Lamb," "Lucy Gray," "We Are Seven."

31. For Lamb's influence in the United States, see Harrison T. Meserole, "Charles Lamb's Reputation and Influence in America to 1835," *Journal of General Education* 16:4 (January 1965), 281–308.

32. First published in January 1822 in the *London Magazine*. Philip Lopate notes in his introduction that the reverie is elegiac for Lamb's older brother John (Charles Lamb, *Essays of Elia*, ed. Philip Lopate [Iowa City: University of Iowa Press, 2003]). Alan Richardson writes of this passage: "Lamb develops in his essays both an intense nostalgia for childhood recalled as a lost paradise, and a sentimentalized and altogether ethereal version of Wordsworth's 'heaven-born' child." *Literature, Education and Romanticism: Reading as Social Practice, 1780–1832* (New York: Cambridge University Press, 1994), 23.

33. Lamb, *Essays of Elia*, 199.

34. Lamb, *Essays of Elia*, 204. Judith Plotz writes of these passages, "Lamb attempts to tease the future out of the past, the not-to-be out of the all-but-gone." *Romanticism and the Vocation of Childhood* (New York: Palgrave, 2001), 116.

35. Hawthorne's 1835 "The Village Uncle" is modeled on Lamb's "Dream-Children: A Reverie," and was first published as "The Mermaid: A Reverie." Hawthorne's bachelor imagines a fantasy spouse who sells "picture books and ballads" (221–22) in a village store by the seashore, and he similarly conjures dream children and disperses them back into the ether. Hawthorne *Tales and Sketches* (New York: Library of America, 1982), 217–27.

36. "Little folk" is current in the eighteenth century for children and family, according to the OED, s.v. "folk." As Andrew O'Malley puts the case, "One effect of the grafting together of childhood and a disappearing popular culture through the temporal displacement of nostalgia was to ensure the two remained at a remove from the present moment. The child and the rural peasant became figures locked together in the past." *Children's Literature, Popular Culture, and* Robinson Crusoe (New York: Palgrave Macmillan, 2012), 12.

37. Ann Weirda Rowland writes of Scott "balladizing" his own childhood in an anecdote in which Scott recounts his nurse trying to kill him. "'The Fause Nourice Sang': Childhood, Child Murder, and the Formalism of the Scottish Ballad Revival," in Leith Davis et al., eds., *Scotland and the Borders of Romanticism* (Cambridge, England: Cambridge University Press, 2004), 225–44, 241. As recent ballad scholars such as Rowland remind us, "Childhood, both personally recalled and metaphorically conceived, is a critical imaginary field for the ballad revival. . . . In the introductory essays that are customary for the collections, the editor often recalls his original childhood attachment to popular poetry" (227).

38. The text is also sometimes titled *The Affecting History of the Children in the Wood*.

39. Parenthetical citations to the novel will be to Clara English, *The Children in the Wood: An Instructive Tale* (Baltimore: Warner and Hanna, 1806), unless otherwise noted. Twenty-seven editions are identified as being by "Clara English," but there are others with the Clara English plot that aren't catalogued under her name. In England, there appear to be far fewer editions. In the United States they might be superseded by the Thomas Morton play, in which the children also survive. In another chapbook version, *The Hermit of the Forest and the Wandering Infants: A Rural Fragment* (attributed to Richard Johnson, published first by Newbery in 1788 and then in several U.S. and a few British editions from 1789 to 1820), the children, abandoned by their uncle, are rescued by Honestus, who had lost his family and estate, and become a hermit; but the children's father turns out not to have died and comes upon them one day; similarly, the hermit's daughters turn out to still live, and all are united in the end. Another novelized version provides an elaborate backstory for the sinister uncle, who murders the babes' parents and succeeds in having the children killed too, usually with the title *The tragical history of the children in the wood. Containing a true account of their unhappy fate; with the history of their parents, and their unnatural uncle. Interspersed with instructive morals* (Boston: S. Hall, 1798, for example). The printed verse ballad seems always to require the children's deaths. The seemingly modernized Clara English versions last into the 1840s and then vanish, their house-of-industry utopianism perhaps too radical for U.S. parents and printers.

40. "The spinning wheels and weaving machines began to move so briskly, that the noise surprised Edgar and Jane" (29). There's a long description of the cloth industry noting that Norfolk is renowned for woolen "manufactures" (30) (Baltimore 1806 edition). These early editions precede cloth manufacturing in Waltham (c. 1813) and Lowell (c. 1820s), but these may undergird the longevity of this version. The most famous Lowell factory girl, Lucy Larcom, notes that her aunt gave

her a "Children in the Wood" (this would be in about 1836), but there's no knowing what edition it is (*A New England Girlhood, Outlined from Memory* [Boston: Northeastern University Press, 1986], 29; St. Armand's "Emily Dickinson's 'Babes in the Wood'" drew my attention to Larcom's recollection.)

41. Hallowell, Maine, 1817. This edition also (uniquely?) reprints *The New England Primer*'s "Dialogue Between Christ, a Youth and the Devil." (American Antiquarian Society Copy B [Cl-pam E58 C5361 1817] is inscribed to Lucretia Earle, who was born in 1841, giving it the cross-generational life characteristic of many children's books in the archive.)

42. Ann Weirda Rowland calls such a child reader a "formalist" (*Romanticism,* 216). Though she's not talking explicitly about the reception of *children*'s ballads by actual children, she makes a similar point: that the (imagined) child reader is meant to channel the form but not the content of the ballad to preserve a national treasure; the infanticide ballads that she's studying disrupt this by staging a scene of child murder by the very singer of the ballad.

43. In an 1803 edition at the American Antiquarian Society (Philadelphia: Jacob Johnson; CL E58 C536 1803), the missing verses have been added by hand: "Then wandered those little babes / Till death did end their grief / In one anothers arms they died / As babes wanting relief / No burial these pretty babes, / From any man received / But robin redbreast painfully / Did cover them with leaves" (63). This corrigendum makes an interesting intervention in the Clara English version's up-to-date political agenda, insisting, as if in the spectral hand of an old wife, on the value of the traditional ballad.

44. For the role of the nurse as old wife, see Rowland, *Romanticism,* 162ff; see also Katie Trumpener, *Bardic Nationalism: The Romantic Novel and the British Empire* (Princeton: Princeton University Press, 1997), especially chapter 5, "The Old Wives' Tale: The Fostering System as National and Imperial Education."

45. Clara English, *Children in the Wood: An Instructive Tale* (Baltimore: Warner and Hanna, 1806), 35.

46. Warning against "gratify[ing] the most licentious appetites," it reminds us further, threateningly and panoptically, "how you must dread the all-searching eye of that BEING, who can bring to light the hidden things of darkness!" (26).

47. *The children in the wood. To which is added, My mother's grave, a pathetic story* (New York: Mahlon Day, 1832), 5–6.

48. This is a somewhat bowdlerized version of the traditional ballad, in which the children die, and includes moralizing verses.

49. I take the expression from Henry James's preface to *What Maisie Knew*: "Maisie to the end . . . treats her friends to the rich little spectacle of objects embalmed in her wonder. She wonders, in other words, to the end, to the death—the death of her childhood, properly speaking" (*Literary Criticism, Volume 2: European Writers and Prefaces to the New York Edition* [New York: Library of America, 1984], 1161). Leon Edel condenses it to "the death of childhood," a preoccupation of Henry James's in the 1890s. *The Treacherous Years: 1895–1901* (Philadelphia: Lippincott, 1969), 181.

50. Rodney Hessinger has explored the tensions between freedom and license as well as between independence and vulnerability in discourses of childhood and youth in early Philadelphia. *Seduced, Abandoned, and Reborn: Visions of Youth in Middle-Class America, 1780–1850* (Philadelphia: University of Pennsylvania Press, 2005).

51. Lawrence Levine, *Highbrow/Lowbrow: The Emergence of Cultural Hierarchy in America* (Cambridge, Mass.: Harvard University Press, 1990), 14, 44. The rhyme of the ballad with the plot of *Richard III* has long been recognized; see *The Tragedy of King Richard III,* ed. John Jowett (Oxford: Oxford University Press, 2000), 24n1. See also Alice Perry Wood, *The Stage History of Shakespear's King Richard III* (New York: Columbia University Press, 1909).

52. Lowell found *Richard III* "a most effective acting play," but so faulty that he proposed that Shakespeare "retouched or even added to a poor play which had already proved popular." *Latest Literary Essays and Addresses of James Russell Lowell* (Boston: Houghton Mifflin, 1896), 128, 125.

53. Susan Stewart describes "distressed" genres of the seventeenth and eighteenth centuries—fables, epics, proverbs, and ballads—as manifesting a "desire to produce speaking objects, objects

both in and out of time. "Notes on Distressed Genres," in *Crimes of Writing* (New York: Oxford University Press, 1991), 67.

54. Roy Strong's exploration of British history painting turns up many images with which the *Goody Two-Shoes* and "Babes in the Wood" popular print images resonate powerfully, especially Millais's *The Princes in the Tower* (1878) and W. F. Yeames's *"And When Did You Last See Your Father?"* (1878), with threatened or victimized children as their focus. Strong, *And When Did You Last See Your Father? The Victorian Painter and British History* (London: Thames and Hudson, 1978), plates VII, X; 119–121, 136–145. Robin Fleming describes the medieval material culture landscape of the nineteenth century in architecture and design: "The mass production and domestication of the medieval led nineteenth-century consumers to have a highly eccentric and anachronistic relationship with the medieval past." Histories and games for children taught "a particular kind of history—one that was virtuous, dramatic, and closely allied to the present." "Picturesque History and the Medieval in Nineteenth-Century America," *American Historical Review* 100:4 (October 1995), 1067, 1075.

55. See especially Reginald Horsman, *Race and Manifest Destiny: The Origins of American Racial Anglo-Saxonism* (Cambridge, Mass.: Harvard University Press, 1981). See also T. J. Jackson Lears, *No Place of Grace: Antimodernism and the Transformation of American Culture, 1880–1920* (Chicago: University of Chicago Press, 1994), 144ff., on late nineteenth and early twentieth-century medievalism and "medieval childishness" in American culture. See also the essays in Allen J. Frantzen and John D. Niles, eds., *Anglo-Saxonism and the Construction of Social Identity* (Gainesville: University Press of Florida, 1997). Robin Fleming notes, "Medieval researchers' longing for a lost world and clear-cut ancestry and their embrace of half-understood science combined to create the central ideology of nineteenth-century American writing on the Middle Ages: that race was the driving force of history and that the 'Aryan race,' in particular its 'Teutonic' branch, was superior to all others." "Picturesque History," 1078.

56. Caroline Levander, *Cradle of Liberty: Race, the Child, and National Belonging from Thomas Jefferson to W. E. B. Du Bois* (Durham, N.C.: Duke University Press, 2006), 33.

57. Steve Newman, *Ballad Collection*, 207.

58. I'm grateful to Lisa Gitelman for this formulation.

59. *The Case of Peter Pan, or the Impossibility of Children's Fiction* (1984) (Philadelphia: University of Pennsylvania Press, 1993), 43.

60. Angela Sorby argues that children are positioned by much nineteenth-century "schoolroom" poetry as "conservators not just of a personal but also of collective—local and national—version of the past" and that "popular verse forms became—and remain—forms of American childhood." *Schoolroom Poets: Childhood, Performance, and the Place of American Poetry, 1865–1917* (Lebanon, N.H.: University Press of New England, 2005), 186, 189.

61. Ann Wierda Rowland sees something similar: "Understanding childhood as an oral, original state places the child on the cusp of the cultural world; the definitive object of acculturation, she is not yet fully a cultural subject, not yet fully subjected. The child who knows not what she sings represents an illusory, because imaginary, relationship to culture in which one can play with and participate in cultural forms without being subjected to their power." *Romanticism*, 239.

62. The *inheritance* of racial features is key to postbellum racial Anglo-Saxonism. Caroline Levander points out that the Daughters of the American Revolution (founded in 1890) "identified a pure, white, Anglo-Saxon child body as the point of origin for all 'true' offspring of Revolutionary forebears." *Cradle of Liberty*, 50–51. The descendants of the revolutionary ancestor carry " 'this bone and sinew and nerve and muscle . . . ours by direct inheritance' " (*American Monthly Magazine*, the DAR organ, quoted by Levander, 51). See also Shawn Michelle Smith, *American Archives: Gender, Race, and Class in Visual Culture* (Princeton: Princeton University Press 1999), 138, cited by Levander, 51.

63. *The Letters of Emily Dickinson*, ed. Thomas H. Johnson (Cambridge, Mass.: Harvard University Press, 1958), 104. The letter is undated but thought to have been written on December 31, 1850. For other Babes references throughout Dickinson's work, see St. Armand, "Emily Dickinson's 'Babes in the Wood.' "

64. I'm grateful to Margaret Hunt for pointing out the aggression in this passage.

Chapter 3. Colonizing Childhood, Placing Cherokee Children

Epigraphs: Joy Harjo and Gloria Bird, *Reinventing the Enemy's Language: Contemporary Native Women's Writings of North America* (New York: Norton, 1997), 469. Quoted in David Wallace Adams, *Education for Extinction: American Indians and the Boarding School Experience 1875–1928* (Lawrence: University Press of Kansas, 1995), 120.

1. A sketch of the phrase's lineage shows how specific to the bureaucratic sensibility and how modern Lancaster's meaning is. The OED misses the 1812 Lancaster source (*The British System of Education* [Washington: William Cooper], 2; the original is in all uppercase), citing a first use in Marryat's 1842 *Masterman Ready*: "In a well-conducted man-of-war . . . every thing is in its place, and there is a place for every thing." Isabella Beeton's 1861 *Book of Household Management* uses the expression in much the same way (OED). Two related dicta emerge from antiquity: Horace on stylistic decorum (*Singula quaeque locum teneant sortita decentem*, let each [style] keep the becoming place allotted it [*De arte poetica*, I.92]) and Augustine, like Horace, relying on rhetorical tradition: "Order is an arrangement of components . . . assigning the proper place to each" (*City of God*, 19, 13). In his 1642 book of aphorisms, *Jacula Prudentum*, George Herbert lades the idea with spiritual anxiety on the one hand—"All things have their place, knew wee how to place them"—and status anxiety on the other: "Sit in your place, and none can make you rise," the latter a version of the traditional "He need not fear to be chidden that sits where he is bidden." Benjamin Franklin's version neatly combines the notion of the decorous style with a tip on general deportment: "Tim and his Handsaw are good in their Place, / Tho' not fit for preaching or shaving a face" (*Poor Richard's Almanack*, 1746). See John Chapin, ed., *Book of Catholic Quotations* (New York: Farrar, Straus and Giroux, 1956); Wolfgang Meider et al., *Dictionary of American Proverbs* (New York: Oxford University Press, 1992); *Oxford Dictionary of English Proverbs*, 3rd ed. (Oxford: Clarendon Press, 1970); Burton Stevenson, *The Home Book of Proverbs, Maxims, and Familiar Phrases* (New York: Macmillan, 1948).

2. Peter Hulme defines "colonial discourse" as "an ensemble of linguistically-based practices unified by their common deployment in the management of colonial relationships. . . . Underlying the idea of colonial discourse . . . is the presumption that during the colonial period large parts of the non-European world were *produced* for Europe through a discourse that imbricated sets of questions and assumptions, methods of procedure and analysis, and kinds of writing and imagery, normally separated out into the discrete areas of military strategy, political order, social reform, imaginative literature, personal memoir and so on." *Colonial Encounters: Europe and the Native Caribbean, 1492–1797* (New York: Methuen, 1986), 2.

3. The New York African Free School, founded in 1787, used the method as well, beginning in 1809. Charles C. Andrews, *The history of the New-York African Free-Schools, from their establishment in 1787, to the present time; embracing a period of more than forty years; also a brief account of the successful labors, of the New-York manumission society; with an appendix.* (New York: Mahlon Day, 1830), 17.

4. National Archive, Bureau of Indian Affairs, War Department, Secretary's Office, Letters Sent, Indian Affairs, E: 151. In a letter dated August 29, 1821, and initialed by Secretary of War John Calhoun's chief clerk, Christopher Vandeventer: "By direction of the Secretary of War, I transmit to you a pamphlet relative to the Lancasterian System of Education, by its founder. This system it appears has been adopted, with advantage, in some of the Indian schools already in operation, and the propriety of adopting it generally is suggested." Robert Berkhofer very plausibly suggests that the pamphlet is Lancaster's 1821 Baltimore manual, *The Lancasterian System of Education, with Improvements.* Berkhofer, *Salvation and the Savage: An Analysis of Protestant Missions and American Indian Response, 1787–1862* (Lexington: University of Kentucky Press, 1965), 27n39.

5. This anecdote is related in David Salmon, *Joseph Lancaster* (London: Longmans, Green, 1904), 2–3. The Clarkson essay would have been either his prize dissertation at Cambridge, *An essay on the slavery and commerce of the human species, particularly the African* (1786), or *An essay on the impolicy of the African slave trade* (1788). Clarkson was a prominent Quaker abolitionist; one of the Pennsylvania Abolition Society's Schools, which also adopted Lancaster's plan, was called the Clarkson school.

6. Jeremy Bentham's *Chrestomathia* (1816) draws heavily on Lancaster as well as on Andrew Bell.

7. Carl Kaestle, *Joseph Lancaster and the Monitorial School Movement: A Documentary History* (New York: Teachers College Press, 1973), 40. It is his nonsectarianism as well as his self-promoting personality and the visuality of his manuals that made Lancaster a success in America. Lancaster drew some aspects of his program from Andrew Bell's Madras system, which, like Lancaster's, relies on and participates in colonial discourses. In addition to Kaestle, sources for Lancaster's biography include Salmon, *Joseph Lancaster;* John Franklin Reigart, *The Lancasterian System of Instruction in the Schools of New York City* (New York: Teachers College Press, 1916); Lancaster's own *Epitome of Some of the Chief Events and Transactions in the Life of Joseph Lancaster, containing an account of the rise and progress of the Lancasterian system of education; and the Author's Future prospects of usefulness to mankind* (New Haven, 1833); and Mora Dickson, *Teacher Extraordinary: Joseph Lancaster 1778–1838* (Sussex, UK: Book Guild, 1986).

8. Kaestle, *Lancaster*, 2: Kaestle, *Pillars of the Republic: Common Schools and American Society, 1780–1860* (New York: Hill and Wang, 1983), 33–37.

9. *Sketch of the Origin and Progress of the Adelphi School in the Northern Liberties, Established Under the Direction of the Philadelphia Association of Friends for the Instruction of Poor Children* (Philadelphia: Meyer and Jones, 1810), 3. Diane Ravitch notes that the first public school in New York was "conceived of as an antipoverty program. . . . Its trustees did not want New York to develop a large pauper class, as was common in big European cities." *The Great School Wars: New York City, 1805–1973* (New York: Basic Books, 1974), 10.

10. Robert H. Bremner, ed., *Children and Youth in America: A Documentary History* (Cambridge, Mass.: Harvard University Press, 1970), viii; Jacqueline Reinier, *From Virtue to Character: American Childhood 1775–1850* (New York: Twayne, 1996), 50.

11. For Lancaster and the market economy, see David Hogan, "The Market Revolution and Disciplinary Power: Joseph Lancaster and the Psychology of the Early Classroom System," *History of Education Quarterly* 29:3 (Fall 1989), 381–417; for Lancaster and architecture, see Dell Upton, "Lancasterian Schools, Republican Citizenship, and the Spatial Imagination in Early Nineteenth-Century America," *Journal of the Society of Architectural Historians* 55:3 (1996), 238–253, and "Another City: The Urban Cultural Landscape in the Early Republic," in *Everyday Life in the Early Republic,* ed. Catherine E. Hutchins (Winterthur, Del.: Winterthur, 1994), 61–118.

12. Kaestle, *Lancaster*, 11–15.

13. Kaestle, *Lancaster*, 14.

14. David Hogan describes Lancaster's pedagogy as "a manufactory of desire and ambition." "The Market Revolution and Disciplinary Power," 384. On manufacturing in the early republic in relation to representational technologies, see Laura Rigal, *The American Manufactory: Art, Labor, and the World of Things in the Early Republic* (Princeton: Princeton University Press, 1998), 13–17. System, notes Kaestle, "was the essence of technology: it was not simply 'efficient,' . . . it was infinitely replicable," and this "idea of a uniform, recursive system is consonant with the developing technological ideology of the nineteenth century." *Lancaster*, 15.

15. At his school in Southwark, London, Lancaster had his own printing press, on which he produced some of these texts. Bound together in one large (17-by-21-inch) volume, for example, are the *New Invented Spelling Book* and *Freames Scripture Instruction,* along with broadside ephemera—Samuel Whitchurch's poems "My Mother" and "The Bible." While the catechism and poems are conventional, the spelling book reveals Lancaster's eccentric methodology, in which the letters are taught out of order, arranged instead according to their visual similarity.

16. Lancaster, *British System*, 93.

17. Lancaster, *Hints and Directions for Building, Fitting Up, and Arranging School Rooms on the British System of Education* (London, 1809),11.

18. See John Bender for tourism and the eighteenth-century British prison. *Imagining the Penitentiary: Fiction and the Architecture of Mid-Eighteenth-Century England* (Chicago: University of Chicago Press, 1987), 14. Prison reform and school reform tended to be inaugurated by citizen committees and government agencies, on whose rolls the same names turn up again and again. The rhetoric of schooling in the early republic always adverts to the costly alternative, the prison; an anonymous letter about Lancaster in *Niles' Register,* April 24, 1819, is one of many examples: "To

enlighten the mind, and thereby *prevent crime*, is better than to punish or commiserate" (150). Joined here in the figure of chiasmus, the two institutions generally share benefactors and theorists as well. In the "Report . . . to the Lancaster School Society of Georgetown" in 1812, the trustees noted that "out of six thousand persons educated by [Lancaster] alone in one school [in London], there has never yet occurred an instance of any one of them being called before a court of justice on a criminal accusation." Lancaster, *British System*, 123.

19. Lancaster, *Hints,* 13.

20. Michel Foucault describes Bentham's carceral system, a plan closely allied to pedagogical schemes like Lancaster's: "Hence the major effect of the Panopticon: to induce in the inmate a state of conscious and permanent visibility that assures the automatic functioning of power. So to arrange things that the surveillance is permanent in its effects, even it if is discontinuous in its action . . . that this architectural apparatus should be a machine for creating and sustaining a power relation independent of the person who exercises it." *Discipline and Punish: The Birth of the Prison*, tr. Alan Sheridan (1977) (New York: Vintage Books, 1995), 201.

21. Lancaster, *The Lancasterian System of Education, with Improvements* (Baltimore, 1821), 3. Dickens's 1854 *Hard Times* (New York: Bantam Books, 1981) is apparently about a Lancasterian school: Sissy Jupe is also known as "girl number twenty," and students "sat on the face of the inclined plane" (3). Consonant with the sentiments of the epigraphs to this chapter, Dickens figures the teacher, Gradgrind, as an embodiment of the square: "The speaker's square forefinger emphasized his observations. . . . The emphasis was helped by the speaker's square wall of a forehead . . . square coat, square legs, square shoulders" (1).

22. The notion of transparency is rooted in Puritan "visible sanctity" but evolves across the eighteenth and into the nineteenth century into what Karen Halttunen calls "sentimental transparency." *Confidence Men and Painted Women: A Study of Middle-Class Culture in America, 1830–1870* (New Haven: Yale University Press, 1996), 57–59.

23. For the history of the optical telegraph, see Gerald Holzmann and Bjorn Pershon, *The Early History of Data Networks* (Los Alamitos, Calif.: IEEE Computer Society Press, 1995). See *Encyclopedia Britannica* (1797), s.v. "telegraph." See also James W. Carey, especially "Technology and Ideology," which calls for a thorough and culturally grounded history of the telegraph, in *Communication as Culture: Essays on Media and Society* (New York: Routledge, 1989).

24. Holzmann and Pershon, *Early History of Data Networks,* 71; OED, s.v. "telegraph" (citing A. Duncan's *Nelson* [1806], 297).

25. Lancaster, *Lancasterian System*, 10.

26. Lancaster, *Lancasterian System*, 3.

27. Upton, "Another City," 84.

28. Dr. Young, *The Bible Recommended to Young People* (Philadelphia: American Sunday School Union, 1827), 6–7.

29. James Clifford, "On Collecting Art and Culture," in *The Cultural Studies Reader*, ed. Simon During (New York: Routledge, 1993), 53.

30. Susan Stewart, *On Longing: Narratives of the Miniature, the Gigantic, the Souvenir, the Collection* (Durham: Duke University Press, 1993), 65.

31. Lancaster, *British System*, 93; emphases in original.

32. David Wallace Adams, *Education for Extinction: American Indians and the Boarding School Experience 1875–1928* (Lawrence: University Press of Kansas, 1995), 117.

33. For an analysis of the transformation of subjects into citizens through children's reading, see Weikle-Mills, *Imaginary Citizens: Child Readers and the Limits of American Independence, 1640–1868* (Baltimore: Johns Hopkins University Press, 2012).

34. This figurative usage of "diffusion" dates from the mid eighteenth century; the OED cites Dr. Johnson (1750) and David Hume (1777) among its earliest citations.

35. "Monitor" originally means "to advise"; its subsequent evolution as a broadcast and electronic media device—substituting for the human—is worth noting.

36. Lancaster, *Lancasterian System*, 10; emphases in original.

37. Edward Said notes that the project of analyzing orientalism shows "that European culture gained in strength and identity by setting itself off against the Orient as a sort of surrogate and even underground self." *Orientalism* (New York: Pantheon, 1978), 3.

38. Lancaster, *British System,* 68–69.

39. Lancaster, *British System*, 75; emphasis in original.

40. An illustration of a "bashaw of three tails" appears in the book of the 1829 children's game *Aldiborontiphoskyphorniostikos* by R. Stennett (New York: Solomon King).

41. Lancaster, *British System*, 74.

42. Sean Shesgreen, *The Criers and Hawkers of London: Engravings and Drawings by Marcellus Laroon* (Aldershot: Scolar Press, 1990), 80.

43. Homi Bhabha uses the figure of mimicry to describe colonialism itself: "If colonialism takes power in the name of history, it repeatedly exercises its authority through the figures of farce. . . . The civilizing mission . . . often produces a text rich in the traditions of *trompe-l'oeil*, irony, mimicry, and repetition. In this comic turn from the high ideals of the colonial imagination to its low mimetic literary effects mimicry emerges as one of the most elusive and effective strategies of colonial power and knowledge." *The Location of Culture* (New York: Routledge, 1994), 85.

44. Hilary Wyss cites a letter from one of the Brainerd students who recounts having to stand and recite Bible verses as punishment, noting that "the Bible is the source of punishment, and publicly reciting from the Bible paradoxically becomes a source of humiliation," suggesting that a similar method of shaming was retained at the mission school. *English Letters and Indian Literacies: Reading, Writing, and New England Missionary Schools, 1750–1830* (Philadelphia: University of Pennsylvania Press, 2012), 224n36. The Brainerd student letters are in the John Howard Payne Papers at the Newberry Library, volume 8. Page numbers refer to a typescript of the letters, hereafter cited as JHPP with volume and typescript page number. The letter Wyss refers to is JHPP, 8, 54.

45. Ronald Rayman assesses what he sees as the failure of the Lancasterian system at the Brainerd School and elsewhere in the Southeast, providing a useful overview of the mission project. He sees the missionary emphasis on "useful work" rather than education as contributing to Cherokee resistance to the mission schools. "Joseph Lancaster's Monitorial System of Instruction and American Indian Education, 1815–1838," *History of Education Quarterly* 21 (1987), 395–409. See also Wyss, *English Letters and Indian Literacies,* and Robert Sparks Walker, *Torchlights to the Cherokee* (New York: Macmillan, 1931), for further accounts of the Brainerd school.

46. Lancaster, *Letters on National Subjects, Auxiliary Education, and Scientific Knowledge; Address to Burwell Bassett, Late a Member of the House of Representatives; Henry Clay, Speaker of the House of Rep, and James Monroe, President of the United States by Joseph Lancaster* (Washington, 1820), 42.

47. Theda Perdue points out that "ethnographers tended to equate Indians to impoverished people in their own societies. Alice Kehoe has described the consequences of this approach for women: 'The traditional [ethnographic] picture of the Plains Indian woman is really that of an Irish housemaid of the late Victorian era clothed in a buckskin dress.'" *Cherokee Women: Gender and Culture Change, 1700–1835* (Lincoln: University of Nebraska Press, 1998), 5. Locke's perception of Indians' failure to improve their property through labor is one of the origins of this error; see William Cronon, *Changes in the Land: Indians, Colonists and the Ecology of New England* (New York: Hill and Wang, 1983), 79–80. It pervades white writing about Indians, who are consistently described by the American Board as "destitute," a term that combines economic and spiritual poverty. As for "civilization," Raymond Williams cites Boswell's account of Johnson's disdain for the term: "'He would not admit *civilization*, but only *civility*. With great deference to him, I thought *civilization* . . . better in the sense opposed to *barbarity*, than *civility*." Williams comments that "Boswell correctly identified the main use that was coming through, which emphasized not so much a process as a state of social order and refinement, especially in conscious historical or cultural contrast with *barbarism*. Civilization appeared in Ash's dictionary of 1775, to indicate both the state and the process." *Keywords: A Vocabulary of Culture and Society* (New York: Oxford University Press, 1985), s.v. "civilization."

48. See Wyss, *English Letters,* for an account of the missionaries' apocalyptic sense of urgency, 111–13.

49. Elijah Parish, *Sermon Preached at Ipswich, Sept. 29, 1815. At the Ordination of Rev. Daniel Smith and Cyrus Kingsbury as Missionaries to the West* (Newburyport, 1815), 11–12.

50. For the history of Cherokees, I have drawn on William G. McLoughlin, *Cherokee Renascence in the New Republic* (Princeton: Princeton University Press, 1986), McLoughlin, *The Cherokees and Christianity, 1794–1870: Essays on Acculturation and Cultural Persistence*, ed. Walter H. Conser Jr. (Athens: University of Georgia Press, 1994); McLoughlin, *Cherokees and Missionaries 1789–1839* (New Haven: Yale University Press, 1984); Theda Perdue's *Cherokee Women*; and James Mooney, *Historical Sketch of the Cherokee* (originally published in 1898 as part of the "Myths of the Cherokees," by the Bureau of American Ethnology, the Nineteenth Annual Report) (Chicago: Aldine, 1975).

51. Margaret Connell-Szasz, *Indian Education in the American Colonies, 1607–1783* (Albuquerque: University of New Mexico Press, 1988), 259.

52. American Board of Commissioners for Foreign Missions, *First Ten Annual Reports of the American Board of Commissioners for Foreign Missions 1810–1820* (Boston, 1834), 193.

53. Sarah Tuttle, *Letters and Conversations on the Cherokee Mission* (Boston: Massachusetts Sabbath School Union, 1830), 74. Tuttle seems here to be drawing on American Board accounts where this anecdote appears in the board's report for 1819; American Board, *First Ten Annual Reports,* 238.

54. David Murray, *Forked Tongues: Speech, Writing and Representation in North American Indian Texts* (Bloomington: Indiana University Press, 1991), 35–36.

55. Murray, *Forked Tongues,* 41. See also Carolyn Eastman's chapter "Mourning for Logan" (*A Nation of Speechifiers: Making an American Public after the Revolution.* [Chicago: University of Chicago Press, 2009], 83–111) for an analysis of the ways in which valorization of Indian eloquence paradoxically served the formation of white publics.

56. American Board, *First Ten Annual Reports,* 192.

57. Berkhofer, *Salvation and the Savage,* 26.

58. Lydia Huntley Sigourney, "Indian Names," in *American Poetry: The Nineteenth Century,* vol. 1 (New York: Library of America, 1993), 111.

59. The renaming constitutes part of what the sociologist Pierre Bourdieu calls a "rite of institution." *Language and Symbolic Power*, tr. Gino Raymond and Matthew Adamson (Cambridge: Polity, 1991), 117–26. He is extending van Gennep's notion of the rite of passage to institutional performances. See also Bourdieu on naming, *Outline of a Theory of Practice,* tr. Richard Nice (Cambridge: Cambridge University Press, 1977), 36. The rite of institution is an "act of communication" that "*signifies* to someone what his identity is" (121). In most Indian school settings these missionary rites are explicitly violent; typical is a description of a Shawnee school in 1850: "The service to a new pupil was to trim his hair closely; then with soap and water, to give him or her the first lesson on godliness, which was a good scrubbing, and a little red precipitate on the scalp to supplement the use of a fine-toothed comb; and then he was furnished with a suit of new clothes, and taught how to put them on and off. They all emerged from this ordeal as shy as a peacock, just plucked. A new English name finished the preparation for the alphabet and the English language." Berkhofer, *Salvation and the Savage,* 36 (quoting Wilson Hobbs, "The Friends' Establishment in Kansas Territory," *Kansas Historical Collections*, VIII, 1903–1904, 253). This account makes explicit the connection between the new name and an initiation into English literacy, which is implicit in the Brainerd accounts. The rhetoric of the *Brainerd Journal* lacks the violence of this account, which is not to say that the effect wasn't quite similar. See Wyss, *English Letters,* 128–29, on renaming at Brainerd; see also Adams, *Education for Extinction,* 108–12, for controversy over naming at federal boarding schools.

60. In the Bellerophon story (*Iliad*, book VI), the only mention of writing in Homer, Proteus, suspecting Bellerophon of seducing his wife, sends him on an errand with a letter of introduction, which conveys instructions to kill the bearer. For an analysis of the story, see Roy Harris, *The Origins of Writing* (La Salle, Ill.: Open Court, 1986), 15–16.

61. Eric Cheyfitz, *The Poetics of Imperialism: Translation and Colonization from* The Tempest *to* Tarzan (New York: Oxford University Press, 1991), 10.

62. Cheyfitz, *Poetics of Imperialism,* 59.

63. James Kincaid, *Child-loving: The Erotic Child and Victorian Culture* (New York: Routledge, 1994), 12.

64. Joyce B. Phillips and Paul Gary Phillips, eds., *The Brainerd Journal: A Mission to the Cherokees, 1817–1823* (Lincoln: University of Nebraska Press, 1998), 423.

65. Phillips and Phillips, *Brainerd Journal*, 406–24.

66. Worcester is American Board corresponding secretary; his nephew Samuel Austin Worcester worked with the (Cherokee) Elias Boudinot on the *Cherokee Phoenix* newspaper, earning the Cherokee name A-tse-nu-sti, "the messenger" (Phillips and Phillips, *Brainerd Journal*, 396). John Knox (1513–1572) was the founder of Scottish Presbyterianism, while John Witherspoon (1723–1794) was a Presbyterian minister and president of the College of New Jersey; Thomas McKenney was superintendent of Indian trade from 1816 to1822 and head of the new Bureau of Indian Affairs in the War Department from 1824 to 1830; Lydia Huntley (Sigourney), by 1829 perhaps the most famous poet in America, was a supporter of Indian rights; one of her first books was a narrative poem called *Traits of the Aborigines* excoriating white behavior toward Indians; Jedidiah Morse was a prominent geographer, founder of the Andover Theological Seminary and on the boards of the American Board and the Society for the Propagation of the Gospel; Jeremiah Evarts, corresponding secretary and treasurer of the American Board, was the author of the "William Penn" letters against Removal; Elias Boudinot, was a federalist force in revolutionary politics and a benefactor of the Cornwall, Conn., Indian school. The newspaper *Boston Recorder* was a student's benefactor.

67. Wyss, *English Letters*, 128–29.

68. Phillips and Phillips, *Brainerd Journal*, July 3, 1820, 182.

69. The Cherokee interpreters who translated the names for the mission records had a daunting task, and doubtless the names lost a lot in translation; nonetheless the Cherokee names are suggestive: Taking Away, Man Strikes, Stone Thrower, Bird Pecking, Swimmer, Making Holes Deeper, A Wren Going Under, Run After, Jumping in the Water, Sleeping Rabbit, Let Us Go Across, Standing, Jumper, John Is Gone, Hid, Howling, Hog Shooter, White Killer, Runner, One Who Runs Too Fast to Be Taken (Phillips and Phillips, *Brainerd Journal*, 407–18).

70. Wyss notes that the students "seemingly did not complain about this wholesale conversion of their personhood and nationality" but wryly draws attention to "those who ran away or never returned from home, a problem that became so acute it had to be addressed through legislation by the Cherokee Council." *English Letters*, 129.

71. James Mooney, *The Swimmer Manuscript: Cherokee Sacred Formulas and Medicinal Prescriptions*, revised and edited by Frans M. Olbrechts, Smithsonian Institution Bureau of American Ethnology, Bulletin 99 (Washington, D.C.: U.S. Government Printing Office, 1932), 127–28.

72. David French and Katherine French, "Personal Names," *Handbook of North American Indians, Volume 17: Languages*, ed. Ives Goddard (Washington, D.C.: Smithsonian, 1996), 212.

73. Wyss, *English Letters*, 118.

74. JHPP, vol. 8, 61.

75. Jefferson told the Indians that "when once you have property, you will want laws and magistrates to protect your property and persons. . . . You will find that our laws are good for this purpose." Quoted in Wilcomb E. Washburn, *Redman's Land, White Man's Law: A Study of the Past and Present State of the American Indian* (New York: Scribner, 1971), 61. Similarly, William Crawford, secretary of war under Madison, thought that "the idea of separate property in things personal universally precedes the same idea in relation to lands." *American State Papers, Class II, Indian Affairs* (Washington, D.C., 1832), 27. White authorities have in mind only particular items of property; specifically, the hoes, plows, spinning wheels, and looms that figure prominently along with slaves, cattle, and pigs in reports of Cherokee progress. See also Reginald Horsman, especially chapter 10, for the relationship between these notions of proper property and the increasing racialization of white and Indian relations. *Race and Manifest Destiny: The Origins of American Racial Anglo-Saxonism* (Cambridge, Mass.: Harvard University Press, 1981).

76. Tuttle, *Letters and Conversations*, Preface, n.p.

77. Phillips and Phillips, *Brainerd Journal*, 423.

78. Wyss notes that one of Nancy Reece's teachers when she was about twelve remarked on her struggles with writing (*English Letters*, 138). When Reece was nine, the Brainerd journal records that she's reading in the "Testament," which suggests that the school wasn't consistently following the Lancaster system of teaching writing early, perhaps because of the language difference (Phillips and

Phillips, *Brainerd Journal,* 423). By the time she was fifteen, she was translating for and teaching younger children herself. Reece is the most prolific of the Brainerd letter writers and has been at the center of other scholarly accounts; see Michael Coleman, "American Indian School Pupils as Cultural Brokers: Cherokee Girls at Brainerd Mission, 1828–1829," in *Between Indian and White Worlds: The Culture Broker,* ed. Margaret Connell-Szasz (Norman: University of Oklahoma Press, 1994). Michael Coleman's article on these child writers as "culture brokers" drew my attention to these riveting letters. For further interpretation and additional excerpts from these letters, see Wyss, *English Letters;* and Virginia Moore Carney, *Eastern Band Cherokee Women: Cultural Persistence in Their Letters and Speeches* (Knoxville: University of Tennessee Press, 2005).

79. JHPP, vol. 8, 6.

80. JHPP, vol. 8, 8.

81. JHPP, vol. 8, 10.

82. Elizabeth Taylor to Miss D. Gould, JHPP, vol. 8, 9.

83. June 23, 1828, JHPP, vol. 8, 40.

84. JHPP, vol. 8, 18.

85. Wyss has teased out the narrative of Reece's intense attachment to her teacher that her letters also reveal. *English Letters,* 138–45.

86. JHPP, vol. 8, 31.

87. Tuttle, *Letters and Conversations,* 136.

88. Tuttle, *Letters and Conversations,* 138–39.

89. Wyss notes that the "letters point to precisely the slippages between the Lancaster erasure of personhood and the relentless family building that is Brainerd." *English Letters,* 145–46.

Chapter 4. "Selling a Boy"

Epigraph. My ellipses. From the opening paragraph of Sylvester Judd, *Margaret: A Tale of the Real and Ideal, Blight and Bloom* (1845), ed. Gavin Jones (Boston: University of Massachusetts Press, 2009). J. G. Whittier uses this quotation as the epigraph to his edited anthology *Child Life in Prose* (Boston, 1873).

1. Viviana Zelizer, *Pricing the Priceless Child: The Changing Social Value of Children* (1985) (Princeton: Princeton University Press, 1994), 11, 5.

2. The references are to Maria Edgeworth's "The Purple Jar" (in *Rosamond,* 1808), and to *Goody Two-Shoes* and "The Children in the Wood," discussed in previous chapters.

3. OED, s.v. "stranger," 4b.

4. Stephen Mintz and Susan Kellogg, *Domestic Revolutions: A Social History of American Family Life* (New York: Free Press, 1988), 54.

5. Barbara Bennett Woodhouse, *Hidden in Plain Sight: The Tragedy of Children's Rights from Ben Franklin to Lionel Tate* (Princeton: Princeton University Press, 2008), 61.

6. Wilma King notes in her history of enslaved children in America, that 56 percent of the slave population in 1860 was under twenty years old. *Stolen Childhood: Slave Youth in Nineteenth-Century America* (Bloomington: Indiana University Press, 1995), vii.

7. A. A. Alryyes sees the "homeless child" at the center of the realist novel's national narrative: "Not only is the suffering of the homeless child a central element in nationalist narratives but also . . . it underpins the rise of the realist novel in the eighteenth century. . . . The rise of the novel, familiarly related to the new middle-class experience, is also fundamentally linked to the experience of homeless children." *Original Subjects: The Child, the Novel, and the Nation* (Cambridge, Mass.: Harvard University Press, 2001), 25.

8. Michael Katz notes that pauper auctions, including of children, a practice of country towns without almshouses, persisted in New England in the early decades of the century and until as late as the 1850s in Rhode Island. *In the Shadow of the Poorhouse: A Social History of Welfare in America* (New York: Basic Books, 1996), 13–22.

9. See, for example, Kirsten Person's bibliography of "lost children" texts, "Child Abduction in Nineteenth-Century American Children's Literature," for the American Studies Seminar at the American Antiquarian Society in 1994.

10. See Laura Wasowicz, "Of Beggars, Ballad Singers, and Sailors: Wayward Children in Early Paper Doll Chapbooks," which describes these editions in detail in *The Child's Turn: Childhood in Text and Image in the Nineteenth-Century United States*, ed. Caroline Sloat and Patricia Crain (University of Georgia Press, forthcoming). The collector and bibliographer A. S. W. Rosenbach found Fanny's story particularly disturbing: "Whatever the author's intention may have been in this story, the results could hardly fail to be disastrous, both on the mind of the small reader, and on her relations with her mother." *Early American Children's Books, with Bibliographical Descriptions of the Books in His Private Collection* (1933) (New York: Dover Books, 1971), 243–44.

11. *The History of Little Fanny, Exemplified in a Series of Figures* (Philadelphia: William Charles, 1812). Parenthetical references will be to this edition.

12. According to Pinchbeck and Hewitt, in England, until 1814, it was the theft of the clothes that was punishable, not of the child. *Children in English Society, Volume 2: From the Eighteenth Century to the Children Act 1948* (London: Routledge, 1973), 360.

13. Robin Bernstein, *Racial Innocence: Performing American Childhood from Slavery to Civil Rights* (New York: New York University Press, 2011), 222.

14. These texts do not use the word "kidnap," which, as Paula Fass notes in *Kidnapped: Child Abduction in America* (New York: Oxford, 1997), was always originally associated with slave labor, 10–11. Fass focuses on the famous Charley Ross ransom kidnapping of 1874, which she sees as having the markers of the modern abduction that the late twentieth and early twenty-first century have been obsessed with. Her introduction offers a useful pocket history of child abduction.

15. Hawthorne, *Tales and Sketches* (New York: Library of America, 1982), 228–35; citations in parentheses will be to this edition. Hawthorne's works for children get scant scholarly attention, but Elizabeth Freeman and Karen Sánchez-Eppler offer smart readings of "Little Annie's Ramble." Freeman reads the tale within a cultural narrative of national expansion, finding a "pedophiliac picaresque" linked to other narratives by Poe, Mayne Reid, and Nabokov: "The narrator uses Annie to teach himself how to have pleasure" and "transforms the little girl into the keeper of his identity rather than vice versa." "Honeymoon with a Stranger: Pedophiliac Picaresques from Poe to Nabokov," *American Literature* 70:4 (December 1998), 881. Sánchez-Eppler sees it as Hawthorne's "meditation on the act of writing for children, and on the conflicting possibilities [for such authorship] of monitor and playfellow." *Dependent States: The Child's Part in Nineteenth-Century American Culture* (Chicago: University of Chicago Press, 2005), 55. Elsewhere, she notes the ways in which Hawthorne "suggests the perverse as well as the innocent possibilities of that role," and the tale's "story of adult lechery and disillusionment." "Hawthorne and the Writing of Childhood," in Richard H. Millington, ed., *The Cambridge Companion to Nathaniel Hawthorne* (Cambridge: Cambridge University Press, 2004), 152. It was Mary M. van Tassel who recuperated the tale from obscurity, positioning it along with Hawthorne's "sketches." "Hawthorne, His Narrator, and His Readers in 'Little Annie's Ramble,'" *ESQ: A Journal of the American Renaissance* 33:3 (1987), 168–79.

16. The very term "keepsake" originates as a print genre designation for the gift book. S.v. "keepsake," OED. Andrew Piper notes the ways in which the gift book, in these dedicatory spaces and elsewhere, *invite* writing, a subject I take up in the next chapter. *Dreaming in Books: The Making of the Bibliographic Imagination in the Romantic Age* (Chicago: University of Chicago Press, 2009), 127. Meredith McGill describes the transformation of such books from commodities to "tokens of affection," via spaces for dedications and presentation that "script[] a relationship between purchaser and receiver." *American Literature and the Culture of Reprinting, 1834–1853* (Philadelphia: University of Pennsylvania Press, 2003), 34.

17. I'm indebted to Blevin Shelnutt's 2010 NYU master's thesis, "Childhood, City Streets, and *Hot Corn* in the Writing of Henry James," for drawing my attention to the position of childhood in Walter Benjamin's description of the flâneur. As Benjamin has it, "The streets conduct the flâneur into a vanished time. For him, every street is precipitous. It leads downward—if not to the mythical Mothers, then into a past that can be all the more spellbinding because it is not his own, not private. Nevertheless, it always remains the time of a childhood." *The Arcades Project,* tr. Howard Eiland and Kevin McLaughlin (Cambridge, Mass.: Belknap Press of Harvard University Press, 1999), 416.

18. Sánchez-Eppler, *Dependent States*, 55.

19. Elizabeth Freeman sees "Annie" in a line that leads to *Lolita.* "Honeymoon with a Stranger."

20. An English edition of Hawthorne's tales headlined Annie—*Little Annie's Ramble, and Other Tales* (1853). McGill, *American Literature and the Culture of Reprinting,* 329n42. By the time of his 1873 reprint (whose epigraph from *Margaret* I have excerpted above), Whittier can write in the preface, "It may be well to admit, in the outset, that the book is as much for child-lovers, who have not outgrown their child-heartedness in becoming mere men and women, as for children themselves; that is as much *about* childhood, as *for* it." *Child Life in Prose,* v.

21. Michael Grossberg, *Governing the Hearth: Law and the Family in Nineteenth-Century America* (Chapel Hill: University of North Carolina Press, 1985), 234.

22. See Cindy Weinstein, *Family, Kinship, and Sympathy in Nineteenth-Century American Literature* (Cambridge: Cambridge University Press, 2004), 52ff.

23. Weinstein, *Family, Kinship, and Sympathy,* 55, 9. Weinstein notes the "two related and contentious developments in the antebellum family and in the legal scene—the diminution of paternal rights and the expansion of maternal ones," 53. See also Carol Singley, *Adopting America: Childhood, Kinship, and National Identity in Literature* (New York: Oxford University Press, 2011), for adoption tropes in nineteenth-century American literature.

24. A modern biography of Jacob Abbott is overdue, not only for his importance to children's literature, but also for his role as a progressive teacher, who, for example, hoped to bring a modern language curriculum to Amherst shortly after its founding. See Larzer Ziff, "Rollo, or How to Raise an American Boy," *Hopkins Review* 5:4 (Fall 2012), 470–89; Gregory Nenstiel, "Jacob Abbott: Mentor to a Rising Generation," Ph.D. dissertation, University of Maryland, 1979; Phillip Kendall, "The Times and Tales of Jacob Abbott," Ph.D. dissertation, Boston University, 1968.

25. Lyman Abbott, *Silhouettes of My Contemporaries* (New York: Doubleday, 1922), 335–36. Lyman Abbott became a distinguished minister and editor. In keeping with Jacob Abbott's narrative style, when the son was changing careers from lawyer to minister in 1859, according to Lyman Abbott's biographer, his father advised that "he should decrease the length of his sermons until the congregation complained that they were too short and then eliminate another five minutes' worth. . . . If he wishes to take his hearers from one idea to another he must go through all the intermediate points, just as in going from one place to another." Ira V. Brown, *Lyman Abbott, Christian Evolutionist: A Study in Religious Liberalism* (Cambridge, Mass.: Harvard University Press, 1953), 22.

26. See the Coda for a discussion of bedtime stories.

27. A number of scholars have recognized the importance of miscellany- or anthology-like print formats in the eighteenth and nineteenth centuries. As Andrew Piper has put it, "The miscellany embodies the etymological origins of reading as an act of gathering," and, further, "the romantic miscellany [in America, the 'gift book'] . . . played a role in marking the transition from the cyclicality to the seriality of cultural production that would become a hallmark of both nineteenth-century literature and twentieth-century mass media more generally." *Dreaming in Books,* 122, 123. See also Meredith McGill, *American Literature and the Culture of Reprinting,* and Leah Price, *The Anthology and the Rise of the Novel: From Richardson to George Eliot* (Cambridge: Cambridge University Press 2000).

28. The first in the series, *The Little Scholar Learning to Talk: A Picture Book for Rollo* (Boston, 1835; in later editions retitled *Rollo Learning to Talk*), was written for parents and older children to read aloud to younger children, engaging them in conversation.

29. Worldcat lists the last as an 1891 edition ("New York: Thomas Y. Crowell & Co., No. 13 Astor Place, [ca. 1891]"). Henry James mentions the "sweet Rollo series" (and the Franconia stories) in his 1913 memoir *A Small Boy and Others* (London: Gibson Square Books, Turtle Point Press, 2001), 127. In a 1911 parody, Robert J. Burdette has Rollo delightedly reading a twenty-three-volume set of Bancroft's *History of the United States.* "Rollo Learning to Read," in *The Wit and Humor of America,* ed. Marshall P. Wilder, vol. 3 (New York: Funk and Wagnalls, 1911), 448–53. Well into the twentieth century, in cultural memory Rollo (like Goody Two-Shoes) is a "prig." Lorinda Cohoon, *Serialized Citizenship: Periodicals, Books, and American Boys, 1840–1911* (Lanham, Md.: Scarecrow Press, 2006), 7, citing a 1947 *Saturday Review* article. And a "sanctimonious little" one at that. William W. Lawrence, "Rollo and His Uncle George," *New England Quarterly* 18:3 (September 1945), 291–302, quote on 291.

30. Abbott, *Rollo Learning to Read* (Boston: Thomas H. Webb, 1835). Citations are from this edition, available online at http://www.merrycoz.org/books/read/READ.HTM.

31. "Amuse" was a word in transition, from early connotations of wonderment, deception, or time wasting (all based on the root "muse," referring to a gaping facial expression) to its modern meaning (OED, s.v.).

32. Steven Mintz notes that the "vast majority of families . . . continued to rely heavily on children's labor and earnings" through the nineteenth century and across rural and urban settings. *Huck's Raft: A History of American Childhood* (Cambridge, Mass.: Harvard University Press, 2006), 135.

33. David Hoffman quoted in Grossberg, *Governing the Hearth*, 235.

34. Hoffman quoted in Grossberg, *Governing the Hearth*, 235. Courtney Weikle-Mills describes the ways in which such "'tacit compacts'" undergird what she calls "imaginary citizenship" for children as for adults, and recognizes ways in which children's literature and schoolroom practices such as rewards of merit functioned as "imaginary versions of children's economic participation" and "helped Americans to claim that social goods could result from economic growth." *Imaginary Citizens: Child Readers and the Limits of American Independence, 1640–1868* (Baltimore: Johns Hopkins University Press, 2012),136. In her view, "As children were imagined as participating in the market with moral values as their guide, they made its transactions seem patriotic, virtuous, and emotionally moving" (137).

35. "When Rollo's father found [Jonas], he meant to have sent him to the poor-house, where all poor boys are taken care of, but he kept him in the house a few days first, and he found that he was a very good boy. . . . And so Rollo's father thought he would let him stay and live with him, and work for him" (116–17).

36. In her chapter on Abbott's contributions to *Youth's Companion*, Lorinda Cohoon notes that "periodicals and series books teach boys how to possess themselves and the materials around them in ways that are legally binding." *Serialized Citizenship*, 29n36.

37. I borrow the notion of the "enterprising" child from Monika Elbert, whose edited collection of essays on nineteenth-century children's literature is entitled *Enterprising Youth: Social Values and Acculturation in Nineteenth-Century American Children's Literature* (New York: Routledge, 2008).

38. Mary E. Quinlivan, "Race Relations in the Antebellum Children's Literature of Jacob Abbott," *Journal of Popular Culture* 16:1 (Summer 1982), 27–36, 28.

39. Donnarae MacCann finds Abbott at best "ambivalent" about African Americans and very much in the thrall of white supremicism, particularly in his first book with an African American character, which I discuss below. MacCann notes that Abbott takes up an antiprejudice theme in the "Rainbow and Lucky" series, while at the same radically limiting his African American characters. MacCann reads this paradox as consistent with Abbott's progressive education theories and conservative political views. *White Supremacy in Children's Literature: Characterizations of African Americans, 1830–1900* (New York: Garland, 1998), 13–16, 58–61, quote on 15. I'm aware of only two articles that have addressed Abbott's black characters: Jeannette Barnes Lessels and Eric Sterling's "Overcoming Racism" (in Elbert, *Enterprising Youth,* [83–96]) and Quinlivan's "Race Relations."

40. Sharpening a knife, *Timboo and Joliba; or, The Art of Being Useful* (New York: Harper's, 1855) 41; telegraphs, *Grimkie, The Florence Stories* (New York: Sheldon, 1860), 234–42.

41. *Mary Gay; or, Work for Girls: Work for Autumn* (New York: Hurd and Houghton, 1865), 79 (scrapbook); *Mary Gay; or, Work for Girls: Work for Spring* (New York: Hurd and Houghton, 1865) (panorama), 18–25 and 100–107 (doll table).

42. Auction in *Caleb in Town* (Boston: Crocker and Brewster, 1839), 67–73; clothesline and book in *Timboo and Joliba*, 28–35 and 89–91.

43. *The Harper Establishment* (New York: Harper and Brothers, 1855 (for presses and type-foundry); *Mary Gay; or, Work for Girls: Work for Spring*, paper mill, 171–72.

44. Jumping bridge in *Congo; or, Jasper's Experience in Command* (New York: Harper Brothers, 1857) 39.

45. *John Gay; or, Work for Boys: Work for Spring* (New York: Hurd and Houghton, 1869), 113–22.

46. *Rodolphus: A Franconia Story* (New York: Harper and Brothers, 1852), 178–79.

47. *Every Day Duty: Illustrated by Sketches of Childish Character and Conduct, with Pictures* (New York: Leavitt, Lord, 1835), 52.

48. *Prank; or, The Philosophy of Tricks and Mischief* (New York: Harper and Brothers, 1855), 34.

49. Abbott, *Timboo and Joliba*, 59.

50. Sánchez-Eppler, *Dependent States,* 154.

51. Abbott, *The Alcove; Containing Some Further Account of Timboo, Mark, and Fanny* (New York: Harper and Brothers, 1856). In an 1878 reader, Timboo appears as "a domestic" from "one of the South Sea Islands . . . but, being good-natured and intelligent, is much liked by the boys, and has a great deal of influence over them." G. S. Hillard, *The Franklin Fourth Reader* (New York: Taintor Brothers, Merrill, 1878), 74. *The Franklin Reader* excerpt notes that it is taken from Abbott's *Dialogues for the Amusement and Instruction of Young Persons*, 1856.

52. *Willie and the Mortgage: Showing How Much May Be Accomplished by a Boy* (New York: Harper and Brothers, 1855); citations to this edition will be in parentheses.

53. *Handie* (Rainbow and Lucky Stories) (New York: Harper and Brothers, 1859); page numbers in parentheses will be to this edition. See also Abbott's *Virginia; or, A Little Light on a Very Dark Saying*. When Virginia was given gifts by her students, she "carried both the money and pencil-case home, and gave them to her father. Indeed, they both belonged to her father. . . . It would only be when she was of age that her earnings would be properly her own. Virginia was well aware of this. She not only knew that the law was so, but she felt that it was just and proper that it should be so" (New York: Harper and Brothers, 1855), 115–16.

54. Ever practical and cautious, Handie says, "Suppose I should not live," and Mr. James says, yes, he must get his life insured for the "amount of the debt" (135).

55. And the contractual nature of just about everything, including family life. There's a print-culture effect at work here: Abbott is immersed in contracts with his publishers, and occasional contract disputes, according to his papers at the Morgan Library, as he had been even in his dealings with Amherst and Mt. Vernon school, and probably also as a minister. See letters to "Messrs Harper & Brothers" at the Morgan Library; on April 14, 1856, for example, Abbott disputes terms of his contract and in a February 7, 1856 letter intercedes on behalf of John S. C. Abbott in a contract issue.

56. Amy Dru Stanley, *From Bondage to Contract: Wage Labor, Marriage, and the Market in the Age of Slave Emancipation* (Cambridge: Cambridge University Press, 1998), 3, 21.

57. Jeannine deLombard, "Slave Narratives and U.S. Legal History," in *The Oxford Handbook of the African American Slave Narrative,* ed. John Ernest (New York: Oxford University Press, 2014), 73.

58. See Quinlivan, "Race Relations," 36n12, for the 1810 ban on "negro mail carriers" that goes "unchallenged until 1862." (She cites Leon Litwack, *North of Slavery: The Negro in the Free States, 1790–1860* [Chicago, 1961], 57–59.)

59. In *Up the River*, Rainbow says he can't be a carpenter because he has no head for calculations and planning; Abbott comments that "he had no talent at all for abstract philosophy in any form" (New York: Harper and Brothers, 1861), 94. Abbott's progressivism here and elsewhere strains against an undertow of such restricting racism.

60. At the end of the novel, Congo, like Rainbow at the end of his series, becomes a coachman. See Susan Ryan's reading of *Congo, The Grammar of Good Intentions: Race and the Antebellum Culture of Benevolence* (Ithaca, N.Y.: Cornell University Press, 2004), 94–95.

61. Abbott, *Juno and Georgie* (New York: Dodd and Mead, 1870), 1.

62. Abbott, *Hubert* (New York: Dodd and Mead, 1870), 108.

63. See, for example, in *Hubert*: "Now, as Georgie's mother almost always concurred with Juno's opinion, Georgie generally considered the question [of any permission] virtually settled, when he had obtained Juno's consent to refer it to his mother" (33).

64. Abbott, *Juno and Georgie,* 172 (italics in original).

65. Abbott, *Juno and Georgie,* 179 (italics in original).

66. Abbott, *Juno and Georgie,* 181.

67. Abbott, *Juno and Georgie,* 186.

68. Abbott, *Juno and Georgie* ,197.

69. Abbott, *Juno and Georgie,* 198.

70. Unlike many African American characters imagined by white authors in this period—Stowe and Twain, for example—Juno lacks the qualities of what film critics have called the "magical negro," whose willing sacrifices support white character's development. See, for example, Matthew W. Hughey, "Racializing Redemption, Reproducing Racism: The Odyssey of Magical Negroes and White Saviors," *Sociology Compass* 6:9 (2012), 751–67.

71. To some extent, Abbott's representations of African American young people (with the very notable exception of Congo) might chime with what Robin Bernstein notes as a "road less taken" in nineteenth-century depictions in her analysis of John Newton Hyde's illustrations. See "Signposts on the Road Less Taken: John Newton Hyde's Anti-Racist Illustrations of African American Children," *J19: The Journal of Nineteenth-Century Americanists,*1:1 (2013), 97–119.

Chapter 5. Children in the Margins

1. Eva Illouz, *Cold Intimacies: The Making of Emotional Capitalism* (Cambridge: Polity Press, 2007), 5.

2. Seth Lerer, "Devotion and Defacement: Reading Children's Marginalia," *Representations* 118:1 (2012), 127. Lerer offers a wealth of insight into children's marks in books, noting as well that "what the annotated book becomes, what later readers find in books marred or manipulated by children, is something very different from what it had been before" (130), a perspective that underlies my thinking in this chapter.

3. H. J. Jackson distinguishes "marginalia" from both what she calls "mere vandalism, that scribbling in books purely to deface them," and professional annotations, but I am here interested in every trace of interaction with a book. "Writing in Books and Other Marginal Activities," *University of Toronto Quarterly* 62 (1993), 217–31, quote on 218–19.

4. In this chapter, I am looking at books catalogued as children's literature ("juveniles") and schoolbooks, though these are not always reliable categories. In these, as in other books, it is sometimes difficult to identify the age of the inscriber, and I will indicate when I have succeeded in doing so.

5. Proverbs 8:17, a verse with wide circulation in texts for and about children in the nineteenth century.

6. The additional verse is "I will be a God to thee, and to thy seed after thee" (a version of Genesis 18:8).

7. Ellen had requested the inscription: "Now, mamma, will you please to write my name in this precious book—my name, and any thing else you please, mother." Susan Warner, *The Wide, Wide World* (New York: Feminist Press, 1987), 42, 41.

8. Carolyn Steedman, commenting on Derrida's "archive fever" in her preface to *Dust,* writes: "If we find nothing [in the archive], we will find nothing in a place; and . . . an absence is not *nothing,* but is rather the space left by what has gone: . . . the emptiness indicates how once it was filled and animated" (Manchester: Manchester University Press, 2002), 11.

9. William Sherman, "Used Books," *Shakespeare Studies* 48 (2000), 146. There's a growing bibliography of work on marginalia, including Sherman's *Used Books: Marking Readers in Renaissance England* (Philadelphia: University of Pennsylvania Press, 2007) and H. J. Jackson's two foundational works on romanticism, *Marginalia: Readers Writing in Books* (New Haven: Yale University Press, 2001) and *Romantic Readers: The Evidence of Marginalia* (New Haven: Yale University Press, 2005). Earlier works include Roger Stoddard, *Marks in Books, Illustrated and Explained* (Cambridge, Mass.: Harvard University Press, 1985). Children's marginalia has attracted fewer studies but is notably treated in M. O. Grenby, *The Child Reader, 1700–1840* (Cambridge: Cambridge University Press, 2011), and Lerer, "Devotion and Defacement," and occasional reports from children's special collections, such as Jeff Barton, "Marks in Children's Books," Cotsen Children's Library Blog, Princeton University, July 28, 2011.

10. These are sometimes the unselfconsciously nostalgia-steeped accounts of book love, sometimes polemics. See, for example, one of the earliest and best of the genre, Sven Birkerts, *Gutenberg*

Elegies: The Fate of Reading in an Electronic Age (New York: Faber and Faber, 1994, 2006). Carolyn Steedman's *Dust* recounts some of the emotions of scholarship, but these are mostly negative (boredom, irritation, anxiety), and Steedman doesn't attach them to artifacts per se.

11. Librarians and cataloguers vary on how they regard things found in books. Vegetation is usually not welcomed. And even the most respectful restorative measures can have the clinical effect of stripping away the presence of former owners, by the application of archival tissue to torn pages, for example, or the enclosing in mylar of paper dolls or other extraneous material inserted between pages.

12. In *The Child Reader* M. O. Grenby provides the most thorough inventory to date of marks in British children's books in the long eighteenth century, using a large corpus of more than five thousand books, uncovering and quantifying reading practices in and out of school.

13. Igor Kopytoff, "The Cultural Biography of Things: Commoditization as Process," in *The Social Life of Things,* ed. Arjun Appadurai (Cambridge: Cambridge University Press, 1986), 83.

14. See Stephen Nissenbaum, *The Battle for Christmas: A Cultural History of America's Most Cherished Holiday* (New York: Vintage Books, 1997), 140–55.

15. Bill Brown, "Thing Theory," *Critical Inquiry* 28:1(Autumn 2001), 1–22; see also this entire issue of *Critical Inquiry.* See Brown, *Material Unconscious: American Amusement, Stephen Crane, and the Economics of Play* (Cambridge, Mass.: Harvard University Press, 1997); Elaine Freedgood, *Ideas in Things: Fugitive Meaning in the Victorian Novel* (Chicago: University of Chicago Press, 200); Peter Schwenger, *The Tears of Things: Melancholy and Physical Objects* (Minneapolis: University of Minnesota Press, 2005).

16. Jackson, *Marginalia*, 19. Jackson has practically single-handedly laid the groundwork for thinking about marginalia, in this book and in *Romantic Readers.*

17. See the next chapter for Henry James's theory of reading, which conjures a spectral child over whose shoulder one reads.

18. Although it's sometimes useful to speak of "the archive," all of the books in this chapter were found from a survey of some three hundred annotated books among the approximately twenty thousand children's artifacts in the library of the American Antiquarian Society, in Worcester, Massachusetts.

19. This ballad's prose incarnation is discussed in Chapter 2. In the Abiah Chapin and some similar cases, it is possible that an adult has inscribed the book on behalf of the child, modeling the practice of owning and the rituals surrounding property. In this case, the inscription takes up the whole inside paper cover of this small chapbook and appears to me to be in an accomplished child's hand, especially since "Abiah" is repeated in the same hand. Abiah Chapin (1806–1864) further inscribed the book to her nephew Seth Dwight Chapin (born in 1824) in 1830. Genealogical details in this chapter are drawn (as in this case) from familysearch.org or from ancestry.com unless otherwise noted.

20. Jackson, *Marginalia,* 90.

21. Alice Comfort's copy is Lindley Murray, *The English Reader: Or, Pieces in Prose and Poetry, Selected from the Best Writers* (Philadelphia: Johnson and Warner, 1811, AAS call number Dated Books). As in many of these books, this inscription is accompanied by library accession marks and, in this case, the stamp of the Harvard College Library. Joseph Bowers marks up Lindley Murray, *The English Reader: Or, Pieces in Prose and Poetry, Selected from the Best Writers* (Poughkeepsie, N.Y.: Paraclete Potter, 1811, AAS call number Dated Books); Maria Bullard's inscription is on a handmade bookplate in *English Exercises, Adapted to Murray's English Grammar* (Bridgeport, Conn.: L. Lockwood and for Collins & Co., New-York, 1815, AAS call number Dated Books) and includes the date of inscription (1816) and the number of the book in the child's or the family's library ("No. 6"), along with a penmanship flourish. Decimus White inscribes Clara English, *The Children in the Wood: An Instructive Tale* (Baltimore: Warner and Hanna, 1806, AAS call number CL-Pam E58 C536 1806).

22. There were exceptions; the Bell system, like Joseph Lancaster's monitorial system, innovatively taught the writing of the alphabetic letters in sand, preceding reading (see Chapter 3).

23. See E. Jennifer Monaghan, "Literacy Instruction and Gender in Colonial New England," *American Quarterly* 40 (1988), 18–41, and *Learning to Read and Write in Colonial America* (Boston:

University of Massachusetts Press, 2005), 276. See also Catherine Hobbs, ed., *Nineteenth-Century Women Learn to Write* (Charlottesville: University of Virginia Press, 1995), 5–12.

24. White literacy approached 90 percent by 1850, though there are broad regional differences. Carl Kaestle, *Literacy in the United States: Readers and Reading Since 1880* (New Haven: Yale University Press, 1993), 25. At the same time, the book trade was booming; from a handful of printers in the late eighteenth century with strong children's lists, between 1821 and 1876, there were some 2,600 "individuals and firms" involved in the business of producing for children. See the Nineteenth-Century Children's Book Trade Directory, American Antiquarian Society. For the emergence of the children's book trade, see also Leonard Marcus, *Minders of Make-Believe: Idealists, Entrepreneurs, and the Shaping of American Children's Literature* (Boston: Houghton Mifflin, 2008), 1–70; Gillian Avery, *Behold the Child: American Children and Their Books, 1621–1922* (Baltimore: Johns Hopkins University Press, 1994). For the book trade more generally in the nineteenth century, from which a great deal can be gleaned about the importance of the children's book market, schooling, and reading practices, see Scott Casper et al., *A History of the Book in America, Volume 3: The Industrial Book, 1840–1880* (Chapel Hill: University of North Carolina Press, 2007).

25. See Holly Brewer, *By Birth or Consent: Children, Law, and the Anglo-American Revolution in Authority* (Chapel Hill: University of North Carolina Press, 2005), especially chapter 7, "The Emergence of Parental Custody, Children and Consent to Contracts for Land, Goods and Labor," for a discussion of the shift in the status of the child's ability to enter into contracts, between 1660 and the early nineteenth century, especially in America; with the publication of James Kent's commentaries on Blackstone (1826–1830), the child was regarded as belonging under the custody of the father (or master) until the age of twenty-one (230–85, 262).

26. Kopytoff, "The Cultural Biography of Things," 64.

27. The signature, in Derrida's account, inscribes both the "having-been present" of the signer in the "signature-event," while at the same time, "in order to function, that is, to be readable, a signature must have a repeatable, iterable, imitable form; it must be able to be detached from the present and singular intention of its production." Jacques Derrida, "Signature Event Context," in *Limited Inc.*, tr. Samuel Weber and Jeffrey Mehlman (Evanston: Northwestern University Press, 1988), 20.

28. The child's relationship to property is complicated by the fact that even the not-enslaved child herself is traditionally understood *as* property. For Blackstone (and other legal authorities in the seventeenth and eighteenth centuries), the child belongs to the father. Brewer, *By Birth or Consent*, 285, and Mary Ann Mason, *From Father's Property to Children's Rights: The History of Child Custody in the United States* (New York: Columbia University Press, 1994), 6. Pinchbeck and Hewitt note without citing dates that "children were legally the property of their parents and were used by them as personal or family assets." *Children in English Society: Volume 2: From the Eighteenth Century to the Children Act 1948* (London: Routledge, 1973), 348. Both Locke and Rousseau thought that children needed to be schooled in property relations. For Locke, of course, property is foundational to personhood, and for Rousseau "the first idea which must be given [the child] is . . . less that of liberty than that of property; and for him to be able to have this idea he must have something that belongs to him" (*Emile; or, On Education*, tr. Allan Bloom [New York: Basic Books, 1979]), 98.

29. See Iona and Peter Opie, *I Saw Esau: Traditional Rhymes of Youth* (London: Williams and Norgate, 1947), for a few traditional examples, and Grenby, *Child Reader*, 276–77. For "traditional flyleaf rhymes," see Kevin Hayes, *Folk Culture and Book Culture* (Knoxville: University of Tennessee Press, 1997), 89–102. Holbrook Jackson cites a number of such verses from the twelfth century onward in *Anatomy of Bibliomania* (London: Soncino Press, 1932), 368–71. Marc Drogin offers a history of the genre, noting that the anathema itself is an ancient form of protection of sacred objects, of graves, and of precodex book forms like tablets and scrolls that becomes adopted for manuscript (by the scribes themselves) and eventually printed codices. *Anathema! Medieval Scribes and the History of Book Curses* (Totowa, N.J.: Allanheld and Schram), 1983. The genre is remarkably durable, attesting to the power of school and child culture.

30. According to Murray's biographer Charles Monaghan, *The English Reader*, its introduction, and its sequel sold some six and a half million copies in America, mostly before 1850; this is not

counting Murray's very popular *English Grammar. The Murrays of Murray Hill* (Brooklyn, N.Y.: Urban History Press, 1998), 96.

31. In England, until "1780, the penalty for over two hundred offences was death by hanging," and a seven-year-old girl, for one example, was hanged for "stealing a petticoat." Pinchbeck and Hewitt, *Children in English Society,* 2:351. According to Holly Brewer, capital punishment of children in England soared once the alternative of transportation to America became impossible (though many were still transported to Australia), leading "many people to reconsider England's bloody criminal code." Brewer notes that in the United States there were two executions of children under fourteen, both nonwhite, in 1786 and 1828, but that by the 1820s children under fourteen were often "presumed innocent," by virtue of "an inability to reason." *By Birth or Consent,* 212–14, 215, 222, 221.

32. Lindley Murray, *The English Reader: Or, Pieces in Prose and Poetry, Selected from the Best Writers* (Fredericktown, Md.: George Kolb, 1819, AAS catalog Dated Books).

33. Inscribed in *The American Tutor's Assistant, Improved* (Wilmington, Del., 1811, AAS call number Dated Books). The inscription continues, after a space, with a version of a more conventional rhyme, in a ritual doubling that is frequent in these books: "Steal not this Book my honnest / friend / For if you do the gallows / They will be your end."

34. Noah Webster, *The American Spelling Book: Containing the Rudiments of the English Language, for the Use of Schools in the United States* (Brattleborough, Vt.: John Holbrook, 1819, AAS call number Dated Books, copy 1.)

35. In Emma Vanlear's copy of a religious tract, *Anecdotes* (Harrisonburg, Va.: Lawrence Wartmann, printer, 1813, AAS call number Tracts Pams V70 No. 006 1813).

36. *Arithmetical Tables, for the Use of Schools* (New York: S. Wood, 1810, AAS call number DP A0750.).

37. This convention may have originated with gift books; see Andrew Piper, *Dreaming in Books: The Making of the Bibliographic Imagination in the Romantic Age* (Chicago: University of Chicago Press, 2009), 128–38, and Meredith McGill, *American Literature and the Culture of Reprinting, 1834–1853* (Philadelphia: University of Pennsylvania Press, 2003), 28–42.

38. *The Children in the Wood: To Which Is Added, My Mother's Grave, a Pathetic Story* (New York: Mahlon Day, at the New Juvenile Book-store, no. 376 Pearl-Street, 1832, AAS call number CL-Pam C5365 C536 1832).

39. See Lisa Gitelman, *Paper Knowledge: Toward a Media History of Documents* (Durham, N.C.: Duke University Press, 2014), especially chapter 1, on the complex ubiquity of the job-printed blank form in the nineteenth century.

40. The original inscription, in a sepia-toned or faded ink, has some overwriting in black ink; "exlent" is revised to "exelent." Lindley Murray, *The English Reader: Or, Pieces in Prose and Poetry, Selected from the Best Writers* (Philadelphia: Johnson and Warner, 1811, AAS call number Dated Books). Grace Comfort's age is gleaned from the American Antiquarian Society catalog record. The book is also inscribed by Alice Comfort.

41. For the long transformation of the economy in America, following the social instability of the postrevolutionary and post–War of 1812 eras, the gradual "commodification of the economy" and the rejection of the premodernist conception "of land as the foundation of proper social and political order, an expression of one's position in a formal social hierarchy and, concomitantly, of political power," see Gregory S. Alexander, *Commodity and Propriety: Competing Versions of Property in American Legal Thought, 1776–1970* (Chicago: University of Chicago Press, 1997), 103, 113.

42. Adam Phillips, *The Beast in the Nursery: On Curiosity and Other Appetites* (New York: Pantheon, 1998),18.

43. M. O. Grenby notes the variety of ways books came into children's hands in eighteenth-century Britain and the practices of borrowing and sharing them. *Child Reader,* 158–67.

44. Murray, *English Reader* (Fredericktown, Md.: George Kolb, 1819, AAS call number Dated Books). The American Antiquarian Society catalog entry notes the several and individual Millers.

45. Murray, *The English Reader* (Fredericktown, Md.: George Kolb, 1819, inscribed by Benjamin Miller et al. AAS call number Dated Books).

46. The generic similarities extend to the communal or sequential ownership of the text, as Lindley Murray's American editions were pirated—with his blessings—and his own contributions to the text were as editor and compiler. See Monaghan, *The Murrays of Murray Hill.*

47. Murray, *English Reader* (Fredericktown, Md.: George Kolb, 1819), 209. Benjamin notes the year 1829 at two other sites, at least, in the book. And presumably another, presumably related, Benjamin Miller also claims it on a flyleaf, on "Jan 28th 1837."

48. *An Abridgment of Murray's English Grammar* (Philadelphia: Benjamin Johnson and Jacob Johnson, 1802). Genealogical information is drawn from the American Antiquarian Society catalog, Samuel Lamborn, *The Genealogy of the Lamborn Family with Extracts from History, Biographies, Anecdotes, etc.* (Philadelphia: M. L. Marion, 1894), and from familysearch.org and http://genforum .genealogy.com/lamborn.

49. In Clara J. Cunningham's copy of Epes Sargent, *The Standard Third Reader for Public and Private Schools* (Boston: Hobart and Robbins, 1857, AAS call number SB Readers S785s3 1857), 211.

50. Sarah Ann Burr's light signature appears on the top of page 132. According to family-search.org, she would have been born in 1814 to Caroline Shelton, though the relationship to Mary Lucretia Shelton is not clear. Lindley Murray, *Introduction to the English Reader: Or, A Selection of Pieces, in Prose and Poetry; Calculated to Improve the Younger Classes of Learners in Reading; and to Imbue Their Minds with the Love of Virtue* (New York: Collins, 1816, AAS call number Dated Books). Subsequent parenthetical citations to Shelton's marginal notes will be to this edition.

51. Though unlike many inscriptions, Shelton's is written in a very clear hand. I have not been able to discover Shelton's age for certain; she may be eight, eleven, or seventeen in 1821, when she dates her inscription.

52. "The Sluggard" ends with the speaker witnessing the (gallows-will-be-your-end) decline of the sluggard, and declaring, "here's a lesson for me; / That man's but a picture of what I might be:/ But thanks to my friends for their care in my breeding/ who taught me betimes to love working and reading!" Murray, *Introduction*, 137.

53. Paul F. Gehl has described the often obscene graffiti in Italian Renaissance grammars. "Owning the Book, Owning the Text, Owning the Mark," paper presented at the SHARP conference, Minneapolis, Minnesota, July 11-15, 2007.

54. Murray, *English Reader* (Fredericktown, Md.: George Kolb, 1819), 35.

55. The book is inscribed by five owners, in Boston and Charleston, Mass., with dates of 1825, 1831, and an undated twentieth-century inscription. *Fables of Æsop, and Others, Translated into English, with Instructive Applications* (Wilmington, Del.: Peter Brynberg, 1802).

56. *Fables of Æsop*, 195.

57. *Childhood* (New York: Samuel Wood, 1815, AAS call number, CL-Pam C536 N532 1815).

58. American Antiquarian Society, Draper-Rice Family Papers, Box 3, Folder 6.

59. According to the biography provided with the Draper papers at the American Antiquarian Society, James Draper was educated in district schools, became a farmer, taught in district schools in "winter seasons," became a justice of the peace in 1810, a magistrate for fifty years, and a representative to the general court. Letters from Lucy's mother, also Lucy Draper, to her husband, when Lucy was a newborn, suggest that they ran a store for a while as well. James Draper is described in an anonymous typescript biography as "a man of strong will and ardent temperament, and sometimes exhibited a hasty temper," moral, "not a professor of religion" but "attendent upon religious worship." Draper-Rice Family Papers, Box 3, Folder 6, 2. Lucy Watson Draper Rider's papers include teenage drawings and inscriptions in her sister's autograph book and a later phrenological analysis, among other documents.

60. Biographical information about the Anthony family is drawn from Charles Lawton Anthony, *Genealogy of the Anthony Family from 1495 to 1904 Traced from William Anthony, Cologne, Germany, to London, England, John Anthony, a Descendant, from England to America* (Sterling, Ill.: Charles L. Anthony, 1904).

61. *Little Kitty Clover and her friends* (Philadelphia: G. Collins: 1856, AAS call number, CL L7781 K62 1856), n.p.

62. *Little Kitty Clover*, 10.

63. *The Blue Pictorial Primer; Designed for the Use of Schools and Families* (New York: Geo. F. Cooledge and Brother, AAS call number Primers B658 P611 1840), 25.

64. *Blue Pictorial Primer,* 34.

65. *Mamma's Gift Book* (New York: D. Appleton, 1854, AAS call number CL M263 G456 1854).

66. *Mamma's Gift Book,* 5.

67. *Mamma's Gift Book,* 91, 55.

68. Lindley Murray, *An Abridgment of L. Murray's English Grammar* (Hallowell, Me.: E. Goodale, 1813, AAS call number Dated Books). Prudence Varnum died young, at seventeen, on the same day (according to familysearch.org) as a younger sibling, which in part may account for the long life of her book. Laura Newton's copy of Murray is *An Abridgment of L. Murray's English Grammar* (Boston: Manning and Loring, 1813, AAS call number Dated Books), and includes an anathema, signed "Nahum Newton, jun."

69. D. W. Winnicott's theory of the transitional object posits that the infant clings to her chosen teddy bear or blanket to navigate separation from the caregiver. Many aspects of the book form make it an ideal transitional object, as the child substitutes a book—or even the book, in general—for the original one. Winnicott allows for all manner of objects to function this way, and sees one of the primary aspects of the transitional object—that it is both found by the baby, and made by the baby—to be a model for cultural life more generally. Winnicott, *Playing and Reality* (New York: Routledge, 1971, 2005), 1–34.

70. Lindley Murray, *Murray's Introduction to English Grammar, Compiled for the Use of the Youth in Baltimore Academy, Tammany-Street. To Which Is Added, An Essay on Punctuation* (Baltimore: Academy Press, 1806. Inscribed by Nancy Smyth. AAS call number Dated Books).

71. I'm grateful to Tom Knoles for pointing out the paper-production history to me.

72. Mark Twain, always alert to the materials of his chosen medium, uses this capacity of the book to function as a communications network to ignite a catastrophic feud with a lovers' note in chapter 18 of *The Adventures of Huckleberry Finn.*

73. Asa Gray, *How Plants Grow: A Simple Introduction to Structural Botany* (New York: Ivison, Blakeman, Taylor, 1872, AAS call number SB Botany G7781h 1872).

74. *New England Primer* (Worcester, Mass.: S. A. Howland, 1845, AAS call number Primers N532 H864 1845).

75. From James's preface to *What Maisie Knew*: "Maisie to the end . . . treats her friends to the rich little spectacle of objects embalmed in her wonder. She wonders, in other words, to the end, to the death—the death of her childhood, properly speaking" (*Literary Criticism, Volume 2: European Writers and Prefaces to the New York Edition* [New York: Library of America, 1984]), 1161. Though James speaks of Maisie in particular here, Leon Edel (among others) has understood James to be preoccupied with this idea in the 1890s.

76. *The History of Miss Kitty Pride* (Windsor [Vt.]: Nahum Mower, [1805?], AAS call number CL-Pam H6734 M6783 1805).

77. *Coverings for the Head and Feet, in All Ages and All Countries* (New York: J. S. Redfield [between 1843 and 1851?]. Inscribed to M. C. Wire. AAS call number CL-Pam C873 F692 1843).

78. Jacob Abbott, *Rollo's Philosophy: Air* (Philadelphia: B. F. Jackson, 1853. Inscribed to Howard Littlefield. AAS call number CL A132 R757 1853).

79. *Little Annie's ABC* (Philadelphia: Appleton, 1851. Inscribed by Harriet Rose Chandler. AAS call number CL L7781 A6131 1851).

80. George Chandler, *The Chandler Family: The Descendants of William and Annis Chandler, Who Settled in Roxbury, Mass., 1637* (Boston: D. Clapp and Son, 1872), 634.

81. *The Newfoundland Fishermen, and Other Books for the Young* ([New York]: American Tract Society [not before 1848?], AAS call number CL A5125 N5475 1848).

82. *The Newfoundland Fishermen,* 15, 13.

Chapter 6. Raising "Master James"

Epigraphs: Simon Nowell-Smith quoted in Muriel Shine, *The Fictional Children of Henry James* (Chapel Hill: University of North Carolina Press, 1969), 22.

Henry James, *A Small Boy and Others* (London: Gibson Square Books, Turtle Point Press, 2001), 49.

Henry James, "Preface to *What Maisie Knew*," in vol. 11, New York Edition (1908), in *Literary Criticism, Volume 2: French Writers, Other European Writers, Prefaces to the New York Edition* (New York: Library of America, 1984), 1163.

Henry James, "The Art of Fiction," *in Literary Criticism, Volume 1: Essays on Literature, American Writers and English Writers*, 62.

1. For a genealogy of the term, see Crain, "New Histories of Literacy," In *A Companion to the History of the Book*, ed. Simon Eliot and Jonathan Rose (London: Blackwell, 2007), 467–79.

2. Muriel Shine, *Fictional Children*, 82.

3. Shine, *Fictional Children*, 172. For Shine, James's child characters register a critique of child-rearing and educational practices, especially indulgent, neglectful American ones. More recently scholars influenced by childhood studies, gender and sexuality studies, and queer theory have returned to James's children. Prominent among these are Kevin Ohi, "Narrating the Child's Queerness in *What Maisie Knew*," in *Curiouser: On the Queerness of Children*, ed. Steven Bruhm and Natasha Hurley (Minneapolis: University of Minnesota Press, 2004), 81–105; Kevin Ohi, *Innocence and Rapture: The Erotic Child in Pater, Wilde, James, and Nabokov* (New York: Palgrave Macmillan, 2005); Maeve Pearson, "Re-exposing the Jamesian Child: The Paradox of Children's Privacy," *Henry James Review* 28:2 (Spring 2007), 101–19; Susan Honeyman, *Elusive Childhood: Impossible Representations in Modern Fiction* (Columbus: Ohio State University Press, 2005); Michael Moon, *A Small Boy and Others: Imitation and Initiation in American Culture from Henry James to Andy Warhol* (Durham, N.C.: Duke University Press, 1998); Teresa Michals, *Books for Children, Books for Adults: Age and the Novel from Defoe to James* (Cambridge: Cambridge University Press, 2014); Michelle Phillips, "The 'Partagé Child' and the Emergence of the Modernist Novel in *What Maisie Knew*," *Henry James Review* 31 (2010): 95–110.

4. Dorothea von Mücke, *The Seduction of the Occult and the Rise of the Fantastic Tale* (Stanford: Stanford University Press, 2003), 148.

5. Many critics, following Leon Edel's biography, see James's child-centered works of the 1890s as recuperative, and some see them specifically as providing narrative modes that serve him in *The Ambassadors*, *The Golden Bowl*, and *The Wings of the Dove*. Edel, *Henry James, Volume IV: The Treacherous Years: 1895–1901* (Philadelphia: Lippincott, 1969). Muriel Shine notes that "young children precede adolescents and adolescents precede his richest and most complex phase as a novelist." *Fictional Children*, 173. Others argue (or argue as well) for the influence of dictation. Michelle Phillips sees *Maisie* as inaugurating a modernist exploration of "'not thinking singly.'" "The 'Partagé Child,'" 76. Barbara Everett counters Edel's therapeutic/biographical notion, reading *Maisie* as inaugurating the late phase stylistically, thematically, and structurally in "the abstract formalism in its plotting," which serves "a new irrealism," expressing "a newly naked inward consciousness." "Henry James's Children," in Gillian Avery and Julia Briggs, eds., *Children and Their Books: A Celebration of Iona and Peter Opie* (Oxford: Oxford University Press, 1989), 325. James had also published *The Other House* in 1896 (from a play scenario written in 1894; serial and book in 1896), in which a young child is murdered; much as in "The Children in the Wood," a will, in this case one that prevents a widow's remarriage as long as her child lives, motivates the murder.

6. James, "The Art of Fiction," *Literary Criticism, Volume 1*, 61–62.

7. James, "Robert Louis Stevenson," *Literary Criticism, Volume 1*, 1251. This essay appeared in the *Century Magazine* in April 1888. In her edition of the James-Stevenson correspondence, Janet Adams Smith dates it by the year of composition, 1887, and notes that James showed it in proof to Stevenson. *Henry James and Robert Louis Stevenson: A Record of Friendship and Criticism* (London: Rupert Hart-Davis, 1948), 123.

8. James, "Robert Louis Stevenson," 1254.

9. The Houghton Library, Harvard University, call number for James's copy of *Treasure Island* (2nd ed., London: Cassell, 1884) is *AC85.J2335.Zz884s2.

10. Others might have used this book after James's death in 1916. Smudges inside suggest child readers. For the fate of James's library, including his copies of Stevenson, see Leon Edel and Adeline Tintner, *The Library of Henry James* (Ann Arbor, Mich.: UMI Research Press, 1987), 2–3.

11. *The X* or cross or + appears on page 144, next to the passage describing Tom Redruth's character as he nears death.

12. The Board of Lady Managers had received funds for a "women's building" but had to raise their own money for the children's building, which would serve as what we would now call a day care center. Karen Manners Smith, "New Paths to Power 1890–1920," in *No Small Courage: A History of Women in the United States,* ed. Nancy F. Cott (New York: Oxford University Press, 2004), 354. The request sent by the Board of Lady Managers was addressed to " 'the laurel-crowned of all countries . . . to aid us by contributing to our volume, a verse—even a line; a sketch (be it ever so small),—a dash of the pencil or brush; some thoughts in music, if only a few chords.' " "Explanatory Note," *Fame's Tribute to Children* (Chicago: A. C. McClurg, 1892), n.p. The tone of the contributions to *Fame's Tribute* ranges widely among a conventional sentimentality, a buck-up disciplining, a mournful nostalgia, and James's and (for another example) Thomas Hardy's more complex visions.

13. *Fame's Tribute to Children*, 15, 39.

14. Thomas Hardy's passage, immediately preceding James's, is darker still: "Helpless creatures who have never been asked if they wished for life on any terms, much less if they wished for it on . . . hard conditions" (from *Tess of the d'Urbervilles*). *Fame's Tribute,* 37.

15. It's not evident that there were other reasons—of economy, for instance—to publish in facsimile rather than typesetting. Thanks to Sharon Marcus for suggesting the celebrity-autograph connection. Thanks to Blevin Shelnutt for researching the history of facsimile publication.

16. George Monteiro notes that Scudder's letter to James, from which these quotations come, exists only in the copy in Houghton Mifflin's letterbooks. "*The Atlantic Monthly*'s Rejection of 'The Pupil': An Exchange of Letters Between Henry James and Horace Scudder," *American Literary Realism, 1870–1910* 23:1 (Fall 1990), 76, 78–79.

17. Edel, *The Treacherous Years*, 100.

18. James, "The Pupil," in *Tales of Henry James,* ed. Christof Wegelin and Henry B. Wonham (New York: Norton, 2003), 137. Further citations in parentheses will be to this edition. George Monteiro notes that Scudder's rejection "has always been told from James's point of view" and suggests that James may have taken the criticism to heart and made changes before publishing it; one can't know, since the copy sent to Scudder is lost. James had written to Scudder, responding to the rejection: "Perhaps I should like it sent to an address in the U.S.—I shall have the MS. recopied and study it afresh—and then perhaps ask you to destroy your copy." Henry James, *Letters of Henry James*, ed. Leon Edel, 4 vols. (Cambridge: Belknap Press of Harvard University Press, 1974–1984), 3:307; Monteiro, "*Atlantic Monthly*'s Rejection of 'The Pupil,' " 75, 80.

19. Others have noted this wonderful passage. Eric Savoy notices a "spectral hand" present here. "Theory *a Tergo* in *The Turn of the Screw*," in *Curiouser: On the Queerness of Children*, ed. Steven Bruhm and Natasha Hurley (Minneapolis: University of Minnesota Press, 2004), 260. Ellen Pifer somewhat misreads the passage, as though James *is* referring to "innocence": "Innocence, James elsewhere writes, both dawns and dies in the 'morning twilight of childhood.' " She notes, also, somewhat misleadingly, that this expression is "oxymoronic." While "morning twilight" may lean in that direction, it's a conventional usage for the period just before sunrise (OED, s.v. "twilight"). That said, Pifer helpfully notes that "this observation could well serve as an epigraph to *What Maisie Knew*," and "a helpful, if ironic, introduction to *The Turn of the Screw*." *Demon or Doll: Images of the Child in Contemporary Writing and Culture* (Charlottesville: University of Virginia Press, 2000), 31. "Morning twilight" may also have been a conventional nineteenth-century trope for childhood. In an 1881 poem, Catherine Parr writes: "The morning twilight: didst though ever mark / Its early breaking, shadowy and dark,/ And not bethink thee of our childhood's feeling— / Vague, indistinct, but full of sweet revealing— / Dim glimpses of the intellect to come, / Like morning break on the midnight gloom." *The Feast of Madain, and Other Poems* (Norwich: A. H. Goose, 1881), 42.

20. In Diana Fuss's description, the aubade "shares important affinities with the elegy. . . . Perhaps more than any other poetic genre, the aubade marries eros and thanatos, joining together love and loss in a centuries-old drama of lovers parting at sunrise." Fuss, *Dying Modern: A Meditation on Elegy* (Durham, N.C.: Duke University Press, 2013), 78.

21. "From His Prefaces, [On 'The Pupil.']," in *Tales of Henry James,* ed. Wegelin and Wonham, 409.

22. His mother calls him "too quaint" (135), which might be understood as part of her unmaternal use of Morgan as an object of sentimental desire. I'm grateful to Ilana Vine's reading of Alcott's *Old-Fashioned Girl* (1870) for thinking through the meanings of the temporal work of "old-fashioned" in her M.A. thesis, "'She will make a charming little woman': Reforming Female Rage in Louisa May Alcott's *An Old-Fashioned Girl*" (New York University, 2013).

23. James describes other characters this way, notably Isabel Archer in *Portrait of a Lady* ("'Isabel's written in a foreign tongue,'" according to her brother-in-law [New York: Norton, 1995], 38), and uses a version of the trope in *Confidence*: "It came over him that it was not a wonder that poor Wright should not have found this young lady's disposition a perfectly decipherable page" (*Novels 1871–1880* [New York: Library of America, 1983], 1108). There are doubtless other examples.

24. For a rich discussion of this figure—"flashing forward (prolepsis) to a flash back (analepsis)," as a "double movement of anticipation and retrospect"—in James but also in a variety of narratives, ancient and modern, see Bruce Robbins, "Many Years Later: Prolepsis in Deep Time," *Henry James Review* 33:3 (Fall 2012), 191.

25. Oscar Maurer, "Andrew Lang and 'Longman's Magazine,' 1882–1905," *University of Texas Studies in English* 34 (1955), 160, 158.

26. Adeline R. Tintner was the first to notice in 1978 the extent to which this tale was in conversation with Stevenson. She saw "The Pupil" as rewriting and responding to *Treasure Island* and *Kidnapped*, in its figurative language of shipwrecks, mutinies, and kidnappings, with, among other things, the Moreens as virtual pirates and Morgan and Pemberton modeled on *Kidnapped's* David Balfour and Alan Breck. "James Writes a Boy's Story: 'The Pupil' and R. L. Stevenson's Adventure Books," *Essays in Literature* 5:1 (1978), 61–73. "Kidnapping" also evokes the spectacular and widely reported Charley Ross case of 1874—the first ransom kidnapping (the child was never found)—which Paula Fass describes in *Kidnapped: Child Abduction in America* (New York: Oxford University Press, 1997).

27. Their warm relationship is captured by Janet Adam Smith's edition of their letters. Of "The Pupil," Stevenson wrote in a letter to James that he read it with "great joy; your little boy is admirable; why is there no little boy like that unless he hails from the Great Republic?" *Henry James and Robert Louis Stevenson*, December 7, 1891, 210.

28. Tony Tanner notes a similar contagion of hands in *What Maisie Knew*, serving to (among other things) "remind us of Maisie's eye-level." *The Reign of Wonder: Naivety and Reality in American Literature* (Cambridge: Cambridge University Press, 1977), 289.

29. Savoy, "Theory *a Tergo*," 260.

30. Moon, *A Small Boy and Others*, 26.

31. Moon, *A Small Boy and Others*, 27.

32. James might have been thinking, in fact, of Whistler's lithograph *Gants de Suède*, of 1890, which depicts a standing woman holding a pair of long gloves, seeming, like Mrs. Moreen, to be "drawing" them through her hands, which rest in front of her hips. As Robert Getscher explains, "The motif of the gloves, from which the lithograph takes its name, was originally explored in *Arrangement in Black: Lady in a Yellow Buskin—Lady Archibald Campbell* (Philadelphia Museum of Art, ill. in Sutton, *Whistler*, pl. 93), first exhibited in 1884." *The Stamp of Whistler: Catalogue* (Oberlin, Ohio: Allen Memorial Art Gallery, Oberlin College, 1977), 41. In a letter to Lizzie Boott in 1884, James wrote of his admiration for this "adorable" painting. *Letters of Henry James*, ed. Edel, 3:43. Lady Campbell's family, however, objected to the image, "claiming it represented 'a street walker encouraging a shy follower with a backward glance.'" Philadelphia Museum of Art's online label for *Arrangement in Black (The Lady in the Yellow Buskin)* c. 1883, http://www.philamuseum.org/collections/permanent/104367.html.

33. Moon, *A Small Boy and Others*, 26.

34. Kevin Ohi describes such belatedness as "the condition of possibility for consciousness itself in late James." In his reading of *The Golden Bowl*, Ohi develops this notion further: "Consciousness is belated, which is to say novelistic: the temporality of consciousness, in other terms, entails a resistance to formalization analogous to that detailed by [James's] essays on the novel—a form, as James repeatedly asserts, legible only in retrospect." *Henry James and the Queerness of Style* (Minneapolis: University of Minnesota Press, 2008), 32, 39.

35. "The Author of Beltraffio" (1884) is another.

36. *What Maisie Knew* (New York: Oxford World Classics, 1996), 54. Further citations to this edition will appear parenthetically in the text.

37. See Edel, *The Treacherous Years*, 15–16. William Veeder extends Edel's therapeutic interpretation of the period of the late nineties, seeing in James a persistent family-romance fascination with female orphans who seemed to him to have escaped the traumas of family life. "The Feminine Orphan and the Emergent Master," *Henry James Review* 12 (1991), 20–54.

38. *The Other House* (1896) is the exception. This interesting if anomalous novel, in which a child is murdered, was based on a scenario for a play that James had made a note of in 1893, and offered a "sketch" of to the producer Edward Compton in 1894. Shine, *Fictional Children*, 77–78; Edel, *The Treacherous Years*, 165.

39. James, "Robert Louis Stevenson," 1236.

40. James, "Robert Louis Stevenson," 1237.

41. James, "The Art of Fiction," 62.

42. "A Humble Remonstrance," in *Henry James and Robert Louis Stevenson*, ed. Smith, 94.

43. In Leon Edel, *The Master, 1901–1916* (Philadelphia: Lippincott, 1972), the first index entry under "James, Henry," reads: "Life at Rye at the turn of the century, Henry James increasingly called 'Master' by contemporaries, 21–31." And yet in those pages, Edel does not say anything about this rubric. In a footnote, Simon Nowell-Smith notes: "The honorific seems to have been bestowed on James early in the 'nineties. Gertrude Atherton who was assiduous at the social and literary salons of London during the 1895 season writes: 'Henry James, and deservedly, was spoken of with bated breath as 'the Master.'" *The Legend of the Master: Henry James as Others Saw Him* (Oxford: Oxford University Press, 1947, 1985), 22n1. Thanks to Blevin Shelnutt for tracking this usage.

44. James, "The Art of Fiction," 62.

45. James, "Preface to *What Maisie Knew*," 1159.

46. Indeed, little girls might grow up to be men. See Catherine Robson, *Men in Wonderland: The Lost Girlhood of the Victorian Gentleman* (Princeton: Princeton University Press, 2001). Sir Claude addresses Maisie often as "old boy" and other masculine tags, whether to protect and distance himself from the implications of her femininity, or in recognition of her incipient masculinity.

47. There doesn't seem to be critical consensus on what links these three narratives. Stuart Culver suggests that the narratives find "centers in consciousnesses that are thoroughly bewildered and fundamentally unable to see their respective stories whole." "Ozymandias and the Mastery of Ruins," in David McWhirter, ed., *Henry James's New York Edition: The Construction of Authorship* (Stanford: Stanford University Press, 1995), 53. Ira B. Nadel describes the narratives as "a set of stories that involved entrapment and the conflict between hope and disillusionment." "Visual Culture: The Photo Frontispieces to the New York Edition," in McWhirter, ed., *Henry James's New York Edition*, 105.

48. *The Complete Notebooks of Henry James*, ed. Leon Edel and Lyall H. Powers (New York: Oxford University Press, 1987), November 12, 1892, 71.

49. Note from August 26, 1893. In a further note of December 21, 1895, before he begins composing in earnest, he lists among topics to work on "the child whose parents divorce and who makes such an extraordinary link between a succession of people." *Complete Notebooks*, 77, 147.

50. Susan Honeyman's acute reading of the novel—especially notable for positioning James within a larger frame of child studies—sees something similar: Maisie is "a medium not a player in the drama," and she "figures the imposed absence of psychological exploration—she is a model for his method. She does not simply reflect social ills; she reflects the process of adults constructing children, and in doing so she reflects James's own grappling with realist representation." *Elusive Childhood*, 42.

51. Media in the shape of typewriters, telegraphs, stenography, and film have come into sharp focus for James scholars. See, for example, Pamela Thurschwell, "Henry James and Theodora Bosanquet: On the Typewriter, *In the Cage*, at the Ouija Board," *Textual Practice* 13:1, 5–23; Richard Menke, "Telegraphic Realism: Henry James's *In the Cage*," *PMLA* 115:5 (October 2000), 975–90; Mark Seltzer, "The Postal Unconscious," *Henry James Review* 21 (2000), 197–206; Hazel Hutchison,

"'An Embroidered Veil of Sound': The Word in the Machine in Henry James's *In the Cage*," *Henry James Review* 34 (2013), 147–62.

52. Edel, *The Treacherous Years*, 175.

53. John Harrison, *A Manual of the Type-writer* (London: I. Pitman and Sons, 1888), 13. The conventional term James often used to describe MacAlpine, amanuensis (a substantive formed of "*a manu*," from or by hand), is distinguished from "secretary"—the keeper of secrets—by its metonymic reduction or distillation of the worker's embodied presence into the writing hand. OED: "L. (in Suetonius) adj. used subst., f. denominative phrase *a manu* a secretary, short for *servus a manu* + *-ensis* belonging to." The earliest OED citation is 1619, but the OED doesn't record the wide common use of the term for secretary and stenographer in the late nineteenth century. In keeping with this sense, James's later typist, Theodora Bosanquet, commented that he liked his secretaries to be "without a mind." Quoted in Seltzer, "The Postal Unconscious," 200.

54. The eighteenth-century literacy described in the first chapter, as "'inalienable possessions'" that you "keep while giving," had now become the obverse: that you keep while not owning.

55. In addition to articles mentioned above, see also Sharon Cameron's exploration of the location and topography of consciousness in *Maisie*, suggesting the influence of dictation, which "exteriorizes thought and moves it between persons." Cameron, *Thinking in Henry James* (Chicago: University of Chicago Press, 1991), 32. See also David Hoover's computational analysis of James's style, which does *not* find a marked difference between dictated and handwritten composition per se. Hoover, "Modes of Composition in Henry James: Dictation, Style, and *What Maisie Knew*," *Henry James Review* 35:3 (Fall 2014), 257–77. *Maisie* typescripts are at the Morgan Library and at the University of Texas at Austin.

56. "Preface to *What Maisie Knew*," 1159.

57. "The Turn of the Screw," 2nd edition, ed. Deborah Esch and Jonathan Warren (New York: Norton, 1999), 1. Further parenthetical citations will be to this edition. Thanks to Molly Kelly for pointing me to the importance of this passage.

58. Lisa Gitelman, *Scripts, Grooves and Writing Machines: Representing Technology in the Edison Era* (Stanford: Stanford University Press, 2000), 188. The machine undergoes various refinements but becomes more or less stabilized—and more or less unchanging—by the early 1890s. For the background of the Remington company, and the likely version that James used, see Hutchison, "'An Embroidered Veil of Sound,'" 147–49.

59. For more on the typewriter and its popular discourses, see Morag Shiach, "Modernity, Labor, and the Typewriter," in *Modernist Sexualities*, ed. Hugh Stevens and Caroline Howlett (Manchester: Manchester University Press, 2000), 114–29; Christopher Keep, "Touching at a Distance: Telegraphy, Gender, and Henry James's 'In the Cage,'" in Colette Colligan and Margaret Linley, eds., *Media, Technology, and Literature in the Nineteenth Century: Image, Sound, Touch* (Aldershot: Ashgate, 2011), 239–55; Pamela Thurschwell and Leah Price, *Literary Secretaries/Secretarial Culture* (Aldershot: Ashgate, 2005).

60. David Reed, "Kitty, the Typewriter Girl" (New York: M. Witmark & Sons, 1894), 4–5.

61. The erotic tales depend on a traditional positioning of the working woman as sexually available; and though most typists were still men until well into the twentieth century, it is women who feature in these stories. See Price and Thurschwell, "Invisible Hands," in *Literary Secretaries/Secretarial Culture*, 1–12. According to Morag Shiach, women clerical workers made up only 13.4 percent of their sector of the labor force in 1901, and 59.6 percent in 1951. "Modernity, Labor, and the Typewriter," 116.

62. In one case, the machine channels James Boswell directly from Hell; in the other, James G. Blaine (who ran for president several times) writes a political polemic from the underworld to the founder of the Yost typewriting company. The last of Henry James's three secretaries, Theodora Bosanquet, neatly merges the two genres in her diary of the 1930s. Pamela Thurschwell has written fetchingly about Bosanquet, who, after James's death, had a long career as a writer and editor, and an avocation as a spirit medium and member of the Society for Psychical Research. A Ouija board session revealed to her that William and Henry James wanted to dictate posthumous works to her, but the spirit she contacted as her go-between to the other world stipulated that she give up her

lesbian companion and become celibate, which she declined to do. "Henry James and Theodora Bosanquet."

63. See also John Matson, "Marking Twain: Mechanized Composition and Medial Subjectivity in the Twain Era," Ph.D. dissertation, Princeton University, 2008; Gitelman on automatic writing, in *Scripts, Grooves*, 184–218; and Jeffrey Sconce, *Haunted Media: Electronic Presence from Telegraphy to Television* (Durham, N.C.: Duke University Press, 2000). Leah Price notes a few mostly post-1900 fictions that "trace textual production to supernatural agents" and notes George du Maurier's 1897 *The Martian*, in which a novelist takes dictation from a female extraterrestrial. "From Ghostwriter to Typewriter: Delegating Authority at the Fin de Siècle," in Robert Griffin, ed., *The Faces of Anonymity: Anonymous and Pseudonymous Publications from the Sixteenth to the Twentieth Century* (New York: Palgrave Macmillan, 2003), 221, 220.

64. Circa the 1890s, as Pamela Thurschwell notes, "new communication technologies such as the telegraph and the typewriter" enable "transgressive fantasies of access" across "gender or class barriers, or that even more difficult-to-negotiate barrier between the living and the dead." "Henry James and Theodora Bosanquet," 1, 5.

65. *Henry James Letters, 1895–1916*, ed. Leon Edel, vol. 4 (Cambridge, Mass.: Harvard University Press, 1984), 55. One more such letter will have to stand in for many. A flirty note to Morton Fullerton (February 25, 1897) begs forgiveness for "a communication, very shabby and superficial . . . through an embroidered veil of sound. The sound is that of the admirable and expensive machine that I have just purchased for the purpose of bridging our silences. The hand that works it, however, is not the lame *patte* which, after inflicting on you for years its aberrations, I have now definitely relegated to the shelf, or at least to the hospital—that is, to permanent, bandaged, baffled, rheumatic, incompetent obscurity. May you long retain, for yourself, the complete command that I judge you, that I almost see you, to possess, in perfection, of every one of your members" *Letters*, vol. 4, 41. The person of MacAlpine breaks through in the metonymic "hand that works it," and in its feminized embroidering of that "veil of sound"; but then the competent mechanic's hand is contrasted to James's wounded paw, which is contrasted in turn to Fullerton's robust and erotically suggestive "members." James "almost see[s]" Fullerton; in "bridging our silence" the "admirable and expensive machine" seems almost to materialize the very person at the other end of the bridge. Hazel Hutchison reads that "veil of sound" as "a permeable barrier through which communication occurs" and notes the paradoxical "obstacle that prevents him addressing Fullerton and the means by which he will bridge the silence between them." " 'An Embroidered Veil of Sound,' " 157.

66. In MacAlpine's only other significant haunt in the archive, James supposedly recounted to William Phelps that "The Turn of the Screw" left MacAlpine comically unmoved: "I might have been dictating statistics. I would dictate some phrase that I thought was blood-curdling; he would quietly take this down, look up at me and in a dry voice, say 'What next?' " (Phelps quoted in *Henry James at Home* [New York: Farrar, Straus and Giroux, 1969], 147). The well-circulated anecdote captures a backtalk that distinguishes MacAlpine's manner from the receptive mode that James appreciated in his later women typists. MacAlpine's "What next?"—the only words he speaks from the archive—mark the sheer implacable presence of others. William Lyon Phelps published at least two other versions of this anecdote ("The Turn of the Screw," Norton edition, 157n). In one, MacAlpine "short-handed" rather than typed "The Turn of the Screw" (*The Advance of the English Novel* [New York: Dodd, Mead, 1916], 324; this version is also published in the Norton edition, 157–58.) One might doubt that MacAlpine ever said or that James ever recounted exactly this, partly because James referred to Phelps as "the boring and vacuous (though so well-meaning) Yale chatterbox." Quoted in Edel, *Master,* 480.

67. The mini-narratives in James's early dictated letters might also be seen as emerging from the strictures of what Mark Seltzer has suggestively called "the technical protocols of interiority." Seltzer positions "The Turn of the Screw" within a material history of letters in which "the novel originates as private letters made public, or . . . designed . . . for interception"; and, further, "once it becomes possible to write on sheets of paper that can be folded back on themselves . . . , and for the handwritten and folded sheet of paper to be inserted in an envelope, sealed, and posted, the technical conditions of interiority and privacy are in place." "Postal Unconscious," 197, 203.

68. In his introduction to "The Turn of the Screw," Peter Beidler notices the similarity between James's and Douglas's performances, focusing on the ways in which dictation is like oral tale-telling. Beidler also notes that James read aloud to the Society for Psychical Research his brother William's report on the medium Mrs. Piper, which underscores James's connection with spiritualism and is also another account of a Douglas-like performance. "The Turn of the Screw," 3rd Edition, Case Studies in Contemporary Criticism (New York: Bedford, 2010), 19, 17.

69. Shoshana Felman notes this originary "transference" of the narrative as expressing what she sees as the psychoanalytic transference at the heart of the narrative. "Turning the Screw of Interpretation," *Yale French Studies* 55–56 (1977), 130.

70. The governess arrives at Bly after "long hours of bumping swinging coach" travel (6); there is no mention of railroads or telegraphs in the tale, and all correspondence is carried out by post.

71. Leon Edel notes the temporal setting of the inside narrative, "the decade of the 1840s . . . also the decade of James's own early childhood." *The Treacherous Years*, 205.

72. Bruce Robbins, among others, notices the class transgressions at the heart of the tale. "Recognition: Servant in the Ending," in the Norton "Turn of the Screw," 238–40.

73. This scene is often noticed, for those interesting O's, although every reading I am aware of posits that Flora *has* been doing her work, that she has written her O's, while it seems to me that the point is just that she has *not*, with her "extraordinary detachment from disagreeable duties." T. J. Lustig in particular notices the O's and sees them as a token of "blankness and circularity," as they are "simultaneously present and absent"; he links them to the excess of dashes in the narrative. He counts "some sixty uses of the word 'oh' in "The Turn of the Screw" (this is before digital text made counting easier). Lustig also links the O's to Hawthorne's "A": "James's 'O' turns in upon itself, leaving only absence." For Lustig the O signifies "blanks and turns, converts the 'ah' of involved sympathy into the 'oh' of detachment, of mystified surprise and suspended meaning." A, for Lustig, is "the sign of sin," O "the disappearance of signs of sin," and he contrasts an American A with the O, a "cipher" that "adds potentially innumerable quintessentially European secrets and values to any given figure." Lustig suggests that "the governess is trying to find the 'A' behind the 'O,'" to impute specific vice, to elicit a scarlet letter instead of all the blanks and turns. *Henry James and the Ghostly* (Cambridge: Cambridge University Press, 1994), 124, 165.

In his introduction to the Oxford edition (1996), Adrian Poole notices a flurry of "Oh"s at the start of sentences in *Maisie*, after about chapter 20 (*What Maisie Knew*, xxiv). Perhaps these round vowels are an artifact of dictation. It may be worth noting that the speech of the automaton Olympia in E. T. A. Hoffmann's "The Sandman" is restricted to "Oh"s.

74. Mark Seltzer sees the governess imbricated in the "'medico-tutelary complex,'" and sees "The Turn of the Screw," like all of late James, "bound up with the excitations and pleasures of the 'power-knowledge' nexus." *Henry James and the Art of Power* (Ithaca: Cornell University Press, 1984), 157.

75. Mark Seltzer even sees the governess's narrative, somewhat extravagantly, as the unsent letter to the master. "Postal," 202. Tessa Hadley understands the child fictions of the nineties as "unwriting all the signs of knowing worldliness," unwriting, in a sense, the social, in order to locate narrative more deeply in subjective experience. *Henry James and the Imagination of Pleasure* (Cambridge: Cambridge University Press, 2009), 44.

76. Lisa Gitelman notes that the one who dictates is sometimes called "the dictator" (*Scripts, Grooves,* 214). Unlike to "narrate" or to "tell," to "dictate" intensifies the transitive relationship between agent or subject and object, deflecting from the content and instead identifying those on either side of the transaction within a hierarchy announced by the dictation.

77. Concerning the ghosts, Shoshana Felman notices "that their manifestations have to do with *writing*, [as] outlined by a remark of the governess herself . . .: 'So I saw him as I see the letters I form on this page.'" Felman notates the case as "to see ghosts = to see letters" and further "what is 'seeing letters,' if not, precisely, *reading*?" It follows that of Mrs. Grose's inability to read, "not to read letters = not to see ghosts." And "the ghosts are thus determined as both a *writing*- and a *reading-effect*." "Turning the Screw of Interpretation," 151, 151n34, 152.

78. Eve Kosofsky Sedgwick, "Queer Performativity: Henry James's *The Art of the Novel*," *GLQ: A Journal of Lesbian and Gay Studies* 1 (1993), 8.

79. Felman, "Turning the Screw of Interpretation," 152.

80. Felman, "Turning the Screw of Interpretation," 152.

81. "I soon possessed myself of a volume, taking care that it should be one stored with pictures. I mounted into the window-seat: gathering up my feet, I sat cross-legged, like a Turk; and, having drawn the red moreen curtain nearly close, I was shrined in double retirement." Charlotte Brontë, *Jane Eyre* (New York: Norton, 2001, 5). Might *this* moreen have suggested Morgan's family name to James?

82. Others have noted the many resonances with *Jane Eyre*. See Lustig, *James and the Ghostly*, 143, and Linda S. Kauffman, *Discourses of Desire: Gender, Genre, and Epistolary Fictions* (Ithaca, N.Y.: Cornell University Press, 1988), 211. See also Alice Hall Petry, who reads the whole text as a dark parody of *Jane Eyre*. "Jamesian Parody, *Jane Eyre*, and 'The Turn of the Screw,' " *Modern Language Studies*, Henry James issue, 13:4 (Autumn 1983), 61–78.

83. James, Preface to the New York Edition of "The Turn of the Screw" (Norton), 124. The first installment didn't actually come out until the end of January 1898. See Melanie Dawson for a discussion of the effort by *Collier's* to entice its middle-class readers by encouraging their identification with elites. "The Literature of Reassessment: James's *Collier's* Fiction," *Henry James Review* 19:3 (1998), 230–38.

La Farge was one of James's oldest friends, whom he found "complex and suggestive." He described a La Farge painting as "a work of an even over-wrought suggestiveness," and found something in it that was "tormented, as the French say, something which fails to explain itself." In its echo of the kinds of things people have long written about James, the passage creates an identification with La Farge, whom James regarded as a mentor—it was La Farge who introduced him to the works of Balzac. It seems likely that illustrator and author would have conferred about the *Collier's* image, but I've found no evidence that they had done so. James, *The Painter's Eye: Notes and Essays on the Pictorial Arts,* ed. John L. Sweeney (Madison: University of Wisconsin Press, 1956), 91–92. Thanks to Patrick Horrigan for bringing James's writing on La Farge to my attention. For other interpretations of the La Farge image, see Amanda Sigler, "Unsuspecting Narrative Doubles in Serial Publication: The Illustrated 'Turn of the Screw' and *Collier's* U.S.S. Maine Coverage," *Henry James Review* 29:1 (2008), 80–97; Jean Lee Cole, "The Hideous Obscure of Henry James," *American Periodicals: A Journal of History, Criticism, and Bibliography* 20:2 (2010), 190–215; for an edition of the text with illustrations and further commentary see Peter Beidler, *The Collier's Weekly Version of The Turn of the Screw* (Seattle: Coffeetown Press, 2010).

84. James, November 18, 1894, *Notebooks*, 109.

85. James, Preface to the New York Edition, in "The Turn of the Screw" (Norton), 124, 125.

86. Sedgwick, "Queer Performativity," 11.

87. Carolyn Steedman, *Strange Dislocations: Childhood and the Idea of Human Interiority, 1780–1930* (Cambridge, Mass.: Harvard University Press, 1995), 12.

88. Steedman, *Strange Dislocations*, 10.

Coda

Epigraph. Lucy Larcom may be self-consciously or unconsciously echoing Robert Louis Stevenson's "To Any Reader," published in *A Child's Garden of Verses* in 1885 (New York: Scribner's [first U.S. edition], 1888), 101, discussed later in the Coda.

1. Andrew Piper, *Dreaming in Books: The Making of the Bibliographic Imagination in the Romantic Age* (Chicago: University of Chicago Press, 2009), 2.

2. Adults had long—and, before electric lighting, very dangerously—read in bed. See Seth Lerer, on contemporary reading in bed, by children and adults, and medieval versions. "Falling Asleep over the History of the Book," *PMLA* 121:1, 229–34. For the fire hazard, see A. Roger Ekirch, *At Day's Close: Night in Times Past* (New York: Norton, 2005), 52. See also Alberto Manguel, *A History of Reading* (New York: Penguin, 1996), esp. 153–61. Manguel's chapter "Being Read To," characteristic of the genre of the history of reading, overlooks bedtime stories for children (see 109–23).

3. On the history of sleep and bedtime, see Peter N. Stearns, Perrin Rowland, and Lori Giarnella, "Children's Sleep: Sketching Historical Change," *Journal of Social History* 30:2 (1996), 345–66; on

nighttime rituals through history, see Ekirch, *At Day's Close*. For children at night in early America, see Peter C. Baldwin, "'Nocturnal Habits and Dark Wisdom': The American Response to Children in the Streets at Night," *Journal of Social History* 35:3, (Spring 2002), 593–611. One does find, here and there in the literature of nineteenth-century childhood, accounts of an adult reading Bible verses to a child in bed.

4. *Nightcaps* has a frame-tale structure, with a mother gathering her children around every evening to hear stories. Like Moulton's *Bed-Time Stories* these are typical nineteenth-century children's fare—somewhat hair-raising moralistic and sentimental stories, involving petted sick children, a child's death and near death, animals and children behaving badly, shaming, and so on. Frances Elizabeth Barrow ("Aunt Fanny"), *Nightcaps* (New York: D. Appleton, 1859); Louise Chandler Moulton, *Bed-time Stories* (Boston: Roberts Brothers, 1873). For drugging children to sleep, see Maria Tatar, *Enchanted Hunters: The Power of Stories in Childhood* (New York: Norton, 2009*)*, 43, and Stearns, Rowland, and Giarnella, "Children's Sleep," 348. For a late twentieth-century sociology of bedtime reading and its effect on later schooling across social classes, see Shirley Brice Heath, "What No Bedtime Story Means: Narrative Skills at Home and School," *Language in Society* 11:1 (1982), 49–76. Many thanks to Pat Pfleiger of merrycoz.org and to Deidre Johnson, Katherine Pickering Antonova, Mary Christianakis, and other members of the Exploring_childhood_studies listserv for sending me references and suggestions for research about bedtime and bedtime stories.

5. See Lee M. Edwards, *Domestic Bliss: Family Life in American Painting, 1840–1910* (Yonkers: Hudson River Museum, 1986), 104–8.

6. As Maria Tatar suggests, in her lovely reading of Guy's *Story of Golden Locks*, from which I have learned a great deal, "the domestic interior space" of the bedroom replaces the "communal hearth" of social storytelling, as the book replaces the traditional teller of tales. She notes, too, the wide-awake, wide-eyed children, and sees the painting's chiaroscuro effects lending "a sense of mystery and apprehension," suggesting that it forms a secular pedant to Georges de La Tour's *Education of the Virgin*. Historically, parents and nursemaids putting children to sleep relied on the discipline of fright, which *Story of Golden Locks* evokes, associated with tales of the bogeyman, such as the classic "sandman." *Enchanted Hunters*, 64–66, 43–50.

7. Richard Brodhead, *Cultures of Letters: Scenes of Reading and Writing in Nineteenth-Century America* (Chicago: University of Chicago Press, 1993), 17–18.

8. In her chapter "Reading Them to Sleep," Maria Tatar headlines this phenomenon as "The Great Migration: From the Fireside to the Nursery." *Enchanted Hunters*, 51.

9. Eve Kosofsky Sedgwick, "Queer Performativity: Henry James's *The Art of the Novel*," *GLQ: A Journal of Lesbian and Gay Studies* 1:1 (1993), 5.

10. Lawrence Grossberg cites John Robinson on the colonization of leisure time by television, which Grossberg identifies as part of Raymond Williams's "long revolution." *Media Making: Mass Media in Popular Culture* (Thousand Oaks, Calif.: Sage Publications, 2006), 255. Jonathan Crary also notes that "the later nineteenth century saw the onset of a relentless colonization of 'free' or leisure time. Initially this was relatively scattered and partial in its effects, allowing oscillations between spectacular attentiveness and the free play of subjective absorptions." *Suspensions of Perception: Attention, Spectacle, and Modern Culture* (Cambridge, Mass.: MIT Press, 2001), 77.

11. For the shift in lighting, see David Nye, *Electrifying America: Social Meanings of a New Technology, 1880–1940* (Cambridge, Mass.: MIT Press, 1992). For the new idea of personal regulation of time, William James famously articulated the coming view in 1892: "We must make automatic and habitual as early as possible, as many useful actions as we can." He exhorts one to "hand over to the effortless custody of automatism" "the details of our daily life," such as "the time of rising and going to bed every day." William James, *Text-book of Psychology* (New York: Macmillan, 1892), 144–45. For the regulation of time, see also Michel Foucault, *Discipline and Punish: The Birth of the Prison*, tr. Alan Sheridan (New York: Vintage Books, 1995), 149–50, and Baldwin, "'Nocturnal Habits and Dark Wisdom,'" for clock time, scheduled time, and curfews for the young in the 1890s. Industrial clock time had become everyone's time. Schooling newly marked out groups of children by chronological age cohort (Carolyn Steedman, *Strange Dislocations: Childhood and the Idea of Human Interiority, 1780–1930* [Cambridge, Mass.: Harvard University Press, 1995], 7). "Punctuality" became

a schoolchild's duty, noted on many rewards of merit. See also Peter Stearns, *Anxious Parents: A History of Modern Childrearing in America* (New York: New York University Press, 2004); Julia Grant, *Raising Baby by the Book: The Education of American Mothers* (New Haven: Yale University Press, 1998); Ann Hulbert, *Raising America: Experts, Parents, and a Century of Advice About Children* (New York: Vintage, 2004).

12. Between 1852 and 1890, most states passed compulsory schooling laws. Michael Katz, *A History of Compulsory Education Laws* (Bloomington, Ind.: Phi Delta Kappa, 1976),17. John Guillory notes (in quite another context, in a discussion of Gray's "Elegy") that "if the cultural capital represented by vernacular literacy signifies to some social groups the possibility of upward mobility, it can also signify the devaluation of the cultural capital possessed by other individuals or groups." *Cultural Capital: The Problem of Literary Canon Formation* (Chicago: University of Chicago Press, 1993), 118.

13. Baldwin, "'Nocturnal Habits and Dark Wisdom.'"

14. The children's periodical *Golden Hours* was published from 1869 to 1880. *The Children's Hour,* published from 1867 to 1874, took its title from Longfellow's poem. See "The Title of Our Magazine," at Pat Pfleiger's website: http://www.merrycoz.org/bib/1872.htm/.

15. Henry James, "Robert Louis Stevenson," in *Literary Criticism, Volume 1: Essays on Literature, American Writers and English Writers* (New York: Library of America, 1984, 1231–55), 1237.

16. Underscoring the increase in the marketability of the child-book matrix, "6 of the 10 overall bestsellers in American between 1875 and 1895" were children's books, including *A Child's Garden of Verses*. Quoted in Christine Pawley, review of Paul Gutjahr's *Popular American Literature of the Nineteenth Century*, citing Anne H. Lundin's "Victorian Horizons: The Reception of Children's Books in England and America, 1880–1900," *Library Quarterly* 64 (1994), 30–59. Pawley review in *Library Quarterly* 72:2 (April 2002), 40.

17. Gillian Brown sees a gendered dimension to this conceit: "If boyhood inspires nostalgia by figuring the origins of human progress, girlhood generates an equally powerful though more difficult form of nostalgia: a longing for the present that projects it into the future condition when it will be the past, and like boyhood, part of the phylogenetic record." Like others, Brown notes the "irretrievable past" that is part of the construction of childhood in the nineteenth century. "Child's Play," *Differences: A Journal of Feminist Cultural Studies* 11.3 (1999–2000), 92, 98. The distinction I am making is that this past is embedded in the construction of childhood *reading* in the nineteenth century.

18. Judith Plotz, *Romanticism and the Vocation of Childhood* (New York: Palgrave, 2001), 3.

Bibliography

Editions of *Goody Two-Shoes* cited in Chapter 1, editions of "Babes in the Wood" cited in Chapter 2, and editions of inscribed books cited in Chapter 5 appear in separate sections below.

Abbott, Jacob. *The Alcove; Containing Some Further Account of Timboo, Mark, and Fanny.* New York: Harper and Brothers, 1856.

————. *Handie* (Rainbow and Lucky Stories). New York: Harper and Brothers, 1859.

————. *Hubert* (Juno Stories). New York: Dodd and Mead, 1870.

————. *Juno and Georgie.* New York: Dodd and Mead, 1870.

————. *Juno on a Journey.* New York: Dodd and Mead, 1870.

————. Letters to Harper and Brothers. February 7, 1856 and April 14, 1856. Misc American Harper. Literary and Historical Manuscripts (LHMS). Record ID 80062. Accession Number MA 1950. Morgan Library and Museum, New York.

————. *The Little Scholar Learning to Talk: A Picture Book for Rollo.* Boston: John Allen, 1835.

————. *Rollo Learning to Read.* Boston: Thomas H. Webb, 1835

————. *Timboo and Joliba; or, The Art of Being Useful.* New York: Harper and Brothers, 1855.

————. *Up the River.* (Rainbow and Lucky Stories). New York: Harper and Brothers, 1861.

————. *Virginia; or, A Little Light on a Very Dark Saying.* New York: Harper and Brothers, 1855.

————. *Willie and the Mortgage: Showing How Much May Be Accomplished by a Boy.* New York: Harper and Brothers, 1855.

Abbott, Lyman. *Silhouettes of My Contemporaries.* New York: Doubleday, 1922.

Acland, Charles R., ed. *Residual Media.* Minneapolis: University of Minnesota Press, 2007.

Adams, David Wallace. *Education for Extinction: American Indians and the Boarding School Experience, 1875–1928.* Lawrence: University Press of Kansas, 1995.

Adams, Gillian. "In the Hands of Children." *The Lion and the Unicorn* 29:1 (2004), 38–51.

Addison, Joseph. *Spectator* 85. *The Spectator Project: A Hypermedia Research Archive of Eighteenth-Century Periodicals*, www2.scc.rutgers.edu/spectator/text/june1711/no85.html.

Alexander, Gregory. *Commodity and Propriety: Competing Visions of Property in American Legal Thought, 1776–1970.* Chicago: University of Chicago Press, 1998.

Alryyes, A. *Original Subjects: The Child, the Novel, and the Nation.* Cambridge, Mass.: Harvard University Press, 2001.

American Board of Commissioners for Foreign Missions. *First Ten Annual Reports of the American Board of Commissioners for Foreign Missions 1810–1820.* Boston, 1834.

American State Papers, Class II, Indian Affairs. Washington, D.C., 1832.

Andrews, Charles C. *The History of the New-York African Free-Schools, from Their Establishment in 1787, to the Present Time; Embracing a Period of More Than Forty Years; Also a Brief Account of the Successful Labors, of the New-York Manumission Society; with an Appendix.* New York: Mahlon Day, 1830.

Anthony, Charles Lawton. *Genealogy of the Anthony Family from 1495 to 1904 Traced from William Anthony, Cologne, Germany, to London, England, John Anthony, a Descendant, from England to America.* Sterling, Ill.: Charles L. Anthony, 1904.

Appadurai, Arjun. "Introduction: Commodities and the Politics of Value." In Appadurai, ed., 3–63.

———, ed. *The Social Life of Things: Commodities in Cultural Perspective*. Cambridge: Cambridge University Press, 1986.

Ariès, Philippe. *Centuries of Childhood: A Social History of Family Life*. New York: Knopf, 1965.

"Aunt Fanny." See Barrow, Frances Elizabeth.

Averill, James. *Wordsworth and the Poetry of Human Suffering*. Ithaca, N.Y.: Cornell University Press, 1980.

Avery, Gillian. *Behold the Child: American Children and Their Books, 1621–1922*. Baltimore: Johns Hopkins University Press, 1994.

Avery, Gillian, and Julia Briggs, eds. *Children and Their Books: A Celebration of Iona and Peter Opie*. Oxford: Oxford University Press, 1989.

Baldwin, Peter C. "'Nocturnal habits and dark wisdom'": The American Response to Children in the Streets at Night." *Journal of Social History* 35:3 (Spring 2002), 593–611.

Barrow, Frances Elizabeth ("Aunt Fanny"). *Nightcaps*. New York: D. Appleton, 1859.

Barton, Jeff. "Marks in Children's Books." Cotsen Children's Library Blog, Princeton University, July 28, 2011.

Bayley, John. "The Child in Walter de la Mare." In Avery and Briggs, 337–49.

Blum, Virginia L. *Hide and Seek: The Child Between Psychoanalysis and Fiction*. Urbana: University of Illinois Press, 1995.

Beidler, Peter, ed. *The Collier's Weekly Version of The Turn of the Screw*. Seattle: Coffeetown Press, 2010.

Bender, John. *Imagining the Penitentiary: Fiction and the Architecture of Mid-Eighteenth-Century England*. Chicago: University of Chicago Press, 1987.

Benjamin, Walter. *The Arcades Project*. Tr. Howard Eiland and Kevin McLaughlin. Cambridge, Mass.: Belknap Press of Harvard University Press, 1999.

Bentham, Jeremy. *Chrestomathia*. (1816). New York: Oxford University Press, 1983.

Berkhofer, Robert. *Salvation and the Savage: An Analysis of Protestant Missions and American Indian Response, 1787–1862*. Lexington: University of Kentucky Press, 1965.

Bernstein, Robin. *Racial Innocence: Performing American Childhood from Slavery to Civil Rights*. New York: New York University Press, 2011.

———. "Signposts on the Road Less Taken: John Newton Hyde's Anti-Racist Illustrations of African American Children." *J19: The Journal of Nineteenth-Century Americanists* 1:1 (2013), 97–119.

Boswell, John. *The Kindness of Strangers: The Abandonment of Children in Western Europe from Late Antiquity to the Renaissance*. Chicago: University of Chicago Press, 1988.

Bourdieu, Pierre. "Forms of Capital." In John Richardson, ed., *Handbook of Theory and Research for the Sociology of Education*. Westport, Conn.: Greenwood Press, 1986. 241–58.

———. *Language and Symbolic Power*. Tr. Gino Raymond and Matthew Adamson. Cambridge: Polity, 1991.

———. *Outline of a Theory of Practice*. Tr. Richard Nice. Cambridge: Cambridge University Press, 1977.

Brayman, Heidi. *Reading Material in Early Modern England: Print, Gender, and Literacy*. Cambridge: Cambridge University Press, 2005.

Bremner, Robert H., ed. *Children and Youth in America: A Documentary History*. Cambridge, Mass.: Harvard University Press, 1970.

Brewer, Holly. *By Birth or Consent: Children, Law, and the Anglo-American Revolution in Authority*. Chapel Hill: University of North Carolina Press, 2005.

Brodhead, Richard. *Cultures of Letters: Scenes of Reading and Writing in Nineteenth-Century America*. Chicago: University of Chicago Press, 1993.

Brontë, Charlotte. *Jane Eyre*. New York: Norton, 2001.

Brown, Bill. *Material Unconscious: American Amusement, Stephen Crane, and the Economics of Play*. Cambridge, Mass.: Harvard University Press, 1997.

———. *A Sense of Things: The Object Matter of American Literature*. Chicago: University of Chicago Press, 2004.

———. "Thing Theory." *Critical Inquiry* 28:1 (2001), 1–22.

———, ed. "Things." Special issue of *Critical Inquiry* 28:1 (2001).

Brown, Gillian. "Child's Play." *Differences: A Journal of Feminist Cultural Studies* 11.3 (1999–2000), 76–106.

———. "*Consent of the Governed: The Lockean Legacy in Early American Culture.* Cambridge, Mass.: Harvard University Press, 2001.

———. "The Metamorphic Book: Children's Print Culture in the Eighteenth Century." *Eighteenth-Century Studies* 39:3, New Feminist Work in Epistemology and Aesthetics (Spring 2006), 351–62.

Carey, James W. *Communication as Culture: Essays on Media and Society.* New York: Routledge, 1989.

Carney, Virginia Moore. *Eastern Band Cherokee Women: Cultural Persistence in Their Letters and Speeches.* Knoxville: University of Tennessee Press, 2005.

Chandler, George. *The Chandler Family: The Descendants of William and Annis Chandler, Who Settled in Roxbury, Mass., 1637.* Boston: D. Clapp and Son, 1872.

Chapin, John, ed. *Book of Catholic Quotations.* New York: Farrar, Straus and Giroux, 1956.

Cheyfitz, Eric. *The Poetics of Imperialism: Translation and Colonization from* The Tempest *to* Tarzan. New York: Oxford University Press, 1991.

Clarke, Norma. "Women Writers and Writing for Children in the Late Eighteenth Century." In *Opening the Nursery Door*, ed. Mary Hilton, Morag Styles, and Victor Watson. New York: Routledge, 1997. 91–103.

Clifford, James. "On Collecting Art and Culture." In *The Cultural Studies Reader*, ed. Simon During. New York: Routledge, 1993. 49–73.

Cohoon, Lorinda. *Serialized Citizenship: Periodicals, Books, and American Boys, 1840–1911.* Lanham, Md.: Scarecrow Press, 2006.

Cole, Jean Lee. "The Hideous Obscure of Henry James." *American Periodicals: A Journal of History, Criticism, and Bibliography* 20:2 (2010), 190–215.

Coleman, Michael. "American Indian School Pupils as Cultural Brokers: Cherokee Girls at Brainerd Mission, 1828–1829." In *Between Indian and White Worlds: The Culture Broker*, ed. Margaret Connell-Szasz. Norman: University of Oklahoma Press, 1994. 122–35.

Colles, Christopher. *A Survey of the Roads of the United States of America.* (1789). Ed. Walter W. Ristow. Cambridge, Mass.: Harvard University Press, 1961.

Connell-Szasz, Margaret. *Indian Education in the American Colonies, 1607–1783.* Albuquerque: University of New Mexico Press, 1988.

Crain, Patricia. "New Histories of Literacy." In *A Companion to the History of the Book*, ed. Simon Eliot and Jonathan Rose. London: Blackwell, 2007. 467–79.

———. "Postures and Places: The Child Reader in Nineteenth-Century U.S. Popular Print." *ELH* 80:2 (Summer 2013), 343–72.

———. "Reading Childishly? A Codicology of the Modern Self." In *Comparative Textual Media: Transforming the Humanities in the Postprint Era*, ed. N. Katherine Hayles and Jessica Pressman. Minneapolis: University of Minnesota Press, 2013. 155–82.

———. *The Story of A: The Alphabetization of America from* The New England Primer *to* The Scarlet Letter. Stanford: Stanford University Press, 2000.

Crary, Jonathan. *Suspensions of Perception: Attention, Spectacle, and Modern Culture.* Cambridge, Mass.: MIT Press, 2001.

Cronon, William. *Changes in the Land: Indians, Colonists and the Ecology of New England.* New York: Hill and Wang, 1983.

Culver, Stuart. "Ozymandias and the Mastery of Ruins." In McWhirter, 39–57.

Darton, F. J. Harvey. *Children's Books in England: Five Centuries of Social Life.* 1932; 3rd edition, revised by Brian Alderson. Cambridge: Cambridge University Press, 1982.

Dawson, Melanie. "The Literature of Reassessment: James's *Collier's* Fiction." *Henry James Review* 19:3 (1998), 230–38.

DeLombard, Jeannine. "Slave Narratives and U.S. Legal History." In *The Oxford Handbook of the African American Slave Narrative*, ed. John Ernest. New York: Oxford University Press, 2014. 67–85.

Derrida, Jacques. "Signature Event Context." In *Limited Inc.* Tr. Samuel Weber and Jeffrey Mehlman. Evanston: Northwestern University Press, 1988. 1–21.

Dickens, Charles. *Hard Times.* (1854). New York: Bantam, 1981.

Dickinson, Emily. *Letters of Emily Dickinson.* Ed. Thomas H. Johnson. Cambridge, Mass.: Harvard University Press, 1958.

Dickson, Mora. *Teacher Extraordinary: Joseph Lancaster 1778–1838.* Sussex: Book Guild, 1986.

Drogin, Marc. *Anathema! Medieval Scribes and the History of Book Curses.* Montclair, N.J.: A. Schram, 1983.

Duane, Anna Mae. *Suffering Childhood in Early America: Violence, Race, and the Making of the Child Victim.* Athens: University of Georgia Press, 2010.

Dugaw, Dianne. "On the 'Darling Songs' of Poets, Scholars, and Singers: An Introduction." *Eighteenth Century Theory and Interpretation* 47:2–3 (2006), 97–113

———, ed. *The Anglo-American Ballad: A Folklore Casebook.* New York: Garland, 1995.

Eastman, Carolyn. *A Nation of Speechifiers: Making an American Public after the Revolution.* Chicago: University of Chicago Press, 2009.

Edel, Leon. *Henry James, Volume IV. The Treacherous Years: 1895–1901.* Philadelphia: Lippincott, 1969.

Edel, Leon, and Adeline R. Tintner. *The Library of Henry James.* Ann Arbor, Mich.: UMI Research Press, 1987.

Edwards, Lee M. *Domestic Bliss: Family Life in American Painting, 1840–1910.* Yonkers: Hudson River Museum, 1986.

Edgeworth, Maria. *Rosamond, Part I.* Philadelphia: Jacob Johnson, 1808.

Elbert, Monika, ed. *Enterprising Youth: Social Values and Acculturation in Nineteenth-Century American Children's Literature.* New York: Routledge, 2008.

Encyclopaedia Britannica; Or, a Dictionary of Arts, Sciences, and Miscellaneous Literature. Philadelphia: Thomas Dobson, 1798.

Everett, Barbara. "Henry James's Children." In Avery and Briggs, 317–35.

Fame's Tribute to Children. Chicago: A. C. McClurg, 1892.

Fass, Paula S. *Kidnapped: Child Abduction in America.* New York: Oxford University Press, 1997.

Felman, Shoshana. "Turning the Screw of Interpretation." *Yale French Studies* 55–56 (1977), 94–207.

Fergus, Jan. *Provincial Readers in Eighteenth-Century England.* New York: Oxford University Press, 2006.

Ferguson, Margaret. *Dido's Daughters: Literacy, Gender, and Empire in Early Modern England and France.* Chicago: University of Chicago Press, 2007.

Fleming, Robin. "Picturesque History and the Medieval in Nineteenth-Century America." *American Historical Review* 100:4 (October 1995), 1061–94.

Fliegelman, Jay. *Prodigals and Pilgrims: The American Revolution Against Patriarchal Authority, 1750–1800.* Cambridge: Cambridge University Press, 1982.

Flint, Kate. *The Woman Reader, 1837–1914.* New York: Oxford University Press, 1995.

Foucault, Michel. *Discipline and Punish: The Birth of the Prison.* Tr. Alan Sheridan. (1977). New York: Vintage Books, 1995.

Fox, Adam. *Oral and Literate Culture in England 1500–1700.* Oxford: Oxford University Press, 2000.

Frantzen, Allen J., and John D. Niles, eds. *Anglo-Saxonism and the Construction of Social Identity.* Gainesville: University Press of Florida, 1997.

Freedgood, Elaine. *The Ideas in Things: Fugitive Meaning in the Victorian Novel.* Chicago: University of Chicago Press, 2006.

Freeman, Elizabeth. "Honeymoon with a Stranger: Pedophiliac Picaresques from Poe to Nabokov." *American Literature* 70:4 (December 1998), 863–97.

French, David, and Katherine French. "Personal Names." In *Handbook of North American Indians, Volume 17: Languages,* ed. Ives Goddard. Washington: Smithsonian, 1996.

Fuss, Diana. *Dying Modern: A Meditation on Elegy.* Durham, N.C.: Duke University Press, 2013.

Gehl, Paul F. "Owning the Book, Owning the Text, Owning the Mark." The Child in the Margin Session. Society for the History of Authors, Readers, and Publishers Conference. University of Minnesota, Minneapolis, 13 July 2007.

Getscher, Robert. *The Stamp of Whistler: Catalogue.* Oberlin, Ohio: Allen Art Museum, 1977.

Gitelman, Lisa. *Always Already New: Media, History, and the Data of Culture.* Cambridge, Mass.: MIT Press, 2006.

———. *Scripts, Grooves, and Writing Machines: Representing Technology in the Edison Era.* Stanford: Stanford University Press, 2000.

Grant, Julia. *Raising Baby by the Book: The Education of American Mothers.* New Haven: Yale University Press, 1998.

Grenby, M. O. *The Child Reader, 1700–1840.* Cambridge: Cambridge University Press, 2011.

Grossberg, Lawrence, et al. *Media Making: Mass Media in Popular Culture.* Thousand Oaks, Calif.: Sage Publications, 2006.

Grossberg, Michael. *Governing the Hearth: Law and the Family in Nineteenth-Century America.* Chapel Hill: University of North Carolina Press, 1985.

Guillory, John. *Cultural Capital: The Problem of Literary Canon Formation.* Chicago: University of Chicago Press, 1993.

———. "Literary Capital, Gray's 'Elegy,' Anna Laetitia Barbauld, and the Vernacular Canon." In John Brewer and Susan Staves, eds., *Early Modern Conceptions of Property.* New York: Routledge, 1996, 389–410.

Hadley, Tessa. *Henry James and the Imagination of Pleasure.* Cambridge: Cambridge University Press, 2009.

Halttunen, Karen. *Confidence Men and Painted Women: A Study of Middle-Class Culture in America, 1830–1870.* New Haven: Yale University Press, 1996.

Hanson, Ellis. "Screwing with Children in Henry James." *GLQ: A Journal of Lesbian and Gay Studies* 9:3 (2003), 367–91.

Harjo, Joy, and Gloria Bird. *Reinventing the Enemy's Language: Contemporary Native Women's Writings of North America.* New York: Norton, 1997.

Harris, Roy. *The Origins of Writing.* La Salle, Ill.: Open Court, 1986.

Harrison, John. *A Manual of the Type-writer.* London: I. Pitman and Sons, 1888.

Hayes, Kevin. *Folklore and Book Culture.* Knoxville: University of Tennessee Press, 1997.

Hawthorne, Nathaniel. "Little Annie's Ramble." (1835). In *Tales and Sketches.* New York: Library of America, 1982. 228–35.

———. "The Village Uncle." In *Tales and Sketches.* New York: Library of America, 1982. 217–27.

Hessinger, Rodney. *Seduced, Abandoned, and Reborn: Visions of Youth in Middle-Class America, 1780–1850.* Philadelphia: University of Pennsylvania Press, 2005.

Hillard, G. S. *The Franklin Fourth Reader.* New York: Taintor Brothers, Merrill, 1878.

The History and Adventures of Little Eliza, a Companion to Little William; Illustrated with a Series of Elegant Figures. Philadelphia: William Charles, 1811.

The History and Adventures of Little Henry, a Companion to Little Fanny. Philadelphia: Morgan and Yeager, 1825.

The History of Little Fanny: Exemplified in a Series of Figures, Engraved on Copperplate. 2nd edition. Philadelphia: Morgan and Yeager, 1825.

Hobbs, Catherine, ed. *Nineteenth-Century Women Learn to Write.* Charlottesville: University of Virginia Press, 1995.

Hogan, David. "The Market Revolution and Disciplinary Power: Joseph Lancaster and the Psychology of the Early Classroom System." *History of Education Quarterly* 29:3 (Fall 1989), 381–417.

Hollander, John, ed. *American Poetry: The Nineteenth Century.* Vol. 1. New York: Library of America, 1993.

Holzmann, Gerard J., and Bjorn Pershon. *The Early History of Data Networks.* Los Alamitos, Calif.: IEEE Computer Society Press, 1995.

Honeyman, Susan. *Elusive Childhood: Impossible Representations in Modern Fiction.* Columbus: Ohio State University Press, 2005.

Hoover, David L. "Modes of Composition in Henry James: Dictation, Style, and *What Maisie Knew.*" *Henry James Review* 35:3 (Fall 2014), 257–77.

Horsman, Reginald. *Race and Manifest Destiny: The Origins of American Racial Anglo-Saxonism.* Cambridge, Mass.: Harvard University Press, 1981.

Hughey, Matthew W. "Racializing Redemption, Reproducing Racism: The Odyssey of Magical Negroes and White Saviors." *Sociology Compass* 6:9 (2012), 751–67.

Hulbert, Ann. *Raising America: Experts, Parents, and a Century of Advice About Children*. New York: Vintage, 2004.

Hulme, Peter. *Colonial Encounters: Europe and the Native Caribbean, 1492–1797*. New York: Methuen, 1986.

Hutchison, Hazel. "'An Embroidered Veil of Sound': The Word in the Machine in Henry James's *In the Cage*." *Henry James Review* 34 (2013), 147–62.

Hyde, H. Montgomery. *Henry James at Home*. New York: Farrar, Straus and Giroux, 1969.

Illouz, Eva. *Cold Intimacies: The Making of Emotional Capitalism*. Cambridge: Polity Press, 2007.

Jackson, H. J. *Marginalia: Readers Writing in Books*. New Haven: Yale University Press, 2001.

———. *Romantic Readers: The Evidence of Marginalia*. New Haven: Yale University Press, 2005.

Jackson, Holbrook. *Anatomy of Bibliomania*. London: Soncino Press, 1932.

James, Henry. "The Art of Fiction." In *Literary Criticism, Volume 1: Essays on Literature, American Writers and English Writers*. New York: Library of America, 1984. 44–65.

———. *The Complete Notebooks of Henry James*. Ed. Leon Edel and Lyall H. Powers. New York: Oxford University Press, 1987.

———. *Confidence*. In *Novels 1871–1880*. New York: Library of America, 1983. 1041–1252.

———. "From His Prefaces, [On 'The Pupil.']" In *Tales of Henry James*, ed. Christof Wegelin and Henry B. Wonham. New York: Norton, 2003. 409–13.

———. *The Letters of Henry James*. Ed. Leon Edel. 4 vols. Cambridge, Mass.: Belknap Press of Harvard University Press, 1974–1984.

———. *The Painter's Eye: Notes and Essays on the Pictorial Arts*. Ed. John L. Sweeney. Madison: University of Wisconsin Press, 1956.

———. *The Portrait of a Lady*. New York: Norton, 1995.

———. "Preface to *What Maisie Knew*." In *Literary Criticism, Volume 2: French Writers, Other European Writers, Prefaces to the New York Edition*. New York: Library of America, 1984. 1156–72.

———. "The Pupil." In *Tales of Henry James*, ed. Christof Wegelin and Henry B. Wonham. New York: Norton, 2003. 133–71.

———. "Robert Louis Stevenson." In *Literary Criticism, Volume 1: Essays on Literature, American Writers and English Writers*. New York: Library of America, 1984. 1231–55.

———. *A Small Boy and Others*. London: Gibson Square Books, Turtle Point Press, 2001.

———. *The Turn of the Screw*. 2nd Edition. Ed. Deborah Esch and Jonathan Warren. New York: Norton, 1999.

———. *The Turn of the Screw*. 3rd Edition, Case Studies in Contemporary Criticism. Ed. Peter Beidler. New York: Bedford, 2010.

———. *What Maisie Knew*. New York: Oxford World Classics, 1996.

James, William. *Text-book of Psychology*. New York: McMillan, 1892.

Judd, Sylvester. *Margaret: A Tale of the Real and Ideal, Blight and Bloom*. (1845). Ed. Gavin Jones. Boston: University of Massachusetts Press, 2009.

Kaestle, Carl. *Joseph Lancaster and the Monitorial School Movement: A Documentary History*. New York: Teachers College Press, 1973.

———. *Literacy in the United States: Readers and Reading Since 1880*. Yale University Press, 1993.

———. *Pillars of the Republic: Common Schools and American Society, 1780–1860*. New York: Hill and Wang, 1983.

Katz, Michael. *A History of Compulsory Education Laws*. Bloomington, Ind.: Phi Delta Kappa, 1976.

———. *In the Shadow of the Poorhouse: A Social History of Welfare in America*. New York: Basic Books, 1996.

Kauffman, Linda S. *Discourses of Desire: Gender, Genre, and Epistolary Fictions*. Ithaca, N.Y.: Cornell University Press, 1988.

Kayman, Martin. "Lawful Possession: Violence, the Polite Imagination and Goody Two-Shoes." In *Violéncia e possessão: Estudos ingleses contemporâneos,* ed. David Callahan et al. Aveiro: Universidade de Aveiro, 1998. 21–28.

Keep, Christopher. "Touching at a Distance: Telegraphy, Gender, and Henry James's 'In the Cage.' " In *Media, Technology, and Literature in the Nineteenth Century: Image, Sound, Touch*, ed. Colette Colligan and Margaret Linley. Aldershot: Ashgate, 2011. 239–55.

Kendall, Phillip. "The Times and Tales of Jacob Abbott." Ph.D. dissertation, Boston University, 1968.

Kincaid, James. *Erotic Innocence: The Culture of Child Molesting.* Durham, N.C.: Duke University Press, 1998.

King, Wilma. *Stolen Childhood: Slave Youth in Nineteenth-Century America.* Bloomington: Indiana University Press, 1995.

Kleist, Heinrich von. "On the Puppet Theater." (1810). In *An Abyss Deep Enough: Letters of Heinrich von Kleist with a Selection of Essays and Anecdotes*, ed. and tr. Phillip B. Miller. New York: E. P. Dutton, 1982. 211–17.

Kopytoff, Igor. "The Cultural Biography of Things: Commoditization as Process." In *The Social Life of Things*, ed. Arjun Appadurai. Cambridge: Cambridge University Press, 1986. 64–91.

Lahr, John. "Ma Rainey's Black Bottom." *New Yorker.* February 17 and 24, 2003. 190–91.

Lamb, Charles. *Essays of Elia.* Ed. Philip Lopate. Iowa City: University of Iowa Press, 2003.

Lamborn, Samuel. *The Genealogy of the Lamborn Family with Extracts from History, Biographies, Anecdotes, Etc.* Philadelphia: M. L. Marion, 1894.

Lancaster, Joseph. *The British System of Education.* Washington, 1812.

———. *Epitome of Some of the Chief Events and Transactions in the Life of Joseph Lancaster, Containing an Account of the Rise and Progress of the Lancasterian system of Education; and the Author's Future Prospects of Usefulness to Mankind.* New Haven, 1833.

———. *Hints and Directions for Building, Fitting Up, and Arranging School Rooms on the British System of Education.* London, 1809.

———. *Improvements in Education, as It Respects the Industrious Classes of the Community.* London, 1803.

———. *The Lancasterian System of Education, with Improvements.* Baltimore, 1821.

———. *Letters on National Subjects, Auxiliary Education, and Scientific Knowledge; Address to Burwell Bassett, Late a Member of the House of Representatives; Henry Clay, Speaker of the House of Representatives, and James Monroe, President of the United States by Joseph Lancaster.* Washington City, 1820.

Larcom, Lucy. *A New England Girlhood, Outlined from Memory.* Boston: Houghton Mifflin, 1889.

Lears, T. J. Jackson. *No Place of Grace: Antimodernism and the Transformation of American Culture, 1880–1920.* Chicago: University of Chicago Press, 1994.

Lerer, Seth. *Children's Literature: A Reader's History from Aesop to Harry Potter.* Chicago: University of Chicago Press, 2008.

———. "Devotion and Defacement: Reading Children's Marginalia." *Representations* 118:1 (2012), 126–53.

———. "Falling Asleep over the History of the Book." *PMLA* 121:1 (January 2006), 229–34.

Lessels, Jeannette Barnes, and Eric Sterling. "Overcoming Racism in Jacob Abbott's Stories of Rainbow and Lucky and in Antebellum America." In Elbert, 83–96.

Levander, Caroline. *Cradle of Liberty: Race, the Child, and National Belonging from Thomas Jefferson to W. E. B. Du Bois.* Durham, N.C.: Duke University Press, 2006.

Levine, Lawrence. *Highbrow/Lowbrow: The Emergence of Cultural Hierarchy in America.* Cambridge, Mass.: Harvard University Press, 1990.

Lewis, Matthew ("Monk"). *Journal of a West India Proprietor, 1815–1817.* Ed. Mona Wilson. London: Routledge, 1929.

Locke, John. *Some Thoughts Concerning Education.* (1693). Ed. John W. and Jean S. Yolton. Oxford: Clarendon Press, 1989.

———. *Two Treatises of Government.* Ed. Peter Laslett. Student edition. Cambridge: Cambridge University Press, 1988.

Lowell, James Russell. *Latest Literary Essays and Addresses of James Russell Lowell.* Boston: Houghton, Mifflin, 1896.

Lucien, Seniel. "'Goody Two-Shoes' Variations on a Theme: From Cinderella through Horatio Alger and Beyond." *Folklore* (Calcutta, India) 23:8 (August 1982), 163–74; 23:9 (September 1982), 194–98; 23:10 (October 1982), 215–220.

———. "Little Goody Two-Shoes: An Early Model of Child Development." *International Journal of Women's Studies* 6:2 (March/April 1983), 148–61.

Lustig, T. J. *Henry James and the Ghostly*. Cambridge: Cambridge University Press, 1994.

MacCann, Donnarae. *White Supremacy in Children's Literature: Characterizations of African Americans, 1830–1900*. New York: Garland, 1998.

Marcus, Leonard S. *Minders of Make-Believe: Idealists, Entrepreneurs, and the Shaping of American Children's Literature*. Boston: Houghton Mifflin, 2008.

Mason, Mary Ann. *From Father's Property to Children's Rights: The History of Child Custody in the United States*. New York: Columbia University Press, 1994.

Matson, John Owen. "Marking Twain: Mechanized Composition and Medial Subjectivity in the Twain Era." Ph.D. dissertation, Princeton University, 2007.

Maurer, Oscar. "Andrew Lang and 'Longman's Magazine,' 1882–1905." *University of Texas Studies in English* 34 (1955), 152–78.

McDowell, Paula. "'The Manufacture and Lingua-facture of Ballad-Making': Broadside Ballads in Long Eighteenth-Century Ballad Discourse." *Eighteenth Century: Theory and Interpretation* 47:2–3 (2006), 151–78.

McGill, Meredith. *American Literature and the Culture of Reprinting, 1834–1853*. Philadelphia: University of Pennsylvania Press, 2003.

McLane, Maureen. "Dating Orality, Thinking Balladry." *Eighteenth Century: Theory and Interpretation* 47:2–3 (2006), 131–49.

McLoughlin, William G. *Cherokee Renascence in the New Republic*. Princeton: Princeton University Press, 1986.

———. *The Cherokees and Christianity, 1794–1870: Essays on Acculturation and Cultural Persistence*. Ed. Walter H. Conser Jr. Athens: University of Georgia Press, 1994.

———. *Cherokees and Missionaries 1789–1839*. New Haven: Yale University Press, 1984.

McWhirter, David, ed. *Henry James's New York Edition: The Construction of Authorship*. Stanford: Stanford University Press, 1995.

Meider, Wolfgang, et al. *Dictionary of American Proverbs*. New York: Oxford University Press, 1992.

Menke, Richard. "Telegraphic Realism: Henry James's *In the Cage*." *PMLA* 115:5 (October 2000), 975–90.

Meserole, Harrison T. "Charles Lamb's Reputation and Influence in America to 1835." *Journal of General Education* 16:4 (January 1965), 281–308.

Michals, Teresa. *Books for Children, Books for Adults: Age and the Novel from Defoe to James*. Cambridge: Cambridge University Press, 2014.

Mintz, Stephen. *Huck's Raft: A History of American Childhood*. Cambridge, Mass.: Harvard University Press, 2006.

Mintz, Stephen, and Susan Kellogg. *Domestic Revolutions: A Social History of American Family Life*. New York: Free Press, 1988.

Monaghan, Charles. *The Murrays of Murray Hill*. Brooklyn: Urban History Press, 1998.

Monaghan, E. Jennifer. *Learning to Read and Write in Colonial America*. Amherst: University of Massachusetts Press, 2005.

Monteiro, George. "*The Atlantic Monthly*'s Rejection of 'The Pupil': An Exchange of Letters Between Henry James and Horace Scudder." *American Literary Realism, 1870–1910* 23:1 (Fall 1990), 75–83.

Moon, Michael. *A Small Boy and Others: Imitation and Initiation in American Culture from Henry James to Andy Warhol*. Durham, N.C.: Duke University Press, 1998.

Mooney, James. *Historical Sketch of the Cherokee*. (Originally published in 1898 as part of the "Myths of the Cherokees," by the Bureau of American Ethnology, the Nineteenth Annual Report.) Chicago: Aldine, 1975.

———. *The Swimmer Manuscript: Cherokee Sacred Formulas and Medicinal Prescriptions.* Revised and edited by Frans M. Olbrechts. Smithsonian Institution Bureau of American Ethnology, Bulletin 99. Washington: U.S. Government Printing Office, 1932.

Moulton, Louise Chandler. *Bed-time Stories.* Boston: Roberts Brothers, 1873.

Mücke, Dorothea von. *The Seduction of the Occult and the Rise of the Fantastic Tale.* Stanford: Stanford University Press, 2003.

Murray, David. *Forked Tongues: Speech, Writing and Representation in North American Indian Texts.* Bloomington: Indiana University Press, 1991.

Murray, Gail Schmunk. *American Children's Literature and the Construction of Childhood.* New York: Twayne, 1998.

Nadel, Ira B. "Visual Culture: The Photo Frontispieces to the New York Edition." In McWhirter, 90–108.

Needham, Lawrence. "'Goody Two-Shoes' / 'Goosee Shoo-shoo': Translated Tales of Resistance in Matthew Lewis's *Journal of a West India Proprietor.*" In *Between Languages and Cultures: Translation and Cross-Cultural Texts,* ed. Anuradha Dingwaney and Carol Maier. Pittsburgh: University of Pittsburgh Press, 1995, 103–18.

Nenstiel, Gregory. "Jacob Abbott: Mentor to a Rising Generation." Ph.D. dissertation, University of Maryland, 1979.

Neuberg, Victor. "The Diceys and the Chapbook Trade." Transactions of the Bibliographic Society. *The Library,* September 1969, 219–31.

Newman, Steve. *Ballad Collection, Lyric, and the Canon: The Call of the Popular from the Restoration to the New Criticism.* Philadelphia: Pennsylvania University Press, 2007.

Nissenbaum, Stephen. *The Battle for Christmas: A Cultural History of America's Most Cherished Holiday.* New York: Vintage Books, 1997.

Nowell-Smith, Simon. *The Legend of the Master: Henry James as Others Saw Him.* Oxford: Oxford University Press, 1947, 1985.

Nye, David. *Electrifying America: Social Meanings of a New Technology, 1880–1940.* Cambridge, Mass.: MIT Press, 1992

Ohi, Kevin. *Henry James and the Queerness of Style.* Minneapolis: University of Minnesota Press, 2008.

———. *Innocence and Rapture: The Erotic Child in Pater, Wilde, James, and Nabokov.* New York: Palgrave Macmillan, 2005.

———. "Narrating the Child's Queerness in *What Maisie Knew.*" In *Curiouser: On the Queerness of Children,* ed. Steven Bruhm and Natasha Hurley. Minneapolis: University of Minnesota Press, 2004. 81–105

O'Malley, Andrew. *Children's Literature, Popular Culture, and* Robinson Crusoe. New York: Palgrave Macmillan, 2012.

Opie, Iona and Peter Opie. *I Saw Esau: Traditional Rhymes of Youth.* London: Williams and Norgate, 1947.

Orme, Nicholas. *Medieval Children.* New Haven: Yale University Press, 2003.

The Oxford Dictionary of English Proverbs. 3rd Edition. Oxford: Clarendon Press, 1970.

Parish, Elijah. *Sermon Preached at Ipswich, Sept. 29, 1815. At the Ordination of Reverand Daniel Smith and Cyrus Kingsbury as Missionaries to the West.* Newburyport, 1815.

Parr, Catherine (Mrs. William Henry Kaye). *The Feast of Madain, and Other Poems.* Norwich: A. H. Goose, 1881.

Payne, John Howard. Papers, vol. 8 (typescript). The Newberry Library, Chicago.

Pearson, Maeve. "Re-exposing the Jamesian Child: The Paradox of Children's Privacy." *Henry James Review* 28:2 (Spring 2007), 101–19.

Perdue, Thea. *Cherokee Women: Gender and Culture Change, 1700–1835.* Lincoln: University of Nebraska Press, 1998.

Perry, Ruth, ed. *The Eighteenth Century: Theory and Interpretation,* Special Issue "Ballads and Songs in the Eighteenth Century." 47:2–3 (2006).

Person, Kirsten. "Child Abduction in Nineteenth-Century American Children's Literature." In "American Studies Seminar Research Papers, 1994: Children's Books and Childhood Reading in Early America." Worcester, Mass.: American Antiquarian Society, 1994.

Petry, Alice Hall. "Jamesian Parody, Jane Eyre, and 'The Turn of the Screw.'" *Modern Language Studies,* Henry James issue 13:4 (Autumn 1983), 61–78.

Phelps, William Lyon. *The Advance of the English Novel.* New York: Dodd, Mead, 1916.

Phillips, Adam. *The Beast in the Nursery: On Curiosity and Other Appetites.* New York: Pantheon, 1998.

Phillips, Joyce B., and Paul Gary Phillips, eds. *The Brainerd Journal: A Mission to the Cherokees, 1817–1823.* Lincoln: University of Nebraska Press, 1998.

Phillips, Michelle H. "The '*Partagé* Child' and the Emergence of the Modernist Novel in *What Maisie Knew.*" *Henry James Review* 31 (2010), 95–110.

Pifer, Ellen. *Demon or Doll: Images of the Child in Contemporary Writing and Culture.* Charlottesville: University of Virginia Press, 2000.

Pinchbeck, Ivy, and Margaret Hewitt. *Children in English Society, Volume 1: From Tudor Times to the Eighteenth Century.* London: Routledge, 1969.

———. *Children in English Society, Volume 2: From the Eighteenth Century to the Children Act 1948.* London: Routledge, 1973.

Piper, Andrew. *Book There Was: Reading in Electronic Times.* Chicago: Chicago University Press, 2012.

———. *Dreaming in Books: The Making of the Bibliographic Imagination in the Romantic Age.* Chicago: University of Chicago Press, 2009.

Plotz, Judith. *Romanticism and the Vocation of Childhood.* New York: Palgrave, 2001.

Porter, Susan L. "'Children in the Wood': The Odyssey of an Anglo-American Ballad." In Porter and John Graziano, eds., *Vistas of American Music: Essays and Compositions in Honor of William K. Kearns.* Warren, Mich.: Harmonie Park Press, 1999. 77–95.

———. "Gendered Expectations: Orphans and Apprenticeship in Antebellum New England." In *The Worlds of Children, 1620–1920: The Dublin Seminar for New England Folklife: Annual proceedings,* ed. Peter Benes and Jane Montague. Boston: Boston University Press, 2004.

Postman, Neil. *The Disappearance of Childhood.* New York: Knopf, 1982, 1994.

Price, Leah. *The Anthology and the Rise of the Novel: From Richardson to George Eliot.* Cambridge: Cambridge University Press, 2000.

———. "From Ghostwriter to Typewriter: Delegating Authority at the Fin de Siècle." In Robert Griffin, ed., *The Faces of Anonymity: Anonymous and Pseudonymous Publications from the Sixteenth to the Twentieth Century.* New York: Palgrave Macmillan, 2003. 211–31.

Price, Leah, and Pamela Thurschwell. "Invisible Hands." In *Literary Secretaries/Secretarial Culture,* ed. Price and Thurschwell. Aldershot: Ashgate, 2005. 1–12.

Quiller-Couch, Arthur, ed. *The Oxford Book of Ballads.* Oxford: Oxford University Press, 1910.

Quinlivan, Mary E., "Race Relations in the Antebellum Children's Literature of Jacob Abbott." *Journal of Popular Culture* 16:1 (Summer 1982), 27–36.

Ravitch, Diane. *The Great School Wars: New York City, 1805–1973.* New York: Basic Books, 1974.

Rayman, Ronald. "Joseph Lancaster's Monitorial System of Instruction and American Indian Education, 1815–1838." *History of Education Quarterly* 21 (1987), 395–409.

Reed, David. "Kitty, the Typewriter Girl." New York: M. Witmark & Sons, 1894.

Reigart, John Franklin. *The Lancasterian System of Instruction in the Schools of New York City.* New York: Teachers College Press, 1916.

Reinier, Jacqueline. *From Virtue to Character: American Childhood 1775–1850.* New York: Twayne, 1996.

Richardson, Alan. *Literature, Education, and Romanticism: Reading as Social Practice, 1780–1832.* New York: Cambridge University Press, 1994

Rigal, Laura. *The American Manufactory: Art, Labor, and the World of Things in the Early Republic.* Princeton: Princeton University Press, 1998.

Robbins, Bruce. "Many Years Later: Prolepsis in Deep Time." *Henry James Review* 33:3 (Fall 2012), 191–204.

Robson, Catherine. *Heartbeats: Everyday Life and the Memorized Poem*. Princeton: Princeton University Press, 2012.

———. *Men in Wonderland: The Lost Girlhood of the Victorian Gentleman*. Princeton: Princeton University Press, 2001.

Rose, Jacqueline. *The Case of Peter Pan, or the Impossibility of Children's Fiction*. (1984). Philadelphia: University of Pennsylvania Press, 1992.

Rosenbach, A. S. W. *Early American Children's Books, with Bibliographical Descriptions of the Books in His Private Collection*. (1933). New York: Dover Books, 1971.

Rousseau, Jean-Jacques. *Emile; or, On Education*. Tr. Allan Bloom. New York: Basic Books, 1979.

Rowland, Ann Wierda. "'The Fause Nourice Sang': Childhood, Child Murder, and the Formalism of the Scottish Ballad Revival." In Leith Davis et al., eds., *Scotland and the Borders of Romanticism*. Cambridge: Cambridge University Press, 2004. 225–44.

———. *Romanticism and Childhood: The Infantilization of British Literary Culture*. Cambridge: Cambridge University Press, 2012.

Ryan, Susan. *The Grammar of Good Intentions: Race and the Antebellum Culture of Benevolence*. Ithaca, N.Y.: Cornell University Press, 2004.

Said, Edward. *Orientalism*. New York: Pantheon, 1978.

Salmon, David. *Joseph Lancaster*. London: Longmans, Green, 1904.

Sánchez-Eppler, Karen. *Dependent States: The Child's Part in Nineteenth-Century American Culture*. Chicago: University of Chicago Press, 2005.

———. "Hawthorne and the Writing of Childhood." In Richard H. Millington, ed., *The Cambridge Companion to Nathaniel Hawthorne*. Cambridge: Cambridge University Press, 2004. 143–61.

Savoy, Eric. "Theory *a tergo* in *The Turn of the Screw*." In *Curiouser: On the Queerness of Children*, ed. Steven Bruhm and Natasha Hurley. Minneapolis: University of Minnesota Press, 2004. 245–75.

Schwenger, Peter. *The Tears of Things: Melancholy and Physical Objects*. Minneapolis: University of Minnesota Press, 2005.

Sedgwick, Eve Kosofsky. "Queer Performativity: Henry James's *The Art of the Novel*." *GLQ: A Journal of Lesbian and Gay Studies* 1 (1993), 1–16.

Seltzer, Mark. *Henry James and the Art of Power*. Ithaca, N.Y.: Cornell University Press, 1984.

———. "The Postal Unconscious." *Henry James Review* 21 (2000), 197–206.

Shelnutt, Blevin. "Childhood, City Streets, and *Hot Corn* in the Writing of Henry James." Master's thesis, New York University, 2010.

Sherman, William. "Used Books." *Shakespeare Studies* 48 (2000), 145–48.

———. *Used Books: Marking Readers in Renaissance England*. Philadelphia: University of Pennsylvania Press, 2010.

Shesgreen, Sean. *The Criers and Hawkers of London: Engravings and Drawings by Marcellus Laroon*. Aldershot: Scolar Press, 1990.

Shiach, Morag. *Modernism, Labour and Selfhood in British Literature and Culture, 1890–1930*. Cambridge: Cambridge University Press, 2004.

Shine, Muriel G. *The Fictional Children of Henry James*. Chapel Hill: University of North Carolina Press, 1969.

Sigler, Amanda. "Unsuspecting Narrative Doubles in Serial Publication: The Illustrated "Turn of the Screw" and *Collier*'s U.S.S. Maine Coverage." *Henry James Review* 29:1 (2008), 80–97.

Singly, Carol. *Adopting America: Childhood, Kinship, and National Identity in Literature*. New York: Oxford University Press, 2011.

Sketch of The Origin and Progress of the Adelphi School in the Northern Liberties, Established Under the Direction of the Philadelphia Association of Friends for the Instruction of Poor Children. Philadelphia: Meyer and Jones, 1810.

Smith, Janet Adam, ed. *Henry James and Robert Louis Stevenson: A Record of Friendship and Criticism*. London: Rupert Hart-Davis, 1948.

Smith, Karen Manners. "New Paths to Power 1890–1920." In *No Small Courage: A History of Women in the United States*, ed. Nancy F. Cott. New York: Oxford University Press, 2004.

Sorby, Angela. *Schoolroom Poets: Childhood, Performance, and the Place of American Poetry, 1865–1917*. Lebanon, N.H.: University Press of New England, 2005.

St. Armand, Barton Levi. "Emily Dickinson's 'Babes in the Wood': A Ballad Reborn." *Journal of American Folklore* 90:358 (October–December 1977), 430–41.

Stanley, Amy Dru. *From Bondage to Contract: Wage Labor, Marriage, and the Market in the Age of Slave Emancipation.* Cambridge: Cambridge University Press, 1998.

Stearns, Peter. *Anxious Parents: A History of Modern Childrearing in America.* New York: New York University Press, 2004.

Steedman, Carolyn. *Dust: The Archive and Cultural History.* New Brunswick: Rutgers University Press, 2002.

———. *Strange Dislocations: Childhood and the Idea of Human Interiority, 1780–1930.* Cambridge, Mass.: Harvard University Press, 1995.

Stevenson, Burton. *The Home Book of Proverbs, Maxims, and Familiar Phrases.* New York: Macmillan, 1948.

Stevenson, Robert Louis. *A Child's Garden of Verses.* (1885). New York: Scribner's, 1905.

———. "A Humble Remonstrance." In Smith, ed., 86–100.

———. *Treasure Island.* 2nd Edition. London: Cassell, 1884.

Stewart, Garrett. *The Look of Reading: Book, Painting, Text.* Chicago: University of Chicago Press, 2006.

Stewart, Susan. *Crimes of Writing.* New York: Oxford University Press, 1991.

———. *On Longing: Narratives of the Miniature, the Gigantic, the Souvenir, the Collection.* Chapel Hill: Duke University Press, 1993.

Stoddard, Roger. *Marks in Books, Illustrated and Explained.* Cambridge, Mass.: Harvard University Press, 1985.

Stone, Wilbur Macey. "The History of Little Goody Two-Shoes." *Proceedings of the American Antiquarian Society.* 49: 2 (October 1939), 333–70.

Strong, Roy. *And When Did You Last See Your Father? The Victorian Painter and British History.* London: Thames and Hudson, 1978.

Tanner, Tony. *The Reign of Wonder: Naivety and Reality in American Literature.* Cambridge: Cambridge University Press, 1977.

Tatar, Maria. *Enchanted Hunters: The Power of Stories in Childhood.* New York: Norton, 2009.

Thompson, Stith. *Motif-Index of Folk Literature: A Classification of Narrative Elements in Folk Tales, Ballads, Myths, Fables, Mediaeval Romances.* CD-ROM ed. Bloomington: Indiana University Press, 1993.

Thurschwell, Pamela. "Henry James and Theodora Bosanquet: On the Typewriter, *In the Cage*, at the Ouija Board." *Textual Practice* 13:1 (1999), 5–23.

Tintner, Adeline R. "James Writes a Boy's Story: 'The Pupil' and R. L. Stevenson's Adventure Books." *Essays in Literature* 5:1 (1978), 61–73.

Trollope, Anthony. *An Autobiography.* (1883). New York: Oxford University Press, 2008.

Trumpener, Katie. *Bardic Nationalism: The Romantic Novel and the British Empire.* Princeton: Princeton University Press, 1997.

Tuttle, Sarah. *Letters and Conversations on the Cherokee Mission.* Boston: Massachusetts Sabbath School Union, 1830.

Twain, Mark. *The Adventures of Huckleberry Finn.* Berkeley: University of California Press, 2001.

Upton, Dell. "Another City: The Urban Cultural Landscape in the Early Republic." In *Everyday Life in the Early Republic*, ed. Catherine E. Hutchins. Winterthur, Del.: Winterthur, 1994. 61–118.

———. "Lancasterian Schools, Republican Citizenship, and the Spatial Imagination in Early Nineteenth-Century America." *Journal of the Society of Architectural Historians* 55:3 (1996), 238–53.

Van Tassel, Mary M. "Hawthorne, His Narrator, and His Readers in 'Little Annie's Ramble.'" *ESQ: A Journal of the American Renaissance* 33:3 (1987), 168–179.

Veeder, William. "The Feminine Orphan and the Emergent Master." *Henry James Review* 12 (1991), 20–54.

Vine, Ilana. "'She will make a charming little woman': Reforming Female Rage in Louisa May Alcott's *An Old-Fashioned Girl.*" M.A. thesis, New York University, 2013.

Walker, Robert Sparks. *Torchlights to the Cherokees*. New York: Macmillan, 1931.

Warner, Susan. *The Wide, Wide World*. New York: Feminist Press, 1987.

Washburn, Wilcomb E. *Redman's Land, White Man's Law: A Study of the Past and Present State of the American Indian*. New York: Scribner's, 1971.

Watt, Tessa. *Cheap Print and Popular Piety, 1540–1640*. Cambridge: Cambridge University Press, 1991.

Weber, Carl J. *A Bibliography of Jacob Abbott*. Waterville, Me.: Colby College Press, 1948.

Weikle-Mills, Courtney. *Imaginary Citizens: Child Readers and the Limits of American Independence, 1640–1868*. Baltimore: Johns Hopkins University Press, 2012.

———. "'Learn to Love Your Book': The Child Reader and Affectionate Citizenship." *Early American Literature* 43:1 (2008), 35–61.

Weinstein, Cindy. *Family, Kinship, and Sympathy in Nineteenth-Century American Literature*. Cambridge: Cambridge University Press, 2004.

Welch, d'Alté. *A Bibliography of American Children's Books Printed Prior to 1821*. Worcester, Mass.: American Antiquarian Society and Barre, 1972.

Welsh, Charles. Introduction, *Goody Two-Shoes: A Facsimile Reproduction of the Edition of 1766*. Detroit: Singing Tree Press, 1970. iii–xxiv.

Whittier, J. G., ed., *Child Life in Prose*. Boston: Houghton Mifflin, 1873.

Williams, Raymond. *Keywords: A Vocabulary of Culture and Society*. New York: Oxford University Press, 1976, 1985.

———. *Marxism and Literature*. New York: Oxford University Press, 1978.

Wishy, Bernard. *The Child and the Republic: The Dawn of Modern American Child Nurture*. Philadelphia: University of Pennsylvania Press, 1969.

Wood, Alice Perry. *The Stage History of Shakespear's King Richard III*. New York: Columbia University Press, 1909.

Woodhouse, Barbara Bennett. *Hidden in Plain Sight: The Tragedy of Children's Rights from Ben Franklin to Lionel Tate*. Princeton: Princeton University Press, 2008.

Wordsworth, William. *The Prose Works of William Wordsworth*. Ed. W. J. B. Owen and Jane Worthington Smyser. Oxford: Oxford University Press, 1974.

———. *Selected Poems*. Ed. Stephen Gill. New York: Penguin, 2004.

Wu, Duncan. *Wordsworth's Reading 1800–1815*. Cambridge: Cambridge University Press, 2007.

Wyss, Hilary. *English Letters and Indian Literacies: Reading, Writing, and New England Missionary Schools, 1750–1830*. Philadelphia: University of Pennsylvania Press, 2012.

Zelizer, Viviana. *Pricing the Priceless Child: The Changing Social Value of Children*. (1985). Princeton: Princeton University Press, 1994.

Ziff, Larzer. "Rollo, or How to Raise an American Boy." *Hopkins Review* 5:4 (Fall 2012), 470–89.

Zipes, Jack, et al. *The Norton Anthology of Children's Literature: The Traditions in English*. New York: Norton, 2005.

Goody Two-Shoes Editions and Versions Cited in Chapter 1

Alphabet of Goody Two Shoes. Philadelphia: Johnson and Warner, 1809.

Child's Delight: Cock Robin, Goody Two Shoes, Tom Thumb. New York: McLoughlin Brothers, 1888.

Goody Two-Shoes: A Facsimile Reproduction of the Edition of 1766. Intro. Charles Welsh. Detroit: Singing Tree Press, 1970.

Goody Two Shoes. Baltimore: Bayly and Burns, 1837.

Goody Two-Shoes. New York: H.W. Hewet [between 1855 and 1856?].

Goody Two Shoes. New York: McLoughlin Brothers [between 1881 and 1882?].

Goody Two Shoes. New York: McLoughlin Brothers, 1898.

The History of Little Goody Two-Shoes. Philadelphia: W. Young, 1793.

The History of Little Goody Two-Shoes. Wilmington, Del.: Peter Brynberg, 1796.

"The History of Little Goody Two-Shoes." In *A Treasury of Pleasure Books for Young Children: With More Than One Hundred Illustrations by John Absolon and Harrison Weir*. New York: D. Appleton, 1853.

Little Goody Two-Shoes. (Miss Merryheart's series.) New York: McLoughlin Brothers [between 1859 and 1862?].

Story of Goody Two Shoes. New York: McLoughlin Brothers, 1869.

Very, Lydia. *Goody Two Shoes.* Boston: Prang [between 1863 and 1868].

"Children in the Wood" Editions and Versions Cited in Chapter 2

The Affecting History of the Children in the Wood. Binghamton, N.Y.: J. and C. Orton, 1840.

Affecting History of the Children in the Wood. New York: Turner and Fisher [between 1837 and 1841?].

Aunt Louisa's Oft Told Tales, Comprising Robinson Crusoe. Children in the Wood. Hare and Tortoise. World Wide Fables. With Twenty-four Pages of Illustratiots. Printed in Colors. New York: McLoughlin Brothers [1875?].

Babes in the Wood: Embellished with Coloured Engravings. Baltimore: J. S. Horton, 1836.

The Babes in the Wood. (Little Folks series.) New York: McLoughlin [between 1871 and 1874?].

The Babes in the Wood, in Verse. New York: Mahlon Day, 1833.

The Babes in the Wood, the Pictures by R. André. New York: McLoughlin Brothers [1888?].

"The Children in the Wood: or, the Norfolk Gentleman's last will and testament." London: Printed and Sold in Bow Church Yard, [1770?]. The Bodleian Library, University of Oxford. Harding B 4 (30).

Children in the Wood. (Aunt Matilda's series.) New York: McLoughlin Brothers [1875?].

The Children in the Wood, To Which Is Added, My Mother's Grave, a Pathetic Story. New York: Mahlon Day, 1832.

The Children in the Wood, Told in Verse by Richard Henry Stoddard, illustrated by H. L. Stephens. New York: Hurd and Houghton, 1866.

English, Clara. *The Affecting History of the Children in the Wood.* Hallowell, Me.: E. Goodale, 1817.

———. *The Children in the Wood: An Instructive Tale.* Philadelphia: Jacob Johnson, 1803.

———. *The Children in the Wood: An Instructive Tale.* Baltimore: Warner and Hanna, 1806.

———. *The Children in the Wood: An Instructive Tale.* Philadelphia: J. Johnson, 1807.

The Hermit of the Forest and the Wandering Infants: A Rural Fragment. London: Newbery, 1788.

History of the Babes in the Wood. New York: Solomon King [between 1822 and 1825].

The History of the Children in the Wood. Harrisburg, Pa.: G. S. Peters [not before 1834?].

Little Lizzie and the Fairies; and Sunny Hair's Dream. Boston: Crosby, Nichols [between 1852 and 1856?].

The Tragical History of the Children in the Wood. Containing a True Account of Their Unhappy Fate; with the History of Their Parents, and Their Unnatural Uncle. Interspersed with Instructive Morals. Boston: S. Hall, 1798.

The Tragical History of the Children in the Wood. Philadelphia: Morgan and Sons [between 1828 and 1834].

Inscribed Books Cited in Chapter 5

Abbott, Jacob. *Rollo's Philosophy: Air.* Philadelphia: B. F. Jackson, 1853. Inscribed to Howard Littlefield. AAS call number CL A132 R757 1853.

The Affecting History of the Children in the Wood. Windsor, Vt.: O. Farnsworth, 1809. Inscribed by Abiah Chapin. AAS call number CL-Pam C5365 A257 1809.

The American Tutor's Assistant, Improved. Wilmington, Del., 1811. AAS call number Dated Books.

Anecdotes. Harrisonburg, Va.: Lawrence Wartmann, printer, 1813. Inscribed by Emma Vanlear. AAS call number Tracts Pams V70 No. 006 1813.

Arithmetical Tables, for the Use of Schools. New York: S. Wood, 1810. AAS call number DP A0750..

The Blue Pictorial Primer. New York: Geo. F. Cooledge and Brother, 1839. Inscribed by Edgar Anthony. AAS call number Primers B658 P611 1840.

Childhood. New York: Samuel Wood, 1815. Inscribed to Lucy Draper. AAS call number, CL-Pam C536 N532 1815.

The Children in the Wood, To Which Is Added, My Mother's Grave, a Pathetic Story. New York: Mahlon Day, 1832. Inscribed by Harvey Copeland. AAS call number CL-Pam C5365 C536 1832.

Colman, Mrs. *The Pearl Story Book.* New York: Samuel Raynor,1850. Inscribed in memory of Carrie. AAS call number CL P359 S884 1850.

Coverings for the Head and Feet, in All Ages and All Countries. New York: J. S. Redfield [between 1843 and 1851?]. Inscribed to M. C. Wire. AAS call number CL-Pam C873 F692 1843.

English, Clara. *The Children in the Wood: An Instructive Tale.* Baltimore: Warner and Hanna, 1806. Inscribed by Decimus White. AAS call number CL-Pam E58 C536 1806.

Fables of Aesop, and Others, Translated into English, with Instructive Applications. Wilmington, Del.: Peter Brynberg, 1802. AAS call number CL A254 C953 1802.

Gray, Asa. *How Plants Grow: A Simple Introduction to Structural Botany.* New York: Ivison, Blakeman, Taylor, 1872. Inscribed, and with traces of pressed plants, by Hattie S. Putnam. AAS call number SB Botany G7781h 1872.

The History of Miss Kitty Pride. Windsor, Vt.: Nahum Mower [1805?]. Inscribed in memory of Relief Crouch. AAS call number CL-Pam H6734 M6783 1805.

Little Annie's ABC. Philadelphia: Appleton, 1851. Inscribed by Harriet Rose Chandler. AAS call number CL L7781 A6131 1851.

Little Kitty Clover and Her Friends. Philadelphia: G. Collins, 1856. Inscribed to Kate Anthony. AAS call number CL L7781 K62 1856.

Mamma's Gift Book. The Little Gift Book. Winter Holidays. Christmas Stories. New York: D. Appleton, 1854. Inscribed to Kate Anthony. AAS call number CL M263 G456 1854.

Manhood. New York: Samuel Wood, 1818. Inscribed to Lucy Draper. AAS call number CL-Pam M2685 N532 1818a.

Murray, Lindley. *An Abridgment of L. Murray's English Grammar.* Philadelphia: Benjamin Johnson and Jacob Johnson, 1802. Inscribed by Carson Lamborn et al. AAS call number Dated Books.

———. *An Abridgment of L. Murray's English Grammar.* Boston: Manning and Loring, 1813. Laura Newton's copy. AAS call number Dated Books.

———. *An Abridgment of L. Murray's English Grammar.* Hallowell, Me.: E. Goodale, 1813. Prudence Varnum's copy. AAS call number Dated Books.

———. *English Exercises, Adapted to Murray's English Grammar.* Bridgeport, Conn.: L. Lockwood, 1815. Inscribed by Maria Bullard. AAS call number Dated Books.

———. *The English Reader: Or, Pieces in Prose and Poetry, Selected from the Best Writers.* Philadelphia: Johnson and Warner, 1811. Inscribed by Alice Comfort. AAS call number Dated Books.

———. *The English Reader: Or, Pieces in Prose and Poetry, Selected from the Best Writers.* Poughkeepsie, N.Y.: Paraclete Potter, 1811. Inscribed by Joseph Bowers. AAS call number Dated Books.

———. *The English Reader: Or, Pieces in Prose and Poetry, Selected from the Best Writers.* Fredericktown, Md.: George Kolb, 1819. Inscribed by Benjamin Miller et al. AAS call number Dated Books.

———. *Introduction to the English Reader: Or, A Selection of Pieces, in Prose and Poetry.* New York: Collins, 1816. Inscribed by Mary Lucretia Shelton. AAS call number Dated Books.

———. *Murray's Introduction to English Grammar, Compiled for the Use of the Youth in Baltimore Academy, Tammany-Street. To Which Is Added, An Essay on Punctuation.* Baltimore: Academy Press, 1806. Inscribed by Nancy Smyth. AAS call number Dated Books.

New England Primer. Worcester, Mass.: S. A. Howland, 1845. Inscribed by Helen Spalding. AAS call number Primers N532 H864 1845.

The Newfoundland Fishermen, and Other Books for the Young. [New York]: American Tract Society [not before 1848?]. Inscribed to Harriet Rose Chandler. AAS call number CL A5125 N5475 1848.

Sargent, Epes. *The Standard Third Reader for Public and Private Schools.* Boston: Hobart and Robbins, 1857. Inscribed by Clara Cunnhingham. AAS call number SB Readers S785s3 1857.

Webster, Noah. *The American Spelling Book: Containing the Rudiments of the English Language, for the Use of Schools in the United States.* Brattleborough, Vt.: John Holbrook, 1819. Inscribed by David Hooper. AAS call number Dated Books, copy 1.

Index

Page numbers in *italics* indicate figures; *pl.* indicates a colored plate.

Acknowledgments

Many friends, colleagues, and institutions have fostered this book. Many thanks to Princeton University for a faculty leave when I was imagining another book entirely; the American Antiquarian Society/American Society for Eighteenth-Century Studies fellowship; the Spencer Foundation Fellowship in the History of Education, Newberry Library; the University of Minnesota Mc-Knight Land-Grant Professorship and McKnight Summer Research Fellowship/Faculty Summer Research Fellowship; the Gilder-Lehrman Institute Fellowship; the American Antiquarian Society/NEH fellowship. Thanks to NYU and to Department of English chairs John Guillory, Phil Harper, Una Chaudhuri, and Chris Cannon for generous leave time and research funding. I am grateful to the Abraham and Rebecca Stein Faculty Publication Fund for helping to subsidize printing the illustrations.

Thanks to colleagues whose invitations to speak helped me to think through crucial moves and gestures: Matt Brown and the University of Iowa Brownell Lecture in the History of the Book; Catherine Jones and the University of South Carolina, Institute for Southern Studies Postdoctoral Forum "Children and Education in the Transmission of Regional Culture," at Hickory Hill; Michael Snediker and the ELH Colloquium, Johns Hopkins University; Leah Price and the History of the Book Seminar, Harvard University; Paul Gehl, at the Newberry Library; the American Antiquarian Society invitation to give the Wiggins Lecture in the History of the Book; Jim Green and Daniel Richter and the McNeil Center for Early American Studies; Deidre Lynch and the English Institute; Jerry Singerman for the Seminar in the History of Material Texts at the University of Pennsylvania; Jordan Stein and Cristobal Silva and Columbia University's American Studies Seminar; The Colloquium on Early Literature and Culture in English, Department of English, New York University; Virginia Jackson, Tufts University American Literature and Culture Colloquium; Martin Brückner, Department of English, University of Delaware; Meredith McGill, Rutgers History of the Book Seminar; Kristen Bluemel, "Ink and Electricity: Advancing Liberal Learning in the Digital Age," Monmouth University; and

Andrea Immel, "Seen and Heard: The Place of the Child in Early Modern Europe 1550–1800" Conference, Cotsen Library, Princeton University.

I am happy to acknowledge my gratitude—and more than this: admiration, adoration, devotion—to curators, cataloguers, conservators, librarians, and all the other experts who have educated and befriended me at the Newberry Library, the American Antiquarian Society, the Pierpont Morgan Library, the Library Company of Philadelphia, the New-York Historical Society, Columbia's Rare Book and Manuscript Library, the Cotsen Children's Library at Princeton, and NYU's Fales Library and Special Collections. Especially: Gigi Barnhill, Joanne Chaison, Alan Degutis, Paul Erickson, Paul Gehl, Babette Gehnrich, Jim Green, Lauren Hewes, Hjordis Halvorson, John Hench, Andrea Immel, Connie King, Tom Knoles, Marie Lamoureux, Doris O'Keefe, Elizabeth Pope, Jenny Schwartzberg, Caroline Sloat, Caroline Stoffel, and Su Wolfe. Laura Wasowicz, the curator of Children's Literature at the AAS, generously shared her vast knowledge of the field, pulling surprising artifacts from the stacks again and again. Jackie Penny took most of the photographs, with skill and good humor. Many thanks to Pat Pflieger, whose website merrycoz.org virtually makes books like this one unnecessary: go there and see what *you* make of nineteenth-century children and their books and reading.

For interventions, conversations, and all kinds of moral support I offer heartfelt gratitude to Laura Agustín, Judy Cohn, Carolyn Eastman, Michael Hancher, Martin Harries, Nancy Hobbs, Patrick Horrigan, Virginia Jackson, Carola Marte, Annie Nayer, Louise Nayer, Paula Rabinowitz, Diana Robin, Doug Stein, and Wings White. For critique, advice, bibliography, and collegial talk, thanks to Steve Bullock, Michael Cohen, Sarah Crosby, Joe Cullen, Richard Fox, Bob Gross, David Hoover, Uli Knoepflmacher, Lucia Knoles, Paula McDowell, Meredith Neuman, Gillian Silverman, Eric Slauter, Lisa Stepanski, and Hilary Wyss.

Special thanks to those who have so kindly and attentively read some, many, or most of these pages along the way: Tom Augst, Amanda Claybaugh, Diana Fuss, Martin Harries, Barbara Hochman, Martha Howell, Margaret Hunt, Heather Love, Sharon Marcus, and Judy Walkowitz. Always very special warm gratitude to Carol McGuirk, whose long friendship and critical (as in clinical emergency) readings have made all the difference. Thanks to Lisa Gitelman for talks and walks and innumerable engaged discerning readings. Thanks to friend and colleague Catherine Robson and our students in Transatlantic Childhood, and to students in various incarnations of the Fictions of Childhood course. Thanks to ace researchers Liz Hutter and Blevin Shelnutt and to the students and now colleagues from whom I learn so much: Annie Abrams, Jane Carr, Tim Cassedy, Laura Fisher, Kristen Highland, Spencer Keralis, Rob Koehler,

Rachael King, Sara Lindey, Joey McGarvey, Alice McGrath, and Michelle Phillips.

I've been inspired and buoyed by work on children and childhood by Robin Bernstein, Anna Mae Duane, Leslie Ginsberg, Lucia Hodgson, Caroline Levander, Carol Singley, and Courtney Weikle-Mills. I owe enormous thanks to Karen Sánchez-Eppler for camaraderie and careful thoughtful readings (twice!) of this book. Martin Brückner too offered a very valuable critique for the Press, for which I am grateful.

Jerry Singerman at the Press has looked after this book and looked out for its author with intellectual acuity, saintly patience and fortitude, kindly good humor, and sensitive attunement. The Penn team—especially Hannah Blake and Noreen O'Connor-Abel—leapt into action with vigor and rigor.

Thanks to John Crain for the Red Cottage writer's studio and to Mary Currid, Jen Hustis, and Pilar Jennings for keeping body and soul together. Warm thanks for the warmth of Sophie (in memoriam), Emi, and Maisie. And a special thanks to the anonymous child outside my window on a summer morning in New York whose excited cry rose up seven stories: "I have an idea! I have an idea!"

Parts of the Introduction along with parts of the Coda were published in a different form in ELH 80 (Summer 2013), 343–72. A version of Chapter 1 on *Goody Two-Shoes* was published in *Childhood and Children's Books in Early Modern Europe, 1550–1800*, edited by Andrea Immel and Michael Witmore (New York: Routledge, 2006). A version of Chapter 3 on Joseph Lancaster was published in *New Media, 1750–1914: Studies in Cultural Definition and Change*, edited by Lisa Gitelman and Geoffrey Pingree (Cambridge, Mass.: MIT Press, 2003). Part of Chapter 6 on Henry James was published, in a different form, in *PMLA*, May 2015. And a portion of Chapter 5 on children's marginalia was published in a different form in *Comparative Textual Media: Transforming the Humanities in the Postprint Era*, edited by Katherine Hayles and Jessica Pressman (Minneapolis: University of Minnesota Press, 2013).

"Patricia Crain has long been one of the handful of scholars whose work I have found truly transformative, changing my sense of the kinds of questions one could ask and of the strategies one might develop for answering them. *Reading Children* is capacious, precise, and at times breathtakingly original in its vision and methods."

— **Karen Sánchez-Eppler**, Amherst College

What does it mean for a child to be a "reader" and how did American culture come to place such a high value on this identity? *Reading Children* offers a history of the relationship between children and books in Anglo-American modernity, exploring long-lived but now forgotten early children's literature, discredited yet highly influential pedagogical practices, the property lessons inherent in children's book ownership, and the emergence of childhood itself as a literary property.

Dozens of colorful illustrations chart the ways in which early literature for children was transformed into spectacle through new image technologies and a burgeoning marketplace that capitalized on nostalgic fantasies of childhood conflated with bowdlerized fantasies of history. *Reading Children* offers new terms for thinking about the imbricated and mutually constitutive histories of literacy, property, and childhood in the eighteenth and nineteenth centuries that ground current anxieties and long-held beliefs about childhood and reading.

Patricia Crain teaches in the English Department of New York University and is author of *The Story of A: The Alphabetization of America from* The New England Primer *to* The Scarlet Letter.

MATERIAL TEXTS

Series Editors: Roger Chartier, Joseph Farrell, Anthony Grafton, Leah Price, Peter Stallybrass, Michael F. Suarez, S.J.

Cover design: John Hubbard
Illustration: Fanny with her book. Cover image adapted from an illustration in *The History of Little Fanny*. Philadelphia: Morgan & Yeager, 1825. Courtesy of the American Antiquarian Society.

UNIVERSITY OF PENNSYLVANIA PRESS
Philadelphia
www.upenn.edu/pennpress
ISBN 978-0-8122-2353-8

90000

9 780812 223538